Symbols and Artifacts:
Views of the Corporate Landscape

COMMUNICATION AND SOCIAL ORDER

An Aldine de Gruyter Series of Texts and Monographs

Series Editor

David R. Maines, *Wayne State University*

Advisory Editors

Bruce E. Gronbeck • Peter K. Manning • William K. Rawlins

Symbols and Artifacts:
Views of the Corporate Landscape

Pasquale Gagliardi

Editor

Aldine de Gruyter • **New York**

About the Editor

Pasquale Gagliardi is professor of organizational behavior and director of ISTUD (Istituto Studi Direzionali) Belgirate, Italy. He was graduated in law from the Università Cattolica del Sacro Cuore in Milan. After working in private industry, he joined the "Centro di organizzazione aziendale" of the University of Padua where he taught organizational behavior from 1964 to 1969. Professor Gagliardi is a consultant to many large Italian corporations. His current research concerns organizational culture and cultural change.

Copyright © 1990 by Walter de Gruyter & Co., Berlin.
All rights reserved, including those of translation into foreign languages. No part of this book may be reproduced in any form—by photoprint, microfilm, or any other means—nor transmitted or translated into a machine language without written permission from the publisher.

First paperbound edition: 1992

published by

ALDINE DE GRUYTER
A division of Walter de Gruyter, Inc.
200 Saw Mill River Road
Hawthorne, New York 10532

LIBRARY OF CONGRESS CATALOGING-IN-PUBLICATION DATA

Symbols and artifacts : views of the corporate landscape / editor,
Pasquale Gagliardi. — 1st pbk. ed.
    p.   cm. — (Communication and social order)
  ISBN 0-202-30428-0
  1. Corporate culture. 2. Signs and symbols. I. Gagliardi,
Pasquale, 1936– . II. Series.
301.3'5––dc20   91-44078
                                     CIP

Printed on acid-free paper.

10 9 8 7 6 5 4 3 2 1

Preface

Origins

The origins of this work by various hands lie in the Third International Conference on Organizational Symbolism and Corporate Culture, arranged by SCOS (the Standing Conference on Organizational Symbolism) and ISTUD (Istituto Studi Direzionali), in cooperation with the Department of Sociology, University of Milan, and the Department of Sociology, Catholic University of Milan, which was held in Milan, Italy, from the 24th to the 26th of June, 1987.

The main theme of the conference was "The Symbolics of Corporate Artifacts," and the call for papers drew the attention of students of contemporary organizations to the following questions:

1. What is the methodological relevance of this theme for organizational research and theory?
2. It is true that the visible elements of corporate culture — such as technology, products, and perceivable patterns of behavior — are the easiest to observe but the least significant for understanding the cultural identity of organizations?
3. What is the relationship between artifacts and cultural codes?
4. Through which subtle mechanisms does cultural identity model the forms of material culture, and
5. How could they be revealed?

This volume contains a selection of the papers given at the Milan conference, chosen mainly from those which — rather than dealing with behavior patterns, themselves definable (and defined by the call for papers) as artifacts in the broad sense of the term — concentrated on aspects so far largely neglected by students of corporate cultures: the buildings, objects, images, forms; all the elements that go into making up the physical setting of corporate life, the perceptual world which is at once product and scenario of action.

This book — like any other book — is a cultural artifact. It testifies to the way in which a certain number of organizational researchers — from different countries, academic backgrounds, intellectual loyalties and tendencies — took up the invitation to reflect on the importance of artifacts for an understanding of organizational phenomena. The authors of the papers printed here are linked, furthermore, by a common interest in looking at organizations from perspectives commonly associated with social constructionist, interpretive, and phenomenological views of the reality, and most of them belong to the Standing Conference on Organizational Symbolism. Some brief introductory information on the nature of SCOS may therefore be of use to the reader in interpreting this book as an artifact produced in a specific cultural context.

SCOS was set up in Europe in 1981 as an independent work group within the European Group for Organizational Studies (EGOS) on the basis that the study of organizations, as human and social phenomena, requires an authentically inter-disciplinary approach, using methods, concepts, and metaphors taken from anthropology, linguistics, history, psychoanalysis, and the other life-sciences, and not just those of sociology and/or social psychology. The basic assumption was that any disciplinary paradigm will tend to restrict the creative interpretation of organizational and social phenomena, and that such paradigms — together with the types of social control operating in any institutionalized scientific context — will tend to smother expressiveness and hinder intellectual exchange. For these reasons SCOS has developed as an informal network asserting the values of toler-ance, expressiveness, and critical awareness of social control mechanisms on intellectual progress in organizational science. The interested reader will find further information on the origins, philosophy, and imagery of SCOS in the contribution by Burkard Sievers.

The Plan of the Work

This book — of equal interest, we believe, to students of contemporary organizations and to people working within them — is designed as a reader's companion on a sort of journey through the world of artifacts, on which he or she is invited to consider how deeply charged with meaning can be the surroundings we habitually treat with indifference, deigning them with a fleeting glance at most, or a stereotyped judgment. Space and artifacts constitute systems of communication which organizations build up within themselves and which reflect their cultural quiddity: artifacts speak, though we seldom listen, and through them we communicate and act, even if unawares: they have the *natural* innocence of the physical world, despite the fact that they are inherently *artificial*, but if we learn to make out their origins, their characteristics, and use, we shall see to what extent they can be emblems of a *socially constructed* reality. It is our hope that, at journey's end, the reader will be able to view the corporate landscape through different eyes and feel urged to give a different meaning to his or her own experience as observer or actor on the corporate scene.

As for the structure of the book, it consists of an introduction by the editor, followed by five sections. The purpose of the introduction is: (1) to define the object of analysis in more analytical fashion than this preface allows; (2) to situate the work within the context of organizational literature in general, and within that of the literature of organizational culture in particular; (3) to outline a conceptual framework on the basis of the editor's research experience and on some of the findings and speculations set out by the authors of the various essays; (4) to discuss some of the problems relating to the epistemological status and methodologies of artifacts analysis in organizational ethnography.

Part I ("Designing Physical Settings in Organizations") is made up of six essays whose authors have a shared interest in exploring the processes by which the corporate stage is conceived, constructed, and invested with meaning. Per Olof Berg and Kristian Kreiner discuss the modes whereby physical settings are turned into symbolic resources, concentrating in particular on the relation between corporate architecture, corporate profile, and corporate identity. Michael Rosen, Wanda Orlikowski, and Kim Schmahmann examine — largely from a macro viewpoint — the dialectical relationship between the organization of labor and the structuring of space, critically analyzing the way in which bureaucratic ideology shapes social life. Brian Rusted discusses modifications to traditional housing on the island of Newfoundland in the light of symbolic and cultural approaches to organizations and communication, showing how restoration, renovation, and demolition practices reflect contextual differences within the social organization of the communities studied. Dennis Doxtater, taking as his starting point the symbolic patterns observable in the structuring of space within traditional societies, suggests that an analogous cultural potential exists in the workplace, available to the designer in his or her struggle to translate and satisfy expressive as well as instrumental requirements in the planning of the corporate setting. Mary Jo Hatch, in an empirical study which compares attitudinal and behavioral responses of employees assigned to private offices with those of employees assigned to non-private offices, claims that the relation between the form of offices and the behavior/ satisfaction of those involved is only amenable to interpretation through the meaning the individuals concerned attribute to offices within their work environments. Claudio Ciborra and Giovan Francesco Lanzara discuss the complex interactions between computer systems — viewed as dynamic artifacts — and organizational culture. They analyze the organization as formative context and look on the making of formative contexts as one of the basic activities in system design.

Part II and III consist of essays illustrating the possibility of using artifacts as cultural indicators for the purposes of research.

Part II ("Disclosing Organizational Cultures Through Artifacts") brings together five essays which examine particular types (or particular qualities) of artifacts as possible clues to cultural themes or to aspects of the culture of an organization. Joseph Sassoon examines from a cross-cultural viewpoint the relationship between cultural codes and color codes, showing — with particular reference to political parties — how changes in the shade and density of colors can express changes in the ideological vectors and in the social meaning of artifacts. Deborah Dougherty and Gideon Kunda propose the content analysis of photographs of customers in ten years of annual reports from five large computer manufacturers as a method of studying organizational beliefs about customers. Burkard Sievers presents his research on the logo of SCOS and discusses the possibility that a symbol of corporate identity, interpreted in the light of a long iconographic tradition and explored in its social and unconscious meanings, can become the expression of a new tradition and of a particular corporate ideology. Christian Scholz constructs a relational model for use in situating, providing parameters for, and interpreting the cultural realities expressed by Computerized Information Systems. Claudia Piccardo, Giuseppe Varchetta, and Gianni Zanarini propose a method for the analysis and interpretation of the language of leadership, viewed as a linguistic artifact which creatively expresses fundamental aspects of the culture of an organization.

Part III ("Root Metaphors Embedded in Artifacts") consists of three essays in which the authors, examining a particular organization's set of artifacts, claim that it is possible to go behind the artifacts to a root metaphor permitting a holistic interpretation of the culture in question. Dick Raspa, analyzing the culture of a large American firm, finds in the game of dominoes the organizing principle of the symbolic field which recreates reality and makes it possible to interpret the relationship between work and play, the outstanding nature of performances, and the features of the physical setting. Janne Larsen and Majken Schultz decode the cultural and organizational syntax of a Danish ministry through the metaphor of the monastery. Howard Schwartz, discussing the cultural roots of the Space Shuttle disaster, sees in the metaphor of "Disneyland in space" the expression and the reason for the parallel degeneration of the N.A.S.A. as an organization and of the American dream.

The three essays in Part IV ("Artifacts and Organizational Control") explore the relationship between artifacts and organizational control. Bob Witkin discusses the relationship between the stylistic quality of artifacts and the sensuous experience of members of the organization, showing how the design of artifacts can be a tool for control in bureaucratic organization. Barbara Czarniawska-Joerges and Bernward Joerges analyze linguistic artifacts as tools for reaching specific goals, and as goods which have a market value since they can be used to create and manipulate social and organizational reality. Barry Turner discusses the creation of artifacts as a project guided by knowledge and information, but also as a passionate manipulation of the world, and failed artifacts as a dramatic demonstration of the organization's incapacity to fulfil given purposes.

Part V ("De-constructing Artifacts") consists of a single essay by Bob Grafton-Small and Steve Linstead which carries to the extreme the theoretical attitude featured in the majority of the previous essays. They apply a deconstructive approach to explore the paradoxes inherent in the relationship between theory and artifact. They argue that the production/consumption duality present in material artifacts is simultaneously present in those theoretical artifacts which accompany their creation and re-creation. The consequence of this for us — as researchers — would seem to be a recognition of the extent to which we are bound up in the complex valuations and revaluations involved in the understanding of what we survey, whether in the symbolism of language or of artifact; and the analytic necessity to deconstruct the variety of theoretical closures which are an inevitable result of our need to escape the paradox of reflexivity and lead active and creative everyday lives. Thus, at the end of our journey through the world of corporate artifacts, Bob Grafton-Small and Steve Linstead invite us to undertake another journey through the world of artifacts within our own field.

Obviously the criterion for grouping the essays in this way is largely arbitrary and reflects my interpretation of the themes *dominant* in each of them: many essays help to illustrate arguments dealt with in other parts of the book and might well have been located elsewhere. In effect, this work is a piece of "bricolage": the building-bricks were not made in function of an overall design, rather the attempt has been to construct a workable building in function of the bricks available, though many of the authors have been kind enough to modify their original papers in the light of the shape our artifact began to take on.

Acknowledgements

With that in mind, I would like to express my lively appreciation to all those authors who generously spent time and energy on modifying and reworking their original papers. I would also like to stress the courtesy of *Social Science Information* (Sage Publications) and of the *Journal of Organizational Change Management* — where after the Milan Conference the essays by Howard Schwartz and Joseph Sassoon respectively appeared — for allowing them to be reprinted in this anthology. Finally I would like to thank Per Olof Berg, Barbara Czarniawska-Joerges, Peter Frost, Kristian Kreiner, Antonio Strati, Barry Turner, and Bob Witkin for their encouragement and for the valuable suggestions they offered.

Editing a work by various hands is not an easy task. It requires the creation of a temporary micro-organization linking publisher, editor, and the various authors, sometimes — as in the present case — scattered over two continents, so as to reconcile the various exigencies, styles, points of view with the need for something reasonably unitary in the outcome. The capable hand of Wilma Bailo held this undertaking on a steady course; her tenacity, her scrupulous efficiency, and her eye for detail have been of inestimable help to me in bringing this publishing venture into safe harbor.

Pasquale Gagliardi

Contents

Part III: Root Metaphors Embedded in Artifacts

Introduction

Introduction

Artifacts as Pathways and Remains of Organizational Life

Pasquale Gagliardi

1 The Field of Analysis

The word artifact has a literal meaning — the one we generally find in dictionaries and to which we refer in current usage — and a conventional meaning among students of organizational culture.

In the first case, the artifact is: (a) a *product* of human action which exists independently of its creator; (b) *intentional*, it aims, that is, at solving a problem or satisfying a need; (c) *perceived by the senses*, in that it is endowed with its own corporality or physicality. Naturally, depending on the dictionaries, languages, cultural contexts in which the word is of current use, the stress given to one or the other of the three elements in the definition will change.

Students of organizational culture, for their part (see for example: Schein 1984, Siehl/Martin 1989), often mean by *artifacts* all the visible expressions of a culture, including therewith (as well as objects and the physical arrangements) patterns of behavior (such as rituals) on the one hand, and, on the other, abstract productions or mental representations (such as stories), which — while having an existence independent of their creators — call on the powers of comprehension of the destinees, rather than on their capacity to experience formal qualities concretely through the senses.

In this introduction and in most of the essays which follow artifacts will be spoken of in this first sense, even though not all the artifacts which come under that heading have the same "concreteness," the same perceptible corporality: some (buildings and workplaces, for example) can be experienced by more than one of our senses, others (for instance, pictures) by only one of them; the presence of some is a hindrance which can only be got rid of by violent and destructive action (think of the shattered statues which so often put their seal on cultural revolutions), others (linguistic labels, for example) entrust their continuance to a written document or merely to the memory of members of the organization.

Obviously the dual distinction proposed (abstract/concrete, product/action) is subtle and ambiguous. The shifting nature of the watershed between the world of theory and the world of objects is acutely shown by Grafton-Small and Linstead in their essay; Rosen, Orlikowski, and Schmahmann stress the dialectical interplay of agency and concrete artifacts; Czarniawska-Joerges and Joerges tell us that a word — apparently immaterial and volatile — can weigh like a stone and that the definition of an object can change physical reality, modifying its loved or painful qualities. Despite this, it seems useful to me to insist on the dual distinction above for the following reasons: (a) by distinguishing between product and action, we have available a precious tool for the diachronic analysis of organizational phenomena and can better appreciate, on the one hand, the power of artifacts to steer and canalize — their being *pathways of action* — and, on the other, their capacity to witness to and reflect social and cultural dynamics — their being *remains and markers* of corporate life; (b) by distinguishing between mental and sensory experience, we can uncover neglected dimensions in organizational processes and perhaps open new and interesting vistas for research and for reflection on the aesthetic dimension of organizations (Jones/Moore/Snyder 1988, Strati 1990). It may not be without interest to note that by stressing, on the one hand, the artifact's nature as a product and, on the other, the way in which it lends itself to aesthetic — in a broad sense — experiences, we come closer to using the term in its strict etymological meaning (*ars*, art + *factum*, made).

The analysis of artifacts in most cases implies the analysis of a fundamental category of experience: space. Every object possesses a physical bound which circumscribes it and sets it off from other objects, a perceptible boundary which marks where it begins and ends (Hall 1959); space defines — or helps to define — the features of an artifact, its relations with other artifacts in the same setting and its meaning. On the other hand, the perception of space is indissolvably linked to the perception of "things" which frame it and define its contours. Thus, by taking the symbolism of corporate artifacts as the object of analysis, our attention is implicitly brought to bear on the symbolism of corporate space: they are faces of one and the same coin, two complementary modes of interpreting the corporate setting.

2 Artifacts in Traditional Organization Theory and Research

"Well, then, is there any record of a successful
war being fought in Homer's day either under
his command or with his advice?"
"No."
"Then had he any practical skill? Is he said to
have invented any ingenious technical or
practical devises like Thales of Miletus or
Anacharsis the Scythian?"
"He did nothing of that sort."
[...]
"And so, Glaucon," I continued, "when you meet
people who admire Homer as the educator of
Greece, and who say that in the administration
of human affairs and education we should study
him and model our whole lives on his poetry,
you must feel kindly towards them as good men
within their limits, and you may agree with them
that Homer is the best of poets and first of
tragedians. But you will know that the only
poetry that should be allowed in a state is hymns
to the gods and paeans in praise of good men;
once you go beyond that and admit the sweet
lyric or epic muse, pleasure and pain become
your rules instead of law and the rational
principles commonly accepted as best."

Plato, *The Republic*, X.

The primacy of reason in western thought and the concern to safeguard the instrumental rationality of action in the utilitarian forms of human association evidently have ancient roots. This dialogue between Socrates and Glaucon would not have been out of place on the cover of any one of the works of the founding fathers of the so-called "classic" theory of organization. And when Socrates claims that art — fosterer of emotions — may be an element in the organization of the state only when it is instrumental to the aims of the state (today we would say: when it is "propaganda" or "state art"), I can't help thinking of the frantic efforts of those theorists who, once informal organization had been discovered and the inevitable interference of feelings in rationally planned production processes, tried and go on trying to trace back these unsuspected energies to the logic and specific purposes of the formal organization. If one thinks of the dominance of the rationalist and reductive paradigm in organization studies up to the end of the 1970s, as documented by Ouchi/Wilkins (1985), it is hardly a surprise to find that the study of the physical setting as source of sensory, emotional, and symbolic experiences has had an altogether marginal role in organization theory.

Steele (1973) observed that Hawthorne's experiments — which originally aimed at studying the effects of the environment on productive behavior — might have opened interesting prospects for research in that direction (even if the research method would today be considered ingenuous and simplistic), but the startling discovery of "group norms" drew attention and research efforts off on quite another tack. Ironically, Steele notes, a re-examination of Hawthorne's findings reveals the influence — slight and mediated though it is — both of the interactions of the workers made possible by the change in setting (Homans 1950), and of the symbolic value that this change had taken on for them in terms of "spatial language." After Hawthorne, the theory of the socio-technical system was, so to speak, another missed opportunity: the theorists of this approach, while recognizing the importance of the physical setting, concentrated their gaze on the fit between technology and the social structure of organizations, devoting only marginal attention to the quality, in terms of artifacts and culture, of the work environment.

A glance at the entry "physical setting" in the index of any textbook on organization analysis will refer you to theories of motivation, in particular to Maslow and Herzberg. Maslow (1943) saw setting as suited to the satisfaction of *primary*, as opposed to *higher, needs*, and Herzberg et al. (1959) described the setting as a *factor of hygiene* or extra-job factor — a possible source of discontent or indifference, but not of satisfaction — as opposed to job factors which are considered the authentic motivators. These notions have probably had a significant role generally in inducing students to underrate the influence of the setting and to judge other problems worthier of attention (Steele 1973, Sundstrom 1987). Independent of the value of these notions — there is no intention of questioning them here — we have here an interesting example of the power of a linguistic artifact — the label (Czarniaswka-Joerges/Joerges in this volume) — to structure a system of meaning: on the basis of labels and underlying assumptions (*primary and higher* needs, *hygiene* factors and *motivators*), the hierarchy of human needs has been fitted with a corresponding hierarchy of research themes which has influenced the stance and choice of field of scholars.

This failure in the working out of organization theory is matched by a visible gap in empirical research. From Sundstrom's (1986) census of 290 studies it emerges that research on work environments is dominated by laboratory experiments in which the level of analysis is that of the individual worker and the hypotheses to be checked deal, on the one hand, with the effect on performance of factors like arousal, stress, distraction, overload, and fatigue, and, on the other, with the effect on job satisfaction of various perceived features of the job, one of which refers to physical working conditions. Some studies examine the relationship between work space, self-identity, status, and satisfaction; and one sole study adopts the organizational level of analysis in attempting to check the fit between two qualities of the organization — bureaucracy and interaction — and two qualities of office environment — differentiation and subdivision: the results turn out to be obvious or contradictory because of the inherent incapacity of the methods used to pick up the symbolic dimension in the observed phenomena. Not one of the empirical studies in the census organically examines the connection between the distinctive culture of the organization and properties of the work environment.

Particular mention in this brief survey should go to Steele's work (1973) exploring the expressive potential and symbolic qualities of the physical setting, within an OD (Organizational Development) perspective. On the basis of his long clinical experience Steele scrupulously reminds us that the attribution of meaning to a physical setting is an empirical question, but only occasionally does he discuss the social and cultural processes which determine it.

The "territory" (in a literal and metaphorical sense) neglected by students of organization has been — and in large measure still is — the domain of efficiency experts and architects/designers. Starting from Taylor's original concern with economy of motion and visual check on workers, efficiency experts have planned the physical setting according, in general, to rigorously instrumental criteria, mitigated by the widespread knowledge that the work environment should also be a status marker. Architects and designers for their part have shown over recent decades a widespread tendency in the plans to "interpret" the *needs* of contemporary society, turning themselves into disciples of theories and ideologies which drew, sometimes in nonchalant fashion, on all kinds of human and social sciences, making themselves proponents/interpreters of fads or supposedly universal criteria of "socially responsible" planning of the work environment ("open plan," for example: see Hatch in the present volume). Summerson (1989) has suggested that this tendency is due in part to the architect's need to redefine his own professional role after witnessing the technical components of his skill and "the purely practical reasons for his existence being undermined by members of a new and flourishing profession," i. e. engineers (1989: 18). This redefinition by architects of their own professional territory has perhaps been abetted by the marginal interest shown by social scientists in the physical setting of organizations. At least for them, what Hall (1959) claims seems particularly true: space is like sex, it's there but that's no reason for talking about it.

3 Artifacts in Organizational Cultural Literature

"The great dancer, Isadora Duncan, was once
asked what dance meant to her. She replied: if it
was sayable there'd be no need to dance it."

Ceruti 1989: 16[1]

When we speak of organizational cultural literature, we refer to the intellectual product of those scholars who — dissatisfied with the rationalistic and
reductive paradigm which dominated organizational science up to the end
of the 1970s — began looking at organizations as expressive forms and as
systems of meaning, to be analyzed not merely in their instrumental,
economic, and material aspects, but also in their ideational and symbolic
features. For these scholars organizations are cultural entities, characterized
by distinct paradigms, and the richness of corporate life can only be grasped
through the use of holistic, interpretive, and interactive models. This intellectual production, from the end of the 1970s onwards, has undergone
exponential development, and corporate culture is today one of the main
domains of organizational research (Barley et al. 1988).

Curiously enough, even this literature has had little to say about corporate artifacts, the most evident, concrete, and tangible manifestations of the
culture of an organization. Reporting on 280 articles and books on corporate culture and organizational symbolism, Berg (1987) found extremely few
pieces explicitly and exclusively devoted to artifacts, and is astounded by
this neglecting of the obvious, by this lack of attention to the most easily
observed manifestations of corporate life. If we consider the definition of
"symbol" most often quoted in this literature — "Symbols are objects,
acts, relationships or linguistic formations that stand *ambiguously* for a
multiplicity of meanings, evoke emotions, and impel men to action." (Cohen
1976: 23) —, we can't escape the conclusion that objects — though they
are what we most readily associate the idea of symbol with — are the
symbol least attractive to these enquirers.

In my review of the literature I have found two shining exceptions
deserving special mention: (1) Pfeffer's (1981) acute, though summary,
analysis of the structuring of the space on a campus as expression of
relationships and as mirroring of conflict between institutions; (2) Martin
and Siehl's (1983) reconstruction of DeLorean's attempt to create a counterculture inside General Motors. The two authors infer with great subtlety
the counterposed cultural stances, the relative power of the actors, and the
limits of acceptable deviance from the formal and stylistic qualities of
particular artifacts (furnishings and dress especially).

Glancing in particular at the literature on the methods of organizational
ethnography, I came across many authors insisting on the importance of

artifacts for the interpretation of culture, but very few who provide analytical indications: sometimes these indications are sketchy and debatable (e. g. Deal/Kennedy 1982: 128 – 129); some authors suggest extrapolating to artifacts methods designed for the analysis of other sources of information such as the behavior of natives or what they say (e. g. Spradley 1979: 9); others stress that the interpretation of artifacts requires a long stay in the field (Schein 1985) and suggest in-depth clinical interview with an informant as the most fitting tool for getting at preconscious assumptions and deep symbolic meanings (Schein 1987; Wilkins 1983a).

Different hypotheses, to some degree linked, can be put forward to explain this tendency of organizational cultural literature to pay lip-service to artifacts while neglecting them in substance. I shall set out these hypotheses below since they constitute the premiss of the theoretical reflections offered in the paragraphs that follow them.

First, organizational cultural researchers are — and remain so, even when they proclaim their interdisciplinarity — social scientists. What they are accustomed to doing, and what they do best, is to examine social behavior. When they study culture, their basic assumption is that behavior is the most important empirical correlative of culture. "A culture is expressed (or constituted) *only* by the *actions* and *words* of its members ..." (Van Maanen 1988: 3, emphasis added). When Beattie defines the purpose of social anthropology as the study of institutionalized social relations, he claims that "... the only *concrete* entities given in the social situation are people" (1964: 34, emphasis added). The analysis of things becomes the privileged object of attention only when they constitute the sole source of information available to us, which obviously only occurs when we study societies of the past whose culture we reconstruct through their remains. It is no accident that, in his *Content Analysis for the Social Sciences and Humanities* (1969), Holsti defines the study of human behavior through the analysis of artifacts as the specific task of archeology. The result is that the social scientist finds himself entirely at ease when analyzing written or verbal communications, but founders in the attempt to grasp the language of things.

This lack of attention towards artifacts may also be due to the fact that — differently from anthropologists who study cultures remote from their own — students of organizational cultures "share with their subjects and readers the same general linguistic and cultural landscape" (Van Maanen 1988: 23) and leave the interpretation of artifacts, which define the contours of that habitual landscape, to a "common sense" they take to be shared.

On the other hand, if the organizational ethnographer turns to cultural anthropologists for tools to analyze material culture, he frequently finds himself dealing with proposed inventories for the classification of objects in function of their use, materials, or techniques employed, often by means of categories which in their turn reflect the ideas and technical knowledge of the observer.

It would be fair to remark that the great anthropologists — or simply the good ones — made and make quite different use of what they have "read out" of material culture, but it is difficult to borrow a gift for interpretation: in many cases competence is only acquired by working alongside those who have it, but this is — yet again — made difficult or impossible by the demarcation disputes, even of an ideological kind, which serve to defend the institutional set-up of the various disciplines. In recent years, for example, students of folklore have shown an increasing interest in organizations, and this might induce us to hope for the beneficial effects of a cross-fertilization of the two disciplines. But if, on the one hand, the presence in this volume of an essay by a scholar of folklore like Dick Raspa gives rise to optimism, I can't, on the other hand, forget the argument that arose at the 1983 Santa Monica conference on organizational folklore, when the folklorists — mainly concerned to safeguard the traditions which arise spontaneously in workplaces — were suspicious that their skills might be exploited by organizational scientists to "interfere" in organizations to instrumentalize the expressive needs of the workers.

Another possible explanation for the neglect of artifacts came to mind on reading what Louis has to say of the universal level of the process whereby meaning is produced: "The universal level refers to the broad set of objective or physically feasible meanings or relevances of each thing ... The basic physical constraints are what Weick (1979) referred to as 'grains of truth.'" (1983: 41). I wonder whether the interest in social reality of organizational cultural researchers — who certainly generally adopt a constructionist perspective in their view of reality — does not betray them into considering only social reality as a socially constructed reality, which would be paradoxical enough and, everything said, tautological, if Cassirer (quoted by Wexler 1983: 237) is right in claiming that "physical reality seems to recede in proportion as man's symbolic activity advances."

I shall illustrate a final (and perhaps the most important) reason for this disregard of artifacts by analyzing a small artifact which is quoted very frequently in the literature, both because it evidently stands for a widespread way of looking at things, and because of the authority of its author, who has a leading role in the development of the cultural approach to the study of organizations. I refer to the table in which Schein sets out the levels of culture and their interaction.

What does this table show us? Three rectangles joined by arrows. The spatial arrangement of the rectangles in the figure immediately and force-fully suggests a *hierarchy* of importance. While we very frequently perceive as more important the things set higher up, the definitions in this case suggest that what is higher up is superficial or apparent, whereas what is lower down is profound, fundamental, thus more worthy of attention. This is exactly what Schein claims, and many students of organizational cultures who have neglected artifacts may have been led to do so by the *logic* of Schein's arguments. What startled me when discussing with many colleagues the possibility of organizing a conference on artifacts was that *many of them remembered Schein's table and the hierarchy* it suggests much better than they remembered the logic of his arguments.

A concrete image is notoriously more mnemonic than a concept, but the formal qualities of this artifact — symmetry, circularity, completeness — may well have reinforced, at the level of aesthetic experience, the mental experience implied by the "understanding" of the concepts the schema summarizes, and the capacity of the form

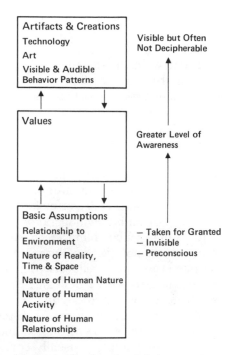

Figure 1: The Levels of Culture and Their Interaction
Source: Schein 1984: 4.

to "persuade" may even have overwhelmed the capacity of the substance to "convince." I believe that these processes are grasped at least intuitively by those used to employing visual aids in their teaching and in communicating and who feel lost without a blackboard, a projector, or a certain number of colored markers.

A second message of the table, more important than the first for the point of the present discussion, is the *suggestion of a pathway*: one does not get to the unconscious assumptions without passing the espoused values, there is no going beyond the frontier of unconscious knowledge without digging into words, tacit knowledge cannot be evoked unless it is drawn up to the level of conscious thought. From this perspective, Schein's schema implicitly formalizes two basic assumptions which in large measure run through organizational cultural literature: (1) the idea that the intellectual unconsciousness can be treated, on the pattern of the psychoanalytic approach, in the same way as the affective unconscious and that iterative interviewing is the best tool for reaching the basic assumptions; (2) the idea that the maps which orient action may be conscious or unconscious but they are solely cognitive, and that the whole of tacit knowledge is in no qualitative way different from conscious knowledge.

The first idea is shared largely by those scholars whose major training was in the area of clinical and social psychology, but it tends to be rebutted by those whose training was largely in anthropology. Often, in fact, ethnographers (for instance, Spradley 1979: 9) insist that tacit knowledge can't always be expressed by an informant, but must be inferred from observation of behavior, from the study of artifacts, and from their use (even if, as we have seen, we are told little about the possible criteria of inference). On the other hand, there is no such thing as an iterative interview which can bring to the informant's consciousness something he does not know he knows. As Piaget puts it: "the subject knows himself very badly, since to explain his own operations and even to glimpse the structures they imply would require him to reconstruct a whole past of which he has never been aware, not even in the moments he was going through the stages: despite everything Freud discovered about the affective unconscious, the intellectual past of an individual is even more unknown to him than his sentimental past" (1967: 120)[1].

The second assumption − i. e. the idea that tacit knowledge is of an intellectual kind − seems more widely shared, implicitly at least: unconscious assumptions are usually considered to be cognitive principles, abstract mental representations, synthetic and general in character, suited to the generation and ordering of cascades of progressively less abstract, more analytical, concepts and mental operations. This conviction seems consistent to me with the equally widespread idea that language constitutes the basic tool in the transmission of culture. But Hall (1959) reminds us that culture is not taught in the same way as language, and that a universe of behavior exists still unexplored, generally ignored, and *hardly observable*, which operates without emerging into consciousness and which lies alongside the universe of words and ideas.

It seems to me that our incapacity to explore this alternative universe is the real reason why a fundamental process of organizational life such as socialization is still a "black-box" for students (Siehl/Martin 1988). Louis, in her interesting essay of 1980 on the way in which individuals in organizational settings cope with entry experiences, particularly surprises, starts from the observation, documented in the literature (Hughes 1958), of the newcomer's experience of sensory overload, and sets herself to study the internal processes through which individuals adapt to the new setting. Nevertheless, she expressly admits that her description of coping bears only on the more rational aspects − the role of conscious thought, in particular − and concludes by saying that the newcomer's "learning the ropes" of the new setting remains inadequately explored.

The emphasis on mental processes and cognition is probably at the origin of our incapacity to give exhaustive explanation to such other fundamental organizational processes as control, persistence, and change (Ciborra/Lanzara, in this volume). I myself proposed a conceptual framework for interpreting the creation and change of organizational cultures, underlining the role of conscious feelings and retrospective rationalization in the genesis of values (Gagliardi 1986), but I often ran into situations which I was led to call "silent cultural changes" and which that scheme does not wholly explain or does not explain at all. I wonder whether our work as enquirers, given its intrinsically intellectual nature, doesn't perhaps lead us to sharpen certain capacities at the expense of others, putting us in the situation of fishermen who perfect their net, making it ever more suitable for catching certain fish, but letting others slip through.

A confirmation that the current approach to the study of organizational cultures has holes in it comes from my observation that in general two orders of factors are considered the components of culture: beliefs and values. Beliefs refer to the ontological and epistemological component of culture ("logos") − corresponding to cognitive experience − values to the ethical and deontological component ("ethos") − corresponding to moral experience. But there exists a third fundamental component to human experience, "pathos," the way we perceive and "feel" reality (and its representations in what we call art). The sensuous experience (see Witkin, this volume) − which can give rise to feelings of attraction and repulsion, pleasure and disgust, suffering and joy − is also culturally conditioned. Geertz (1973) includes in ethos the aesthetic component in culture: "A people's ethos is the tone, character, and quality of their life, its moral and aesthetic style and mood" (p. 127). But organizational culture researchers seem in general little inclined to recognize and describe the aesthetic component when they discuss the value systems of modern bureaucratic organizations. The distinction between ethos and pathos may be useful both in calling their attention to a neglected dimension, and − above all − because it is probable that the *mechanisms of influence* on behavior and the *modes of enquiry* into these two aspects of the cultural order are different. The basic hypothesis of this essay − and of this book − is that artifacts can provide a key giving privileged access to the sensory and aesthetic dimensions of corporate life. In the paragraphs that follow I shall attempt to explore − on the basis of my own research experience and of certain suggestions contained in the other essays in this book − the *pragmatic* dimension of artifacts (the relationship between artifacts and organizational action) and their *hermeneutic* dimension (what and how may artifacts speak to us when we are seeking to interpret the culture of an organization).

4 The Potency of Artifacts in the Structuring of Sensory Experience

> "... no man need ever despair of gaining
> proselytes to the most extravagant hypothesis,
> who has art enough to represent it in any
> favourable colours. The victory is not gained by
> the men at arms, who manage the pike and
> sword; but by the trumpeters, drummers, and
> musicians of the army."
>
> *Hume*[2]

Let me introduce this theme by recounting something that happened to me recently.

The Istituto di Guerra Marittima — a training and refresher-course center for the Italian Navy — invited me to give a lecture on recent trends.in organization theory, as part of a refresher course for Staff Officers. Beforehand I told my contact (the officer responsible for the course) that I wanted to preface my lecture with a brief discussion: it was my intention, I explained, to center what I had to say on the interests, knowledge, and language of my listeners. At this proposal, my interlocutor, on the other end of the phone, fell silent. As the silence went on I realized there was something wrong and asked if my suggestion would cause problems. The somewhat embarrassed reply was that it would be better if the formula was more traditional: first there should be the lecture, and then there'd be a discussion. I understood there was no point in arguing the matter or insisting.

On the day, I went to the Institute and was welcomed with great courtesy by the admiral who ran it. When the small group comprising the admiral, the people in charge of the programme, and myself entered the hall where I was to give the lecture, we were greeted with a brief service ritual of salute from the participants who were standing in wait in front of their chairs. The hall was rectangular (I *remember* it as windowless: if there were any, they were closed and/or hidden behind curtains, the lighting was certainly artificial, even though it was a lovely sunny day), taken up on one side by a platform on which towered the speaker's lectern and seats were set for the "authorities" who accompanied me. In front of the platform were aligned the rows of seats for the course participants. I noticed that they had to bend their heads slightly backwards so as to look me in the face. The victim of habit, I scanned my lecture with questions of the "Is that clear?" kind, or comments like "I don't know whether that's clear" followed by a pause. I quickly cut down the pauses and avoided asking questions, even if merely rhetorical, because I "sensed" the unease of my hosts and of the participants.

At the end of the lecture there was a break for coffee in a room across from the hall. When the time for the break was up, one of my hosts said: "Good, now we move on to the discussion," and I made to cross back over the corridor to the hall where I'd given the lecture, but was immediately rerouted. "No, Professor," I was told, "the discussion takes place elsewhere." And off we went elsewhere, quite some way from the hall: one of those handsome lecture theaters, where everybody can see each other, functional, in no way off-putting, with large windows and plenty of daylight, lots of blackboard space, and comfortable benches for the trainees. I couldn't hide my surprise and, congratulating them on the splendid room, asked why on earth they hadn't arranged for me to give my lecture there. "Ah, no! ... you see, Professor, this is the ..." and the man who was telling me lowered his voice — "bollockdrome. The place where trainees can come out with all the bollocks they like." I was stunned for a moment and had to think, but then I couldn't prevent myself from coming out with my admiration for what I had to call "the unconscious organizational wisdom" of the institution.

This case, in my view, illustrates very clearly the possibility of using space to structure organizational relationships, to define and reinforce behavior patterns, and to handle contradictions through loose-coupling.

We are in a service institution: very high value indeed is placed on respect for authority, whether hierarchical or academic. When authority speaks, what it says is not subject to discussion, nor is it conceivable that what it says isn't clear, because that would already be to "undermine" it. When authority speaks, the setting permits of only certain visual relationships and not others, it obliges people to dispose themselves in such a way as physically to acknowledge the distinction between social groups and maintain stability (Goffman 1959), it enforces particular postures which produce the sensory experience of dependence. Every detail of the setting reminds us, physically and symbolically, with all the motionless and unmoveable persistence of objects, what we are, what we must do, what we cannot do.

But the Navy is known for the quality of its officers, for its capacity to train them efficiently, for its openness to the outside world and to progress. (After the Second World War, when Italy went through its great economic development, the Navy was one of the sources that industry drew on for its executives.) Training in modern techniques requires the participation of students, interaction between them and the teacher, the possibility of discussion and of verifying the success of the learning process. All this must therefore take place, and it does take place: but elsewhere, in a place which inverts the initial situation, offering almost a mirror-image of it, in a setting which allows, suggests, promotes — physically and symbolically — everything that the first setting denied. The contradiction is dealt with through temporal and especially physical loose-coupling: the two values are enacted and testified to at different moments and in different places. But the hierarchical relationship between the two values must not be left in ambiguity, nor left to be inferred solely from the temporal succession: what happens *afterwards* might be the more important, not what happens first.

The problem is solved through a linguistic artifact: the definition of the second setting as the "bollockdrome." "Drome" is the second element in compound words like hippodrome and autodrome, and indicates a place where racing (for pleasure or in competition) takes place: the second element of the word thus underlines the message of absolute freedom — essential to the learning-process. But what race or compete are, by definition, "bollocks." The hierarchy of values is re-established, unmistakably, through a linguistic artifact the features of which express the intention of alleviating the emotional tension which the definition of a hierarchy between values can bring about (Martin et al. 1983), shifting the discourse from the *serious* plane of logical congruence to the *jesting* plane of the amusing paradox.

4.1 The Pathways of Action

Artifacts are pathways of action and constitute a concrete element in the social structure: actors daily create and recreate the reality of their own identity and of the mutual relationships within bounds which are the result of previous choices, made by other actors or by themselves at different moments (see the contributions in this volume by Rosen/Orlikowski/ Schmahmann and by Rusted). The most immediately perceptible of these bounds is the field within which the actors move, which is at the same time a physical and symbolic ground, the properties and contours of which are defined by artifacts. It embodies institutional arrangements, routines, cognitive frames, and imageries, and is at the same time part and expression of what Ciborra and Lanzara call the formative context, the deep-seated structure which influences the behavior of the actors and which "accounts for their skills, the inertia of their learning, and the unawareness of their actual practices" (Ciborra/Lanzara, this volume: p. 150).

Every organization over time constructs its own cultural identity, and the process of institutionalization has been thus defined as the progressive infusion of values into an arrangement originally conceived according to a strictly instrumental logic (Selznick 1957). The maintaining of this identity, which is the product of history and circumstances, becomes the main aim of the organization (Selznick 1948), and the set of values which uphold the cultural identity circumscribes the range of options available for organizational action. The alternatives for design and for physical and symbolic manipulation of the setting are similarly limited to a range of options which reflect both the contextually operating system of assumptions (Gagliardi 1986) and the previous design decisions inscribed in the corporate biography and which shape its future evolution (Kimberly 1987, 1988).

Through what processes do the physical setting and artifacts influence the behavior of the actors? And through what processes do the actors cope with the physical setting, whether that represents a familiar situation — as happens with those already "inside" the culture of an organization — or whether it represents a new and unexpected situation — as happens with newcomers? Obviously, the two types of process can be distinguished only analytically — and to a limited degree — since they are inextricably linked and the existence of one cannot be posited without the existence of the other: it is more just, therefore, to consider them as two complementary and interactive aspects of a single process, the interplay between the physical setting and the person dwelling or arriving within it.

As we have already observed, this interrelationship has been studied only marginally with specific regard to the physical setting; generally it has been explored as an interrelationship between the individual and the overall organizational setting, viewed as a social and cultural reality and only implicitly as a "tangible" phenomenon. On this view, the analytical categories employed refer, directly or indirectly, to the cognitive capacities of the actors — individuals or social groups — and to the role of information elaborated in the mind. When the enquiry passes from the level of the overt information transmitted by the setting, and from the role of conscious thought in working it out, to go on to investigate less explicit and visible processes, the constructs more frequently encountered in the literature are those of script (Abelson 1976), schema (Bartlett 1932), frame (Bartunek 1988), theories-in-use (Argyris/Schön 1974). These constructs have been elaborated within a theoretical approach which views organizations as "bodies of thought" and as "sets of thinking practices" (Weick 1979: 45). They refer to (generally unconscious) *mental* processes, though it is sometimes stressed that these stimulate or are stimulated by emotions (e. g. Bartunek 1988).

It has been observed that cognitive maps can be encoded within material artifacts: for example, the schematic drawings of office space or a building itself may be "public representations of organizational theory-in-use to which individuals can refer," revealing patterns of communication and control (Argyris/Schön 1978: 17); more frequently, however, students of organizational culture have looked for scripts in immaterial artifacts such as the stories which are recounted and passed down in an organization and which satisfy cognitive needs in members and the organization's exigencies of control (Wilkins 1983b). These authors (who have tended — as we have seen — to neglect material artifacts) have mainly concentrated on the mental representations (such as the myths and stories) of a culture and on behavior patterns (such as the "rituals" in modern bureaucratic organizations): if their interest in social behavior brings out their epistemological affinity with sociological — rather than with anthropological — ethnography (Van Maanen 1988), their interest in mental representations brings out their epistemological affinity with the cognitive approach. The widespread emphasis placed on the definition of culture — or of the organization as culture — in terms of "system of meanings" (Smircich 1983a, 1983b) is itself an indication of this general leaning. One may well wonder, however, whether in our search for "sense" we haven't too hastily skimmed over the "senses," and whether paying more attention to the "filters" which culture imposes on sensory experience might not improve our understanding of culturally specific mental representations and behavior patterns.

Clearly the physical setting influences the behavior of the actors since the first thing it does is to limit and structure their sensory experience. A specific setting allows us to do some things but not others — i. e. it sets us physical bounds in a strict sense — and it gives rise to certain sensations and not others. The selective stimuli — visual, aural, olfactory, tactile — transmitted by the habitat created by the organization accustom us (more rapidly perhaps than is usually thought or than we ourselves are aware of) to use our senses in a different way, so that the same event can be perceived in one setting entirely differently from the way it is perceived in another (Hall 1966).

The symbolic potency itself of artifacts — their capacity, as symbols, to rouse feelings and urge to action — is all the greater the more the symbol engenders sensations. Representing victory (Nike) as a beautiful half-naked woman, the Greeks did not aim at evoking in their warriors the idea of woman, but the sensations of erotic pleasure and the association of a panted-for victory with the instinctual desire for sexual conquest. For this reason the meaning of a symbol is often "intuitively sensed, not consciously interpreted" (Geertz 1973: 128); symbols — as products of creative work shaped to rouse sensations and emotions — have an internal dramatic structure, and their study is partly a study in the sociology of art (Cohen 1976: 30). Obviously, the tendency itself to associate pleasant or unpleasant sensations, attraction or disgust, with specific stimuli is not universal. Against a pre-cultural background, which has its roots in the biological past of mankind, patterns of association and reaction are structured which are the fruit of experience and history, and which are therefore culturally conditioned. The sense of beauty is a cultural product just like artifacts themselves:

The artist works with his audience's capacities ... And though elements of these capacities are indeed innate — it usually helps not to be color-blind — they are brought into actual existence by the experience of living in the midst of certain sorts of things to look at, listen to, handle, think about, cope with, and react to; particular varieties of cabbages, particular sorts of kings. Art and the equipment to grasp it are made in the same shop (Geertz 1983: 118).

Paraphrasing the famous assertion of Max Weber quoted by Geertz (1973), we may say that people are prisoners not only of webs of significance, but also of subtended webs of sensation they themselves have spun.

4.2 Cognitive Maps, Sensory Maps, and Fourth-Level Controls

The wealth of associative and reactive capacities that people construct living in a specific organizational culture probably constitutes an important part of what is usually defined as tacit (Polanyi 1966, Spradley 1979) or informal (Hall 1959) knowledge, basic assumptions (Schein 1985), or mute learning (Ginzburg 1979).

Genetic epistemology suggests that a clear distinction must be made between two fundamental aspects of the subject's behavior, that is to say "... on the one hand, his *actions* (*conduites*), on the other, the *knowledge* the subject himself has of them," and that there is a "recurrent gap between epistemological consciousness of the constructive matrices and effective knowledge (action)" (Ceruti 1989: 125−126)[1]. While philosophical psychology attributes to introspection a limitless power extending to the whole of mental life, the scientific psychology of action (*conduites*) bases itself on the premise that consciousness begins to be centered on the outcome of activity before it reaches its mechanism, and that corresponding to the relative consciousness of outcome there is an almost total unconsciousness of the mechanisms (Piaget 1974). "The real process of knowledge-formation does not consist, therefore, of a succession of states of consciousness ... On the contrary, we must refer to a succession of *activities* (both in the sense of actions and of operations) largely outside the field of consciousness" (Ceruti 1989: 127)[1].

The confines between the form of learning which implies unconscious mental operations and instinctual or intuitive learning are probably very shaky and perhaps not really conceivable. Hall (1959) alludes to these same processes when he claims that so-called informal knowledge consists of a set of activities learnt without the awareness of learning and automatically integrated into daily life.

Starting out from these considerations, we may propose a new construct, to be termed "sensory maps" − having their roots in the last and deepest level of the processes of adaption to the environment, i.e. the physio-biological level, while remaining culturally conditioned − reserving the term cognitive maps for those mental schemata which may be conscious or unconscious but which are "knowable" to the subject. Clearly sensory maps are not in the mind, nor even in the body, but come into operation in the interaction between the senses and a culturally and/or physically characterized setting. Perhaps they correspond to what Van Maanen (1977) terms the maps of space and time which the newcomers construct when their senses undergo the impact of a new setting.

The possible connection with the maps Van Maanen speaks of was suggested to me by the Kantian distinction between passive intuition and intellectual knowledge: intuition corresponds to the "capacity to let oneself be soaked through by the sensory,"[3] ordering it through the *a priori* categories of space and time, *before* (and often *without*) the intellect's conferring of unity on the data of sensory experience through concepts.

The suggestion being made here is that the sensory maps are structured in reference to primordial needs of survival and primordial life experiences, and that they classify the stimuli of a setting along the reassurance/threat axis, to which the parallel inaction/flight/defence/attack axis corresponds. The newcomer's sense of sensory overload can now be interpreted as the frenetic effort to adapt maps activated in previous situations, in the aim of redefining the codes of instinctive reaction to people and things — according to their positioning in space and time and of their every other perceptual feature — and the codes associating stimuli with pleasant/unpleasant sensations. The adaption of the corporal schema, i. e. of the perception we have of our body, may be an example of the activation of sensory maps and perhaps constitutes their basis: people used to moving in a space that can be seen and is free of obstacles, finding themselves in a dark place and/or with different artifactual surrounds, are forced to rapidly redefine their corporal schema, activating different senses and learning at speed — from their experience of impact with tangible reality — to use different patterns of adaptive reaction. These activities are probably at the heart — or, at all events, an important part — of what Berger and Luckmann (1966) term "habitualization."

Sensory maps, which become active in the interaction between our senses and the artifacts of the organization in which we live, belong to what has been termed the "knowledge by clue," which rises out of concrete and sensory experience and relies on subtleties not formalizable and often ineffable; a capacity of *low* intuition as distinct from *high* intuition:

... low intuition is rooted in our senses (though going beyond them) — and as such it has nothing whatever to do with the suprasensory intuition of the various eighteenth and nineteenth century irrationalisms, ... it is far removed from any higher consciousness, ... it links animal man tightly to other animal species (Ginzburg 1979: 156)[1].

Students of organizational culture often refer to Kuhn (1962). It may be worthwhile to recall the importance that Kuhn sets on exemplars — i. e. the *concrete* solutions to problems — in the spread of a paradigm: exemplars serve to carry tacit knowledge, and through them one learns to see things accordingly on the basis of perceptual processes over which we can exert no mental control. In a similar vein, Hall (1959) claims that the main agent of informal knowledge is the imitation of concrete models which permit us to learn in one go a whole set of linked activities without knowing what or which rules govern the thing one learns. This view is consistent, for that matter, with the importance of imitation and of model-following in the learning of work values in organizations, documented in the literature (Bandura 1977, Weiss 1978).

As we know, Perrow (1972) picked out three levels of organizational control: (1) control which is expressed in direct orders; (2) control operating indirectly through programmes and procedures; (3) control exerted by operating on the *ideological* premises of action. The preceding set of considerations leads one to believe that the three levels picket out by Perrow should be increased by a fourth: that exercised by operating on the *sensory* conditions and premises of action, and for which organizational artifacts constitute the vehicle and the expression (see in particular Witkin in this volume).

An interesting question — which would merit detailed exploration — is the relationship between the control of sensory premises and control of the value premises which govern the criteria, more or less explicit, on the basis of which a thing is judged beautiful or ugly. From this viewpoint the distinction between the two levels of control reflects the distinction between general aesthetic experience (the perception of form) and "special" aesthetic experience, which implicates a *judgment of taste* on sensory experience[4]. Control of the sensory premises is achieved by operating on the construction and manipulation of the setting, control of the value premises of an aesthetic kind is achieved by encouraging the spread and interiorization of a specific aesthetic "discourse." The two levels can be consistent, mutually reinforcing each other, or *vice versa* they can diverge: in the second case, the divergence is an indicator of the dialectical interplay of agency and structure, and reflects the diversity or the shift in relative power, in aspirations, and in the strategies of the corporate actors.

5 The Hermeneutic Dimension of Artifacts

> "A simple artifact often holds the essence of a whole social system."
>
> Wuthnow et al. 1984: 4

This section will be introduced by a succinct illustration from my research experience with an Italian firm. I'm not going to give an accurate ethnographic account, both because the need to disguise the firm prevents me from giving certain details, and because the introduction to a collection of essays is perhaps not the most suitable place for giving a full description of a specific organizational culture. My aim is to give the reader the flavor of an experience which significantly influenced my way of studying cultures and of identifying their essence.

The I.T.I.[5] was a limited company producing instrumental goods for domestic and industrial use, selling in Italy and abroad, and considered — by customers and competitors — technically advanced and reliable. The firm had been set up about sixty years earlier as a small repair workshop, inherited by three brothers who had transformed it into a proper factory. I.T.I. had gradually expanded and had finished by taking on national importance. One of the brothers, an engineer with a marked capacity for innovation and technical design, had been the undisputed leader of the enterprise, running it up to the time of his death a few years previously. The firm had passed to the heirs of the three brothers who — after a period of uncertain interregnum — had designated as chairman and managing director a member of the family thought to be an able administrator and a clever negotiator. The firm, employing about 1500 people, was located in Serrato[5], a town of about 20 000 inhabitants, founded in the remote past as a fortress and continuing as such up to the last century, as its position overlooking a river was considered strategically important and readily defended in case of war.

The occasion for my research came from the managing director, who declared that he wanted to "modernize" the firm. It was his view, on the basis of chance information from clients and competitors, that the market share was gradually decreasing, and he thought I.T.I. unsufficiently open to the outside world and poorly integrated within itself. What exasperated him most was the futility of his attempts to get top management to work together. He wanted assistance in understanding the situation.

I spent some weeks looking at what was going on, collecting data, and interviewing people at various levels. I was mainly concentrating on observable behavior patterns and/or those to be inferred from the interviews, my aim being to reconstruct them and interpret them.

I.T.I. had a functional organization which took the form of two large groupings of activities: a technical section and a sales section for Italy. The technical section was split into four departments: product design, planning and organization of production, factory, buying. The domestic sales department consisted of a central office and a sales network using representatives who covered the country. The administration mostly handled the paperwork for the accounts and dealings between the two operative sections; the personnel department hardly existed. A few years previously a retired elderly man, with a successful past as an executive in a large company, had been taken on as general manager: he had quickly ceased to concern himself and had set about expanding and managing export sales, which was a separate department located in a town about 40 kilometers from Serrato. The offices and the factory occupied a single large building set across the river from the "old" fortified township, marking one of the edges of the "new" town. Inside the building, in a long narrow courtyard, stood a statue of the founder.

The two large sections into which I.T.I. was divided were run very independently by managers who had been many years with the firm and who only came together on official occasions, addressed each other formally though they had been working in the same firm for decades and communicated mainly in writing or through "emissaries." Horizontal relationships between intermediate levels in the two structures were strictly forbidden. The setting of production schedules followed on the whole a sequential logic: the technical section let it be known what kind of products would be available, the domestic sales department (and, on its part, the export sales department) let it be known what quantities they could sell, and on this basis production was planned and carried through. Variations to the programme were minimal, both because — the fact was admitted — forecasts were conservative, and because each of the parties adopted their own mechanisms to buffer oscillations, and individual policies aimed at influencing their respective contexts of reference. When it was absolutely necessary to modify a programme, modifications were agreed upon following the strict and formal procedure already mentioned.

The most surprising thing was the repetition of this model on the inside of the two sections. Each of the four departments in the technical section was organized so as to minimize its dependence both on the outside of the section and on the other departments in its own section. In consequence of this arrangement, the department which designed the product also designed even its most elementary components, and the factory made practically all the components of the product, often including the screws which — for one reason or another — were thought to be "special" and unavailable on the market. All the inevitable interdependencies between the four departments were dealt with by the respective heads through rigorously controlled and formalized mechanisms. The managing director's attempt to question the wisdom of making everything themselves had been answered with a great display of figures to the effect that everything produced in-house was produced more cheaply than could be bought: in consternation the managing director wondered whether the principle of the "experience curve" did not hold for his firm. Within the domestic sales department there was no marketing in the usual sense: there was no market-research, nobody was concerned with product management, they did not employ advertising agencies, all the promotional material was produced in-house. In fact, what the firm bought in was almost exclusively raw materials, and the buying was done independently and autonomously — in line with their own needs — by the technical management and by the sales management, always with more than ample safety margins.

In appearance the situation could be interpreted according to the widespread stereotype of the technologically inclined firm used to dominating its market, but this interpretation did not explain the specificity of the patterns of behavior, their persistence, or the internal consistency of the overall structure. I was also puzzled by a sort of instinctive tendency of the managing director to not really put in question the existing structure and the men who ran it, despite the ample powers delegated to him by the other partners. All doubts about the rationality of the arrangement, all reference to the risks involved and to the eventual need of changing it ran up against a widespread belief in the obviousness, inevitability, and — at bottom — unquestionable rightness of the arrangement.

On the occasion of yet another visit to the firm, I was in taxi travelling the 30 kilometers separating Serrato from the chief town of the province. I was musing on another odd circumstance: as opposed to what usually happens in Italy when a firm is a basic element in the economy of a local community, neither the family owning I.T.I. nor members of the management had ever shown the slightest interest in local politics and had never sponsored social or cultural initiatives for the community. One couldn't get away from the fact, I was thinking, that the founder's statue didn't stand — as so often happens — in the town square, but in the internal courtyard of the factory. My thoughts were interrupted by the taxi-driver asking me: "You see this fine road? Did you know that it was laid against the wishes of the people of Serrato? Did you ever hear the like, a town not wanting better connections with the big city?!" Then I suddenly understood: the fortress was the underlying metaphor, the concrete image hidden perhaps in the collective unconscious, perhaps taken in through the old people's stories, certainly incorporated and expressed in perceptible manner in the artifacts. With fresh eyes and a different viewpoint I thought of the contours of the physical space through which I had been wandering unknowingly till then.

The building housing the firm was protected on one side by the river. On one of the flanks overlooking the "new" city there was not a single aperture, on the others, very few windows, long and narrow, which no one ever looked out of and the shutters of which I had always seen closed, whereas there were tall wide windows opening onto the courtyard where the founder's statue had been erected. The two big sectors into which the firm was divided confronted each other across the neutral space of the courtyard, and were accessible only from the courtyard and only by means of an unavoidable narrow passage. In the same way, a single tortuous route permitted passage between the departments into which the technical section was subdivided; and the agents who arrived at general headquarters to deliver or obtain information were received in a room where a counter and a glass panel separated them from their central-office counterparts. Yet again I was conscious of the awkwardness and constraint of those enforced passageways, the reason for which I had not grasped and of which I had been given evasive explanations or rationalizations as rambling as the passageways themselves.

The fortress is the place to which access is controlled, where one learns to distrust outsiders and to rely only on oneself and one's own resources during long siege. The fortress was the code in operation, acting according to the syntactic principle of parallel repetition: as in a game of Chinese boxes, the fortress-city — cut-off, mistrustful, and self-sufficient — produces the fortress-firm, cut-off, wary, and self-sufficient, and this in turn generated fortress-sections and fortress-departments in its own likeness, shaping the physical and organizational structures with the cogency of a seal moulding wax.

"The responses which a specific culture gives to nature are the garments with which to clothe the ignorance of man" (Di Chiara 1986: 349)[1], and these garments are woven out of perceptual forms even before conceptions. The first way in which man protects his natural weakness is by building a shelter: perhaps it is because of this ancestral importance of the shelter that the constructed setting is deliberately or spontaneously used to recount the story of our security, of the certainties which allow us to live and to act. And it is probable that the bolder the convictions of an organization — and, in general, of a social group — the more it will be concerned to reify them, to immortalize them in lasting things, passing them on to succeeding corporate generations through the language of the senses. From this point of view, the constructed setting of an organization is its "monument" and the reflection of its culture.

5.1 The Remains of Organizational Life

Siehl and Martin (1988) claim that cultural forms — as against the practices, formal above all, which constitute the object of study of traditional organizational research — are less susceptible to social desirability biases and more apt to reveal "enacted" themes, as opposed to "espoused" themes; I myself would add that artifacts and the organization of space are the cultural forms least likely to succumb to that risk: we can, in fact, "rehearse" for the time a ritual that no longer has meaning for us, we can send out false messages about our identity, we can give an artificial image of ourselves during a conversation, but we can't live for too long in an artifactual setting inconsistent with the "pathos" of our culture. It is a matter of perceptual dissonance, so to speak, prior even to its being cognitive: by dint of wearing a cultural "garment," we end up by adapting our way of "feeling" to it or we try to change clothes. It is important to note here that adapting oneself to the artifactual environment does not necessarily mean to enjoy it. On the contrary, it is possible that adaption implies suffering: this suffering can be endured dutifully — by those who inwardly share that way of feeling — or felt as ineluctable — by those who lack the power to make the setting consistent with their own different way of feeling.

One hypothesis which the study of the fortress-firm suggested to me was that artifacts can function as a "lapsus" of the collective unconscious, revealing profound modes of feeling different from or opposed to the rationalizations that the members of the culture offer, in perfect good faith, even to themselves. My idea is that organizations, *as utilitarian forms* of human association constructed and reconstructed for the achieving of certain specific goals, tend to censor the expression of the need for persistence and loyalty to themselves which they have *as cultures*, when this need clashes with the necessity to readapt to circumstances the fit of ends and means: failure to readapt would in fact do injury to the basic legitimizing principle of organizations in modern society, i. e. their instrumentality. But mythic significations do not give way to instrumental goals: the scansion of space according to the binary code "sacred/profane" — the fundamental antithesis which, according to Cassirer (Bolognini 1986), structures experience — corrects or underpins the scansion of space according to the rational claims dictated by the exigencies of practical life (Doxtater in this volume).

The possibility that artifacts evade censorship depends on two intrinsic features present in different measure in the various artifacts: the tendency,

proper to matter, to endure over time — something not always easy to
manipulate — and the characteristic they have of being "ornament," of
being "innocent forms," apparently without influence on the "important
things" which are said and done. This hypothesis has often helped me to
uncover unconscious messages, opposed to the stated claims (and *even* to
those inferable from behavior), by analyzing, for example, the formal
features, the illustrations, and all that goes into making up the "decoration"
of a communication (on this point, see the essay in this volume by Dougherty and Kunda).

Obviously, a new building can reflect the cultural changes hoped for by
the top management rather than the traditional values of the organization,
office design may contradict the aspirations and conceptions of workers
about what is to be understood as a satisfactory working environment (see
Hatch in this volume), and members of the organization snatch every
malleable possibility of the setting to express their values and personal
ambitions — creating what Larsen and Schultz (in this volume) call "artifacts of style." This simply means, in line with our argument, that artifacts
evince and reflect social and cultural dynamics, our task is simply that of
carefully decoding them as traces of organizational life. The physical setting
is an arena in which diverse visions and interests, conflicts and bargains,
the *tension*, in a word, implied by the actors' constant attempt to create
and recreate social reality become manifest (see all the contributions to the
first part of this volume, as also the essay by Grafton-Small and Linstead).
But if there is a dominant vision, this will be faithfully reflected by the
artifacts.

The experience I just now related and all the essays in the third part of
this book suggest more than anything the possibility that artifacts reveal a
root metaphor explanatory of the *cultural order* and its translation into
organizational order. If the explanation of structural variability is a central
issue in organization theory, this possibility requires us to reexamine the
supposed secondary and ancillary character of artifacts in the identification
of the distinctive features — cultural and structural — of an organization,
and attribute a different epistemological status to the analysis of artifacts
in the hierarchy of possible research tools.

5.2 Root-Metaphors, Concrete Images, and Organizational Order

A root metaphor, according to Pepper (1942), is the area of common-sense
fact which mankind uses as a basic analogy in its striving to understand
the world. In Pepper's view, there exists a constant tension between common

sense and refined knowledge. Starting from common sense, the person who poses himself the problem of responsible cognition seeks to reduce his doubts through two main types of corroboration: multiplicative and structural corroboration. "Multiplicative corroboration consists in attesting to the repetition of the 'identical' item of evidence in many different instances ... Structural corroboration consists in the convergence of qualitatively different items of evidence in support of a single item" (1942: 104−105). But structural corroboration requires a theory or hypothesis for the connection of the various items of evidence, and this theory or hypothesis is also drawn from common sense. Morgan (1986) claims that organization theorists, in their effort to develop expert knowledge on organization, use the same procedure, and that every theoretical view they work out is in fact a metaphor, a representation of organizational reality in terms of a situation or an object belonging to experience and common sense. Thus, if the very people who in an explicit and conscious way set themselves the problem of understanding and explaining the world are themselves caught in the ineluctable circle which binds expert knowledge to common sense, *a fortiori* it will be not different for a human group whose project is not that of providing itself and others with a systematic and conceptually formulated "theory," but whose main concern is to survive and to act in face of the problems set by the environment. For this reason it seems plausible that at the deepest levels of a culture, at the heart of tacit or informal knowledge, what are to be found are concrete images rather than philosophies.

The strategies adopted by researchers in their efforts to give a holistic interpretation to culture tend to follow two main lines of argument, distinguished at bottom by the two differing epistemologies mentioned in section 4 above. Some students seek, in the deepest layers of culture, for the philosophies and cognitive principles which underpin the cultural order, and use the analysis of symbols and artifacts as confirmation of the abstract conceptions governing action (for example: Schein 1985, Schneider/ Shrivastava 1984, Shrivastava/Schneider 1984). For those who adopt this approach (which we may term a "neo-platonic" approach), the essence or paradigm of a culture is a system of interrelated ideas. Other students instead seek to interpret the cultural order on the basis of a dominant drive (Benedict 1934) or an integrating theme (Barley 1983, Opler 1945) which can be stored in synthesizing symbols (Geertz 1973).

The hypothesis put forward here − of a concrete form which enables us to give a holistic interpretation of an organizational culture and which gives form to the culture in that it is an organization, clearly has more affinity with the approach of students of the second camp rather than the first. In our hypothesis, the basic assumptions − understood as general tendencies to see things and to act in specific ways − derive from a "mould" which defines their hierarchy and reciprocal relationships. What particularizes the specific organizational culture described earlier is not "distrust" or "self-sufficiency," but the stylistic and perceptual context which we have described in the image of the fortress.

It should be noted that the concrete image is not necessarily present to the minds of those who adopt behavior patterns homologous with it, precisely because the patterns may have been learned in an imitative way and absorbed through sensory experience without the subject consciously asking himself about their structure. It is also important to stress that in using the word "image" we are here making reference to the most common way of perceiving a sensory form, that is, by way of the eyes. But there exist equivalents to the image printed on the retina: the global perception of a form may be tactile (as with the blind), olfactory (such as that given to Proust by his "madeleine"), or aural (such as we receive from a musical composition, or in any case through hearing). And I believe it is to this multi-sensory valency that we can attribute the "concrete image's" capacity to simultaneously activate self-consistent associative and reactive patterns. And it is in virtue of this multi-sensory valency that the concrete image which structures experience can be incorporated and transmitted by the whole setting of artifacts and not exclusively or necessarily by the iconography of an organization.

The idea that concrete forms can incorporate mental and value structures has been asserted by various writers, students of symbolism, art historians, and anthropologists. Bolognini, with Cassirer in mind, has claimed that "the logical space of geometry is analytic: it serves to order things and has value only as a logical condition of this order. Mythical space is synthetic: it is like a receptacle which gathers things and events and which takes on their axiological features. This is why it is a carrier of values, the very expression of the ways in which values are divided and shared" (1986: 91)[1]. Douglas and Isherwood (1979) claim that goods establish and dramatize cultural categories. Csikszentmihalyi and Rochberg-Halton (1981) have explored the relationship between objects, the home, and the development of the self. Others have investigated the structural correspondencies between different formal and conceptual orders of social reality: Vernant (1969), for instance, sees in the structuring of space and in the political organization of ancient Greece the imprint of the same *habitus*; Panofsky (1974) has analyzed the relationship between Gothic architecture and scholasticism. However, it is Geertz (1983) who, in my view, grasps the nub of the question when, in his essay on art as a cultural system, he stresses that artifacts are not necessarily illustrations of conceptions already in force, but equally primary documents (Goldwater 1973) which materialize a way of experiencing and of feeling.

The relationship between artifacts and intellectual knowledge is ambiguous and probably of reciprocal interdependence. Perhaps we shall never know whether concrete forms are the product of certain ideas, whether the ideas we receive are rationalizations of ways of feeling or whether the ideas we read off from forms are only *our* way of interpreting them. For this reason, if I were to claim that the specific metaphor used by a researcher to explain the structure and the behavior patterns of a particular organization is valid only if we are *certain* that it corresponds to the concrete image imprinted on the senses of its members, I would contradict everything I have said so far. The metaphor we latch onto may be an idea of our own, a rationalization we are forced to adopt by the necessity of communicating to others what we have intuited about another culture: its heuristic value lies solely in its plausibility as an overall criterion of interpretation of all we have observed and described. This observation takes us on to the problem of the methods available for the study of organizational cultures through their artifacts, which we shall investigate in the following section.

6 The Study of Artifacts

The research strategies available for the study of artifacts — as of other cultural forms — seem to fall under two distinct heads: (1) formalist and analytic approaches which tend to interpret artifacts by abduction — i.e. on the basis of general rules governing the conventions of signification (Manning 1987); (2) antiformalist, relativistic, contextual approaches which tend to interpret artifacts on the basis of "local" and inductive logics (Geertz 1983).

The two approaches can be combined in use. Barley (1983), for example, studying the culture of a funeral home, used the semiotic approach to interpret objects — though still through the linguistic mediation of members of the organization — and to identify an organizational theme integral to the culture which functions as a local syntactical principle, like the image of the fortress in the case of I.T.I. which I have described.

The limits of the semiotic approach in studying cultural artifacts derive from the fact that — as Barthes (1964) has observed — semiotics is not (as Saussure postulated) the general science of signs of which linguistics is a part, but a copy of linguistic knowledge which has been very timidly applied to non-linguistic objects. Bromberger (1979) has stressed that the significance of an object's form depends on the "semantic dosage" — variable according to culture — of three functions: (1) the practical function, i.e. the *instrumentality* of the object as regards specific contextual needs; (2) the function of *social distinction* performed by the object as a sign uniting a form and a meaning in an explicit relationship on the basis of a system of culturally recognized conventions; (3) a function *expressive* of specific values and ideologies, manifested analogically and for the most part in an implicit way, escaping individual consciousness. The meaning of an object as sign is consciously linked to the system of acquired expectations and habits which culturally define its use: from this viewpoint the semiotic-formalist approach is very useful. As symbol, however, the object must be interpreted on the basis of the subtle correspondences between its stylistic modalities — i. e. its formal particularities — and the culture that produces it. We are no longer in the field of semiotics but of general aesthetics, understood as a general theory of sensibility[4].

The essays in this volume exploring the possibility of using artifacts as cultural indicators for the most part employ approaches which are more inductive and qualitative, postulating, more or less implicitly, the research-er's *identification* with the situation being investigated (see, in particular, the beginning of Schwartz's essay and the methodological proposal in Larsen and Schultz). To the reader this preference ought to appear consist-ent with the emphasis we have put on the artifact's being the expression of an organization's specific *way of feeling* (pathos).

Rosen (1989) has discussed the special epistemologically based problems rising out of the fact that in organizational research the studied and the studier most often inhabit the same society. At least as regards the analysis of artifacts and the sensory dimension of organizational life, it seems to me that this position offers opportunities foreclosed to the anthropologist studying isolated and exotic communities: it is unlikely, in effect, that a student of civilizations far removed from his own manage to "get inside the skin" of the natives, and Geertz's assertion (1983: 44) remains true: "we can never apprehend another people's or another period's imagination neatly, as though it were our own." But all those of us who study formal contemporary organizations may belong (or even do belong: see Sievers' essay) to the organizations under investigation. The way of feeling of the particular organization we are studying — should it have a distinct cul-ture — is different from our own if we belong to other culturally charac-terized organizations, but we can quickly learn to feel in the same way as the organization we are studying feels: culturally specific codes can suspend or invert institutional codes (see the essay by Berg and Kreiner in this volume), but just because of this they tend to be structured *in relation* to those institutional codes spread throughout the society to which both the studied and the studier belong.

Since my experience at I.T.I. I have often wondered whether we wouldn't become more adept at grasping the language of artifacts if we were forced to use *them alone* for interpreting a culture, if we were in the position of the archeologist. I have thus adopted the habit — whenever possible — of staying behind in the setting of the organization I am studying when everybody else has left: every "locus" has its "genius," and I believe it is less improbable to take hold of it when the din of voices has died away, the actors exit, and the stage is left empty. The voices and the actors are fundamental elements of the perceptual context: words, sentences, discourses can be creative products which rouse sensations and feelings, and it is mainly for their stylistic qualities that words, sentences, and discourses are discussed in this volume as "linguistic artifacts" (see the essay by Piccardo/Varchetta/Zanarini and that by Czarniawska-Joerges/Joerges in this volume); in the same way, people "resound," smell, are made visible through the way they dress, gesticulate, act. Nevertheless, the prevalence, on the one hand, of the pragmatic element in organizational communication and behavior, and our *cognitive* attitude towards them (our effort to *understand* their meaning, even symbolic), tend, on the other, to overwhelm our capacity to "let ourselves become soaked through" with their formal qualities.

Mirvis and Louis (1985) have claimed that a particular relationship gets established between the researcher and the human system he or she studies. An analysis of the emotional dynamics implicated in this relationship constitutes an important element in the process of research, in the same way that the examination of countertransference is an integral part of psychoanalytic practice. This claim provides the occasion to make two points crucial for my argument: (1) the researcher establishes transference with the physico-perceptual setting as well as with the human and social system; this relationship should not be hindered or immediately rationalized but lived without misgiving; (2) it is at the same time indispensable for the researcher to assume a *reflective* attitude enabling him or her to get a clear grasp of the specificity of the sensory maps which are structured in the setting. From this viewpoint a long stay in the setting hampers rather than fosters the capacity for reflection: the researchers — like the newcomers — adapt rapidly to the perceptual context so as to reduce the sensory overload, to harmonize with the physical setting and to give themselves over to what they best control — the relationship between their mind and the organization as a "body of thought."

The reader who has followed the thread so far will not be astonished by the final corollary to be drawn from the conceptual framework proposed: the ideal report of what we have "felt" that the natives "feel" can only be given in a way that enables our audience to "feel," and it demands that we use our creative imaginations. The aesthetic experience should be transmitted in ways consonant with its nature.

In treating this latter point, I shall need to refer yet again to a personal experience. Having finished a research project, I asked a member of the team to make a brief report on what she felt were the most important

findings in her field work, to be written up in whatever way she felt
respected them best. She wrote a fairytale and we decided to include it in
the research report. The research had been commissioned by the managing
director of the organization we had been studying, a recent appointee from
outside. In presenting the report, we spoke to our client about beliefs,
values, and ideologies, and he made a visible effort, without great success,
to follow our reasoning. Then, when the fairytale was read out, he blanched
and said: "At last! Now I'm with you!"

7 Towards a Theory of Corporate Artifacts

Our starting point, in this introduction, was the definition of the artifact
as an intentional product of human action perceptible through the senses,
and we have surveyed the marginal role played by the study of the physical
setting — as a source of sensory and emotional experience — in organization
theory and organizational culture research.

Among the possible reasons for this neglect particular attention was
given to the tendency to employ a cognitive paradigm even in the study of
the symbolic aspects of the organization. We then suggested that organizational cultures be studied not just by picking out the ontological element
(the logos) and the deontological element (the ethos), but also the sensory
and aesthetic element (the pathos), formulating the hypothesis that corporate artifacts represent and are the vehicle of the pathos of corporate
culture.

In exploring the pragmatic dimension of artifacts — their being the
pathways for organizational action — and their hermeneutical dimension —
their being remains of corporate life, documenting and reflecting its social
and cultural dynamics —, a chain of linked ideas has been offered, which
I shall now briefly run through for the sake of the reader.

Artifacts constitute a concrete element in the social structure and are
most immediately perceptible of all the physical and symbolic bounds within
which the actors move and which they strive to modify and manipulate ...

The physical setting influences the behavior of the actors because it
selectively steers and structures their sensory experience ...

The wealth of associative and reactive capacities which people construct
living in a specific setting is an important part of so-called tacit or informal
"knowledge" ...

This wealth gets translated into "sensory maps" which become activated
in the dynamic interaction between the senses and a specific physico-cultural

setting, and which can be distinguished from unconscious mental schemata ...

Sensory maps classify the stimuli in a setting along the reassurance/threat axis, to which the parallel inaction/flight/defence/attack axis corresponds ...

Adaption to a new setting implicates the redefinition of codes of instinctive reaction to people and things — according to their formal qualities — and of codes associating stimuli to pleasant/unpleasant sensations ...

The possibility therefore exists of a fourth level of organizational control (as against the three indicated by Perrow), which is exerted by operating on the sensory conditions and premises of action, and of which artifacts are the vehicle and expression ...

Organizational cultures tend to reify their basic assumptions and particular way of feeling (pathos) in the setting constructed by the organization ...

Material artifacts and the organization of space are less susceptible to social desirability biases than other cultural forms and more apt to reveal the enacted cultural themes and the tension implied by the actors' constant efforts to create and recreate social reality ...

In particular, artifacts can reveal the root metaphor which explains the cultural order and its translation into the organizational order ...

The root metaphor incorporated and transmitted by the artifactual setting tends to be a concrete multi-sensory image which simultaneously activates self-consistent patterns of association and reaction ...

Artifacts, as the expression of an organization's way of feeling (pathos), can be studied by means of inductive and qualitative approaches which postulate both the researcher's identification with the situation under investigation and his or her capacity — at the same time — to reflect on the sensations he or she feels ...

Reporting on what the researcher has picked up of the pathos of an organization requires the use of creative imagination and of ways of communicating consonant with the aesthetic nature of the experience to be communicated ...

The ideas set out above were developed out of the literature, out of my research experience — but above all in response to stimuli from the essays in this volume. From a certain point of view, it would have been more appropriate to have placed this sketch of a theory at the end of the book. Nevertheless, I have adopted as my own Weick's thesis (1987: 122) that: "Ideas ... gain their value from what they allow us to see in organizations. Evocative ideas need to be cultivated by theorists from the beginning because belief, not skepticism, precedes observation ... If believing affects seeing, and if theories are significant beliefs that affect what we see, then theories should be adopted more to maximize what we see than to summarize what we have already seen." I hope that this attempt at theorizing will help the readers *to see more* in the essays which follow and in the organizations they study or in which they live.

Notes

1 The translation is my own.
2 Quoted in C. K. Ogden and I. A. Richards (1949): *The Meaning of Meaning*. London: Routledge & Kegan Paul, p. 139.
3 I owe this trenchant formulation of the Kantian view to Fulvio Carmagnola, in conversation.
4 I owe the sharpness of this distinction to an exchange of ideas with Fulvio Carmagnola. On the difference between Aesthetics as a general theory of sensibility and Aesthetics as a theory of art, Formaggio has said: "... Throughout its history since the Greeks, it [Aesthetics] has dealt with two distinct classes of event: the facts of sensibility and artistic facts or events, i.e. sensory facts or events and those of artistic praxis and experience. Aesthetics has always claimed that they were confused together: by dealing with two totally different, even if mutually related, sets of event, Aesthetics has often been active in this confusion. Meanwhile in the modern world it has become evident that the events which constitute the artistic experience have nothing to do with those that constitute the aesthetico/sensory or contemplative experience. To create art is one thing, to contemplate a beautiful sunset is another. They belong to two different classes even on theoretical grounds. Today Aesthetics has no alternative but take this old story for granted and thus become a general theory of sensibility since it deals with the body, perception, memory, and by so doing becomes a prefatory science for physiology, psychology, the human sciences in general" (*Domus* 1986: 16).
5 The name is fictitious.

References

Abelson, R. P. (1976): Script Processing in Attitude Formation and Decision Making. *Cognition and Social Behavior*. J. S. Carroll/J. W. Payne (Eds.). Hillsdale, NJ.: Lawrence Erlbaum, pp. 33–46
Argyris, C. and D. A. Schön (1974): *Theory in Practice*. San Francisco, CA: Jossey-Bass
Argyris, C. and D. A. Schön (1978): *Organizational Learning: A Theory of Action Perspective*. Reading, MA: Addison-Wesley
Bandura, A. (1977): *Social Learning Theory*. Morristown, NJ: General Learning Press
Barley, S. R. (1983): Semiotics and the Study of Occupational and Organizational Cultures. *Administrative Science Quarterly* 28, pp. 393–413

Barley, S. R., G. W. Meyer, and D. Gash (1988): Cultures of Culture: Academic Practitioners, and the Pragmatics of Normative Control. *Administrative Science Quarterly* 33(1), pp. 24−60

Barthes, R. (1964): *Éléments de semiologie*. Paris: Seuil

Bartlett, F. C. (1932): *Remembering*. Cambridge: Cambridge University Press

Bartunek, J. M. (1988): The Dynamics of Personal and Organizational Reframing. *Paradox and Transformation*. R. E. Quinn/K. S. Cameron (Eds.). Cambridge, MA: Ballinger Publishing Company, pp. 137−162

Beattie, J. (1964): *Other Cultures*. London−Henley: Routledge & Kegan Paul

Benedict, R. (1934): *Patterns of Culture*. Boston: Houghton-Mifflin

Berg, P. O. (1987): Some Notes on Corporate Artifacts. *SCOS Note-Work* 6(1), pp. 24−28

Berger, P. L. and T. Luckmann (1966): *The Social Construction of Reality: A Treatise in the Sociology of Knowledge*. Garden City, N.Y.: Doubleday

Bolognini, B. (1986): Il mito come espressione dei valori organizzativi e come fattore strutturale. *Le imprese come culture*. P. Gagliardi (Ed.). Milano: ISEDI, pp. 79−101

Bromberger, C. (1979): Technologie et analyse sémantique des objets: pour une sémio-technologie. *L'Homme*, janvier-mars, XIX(I), pp. 105−140

Ceruti, M. (1989): *La danza che crea*. Milano: Feltrinelli

Cohen, A. (1976): *Two-Dimensional Man*. Berkeley−Los Angeles: University of California Press

Csikszentmihalyi, M. and E. Rochberg-Halton (1981): *The Meaning of Things: Domestic Symbols and the Self*. Cambridge: Cambridge University Press

Deal, T. E. and A. A. Kennedy (1982): *Corporate Cultures: The Rites and Rituals of Corporate Life*. Reading, MA: Addison-Wesley

Di Chiara, G. (1986): Psicoanalisi: natura e cultura. *Rivista di Psicoanalisi* XXXII(3), pp. 343−351

Domus (1986): Dino Formaggio: progettare con il corpo. *Domus* N. 676, pp. 16−24

Douglas, M. and B. Isherwood (1979): *The World of Goods*. New York: Basic Books

Gagliardi, P. (1986): The Creation and Change of Organizational Cultures: A Conceptual Framework. *Organization Studies* 7(2), pp. 117−134

Geertz, C. (1973): *The Interpretation of Cultures*. New York: Basic Books

Geertz, C. (1983): *Local Knowledge. Further Essays in Interpretive Anthropology*. New York: Basic Books

Ginzburg, C. (1979): Spie. Radici di un paradigma indiziario. *Crisi della ragione*. Aldo Gargani (Ed.). Torino: Einaudi, pp. 57−106

Goffman, E. (1959): *The Presentation of Self in Everyday Life*. New York: Doubleday

Goldwater, R. (1973): Art and Anthropology: Some Comparisons of Methodology. *Primitive Art and Society*. A. Forge (Ed.). London: Oxford University Press

Hall, E. T. (1959): *The Silent Language*. New York: Doubleday

Hall, E. T. (1966): *The Hidden Dimension*. New York: Doubleday

Herzberg, F., B. Mausner, and B. B. Snyderman (1959): *The Motivation to Work*. New York: John Wiley and Sons

Holsti, O. R. (1969): *Content Analysis for the Social Sciences and Humanities*. Reading, MA: Addison-Wesley

Homans, G. C. (1950): *The Human Group*. New York: Harcourt, Brace

Hughes, E. C. (1958): *Men and Their Work*. Glencoe, IL: Free Press

Jones, M. O., M. D. Moore, and R. C. Snyder (Eds.) (1988): *Inside Organizations*. Beverly Hills, CA: Sage

Kimberly, J. R. (1987): The Study of Organization: Toward a Biographical Perspective. *Handbook of Organizational Behavior*. J. W. Lorsch (Ed.). New York: Prentice-Hall, pp. 223–237

Kimberly, J. R. (1988): Reframing and the Problem of Organizational Change. *Paradox and Transformation*. R. E. Quinn/K. S. Cameron (Eds.). Cambridge, MA: Ballinger Publishing Company, pp. 163–168

Kuhn, T. S. (1962): *The Structure of Scientific Revolutions*. Chicago, IL: University of Chicago Press

Louis, M. R. (1980): Surprise and Sense Making: What Newcomers Experience in Entering Unfamiliar Organizational Settings. *Administrative Science Quarterly* 25, pp. 226–251

Louis, M. R. (1983): Organizations as Culture-Bearing Milieux. *Organizational Symbolism*. L. R. Pondy/P. J. Frost/G. Morgan/T. C. Dandridge (Eds.). Greenwich, CT: JAI Press, Vol. 1, pp. 39–54

Manning, P. K. (1987): *Semiotics and Fieldwork*, Beverly Hills, CA: Sage

Martin, J. and C. Siehl (1983): Organizational Culture and Counterculture: An Uneasy Symbiosis. *Organizational Dynamics* 12(2), pp. 52–64

Martin, J., M. S. Feldman, M. J. Hatch, and S. B. Sitkin (1983): The Uniqueness Paradox in Organizational Stories. *Administrative Science Quarterly* 28, pp. 438–453

Maslow, A. H. (1943): A Theory of Human Motivation. *Psychological Review* 50, pp. 370–386

Mirvis, P. and M. R. Louis (1985): Self-Full Research: Working through the Self as Instrument in Organizational Research. *Exploring Clinical Methods for Social Research*. D. N. Berg/K. K. Smith (Eds.). Beverly Hills, CA: Sage, pp. 229–246

Morgan, G. (1986): *Images of Organization*. Beverly Hills, CA: Sage

Ogden, C. K. and I. A. Richards (1949): *The Meaning of Meaning*. London: Routledge and Kegan Paul

Opler, M. E. (1945): Themes as Dynamics Forces in Culture. *American Journal of Sociology* 3, pp. 192–206

Ouchi, W. G. and A. L. Wilkins (1985): Organizational Culture. *Ann. Rev. Sociol.* 11, pp. 457–483

Panofsky, E. (1974): *Architecture gothique et pensée scolastique*. Paris: Editions de Minuit

Pepper, S. C. (1942): *World Hypotheses: A Study on Evidence*. Berkeley, CA: University of California Press

Perrow, C. (1972): *Complex Organizations: A Critical Essay*. Glenview, IL: Scott, Foresman

Pfeffer, J. (1981): Management as Symbolic Action: The Creation and Maintenance of Organizational Paradigms. *Research in Organizational Behavior*. B. M. Staw/ L. L. Cummings (Eds.). Greenwich, CT: JAI Press, Vol. 3, pp. 1–52

Piaget, J. (1967): *Logique et connaissance scientifique*. Paris: Gallimard

Piaget, J. (1974): *La prise de conscience*. Paris: PUF

Plato (1987): *The Republic*. Desmond Lee (Trsl.). Harmondsworth: Penguin Books

Polanyi, M. (1966): *The Tacit Dimension*. Garden City, NY: Doubleday

Rosen, M. (1989): Coming to Terms with the Field: Understanding and Doing Organizational Ethnography. Paper presented at the 4th International SCOS Conference, Fontainebleau, June

Schein, E. H. (1984): Coming to a New Awareness of Organizational Culture. *Sloan Management Review* 25(4), pp. 3–16

Schein, E. H. (1985): *Organizational Culture and Leadership*. San Francisco, CA: Jossey-Bass

Schein, E. H. (1987): *The Clinical Perspective in Fieldwork*. Beverly Hills, CA: Sage

Schneider, S. C. and P. Shrivastava (1984): Content of Basic Assumptions. Paper presented at the First International Conference on Organization Symbolism and Corporate Culture, Lund, Sweden, June

Selznick, P. (1948): Foundation of the Theory of Organization. *American Sociological Review* 13, pp. 25–35

Selznick, P. (1957): *Leadership in Administration*. Evanston, IL: Harper and Row

Shrivastava, P. and S. C. Schneider (1984): Organizational Frames of Reference. *Human Relations* 37(10), pp. 795–809

Siehl, C. and J. Martin (1988): Measuring Organizational Culture: Mixing Qualitative and Quantitative Methods. *Inside Organizations*. M. O. Jones/M. D. Moore/R. C. Snyder (Eds.). Beverly Hills, CA: Sage, pp. 79–103

Siehl, C. and J. Martin (1989): Organizational Culture: A Key to Financial Performance? *Organizational Culture and Climate*. B. Schneider (Ed.). San Francisco: Jossey-Bass

Smircich, L. (1983a): Concepts of Culture and Organizational Analysis. *Administrative Science Quarterly* 28(3), pp. 339–358

Smircich, L. (1983b): Organizations as Shared Meanings. *Organizational Symbolism*. L. R. Pondy/P. J. Frost/G. Morgan/T. C. Dandridge (Eds.). Greenwich, CT: JAI Press, Vol. I, pp. 55–65

Spradley, J. P. (1979): *The Ethnographic Interview*. New York: Holt, Rinehart and Winston

Steele, F. I. (1973): *Physical Settings and Organization Development*. Reading, MA: Addison-Wesley

Strati, A. (1990): Aesthetics and Organizational Skill. *Organizational Symbolism*. B. A. Turner (Ed.). Berlin: de Gruyter, pp. 207–222

Summerson, J. (1989): The Mischievous Analogy. *Domus* 702, February, pp. 17–29

Sundstrom, E. (1986): *Work Places: The Psychology of the Physical Environment in Offices and Factories*. New York: Cambridge University Press

Sundstrom, E. (1987): Work Environments: Offices and Factories. *Handbook of Environmental Psychology*. D. Stokols/I. Altman (Eds.). New York: John Wiley and Sons, Vol. 1, pp. 733–782

Van Maanen, J. (1977): Experiencing Organization: Notes on the Meaning of Careers and Socialization. *Organizational Careers: Some New Perspectives*. J. Van Maanen (Ed.). New York: Wiley, pp. 15–45

Van Maanen, J. (1988): *Tales of the Field*. Chicago–London: The University of Chicago Press

Vernant, J. P. (1969): *Mythe et pensée chez les Grecs*. Paris: Maspero

Weick, K. E. (1979): Cognitive Processes in Organizations. *Research in Organizational Behavior*. L. L. Cummings/B. M. Staw (Eds.). Greenwich, CT: JAI Press, Vol. 1, pp. 41 – 74

Weick, K. E. (1987): Theorizing about Organizational Communication. *Handbook of Organizational Communication*. F. Jablin/L. Putnam/K. Roberts/L. Porter (Eds.). London: Sage, pp. 97 – 122

Weiss, H. M. (1978): Social Learning of Work Values in Organization. *Journal of Applied Psychology* 63(6), pp. 711 – 718

Wexler, M. N. (1983): Pragmatism, Interactionism and Dramatism: Interpreting the Symbol in Organizations. *Organizational Symbolism*. L. R. Pondy/P. J. Frost/G. Morgan/T. C. Dandridge (Eds.). Greenwich, CT: JAI Press, Vol. 1, pp. 237 – 253

Wilkins, A. L. (1983a): A Culture Audit: A Tool for Understanding Organizations. *Organizational Dynamics* 12(2), pp. 52 – 64

Wilkins, A. L. (1983b): Organizational Stories as Symbols which Control the Organization. *Organizational Symbolism*. L. R. Pondy/P. J. Frost/G. Morgan/T. Dandridge (Eds.). Greenwich, CT: JAI Press, pp. 81 – 92

Wuthnow, R., J. Davison Hunter, A. Bergesen, and E. Kurzweil (1984): *Cultural Analysis*. London – New York: Routledge & Kegan Paul

Part I:
Designing Physical Settings in Organizations

Corporate Architecture: Turning Physical Settings into Symbolic Resources

Per Olof Berg and Kristian Kreiner

1 Corporate Architecture — Vanity or Asset

It is an indisputable fact that organizations increasingly care about their physical appearance. Huge amounts of money are being invested in improved corporate "looks," in terms of slick, stylish corporate buildings, new office lay-outs and decorations, landscape gardening, graphic designs, corporate "uniforms" and colour codes, visual identities, etc. This apparent "corporate vanity" has infected organizations in most industrial sectors, for example in the corporate identity programmes in the petrol industry (Q8, Statoil, Mobil Oil, Caltex, Norsk Hydro, etc.), in corporate graphics in the airline industry (e. g. British Airways' visual identity programme), and in image programmes in the telecommunication industry (e. g. AT & T and KTAS, Copenhagen). Even contractors, ordinarily known for their stolidity and distaste for bureaucratic red tape, nowadays paint their heavy equipment in carefully selected colours and develop professional graphic design for their stationery and forms. Also hospitals now renovate their facilities in order to look more inviting (Sponseller/Hatfield 1986)! The "styling" of corporations is, however, not limited to the surface of the organization but includes also the interior design and the lay-out of production plants and retail outlets (e. g. as in McDonald's restaurants and Pizza Huts).

In this chapter we will focus on one facet of the physical appearance of organizations, i. e. the *physical setting* (the immediate built environment) in which organizations operate and with which they are identified. By physical setting we simply mean the *exterior and interior design of corporate buildings*. Of particular interest to us in this study are those aspects of the physical settings which are said to express particular and strategic aspects of the organization or its business (the corporate profile), or which delineate the organization as a whole, as experienced by its members (its identity). In modern managerial terms, this is often referred to as "corporate architecture" (when referring to the overall architectonic aspects of the buildings), as "interior design" (when referring to the inside of the buildings with their space lay-out, choice of colours, furniture, etc.), as "visual identity" (when referring to all forms of visual material, such as logos, office design, retail outlet design, colours, and uniforms), and as "corporate design" (when referring to products — and the way in which they are packaged and sold —, buildings and settings). In this chapter we will mainly use examples of corporate architecture. However, our discussion can be used in a discourse on any of the corporate activities mentioned above.

In a strictly "instrumental" perspective it is easy to ridicule this preoccupation with corporate surfaces and physical appearance. How could one ever justify a $ 50 million investment in a corporate identity programme? Are not the buildings of many new corporate headquarters signs of megalomania or self-inflation on behalf of a corporate president rather than the result of a carefully calculated facility plan?

However, when seen in a symbolic perspective, buildings and other physical artifacts take on a new meaning that does not lend itself easily to pure instrumental explanations. In this perspective, buildings may be seen as symbolic artifacts that reflect (and as such may inform us about) some basic traits of the organization inhabiting them. While the physical setting is not ascribed great significance in conventional organization theory, it is indeed a common understanding that the individuality of organizations somehow surfaces in the way they build and dwell:

The individuality of the great [British Railway] companies was expressed in styles of architecture, typography and liveries of engines and carriages, even down to the knives and forks and crockery used in refreshment rooms and dining cars. The Midland favoured Gothic, and so, in a less expensive way, did the Great Eastern. The Great Western remained its strong Gooch-and-Brunel self. Greek learning dominated the London and North Western. The Great Northern went in for a reliable homeliness rather than beauty. The Midland Railway was the line for comfort rather than speed. It introduced dining cars in the very early days and its rolling stock was always particularly agreeable to travel on, although rarely quite as fast as its competitors. St Pancras Station, its scarlet brick terminal in London, was much grander than next door King's Cross, London terminal of the rival Great Northern Railway. The Great Northern was, as Betjeman says, "noted more for its trains than its buildings." The Midland put Sir Gilbert Scott's fantastical Gothic palace in front of Barlow's magnificent engine shed, but the Great Northern's workman-like King's Cross was designed by Lewis Cubitt with the minimum delay, cost and fuss (Olins 1978: 19—21).

While the individuality of organizations, presumably to a large degree unwittingly, is expressed in their physical settings, the phenomenon of corporate vanity signifies a greater intentionality in the choice of physical expression. Coinciding with the enlarged notion of management, now also to include the task of meaning creation and maintenance (Pfeffer 1981), corporate buildings have in the hands of contemporary management been transformed from "containers" of organized behaviour to impelling symbols of corporate virtues and managerial intentions. As such, buildings and other physical artifacts have become powerful managerial tools as well as tools of production. This is almost an institutionalized truth by now, and at any rate the kind of argument which is brought forward as managerial justification for the often heavy investments in the physical appearance of the organization.

Furthermore, the emphasis on corporate surfaces can be seen as a purposeful adaptation to postmodern society with its emphasis on appearance and mass communication. What counts today is as much the appearance of an organization — and thus its credibility — as its performance.

However, as we will show in this chapter, the relationship between the building as such and what it is meant to signify in the life of the organization or in society is not only a largely unexplored empirical field, but also a highly problematic theoretical territory. How do we, for example, know that a certain design will evoke a certain emotional, aesthetic, or intellectual collective response, and through which processes is the dead material of buildings (the bricks and beams) turned into living symbolic assets?

Thus, the aim of our study is to clarify the mechanisms by means of which the physical settings of organizations may indeed become symbolic resources. We are convinced that the intended symbolism in corporate buildings is commonly known by organizational members and others. At the same time, however, the technology of symbolic management appears, in our analysis, to be extremely unclear. Untangling this paradox helps us to understand more precisely which role physical symbols play in contemporary organizations.

2 The State of the Art

The symbolic aspects of the physical settings, especially the built environments which man inhabits, have been recognized as important and valid phenomena in most of the social sciences. Archaeologists have studied the remains of buildings of past civilizations, which has enabled them to grasp the way in which people of a particular civilization lived, produced, and interacted. Anthropologists and sociologists have studied existing buildings and recognized the social structure and social relationships of the cultures under study. There are even today sub-sciences primarily concerned with the way in which man interacts with his physical settings in symbolic terms.

One example is "environmental psychology" which is dealing with the subtle and complex consequences of physical conditions on human behaviour.

While earlier research in this field was mostly concerned with physical structures and physical stimuli and their effects on performance and comfort, recent efforts have been directed also towards studying physical settings as symbolic artifacts (Davis 1984). This leads to a perspective which claims that:

... the dominant influence of the physical surroundings ... is via its significance. It is what the existing surroundings and proposed modifications mean to people involved which carry their influence, much more than any direct effects on behaviour (Canter 1983: 12).

Theory of architecture has undergone a parallel development. Recent reformulations of the role of architecture amend the previous preoccupation with manipulating only space:

... an essential aspect of people's interaction with buildings is the meanings they associate with those buildings; therefore, good design should encompass a conscious manipulation of intended meanings (Groat/Canter 1979: 84).

When applied to the business world, there is even a greater emphasis on the meaning-bridging aspect of buildings. Corporate architecture, as well as plant and environmental design, is seen as a way of infusing the corporation, its activities, and its products with meaning.

However, within *organization theory* the interest in physical settings (in physical as well as in symbolic terms) is conspicuously little. This void has been noticed occasionally, and a few exceptions to the above rule can be found (Davis 1984, Pfeffer 1981, Steel 1973). However, these studies mainly fail to integrate the physical settings into an overall theoretical framework relevant to organizations, and, instead, tend to consider buildings another variable in the organization equation.

Even in the organizational symbolism literature corporate buildings are studied as symbols only occasionally (Grafton-Small 1985, Grafton-Small/ Linstead 1986, Schneider/Powley 1986).

We are bound to conclude that at the level of organizations the significance of physical settings (especially that of corporate buildings) is almost entirely without theoretical underpinnings. On the other hand, much practical experience on this issue seems to have been gained in the field of corporate architecture and environmental design. The practical use of corporate buildings as symbolic artifacts seems to have been spurred by two developments.

First, there is an increased demand among employees (or at least an increased awareness of such demand) for physical signs of their standing within the organization (in terms of status, reputation, performance, etc).

This is also manifested in the increase of narrative or popular accounts of corporate culture (Holm-Löfgren 1980, Page 1974). A quick review of the vast bulk of literature on corporate culture has convinced us that buildings, settings, equipment, products, and other physical artifacts are not only recognized but also considered important in the shaping and maintenance of corporate culture.

Second, there seems to be an increased desire among corporate managers for giving the corporate profile a physical expression in the buildings they inhabit, for internal as well as external purposes. Whether this is only an expression of managerial megalomania or a purposeful corporate adaptation to postmodern society, we do not know. The fact remains, however, that buildings tend to become increasingly important in expressing corporate identity.

Assertions as to the symbolic functions of corporate buildings on which corporate architecture is practiced are frequently explicitly stated in corporate communications. The intended meanings of newly constructed or remodelled buildings are recurrent topics in annual reports, anniversary brochures, information leaflets, public statements, and circulated anecdotes. The same is true of reviews of commercial buildings which more and more business and professional magazines run on a regular basis.

If corporate buildings are increasingly designed in compliance with such tenets in corporate architecture in practice, a review of these seems a proper point of departure for our effort, even if they lack proper theoretical and empirical foundation. In doing so, we will also speculate on the possible symbolic mechanisms which may link the claimed effects of physical settings on human behaviour and thinking.

3 Corporate Architecture — Assertions and Perspectives

Let us now review the literature and the present debate on corporate architecture and outline the most common assertions made about the symbolic functions of buildings. However, we will not concern ourselves with the assertions made about buildings as physical structures and filters of physical stimuli. This selectivity is justified by our particular interest in corporate buildings as symbolic artifacts.

It should be noted that our classification of perspectives and assertions below is not primarily intended as a review of the literature but rather as an attempt to trace some of the tacit assumptions upon which much of recent research seems to rest. Thus, a reference might well be referred to in more than one of the the the six categories.

3.1 The Symbolic Conditioning of Organizational Behaviour

A basic proposition of corporate architecture is that the architectural, interior, and environmental design of corporate buildings and settings has a profound impact on human behaviour in general (in terms of interaction patterns, communication styles, service mindedness, etc.) and on human performance in particular (productivity, efficiency, creativity, etc.). The following quotation (from a brochure on "Arlanda City," a high-tech, multi-business centre in the vicinity of Stockholm) is a good illustration of the "assumed logic" behind corporate architecture:

A couple of years ago *Business Week* presented a study of several American companies investing much in "corporate architecture" (good working environment implying creative stimulation). The study showed that almost all companies had decreased their personnel turnover radically. Everybody was talking of increased productivity and increased identification with the company — among personnel, clients, and suppliers alike. Most of the companies had also been able to reduce their advertising costs since the architecture itself gave a lot of publicity. And finally it should not be disregarded that the sales value of the house was regarded considerably higher than that of the ordinary office buildings.

Thus, what sets these buildings apart from ordinary office buildings is not their efficiency as physical structures, nor their adequate infusion of physical stimuli on the work-force — modernist buildings were designed to achieve exactly that already. It is rather the fact that they provide "creative stimulation" which in turn produces the desirable effects. But in what way are physical settings able to provide creative stimulation?

It is entirely plausible that people respond spontaneously upon recognizing certain physical cues in the setting. The recognition may be based on familiarity and/or association. For example, it has been noticed that churches elicit religious behaviour even in people who are not religious. Likewise, clean rest-rooms have been claimed to elicit tidier behaviour amongst users. Moving from the conference table to the easy-chairs in the executive suite often produces less formal interaction. Less trivial is perhaps the case of airline stewardesses who are trained mentally to imagine the cabin as their own home, whereby feelings are aroused which enable them spontaneously to act out the role of hostesses (Hochschild 1983).

All these examples indicate that behaviour in organizations may be symbolically conditioned by certain cues in the physical settings. The conditioning may function when physical cues help invoke what Stanislavsky terms "emotional memories" (individual or collective) or when they help persons to adapt to model-behaviour which has been learnt, trained, or merely experienced in other situations. Such symbolic conditioning may help explain the logic of the one-look concept of e. g. hamburger chains, whose rigidly standardized outlets are claimed to produce standardized responses from employees and customers alike.

A symbolic conditioning of behaviour may be the intended effect of the design of the ABV corporate headquarters, a leading Swedish contractor (Illustration 1). The architect describes the building in the following way:

The ABV building is ... a friendly, pink brick building with an inviting main entrance which leads directly into the glass-covered court-yard, an oasis for visitors, coffee-drinking restaurant guests, and passing personnel. A lot of offices and almost all the conference rooms face the yard and give life to it. From the yard one can see the glass lift cages going up and down which contributes to the vitality of the yard. A ride in the lift gives the people working in the building as well as the visitors a stimulating impression of the company as a whole and its activities.

It is not improbable that such a stimulating impression of vitality elicits vitality on the part of the employees and visitors to ABV. It is at least plausible that the responses will be very different from the ones elicited by the main entrance of the corporate headquarters of a leading Swedish pharmaceutical company (Illustration 2).

Illustration 1

Illustration 2

3.2 Buildings as "Totems"

It has been claimed that, in the same way that civilizations, societies, cultural epochs, or tribes can be characterized by their buildings, corporations — which can be seen as micro-societies — tend to choose to dwell in buildings that conform with their identity. In this way, the building comes to serve as a "totem," a uniting symbol for all the people working in the company. One of the most striking examples is Bonniers (the major publishing company in Sweden) who, in a corporate advertising campaign, presented all their subsidiary companies, using an image of the façades of their main entrances (Illustration 3).

3.3 Buildings as Symbols of a Strategic Profile

Evidently corporate buildings are becoming an important part of the corporate profile and strategy. Seiler (1984), for example, states:

When buildings reflect the purpose of the business and encourage important work relationships, they can become significant elements of corporate strategy (p. 111).

This argument seems to be underlying corporate architecture of the present, as the following example shows. Round Office, one of Sweden's leading office furniture manufacturers, has developed a round work station design. The work station forms a semi-circle round the individual operator/secretary. This "round office" concept is also reflected in most of their corporate graphics and in the design of their Örebro headquarters (Illustrations 4 and 5). The marketing manager of the company describes the idea behind the design in the following way:

The building had to be flexible and emphasize the strong identity proper of our product. As we are located in an industrial area, our exterior identity was important, i.e. our clients should be able to find us easily. The domed roof, in its form and design, consequently symbolizes the rounded details in our assortment. In the interior we have rounded doors and some corners are similarly rounded instead of being right-angled in order to accentuate the identity of the product.

The company's way of thinking is further expressed in this way:

The business idea and identification behind Round Office is a model in its conception. In the exterior, logo, architecture, and product programme we are everywhere confronted with the same round basic form. From the moment we enter the reception we are also confronted with the positive sense of well-being associated with success. No communication problems here.

Another example is the headquarters of Levi's Jeans in San Francisco. The following account was related to us by a consultant:

Illustration 3

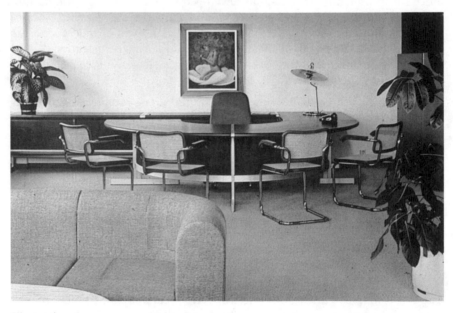

Illustration 4

Illustration 5

Illustration 6

They were going to move, you know, and decided to build a high-rise downtown San Francisco. As it turned out, though, they never really settled there. It sort of didn't fit with their value system. A high-rise creates more of the pin-striped type of atmosphere, you know. So they decided to move and build another housing complex down in the wharf area. Sort of a campus-styled headquarters with many terraced buildings with a plaza in the middle. That sort of students atmosphere was just right for their jeans concept (Illustration 6).

Another feature of corporate architecture is the attempt to embody the "soul" of the corporation in the buildings (Leibson 1981, Olins 1978, Seiler 1984). The popular press is full of headings such as: "The Offices for the Souls" (*Veckans Affärer* 1986, 19/5) and "The Environment Should Reflect the Corporate Soul ..." (*Ledarskap* 1986). One way in which architects attempt to embody the corporate soul is by means of the design of "social main rooms." A social main room may be a large hall, a glass-covered courtyard, or a main passage, i. e. any space where people pass or come together during the day (Illustration 7). Olivegren (1987) writes the following about these social main rooms:

In some Swedish corporate buildings the personnel has experienced how rooms like these, i. e. rooms which every one of the employees passes at least once a day and which in some way represent the company, its business, or its idea, have contributed to a feeling of community, a "we-spirit," which is communicated through the common room (p. 4).

Not only business concepts and the overall profile, but also management philosophy may be symbolized in the corporate buildings. A good example of this is the new SAS headquarters under construction. The managing director, Jan Carlzon, has published his management philosophy in a book which, in literal translation from Swedish, is entitled "Demolish the Pyramids!" The low, flat design of the headquarters seems to be a physical implementation and symbolization of these ideas, or — as Jan Carlzon says — "the fewer pinnacles and towers, the easier to do away with hierarchy" (Illustration 8). Compare this with the building of the West German insurance company, Allgemeine Rechtsschutz AG in Düsseldorf (Illustration 9). The president of the company, Heinz G. Kramberg is quoted as saying that he ordered the staircase design to "encourage ambition and provide a visual image of our organization structure" (taken from Steel 1973).

Illustration 7

3.4 Buildings as Packaging

The physical settings in which goods and services are produced and exchanged may sometimes influence the characteristics of the goods and services as experienced by the people involved. Corporate buildings are in these cases "extensions" of the products or service. They produce the same effect as packaging in general: they symbolize the characteristics and quality of the goods and services being produced and exchanged.

Consider the following example. Architectural firms are predominantly located in the centre of Copenhagen near the Royal Academy of Art and housed in old but remodelled buildings. One major architectural firm is however located in a building complex on the outskirts of the city, a complex which predominantly houses consulting engineering firms and which is designed in the modernist tradition of architecture. Whether this architectural firm is designing less artistic buildings than other firms is difficult to say, but that is exactly the reputation it has in some quarters. It could be claimed that its physical setting might suggest such a character of its performance.

The visual identity programmes which most consumer oil companies are presently launching — providing new corporate trademarks, repainting and rebuilding filling stations, redressing the pumps, etc. — could also be

Illustration 8

Illustration 9

understood as a way of adding differential experiences to basically homogeneous products. The aim is, of course, to develop consumer preferences by means of the manipulation of physical settings.

A good illustration of this "packaging" function is Schwantzer's (1986) study of how corporate architecture influenced the image of the organization. His findings indicated that particular types of design — a special type of vaults over the entrance — were preferred to others.

3.5 Buildings as Symbols of Status, Potency, and Good Taste

It is common understanding that organizations demonstrate their command of resources by means of constructing and inhabiting large, lavish corporate buildings. Likewise, individual members of the organization signal their status by the size of their office, its furniture and decoration, etc. These symbolic functions are too well known to warrant further elaboration in the present context.

Less commonly described is the fact that corporate buildings may also symbolize good taste and appreciation of quality. It is striking how much attention and publicity is given to the identity of the architect when he is of a certain standing within a community. One often gets the impression that *who* designed the building is more important to the corporation than what he designed. In this sense, corporate buildings almost become (de)signed objects of art, the possession of which has a favourable repercussion upon the corporation in terms of reputation and identity. Publicly renowned corporate buildings easily come to serve as physical symbols which foster identification with the company and feelings of corporate pride.

1950-1964

Illustration 10

3.6 Buildings as Markers of Time, Ideas, and Existence

Organizations often seem to mark discontinuities in their history with a change of physical setting. Dramatic changes in market conditions or in strategies are accompanied with remodelling of old facilities or construction of new ones. While this may reflect changing functional needs, it does also take on symbolic significance. The different buildings come to stand for different epochs in the corporate saga and are often used in anniversary brochures to illustrate the development and progress of the company. The construction of a new headquarters is in itself a strong and powerful signal to the employees and the environment that a new time has come. The construction of the AT & T headquarters in New York would be a case in point. The decentralization which was forced upon the company by the deregulation of the telephone industry was marked with what became an urban event in architectural terms (Schneider/Powley 1986).

However, buildings are also frequently used to symbolize history and tradition. IKEA is one example. Information material from that company frequently includes a picture of the old barn "where the whole thing started" (Illustration 10). Buildings from the company's earlier days are almost regarded as sacred places and symbolize the historical roots of the company.

Further, buildings are also frequently used to signal corporate ideas and managerial intentions. Consider the following story about the way in which the Volvo Kalmar Plant was designed:

The team, which was designing the new body assembly plant in Kalmar, had been working for about a year when they finally came up with a proposal. At the meeting where the proposal was presented, P. G. Gyllenhammar, the President of Volvo, abruptly said: "No, this is no good. We want a plant that really tells people we are serious when we talk about work democracy, creativity, and technical innovation. This plant is too old-fashioned! Come back in fourteen days with a more unconventional design." After fourteen days the team, having worked day and night, turned up with the pentagon-shaped Volvo Kalmar plant design.

Later, Bert Jonsson, The Vice President of Corporate Planning, said:

"In retrospect one can say that the important part of the Kalmar plant was not the design of the plant itself (in fact, the pentagram idea was never used again in any new plant) but rather its symbolic value. It was a signal to the whole company that we were fully backing up what we were saying about work democracy, technological innovations, etc."

In this case, the plant design became a public statement (not least to the Volvo employees) used as part of an intervention strategy to accomplish a change in a given direction.

Finally, buildings are used to mark the existence and presence of a company in a social, cultural, and geographical context. The selection of a site, the form and size of the building, the degree of idiosyncrasy in the design, etc. may all reflect a choice on how to position the company in its environment. The new HP building in Birkerød, Denmark, makes no secret of its existence, being totally dominant of the surrounding landscape (Illustration 11). The local branch of a leading Danish bank in a rural town, housed in a traditional farm house, also makes a claim on existence, but in a different language (Illustration 12).

Illustration 11

Illustration 12

4 Some General Notes on Buildings as Corporate Artifacts

Organizational (or corporate) culture has a somewhat unclear conceptual status. On the one hand, organizations are embedded in wider cultural contexts (societies, civilizations, etc.). The symbolism of organizations must somehow build on, and reflect, the symbolism which is institutionalized in these wider cultural context. On the other hand, the need for a concept of organizational culture arises specifically when the individuality of each organizational culture is recognized. To some extent the culture of one organization is distinguishable from the culture of other organizations — and as such it is also distinguishable from culture at large. Being embedded in the same overall culture, all corporate cultures are bound to be similar; being attributable to individual organizations, all corporate cultures are bound to be different.

This problem is nicely illustrated in the above discussion of symbolic artifacts in organizations. The propensity of man to read socially and behaviourally significant meanings into physical settings is taken for granted. The codes which guide the interpretation of physical settings are, however, socially defined and culturally bounded: the link between the symbolic artifact and the meaning it signifies is only established by means of arbitrary conventions. Environmental psychology studies how people are culturally trained to associate certain meanings with physical arrangements. Such mental programmes are of course not left at the doorstep of formal organizations. And most of the illustrations of symbolic artifacts above are consequently illustrations of the application of general symbolic codes as they are applied in an organizational context.

Yet the basic rationale for corporate architecture is to a large extent to establish the individuality of the organization in the eyes of the employees and of the general public. Partly, corporate buildings are designed consciously to exploit general symbolic codes, but partly also organization-specific symbolic codes are consciously established to set the corporation apart from its environment. Certainly, much of the symbolism which is surrounding corporate artifacts is not institutionalized in the wider cultural context. However, this potential inconsistency between general symbolic codes and custom-made symbolic codes is not widely recognized in the literature on corporate architecture even though it merits a more thorough study.

4.1 Suspending Institutionalized Symbolic Codes

The institutionalized symbolic codes which allow the members of a society to infuse artifacts with meaning are in many ways a resourceful tool in the hands of corporate management. These codes allow managers to communicate to the employees and the general public in easily understood terms. However, the meaning communicated through buildings is not the sole design criterion, of course. One has to recognize the fact that corporate buildings are means of production and as such they must be designed with an eye on the cost effectiveness with which they facilitate directly productive activities. Occasionally, corporate management will find itself in the situation where the efficient building (in terms of physical structuring of activities) carries an institutionalized meaning which is unfavourable or unintended. Consider the following case in this connection.

In a recent round table discussion between corporate architects (reported in *Architectural Record*, No 1, 1985) the design of a new Union Carbide building in Danbury was being discussed. Said one of the discussants:

I worry a lot about corporate standardization of the environment. The new Union Carbide building in Danbury, designed so that everyone has exactly the same size office and in fact an almost identical view of the forest outside, and much talked about in the magazines, ... worries me. As opposed to it being boring, I found that kind of standardization depressing. I wonder about the philosophical and managerial implications of so standardizing spaces ...

Another discussant, who at the time had actually worked with the architect involved commented:

The intent of the decision to standardize office size was not at all to dehumanize the office environment, but rather to humanize it by eliminating the kinds of jealousies that result from the corporate pecking order — "I've got three windows and you only have two." There was also an economic judgement based on the enormous cost of moving the movable partitions and redistributing the space. At General Foods, after we saw what Kevin (Roche, the architect) had done at Union Carbide, we went at least part of the way down that road and eliminated the division between the two most prevalent salary grades that caused the most partition moving. When you pass from one grade to another you can get new upholstery or some adjustment of furniture, but most of our employees have simply foregone that corporate perk. So it was not an effort to overstandardize — it was a programmatic issue to try and cut down one of the problems of the pecking order that all corporations live with.

The case illustrates a number of points. First of all, economic considerations may arrest the inclination to conform with institutionalized symbolic codes when corporate buildings are designed. Secondly, such symbolic codes are actually applied when outsiders interpret the buildings: they were actually made to signal dehumanizing standardization also of social statuses. And thirdly, such institutionalized symbolic codes may in fact be suspended in particular organizational circumstances, as illustrated by the fact that the employees at General Foods did not claim the adjustments in furniture and upholstering when they climbed up the organizational hierarchy. The last mentioned point makes a strong case, since few other symbolic codes are as institutionalized as the ones linking office size, view, furniture, etc. to social status.

We lack information about how this suspension of institutionalized symbolic codes was precisely achieved. However, the reference to the "jealousies that result from the corporate pecking order" might suggest that an appeal to the arbitrariness (or irrationality) of such physical symbols of status may have been successfully made. Laying bare this arbitrariness apparently made it illegitimate to collect even the entitlements which were left at General Foods, since to do so would signal not status, but status consciousness. Since most symbols are arbitrary, we may come to the conclusion that symbolic artifacts in organizations are made of volatile matter. Their ability to enchant may disappear when made subject to conscious consideration.

The corporate management's ability to, and interest in, suspending institutionalized symbolic codes depends upon the specific organizational context, however. The use of status symbols in organizations supposedly reflects a human need for ascertaining a position in the social and formal hierarchy. This needs not be achieved with the help of status symbols, of course. Writes Steel (1973: 53): "I believe that the social variable that most influences the amount of emphasis on status symbols is the extent to which people receive direct, concrete feedback about their standing and performance in the organization." If such feedback is low, and if the corporate management does not provide physical symbols of social standing, a sense of uncertainty and insecurity may develop which may in turn influence morale and performance. Thus, for example, we know of one company where it indicates status to have one's wastepaper basket next to one's table in the canteen. Informal competitions and fights over wastepaper baskets are not likely to further collaboration and satisfaction.

In conclusion, we might hypothesize that the corporate management may suspend any one of the institutionalized symbolic codes which constitute symbolic artifacts in an organization — but not all of them.

4.2 Supplementing Institutionalized Symbolic Codes

Physical settings, when they are approached as symbolic artifacts, inform members of a certain culture of the meaning of some particular setting. The members "read" the meaning from the physical aspects of an artifact.

In the case of corporate architecture, intentionality is added to this process. The physical setting is arranged so as to *communicate* an intended meaning to members of the culture.

It is quite obvious that corporate managers have increased their ambitions in relation to the communicative functions of buildings. As it will be clear from our review of corporate architecture above, more and more subtle and complex intended meanings are designed into corporate buildings. However, the more subtle and complex the intended meanings, the more likely the message will get lost.

When considering the architectural design of corporate buildings, institutionalized symbolic codes are probably too vague and general to decipher the intended meanings of the buildings. To illustrate the point, stop and look at Illustration 13 before you continue reading!

Our hunch is that you will have no clue as to what kind of organization will dwell here: it might just as well be a computer company as a school or even some kind of official institution. In this case it is a chemical producer and a wholesaler in plastics. But the intended message of the design was much more specific than that. The company, CPS Kemi in Copenhagen, has developed a line of water-soluble products and takes pride in being a hygienic and environment conscious company. In the brief for the new headquarters the architect was required to express those virtues in the building design. That is what the building signals to everyone.

No institutionalized symbolic code would seem to allow the general public to read the building in that way if it were left to speak for itself.

It might be argued that there exists a more specific code of architecture which might help to interpret buildings. It is true that also the architectural profession communicates with itself by means of buildings, also corporate buildings. However, the target group of corporate communication by means of buildings is not the architects. Furthermore, as Groat and Canter (1979) and Groat (1982) have experimentally proved, architects and accountants employ different codes when evaluating buildings. Whitfield and Wiltshire (1982) have shown the same to be true in relation to chairs.

At best one might claim that the building design does not directly contradict the intended meaning. But corporate buildings are seldom left to speak for themselves. They are described, reviewed, and interpreted over and over again in direct communications from the organizations. In such communications a custom-made code is established, a rudimentary code which links a specific message to that particular building directly, and a code which will not be applicable to other corporate buildings. Nevertheless, they may eventually come to carry the intended meaning.

Originally, the corporate buildings do not communicate at all. They are rather topics in the conversations that organizations carry out with themselves and with their environment. A new or remodelled corporate building

Illustration 13

constitutes a legitimate opportunity for signalling the profile of the corporation, by means of something concrete rather than with ambiguous symbols. Potentially, employees and the general public may become indoctri-
nated to read the building in the intended way.

Buildings are in general a common topic of conversation between the
organization and its environment. Before starting to write this chapter we
had observed that banks very often use pictures of their local branches in
annual reports, etc. We found this fact puzzling, since these physical settings
seem vaguely related to the kinds of services banks provide. Furthermore,
the expressiveness of the architecture used for branch offices is quite low
(compared to what is true for headquarters). The best interpretation of the
use of these pictures is perhaps that buildings are tangible and therefore
possible to picture. Whether or not they communicate anything in themselves, they do lighten the message being conveyed in texts and figures.

Devising its own codes of interpretation would seem to give the corporate
management almost complete freedom to convey a specific meaning by
means of the organization's physical settings. However, prior public knowledge about the organization can limit the credibility of the message conveyed. This dilemma is illustrated by Banham (1981) when he reviews the
Silicon style of corporate architecture:

The whole design clearly aims to make a strong public statement that this is a
sensitive, energy-conscious, ecologically aware company, not a bunch of High-Tech,
high-energy show-offs such as some of the earlier denizens of the Vale of Chips are
now deemed to be.

By their bush work shall ye know them ... (But) whom does the greenery benefit?
... (Is) it anything more than public relations − vegetable flack aimed at putting a
new and less intimidating face on an industry whose links to power may not appeal
to the current preferences for softer technology and a simpler society?

There are, however, a lot of rather fundamental aspects of the basic High-Tech
box that can't change very much. The need for a clean, well-lighted place to work
is almost absolute. In the present state of industrial economics, that necessity means,
almost unavoidably ..., rectangular, lightweight one- or two-story structures with
big, clear spaces between skinny columns placed at infrequent intervals. It means a
lot of light (usually artificial), air conditioning and other energy-consuming environmental gizmology ... And it also means that a lot of the work force will be a long
way from the comforts − and distractions − of outside views, regardless of how
the windows are arranged. But truth in architecture will out, sooner or later.
Whatever the present preoccupation with external imagery and cosmetic shrubbery,
it will need only a slight shift of corporate vision for the basic box to be found
admirable for its simplicity and for Digital and IBM Santa Teresa to be praised for
their naked honesty. For the moment, though, fig leaves are in, full frontal industrial
nudity is out.

Keeping in mind that this is an architect's informed opinion, and realizing
that the public relations effort might actually work with less informed

observers, the point of honesty is relevant in general. It is not likely that the greenery surrounding the corporate headquarters of Superfos, a renowned environmental polluter, will signal ecological awareness to visitors or to the general public. When corporate architecture is seen as architecture of illusion, the intended message will get lost.

5 Conclusion

This chapter started with the observation that organizations of present times take greater care and more pride in the way they physically present themselves. Our review of the corporate architecture literature and debate suggested that such corporate vanity should be understood in terms of the manipulation of intended meanings which the "architecture" of the physical setting is conveying.

While we were able to distil from the literature some of the ways in which physical settings may convey meaning, and some of the consequences on behaviour and performance that such meanings might have, we were not able to find coherent theoretical frameworks which might explain in an organizational context how, and to what degree, such intended meanings become an integral part of corporate culture. It still appears that the mechanisms by means of which employees and the general public assign meanings to the physical settings created by organizations are vaguely understood.

We do not claim that we have provided a coherent framework for understanding the role of symbolic artifacts in organizations. But hopefully we have taken a few initial steps in that direction by highlighting some obstacles to, and some options for, the development of organization-specific reading of corporate buildings.

Further theoretical development in this field will likely require a framework which at least includes the following basic factors:

- the wider cultural context of organizations, in terms of institutionalized symbolic codes for interpreting physical artifacts;
- man's fundamental need for feedback and identification and his disposition to read physical phenomena as symbols;
- the volatile matter symbolic artifacts (even physical ones) are made of;
- post-modern society's demand for visibility and individuality of individuals as well as of organizations;
- current trends in architecture and in management science;

— the history of the organization, its profile and image with employees and the general public;
— the economical and functional parameters of buildings and physical work settings.

To develop such a theoretical framework is of course not a trivial task. On the other hand, since the phenomenon of corporate vanity is so conspicuous, and the concept of corporate artifacts so intriguing, it might prove worth the effort to pursue a theory of organizational symbolism along these lines. Corporate architecture may, as some would argue, turn out to be just another fad amongst managers. But whether it is or not, it still provides us with the kind of data and puzzles that goad theoretical development.

References

Banham, R. (1981): Silicon Style. *Architectural Review* Vol. CLXIX, pp. 283 – 290
Canter, D. (1983): The Physical Context of Work. *The Physical Environment at Work*. D. J. Oborne/M. M. Gruneberg (Eds.). New York: Wiley, pp. 11 – 38
Davis, T. R. V. (1984): The Influence of the Physical Environment in Offices. *Academy of Management Review* 9(2), pp. 271 – 283
Grafton-Small, R. (1985): Making Meaning Concrete: Exchange Processes and the Cultural Determination of Physical Space. *Cebes* 1(1), pp. 62 – 75
Grafton-Small, R. and S. Linstead (1986): Bricks and Bricolage: Deconstructing Corporate Images in Stone and Story. *Dragon* 1(1), pp. 8 – 27
Groat, L. (1982): Meaning in Post-Modern Architecture: An Examination Using the Multiple Sorting Task. *Journal of Environmental Psychology* 2, pp. 3 – 23
Groat, L. and D. Canter (1979): Does Post-Modernism Communicate? *Progressive Architecture* 12, December, pp. 84 – 87
Hochschild, A. R. (1983): *The Managed Heart: Commercialization of Human Feeling*. Berkeley, CA: University of California Press
Holm-Löfgren, B. (1980): *Ansvar Avund Arbetsgladje*. Stockholm: Askild & Karnkull
Leibson, D. E. (1981): How Corning Designed a "Talking" Building to Spur Productivity. *Management Review* 70(9), pp. 8 – 13
Olins, W. (1978): *The Corporate Personality: An Inquiry into the Nature of Corporate Identity*. London: Design Council
Olivegren, J. (1987): *Corporate Brochure FNRS*.
Page, M. (1974): *The Company Savage: Life in the Corporate Jungle*. London: Coronet
Pfeffer, J. (1981): Management as Symbolic Action: The Creation and Maintenance of Organizational Paradigms. *Research in Organizational Behavior* Vol. 3, pp. 1 – 52
Schneider, S. C. and E. Powley (1986): The Role of Images in Changing Corporate Culture: The Case of AT & T. *Dragon* 1(2), pp. 5 – 44
Schwantzer, B. (1986): *Die Bedeutung der Architektur für die Corporate Identity eines Unternehmens*. Wien: Modulverlag

Seiler, J. A. (1984): Architecture at Work. *Harvard Business Review* Sept.—Oct., pp. 111—120

Sponseller, M. and H. A. Hatfield (1986): New Hospital Designs Stress Looking Good: As Use Declines, Facilities Must Attract Customers. *Engineering News Record* December, 18, pp. 70—72

Steel, F. I. (1973): *Physical Settings and Organization Development*. Reading, MA: Addison-Wesley

Whitfield, A. and J. Wiltshire (1982): Design Training and Aesthetic Evaluation: An Intergroup Comparison. *Journal of Environmental Psychology* 2, pp. 109—117

Building Buildings and Living Lives: A Critique of Bureaucracy, Ideology and Concrete Artifacts

Michael Rosen, Wanda J. Orlikowski, and
Kim S. Schmahmann

> "It's exactly this kind of communal street
> life that the highrise block is destroying ..."
> — from *The Young Ones*, a contemporary
> British sitcom.

1 Introduction

This paper explores the relationship between the labor process in bureaucratized organization and the physical space in which this labor is transacted and workers housed, that is, in the office buildings, retail places, and manufacturing plants in which we work and the homes in which we live. This relationship between the organization of labor and the structuring of space is presented as dialectical, where the arrangement and provision of physical space is seen not as unrelated to or as an epiphenomenon of bureaucratized relations of production, but as an integral aspect of the system of such production, and as incomprehensible apart from it.

It should be understood that we take bureaucracy here as essentially the rational — legal bureaucracy of Weber. This is not synonymous with capitalism, but instead one of many organizational forms emerging within capitalism enabling managerial control and the appropriation of surplus value (Burawoy 1979, Clawson 1980).

Like all official realms of bureaucratic organization, the design, allocation, and use of space within this form has become rationalized and commodified. And precisely as the design and use of space is influenced by the social relations and ideology of bureaucracy and capitalism, such design and use is reflected and recursively implicated in the social relations and ideology of bureaucracy and capitalism.

The case has been made that within capitalist society the labor process is a largely isolated realm independent unto itself, which can be understood without relationship to and exploration of other fields of activity. This position is related to Gramsci's (1971: 285) stance that "hegemony here [in the United States] is born in the factory." Burawoy, for example, adopts this perspective in his analysis of shop floor production, taking as his point of departure that consent towards the labor process "is produced at the point of production — independent of schooling, family life, mass media, and so forth" (1979: xii).

This labor-centric position, however, minimized the holistic nature of capitalist relations. Commodification, the production and exchange of goods and services to obtain profit, is the defining characteristic of capitalism. And while commodification certainly typifies the sale and purchase of labor power under varying conditions that appropriate surplus value, commodification also typifies many other aspects of daily life, in particular the way we create and inhabit space. Thus the relevance of this study.

We understand commodification to be an ongoing process of transformation, wherein the expression of an object or phenomenon — here space — as abstract and instrumental, as quantifiable and universal, under capitalism comes to predominate over the qualitative experience of this object or phenomenon in non-capitalist forms of society (Giddens 1981, Marx 1976). Adapting Marx's (1976) concepts of use-value versus exchange-value, Giddens (1981: 134) thus proposes that commodities have a double existence, as phenomena with definite qualities, and as pure transformative mediation relations. The subjugation of the former to the latter vis-à-vis the expression of space is of interest here.

2 The Dialectics of Space and Labor

In an often quoted phrase, Marx notes that "men [read humans] make history, but not in circumstances of their own choosing" (see Bernstein 1986: 241). In other words, people create the world through actions they largely choose, but such choices are constrained by the previous outcomes of previous choices.

From this perspective, we approach building within the framework of structuration. Herein, a building is viewed as an element, albeit a concrete one, of social structure, the nature of which cannot be grasped as separate from an exploration of how human agency is reflexively and recursively implicated in it. An aim inherent in this approach, therefore, is to illuminate the duality and dialectical interplay of agency and structure (Bernstein 1986: 235).

Paraphrasing Giddens (1984), to conceive of structure as recursively organized sets of rules and resources is to conceive of it acontextually, and marked by an absence of the subject. Herein,

the social systems in which structure is recursively implicated ... comprises the situated activities of human agents, reproduced across time and space. Analysing the structuration of social systems means studying the modes in which such systems, grounded in the knowledgeable activities of situated actors who draw upon rules and resources in the diversity of action contexts are produced and reproduced in interaction. Crucial to the idea of structuration is the theorem of the duality of structure ... The constitution of agents and structures are not two independently given sets of phenomena, a dualism, but represent a duality. According to the notion of the duality of structure, the structural properties of social systems are both medium and outcome of the practices they recursively organize. Structure is not 'external' to individuals ... Structure is not to be equated with constraint but is always both constraining and enabling" (Giddens 1984: 25).

A building may be conceived in this vein. A building is a concrete social artifact, for unlike a kinship pattern or status hierarchy, its corporal form possibly exists regardless of the continued existence of its creators or those following; the same physical structure may remain through fully different culture systems. In addition, precisely the same structural form may survive in use from one epoch to another. Nevertheless, the spacial characteristics of buildings, both internally and in patterned relationship to other buildings designed for similar or differentiated purposes, are both medium and outcome of actions they recursively organize.

The physical settings in which people experience their work, leisure, and home life therefore emerge from a largely implicit set of assumptions people have about themselves and others. These assumptions are reinforced or changed as people's day-to-day experiences are played out, and will be reflected in the physical structures we create. But insofar as the physical structures which we inhabit participate in channelling our experiences and influencing our range of interactions, the physical space, in turn, plays a role in recreating and changing our social being.

3 Building and Being

As an over-simplified example of the relationships proposed above, the Egyptian pharaohs were deities within an elaborate system of deities insofar as they and others perceived them as such. Among other symbol systems, their deification was also objectified in the magnificent structures they had created for themselves and the other gods. And as the meaning systems of Egypt were integrated with this stonework, the deity of the pharaohs was recreated.

We, several millenia removed, live in an age of formal, bureacratic organization (Perrow 1986). Megacorporations build the cars we drive, refine and sell the gasoline we buy, grow and process the food we eat, manufacture the desire for the clothes we wear, and pay us the money to do all the above through the work we do within them. And just as contemporary economic life is dominated by these megacorporations, so is social life within the contemporary megalopolis. It is a metaphoric corollary to the Egyptian pyramids that the Manhattan skyline (taking Manhattan as one apotheosis of the urban built environment) is dominated by the honorific monoliths to the megacorporation. The Chrysler Building, the Pan American Airlines Building, the AT & T Building, the Citicorp Center, One Chase Manhattan Plaza, the IBM Building, the Woolworth Building, the Merrill Lynch Building, Trump Tower, the World Trade Center, and so on, dominate New York's business districts, dwarf any construction from the ancient world, and dwarf those who made them and who subsequently play out their lives around and within them.

As corporations amass the resources to construct and inhabit these edifices, their existence is recursively implicated within the internal arrangements and exterior designs of such spaces. This process likely involves not only a perception of the corporation's existence as part of the natural order of things, but also a likely perception of the bureaucratized social relations fundamental to such organization as natural and neutral.

4 Building in Sociohistoric Context

It is perhaps difficult to conceive the influence of capitalist relations of exchange on the urban and suburban landscape without first generally referring to the basic nature of precapitalist life and to the architectural design of cities before the rise of capitalism.

Broad-based capitalist relations of production and exchange date only from the sixteenth century, while industrial capitalism — the form of production, exchange, and consumption with which we are most familiar — dates only from the late eighteenth century (Galbraith 1983).

Prior to the sixteenth century, exchange was largely not commodified, and relatedly, space was either not alienable, or subject to limitations on its alienability. That is, land and housing could not, at least readily, be transferred from one owner to another through private monetary exchange (Giddens 1987: 101). Ownership and exchange without commodification clearly existed, as with conquest and aristocratic grants of land ownership under feudalism, but such space was not readily alienable, at least through commodified exchange, and is not of interest here.

Physically, pre-modern cities were generally clearly differentiated from the country-side. They were ordinarily walled and compact. The central area would be occupied by the temple, palace, and market place, with a stable distribution of surrounding neighborhoods (Sjoberg 1960: 5). Although an extensive road system might have existed between the city, the country-side, and other cities, the average citizen travelled very little. Populations were small compared to those of modern cities, and life was slow paced (Giddens 1987: 92).

To conceive of the difference in social and physical structure between then and now, Giddens (1984: 144) asks us to consider a situation in which

the formal order of the universe could be reduced to a diagram of two intersecting coordinates in one place. Yet this is exactly what did happen in antiquity: the Roman who walked along the *cardo* knew that his walk was the axis around which the sun turned, and that if he followed the *decumanus*, he was following the sun's course. The whole universe and its meaning could be spelled out of his civic institutions — so he was at home in it.

As so designed and conceived, the pre-capitalist city does not exist in commodified and alienable time and space. In comparison, however, most of what we do in our day-to-day lives is strictly instrumental. This holds for the clothes we wear, the way we approach labor, our approach to face-to-face interaction, as well as to most features of the buildings and cities in which we live and work (Lefebvre 1971). This is not as things have always been, however. As Lefebvre (1971: 29) writes,

with the Incas, the Aztecs, in Greece or in Rome, every detail (gestures, words, tools, utensils, costumes, etc.) bears the imprint of a style, nothing has as yet become prosaic ... the prose and the poetry of life were still identical. The spread of capitalism ensured the pre-eminence of the "prose of the world" — the primacy of the economic, the instrumental, and the technical — such that it involves everything — literature, art and objects and all the poetry of existence has been evicted.

This description, Giddens (1987: 113) argues, is not an overly romantic version of pre-capitalist society. Instead, it is the face of interaction based on morally grounded tradition, integrated also with broader aspects of human existence.

The lack of social differentiation in pre-capitalist societies is reflected in the physical settings for such interaction. For example, Giddens (1984: 121) notes that prior to the eighteenth century in Western Europe the homes of the poor frequently consisted of one or two rooms, in which communal living and sleeping arrangements were all conducted. Even the homes of the aristocracy favored communal interaction, for rooms were generally connected directly with one another, without the use of hallways that permit the differentiation of areas for specialized purposes and also allow a privacy of individual and social action.

In this sense, in pre-capitalist society the organization of regions of social interaction in both time and space, what Giddens (1984: 122) calls the time — space organization of regions, occurred within far more embracing social systems than does such regionalization within capitalism, reflecting the extensive differentiation and instrumentalism of capitalism. In pre-capitalist society, the "home," the dwelling, is often the physical focus of both family and production relationships, the latter occurring either in the dwelling itself or in closely adjoining land or outbuildings (Giddens 1984: 122).

With the emergence of large-scale industrial capitalism, however, land and buildings not only became largely commodified, but the basic design of such space changed as well. Reflexively, a dissolution of integrated society occurred. "Home" is differentiated from "workplace," with such an extensive separation found only in the modern West (Giddens 1984: 152). This has considerable implications for the overall organization of productive relationships. This relates, but is not limited, to the emergence of a predominantly instrumental, contractual organizational self, in contradistinction to the moral self of non-contractual, non-utilitarian roles that existed prior to capitalism (Cohen 1974: 55).

In the beginning of British industrial capitalism, industrialists and others who could so afford built homes with easy access to central production facilities, "but avoiding the grime and soot of the factories" (Giddens 1987: 104). Workers' family cottages, on the other hand, were distributed immediately around factories or railways. These workers were placed in housing without the communal elements of traditional argricultural villages they had often forcibly been removed from through the "fencing in" of pastoral lands (Marx 1976).

Within the emerging cities, the new built environments, large numbers of people lived in close proximity. Social interaction with all but a few people tended — and tends — to be fleeting and fragmentary, based on an instrumental means-ends algebra (Giddens 1987: 96). Such relations are stripped of the "spontaneous self-expression, the morale, and the sense of participation that comes from living in an integrated society" (Wirth 1938: 13). The dissolution of integrated social relations entails the emergence of orderly routines, wherein control is established through impersonally defined rules governing behavior (see Durkheim's [1933] representation of instrumentalized social relations inherent to and enabling control within "organic solidarity") (Giddens 1987: 96), the corollary of which is found in Weber's characterization of bureaucracy.

Further, the sort of distribution of neighborhoods described above creates clearly differentiated front and back regions in architectural time-space. For example, industrial plants were once the most visible aspect of the built environments of early industrial capitalism, with "factories and mills proudly displayed" (Giddens 1984: 130). However today, as anyone familiar with contemporary urban landscapes knows, such areas, including the accompanying worker housing, have been enclosed as back regions. They have either been pushed to the edges of town, pushed to less affluent adjacent municipalities, or architecturally screened from sight.

A differentiation and segmentation of the same space occurs, a zoning of time-space in relationship to social practices. In contemporary capitalist society, as noted, this is seen in the dissolution of the unified work-place — homeplace into differentiated residential and commercial neighborhoods. It is also evident within the social and physical structure of bureaucratic organizations, as it is in the home. It is to each of these that we now turn.

5 Bureaucratic Control in Physical Space

Individualization, an engagement of the self with the organization trans-acted to satisfy individual — rather than group and/or class — based interests, is prevalent in bureaucratic organizations. A person interacts with the organization as an individual, rather than as a member of a family, social group, or class, with presumably only individual interests to satisfy. This individualization is evidenced in all of bureaucracy's defining characteristics; in its hierarchical arrangement of positions, the career concept, the specialization of tasks, differential pay according to position, and so on. Through this structure of affiliation a person engages with the organization on a fully individualized basis, navigating his or her own, unique, personal career through the organization, and sells his or her labor to the organization accordingly.

Individualization is also evidenced in the physical distribution of offices in bureaucracy, wherein offices are insulated one from another by walls, doors, and so on. This insulation gives a significant degree of autonomy to those within them, or at least the illusion of this, and serves as a palpable marker of hierarchical power and control to all within the organization (Giddens 1984: 152).

Control through individualization in the physical sense uses space to achieve discipline. Control derives from discipline, and organizational discipline in part depends upon the calculative division of space (Foucault 1979). It is not any one particular part of a building that matters in the achievement of this disciplinary spacing, nor an association of the organization with any particular piece of territory. Instead, it is the farming of space through the use of lines, columns, and measured walled intervals that achieves an overall relational form tending to individualize and control organization members (Giddens 1984: 147). Disciplinary spacing is thus fundamental to bureaucratic control within the place of the organization.

At Financiers Faith, for example, the fictitious name of a major U.S. financial institution, an Executive Vice President is entitled to a maximum of 275 square feet of private office space. He or she is allowed three pieces of artwork, which are limited in cost from $ 75 to $ 350 each. Being a Department Head, he or she is also entitled to a piece of "foliage," a green plant, in this office. She or he is also entitled to drapes covering the office windows, for only Senior Vice Presidents and above are allowed drapes. Finally, as Exhibit 1 illustrates, his or her office comes with two filing cabinets, one desk and desk chair, two upholstered office chairs, one coffee-table sized conference table with four accompanying padded chairs, and one side table and accompanying lamp.

Senior Vice Presidents and Vice Presidents are also entitled to private offices, of 225 square feet and 150 square feet, respectively. As Exhibits 2 and 3 illustrate, not only the allowed space, but also the quality and quantity of furnishings also diminishes according to the rank of the officer.

An Assistant Vice President, ranked immediately below the Vice President, is not entitled to a private office, but instead occupies an open partitioned office of 100 square feet (see Exhibit 4).

Allocated space for non-officers, the organizational rank and file, varies from 75 square feet for a Senior Professional and System Analyst (see Exhibit 5) to 30 square feet for two low-level clerical workers (see Exhibit 6), with an accompanying decline in the quality and quantity of furnishings.

We see in the above a carefully systematized objectification of bureaucratic social relations and control worked out in vinyl wall covering, wood laminated furniture, bent chrome tubing, incandescent lighting, acrylic carpeting, and floor area; that is, in the rationalized farming of space.

This individualization of space in bureaucratic, capitalist society occurs not only in the places we work, as discussed above, and the places we live, as will be discussed below, but also in the places we play. For example, in their seminal architectural critique of Las Vegas, Venturi, Brown, and Izenour (1972) discover that unlike the communal organization of what they call monumental spaces in pre-capitalist society — cathedrals, piazzas, etc. — such space within our society is organized for anonymous individuals

Exhibit 1: Financiers Faith Company, EVP/SVP-Dept. Head Office, 275 sq.ff.

Exhibit 2: Financiers Faith Company, SVP Office, 225 sq.ff.

yoked together. That is, such space is designed to bring people together in close physical proximity, yet to retain individual modes of thought and action. They write, for example, that

Exhibit 3: Financiers Faith Company, VP Office, fixed wall, 150 sq.ff.

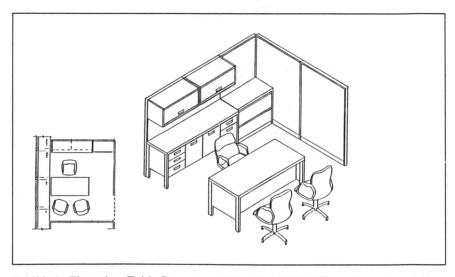

Exhibit 4: Financiers Faith Company, AVP, AT, ACCT. Officer, Supervisor Office, all buildings, 100 sq.ff.

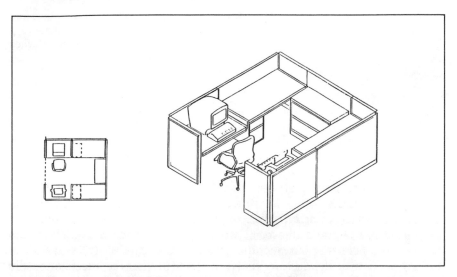

Exhibit 5: Financiers Faith Company, Word Processing/Secretarial Station, all buildings, 75 sq.ff.

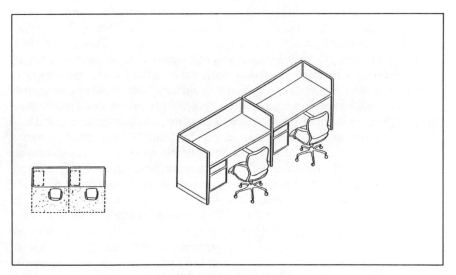

Exhibit 6: Financiers Faith Company, Clerical/Systems Station, all buildings, 30 sq.ff.

perhaps we should admit that our cathedrals are the chapels without the nave and that, apart from theaters and ball parks, the occasional communal space that is big is a space for crowds of *anonymous individuals* without explicit connection with each other. The big, low mazes of the dark restaurant with alcoves *combine being together and yet separate* as does the Las Vegas casino (1972: 50, emphasis added).

6 Housing the Individual

Aspects of bureaucratic organization — individualization, hierarchy, the sale of labor, and so on — are reflected not only in the physical structure of the office place, as described above, but also in the physical organization of private housing and the social structure of the nuclear family. We do not propose here that bureaucratic organization "causes" the structure of private housing or the nuclear family, but instead, that the interrelationship among these factors is dialectical, one tending to reflect and affect the other, with the absence of community and the primacy of individualization typifying each.

For example, given the primacy of individualization the provision of communal space under the influence of capitalism is not a priority, as it may perhaps undermine control. Fittingly, significant communal space is absent in the structure of the typical high-rise apartment building, just as it is in the suburban single-family development project. On the other hand, the traditional African living within a kraal inhabits a time—space framework irrational within the bureaucratized world. This person lives within a consistently arranged, clearly delineated compound, housing family and other tribal members together with their cattle. Such space is non-alienable — it is not exchangeable for monetary compensation as typifies commodity exchange — and considerable activities are carried out communally within communally held space. These include food preparation and childcare activities, vegetable gardening by females, and cattle tending by younger males. The "nuclear" family living alone and transacting its relationships largely autonomously, as this concept is enacted in the contemporary West, has no distinct meaning in this context. Accordingly, commodified and alienable individualized space is not provided for.

The nature of housing on the Israeli kibbutz — and of numerous other aspects of this organizational form as well — is a contemporary example of decommodification developed in response to the capitalist mode of production. The kibbutz is a collective in both its production and consumption structures, with linkages to secondary and tertiary cooperatives. Although most kibbutzim were established with agricultural production as their economic basis, industrial production has currently become at least as important a source of revenue for the majority of kibbutzim.

Kibbutz members live and work in a substantially de-differentiated region. The "village" area — housing and service facilities — is generally surrounded by the fields and factories in which members work. Family units occupy small apartments or garden houses, and make community use of the dining hall (where all meals are eaten communally), the recreation room or hall, sporting facilities, and so on.

The concept of private ownership on kibbutzim extends only to relatively inexpensive personal objects, such as clothing, books, household furniture, and bicycles. Land, production equipment, motorized transport, food, housing, and so on are collectively owned, subject to extensive limitations on their alienability, and are not commoditized in the sense described earlier. As also in the case of the kraal, commodified and alienable individualized space is not provided for.

On the other hand, the ontological base of commodified production and exchange as pertains under capitalism, particularly as this is realized within bureaucratic organization, lies in the human as an individual being and producer. The self is defined as an organizational self, with the interests that lie outside the production framework — family, religion, social, etc. — being potentially in conflict with production, and thus the organization. A force towards insulation of the organizational self from the development of other selves is present. This force is most clearly seen in instances where domination is given relatively free reign, as is currently the case in South Africa.

Here rural black laborers seeking employment from white capitalists in urban areas tend to find jobs with the requirement that they live in company housing-blocks, often with thousands of other black workers similarly separated from their families, friends, and tribes. Family living is prohibited, with even visits strictly limited, all enforced at the cost of unemployment. The housing-block thus emerges within the racist, capitalist state as a clear instrument of bureaucratic control, homogenizing the labor force and delimiting resistance.

While this example is not the norm within bureaucratic organization, its extremity does reveal possible underlying tendencies of this form of organization. In the "free" West, where capitalist forces are less based on domination than hegemony (Burawoy 1979), the nuclear family arrangement emerges as a shorn-down familial unit as compared to the community or extended family unit of traditional and agrarian-based societies. Most basically, the nuclear family arrangement emerges as a compromise to the individualization of bureaucratic labor and the human propensity to familial relationships, social accompaniment, sexual activity, biological reproduction, and so on. Here, the nuclear-family and single-family housing, which may be purchased and sold and thus readily acquired and disacquired, accord well with the bureaucratic relations of an individual's employment, or "career," through one or several organizations. Needs for worker relocation arising through promotion or demotion, job loss or change, and so on, are met as the nuclear family is moved and housing exchanged. Resistance is limited as the worker is less exposed to social interests arising from extended family and/or community relationships existing with other forms of social organization. This leads Horkheimer and Adorno (1944) to observe that the individualization of housing units discussed here makes individuals more, rather than less, dependent on and subject to domination by capital.

The city housing projects designed to perpetuate the individual as a supposedly independent unit in a small hygienic dwelling make him all the more subservient to his adversary — the absolute power of capitalism. Because the inhabitants, as producers and as consumers, are drawn into the center in search of work and pleasure, all the living units crystalize into well-organized complexes (1944: 120).

7 Conclusion

It should be noted, of course, that resistance is also enabled through the privatization of space. For example, privatized space within bureaucracy makes surveillance for control problematic, requiring trust in its place. But the break of trust behind closed doors is readily possible without detection, played out in such non-bureaucratic forms of behavior in one's office as sleeping, "goofing-off," consumating an office affair, doing work for oneself, and so on.

Countervailing tendencies are also evident within the commodification of the modern built environment. The municipal and/or state provision of public housing, rent and investment controls, and the provision of parks and other recreation areas are all examples of planned de-commodification from above (Giddens 1987: 109). In the urbanized U.S., block associations representing neighborhood interests vis-à-vis private real estate development forces and the delivery of municipal infra-structural services, as well as tenant groups in public housing projects established to self-manage the projects to maximize tenant interests, are examples of grass-root resistance to the commodification of housing.

The squatter camps of South Africa are among the most dramatic examples of housing used to resist control. The camps, established on the outskirts of such industrialized areas as Capetown and Durban, are home to many thousands of blacks illegally living on appropriated land, housed in shacks made of corrugated iron scrap, cardboard milk cartons filled with dried earth, and so on.

The camps tend to have a strongly knit social character, with day-care centers, schools, shebeens (illegal bars), and well-developed markets constituting the "informal economy." Many inhabitants perform illegal jobs in the nearby white-owned industrial and service facilities, without the privilege of working passes, while others find their way to the squatter camps if otherwise without a home or job.

Cross-Roads, Malakazi, and numerous other camps, centers of community solidarity, tend to be the loci of visible and invisible resistance to the policies of apartheid and the domination of capital, a combination related precisely as with the fascism of Nazi Germany.

Just as with kibbutz, the physical organization and elements of social solidarity within these squatter camps indicates the possibility and possible direction of transcending the internal limits of commodified and alienable — and hence, alienating — building within the built environment. While a full analysis of such praxis will be left to another discussion, we propose that the *deconstruction of bureaucratized building* offers a partial program of practical dis-alienation. The proposal is based on the premise that even the partial socialization of private property, and the design of self-managed habitats encouraging the participation of individuals in social communities in which they live and work, may be action towards emancipation. Surely, the socialization of property within a discrete, localized community, and the involvement of people in self-designed communal and cooperative spaces, might only be palliative steps towards emancipation given that such practical action occurs within an overarching bureaucratic structure, and is subordinate or subject to pressures from this structure (Markovic 1982: 6). However, if taken as first steps in the process of human emancipation, the deconstruction of bureaucratized space provides the opportunity for transcending limiting social relations, replacing these with structures allowing further emancipation. In other words, this deconstruction provides the opportunity for revolution, for as Markovic (1974: 191) notes, "the essential characteristic of revolution is a radical transcendence of the essential internal limit of a certain social formation." As such, revolution needs not be sudden, forceful, or even involve the transformation of a whole social system. Instead, revolution necessitates the establishment of those basic social institutions which make a society non-rational and inhuman, and the establishment of the possibility and a program for transcending such institutions with others more rational and humane (Markovic 1974: 191). An aim of this paper, therefore, has been to explore — through critique — the essential limitations of the design and use of space within bureaucracy and capitalism, and to indicate characteristics for transcendence. Indicating the path or paths for transcendence, another moment in praxis, will be left for further works.

84   Michael Rosen, Wanda J. Orlikowski, and Kim S. Schmahmann

References

Bernstein, R. J. (1986): Structuration as Critical Theory. *Praxis International* 6(2), pp. 235–249

Burawoy, M. (1979): *Manufacturing Consent.* Chicago, IL: Chicago University Press

Clawson, D. (1980): *Bureaucracy and the Labor Process.* New York: Monthly Review Press

Cohen, A. (1974): *Two-dimensional Man.* Berkeley, CA: University of California Press

Durkheim, E. D. (1933): *The Division of Labor in Society.* New York: Free Press

Foucault, M. (1979): *Discipline and Punish.* Harmondsworth: Penguin

Galbraith, J. K. (1983): *The Anatomy of Power.* Boston: Houton Mifflin

Giddens, A. (1981): *A Contemporary Critique of Historical Materialism.* Berkeley, CA: University of California Press

Giddens, A. (1984): *The Constitution of Society.* Berkeley, CA: University of California Press

Giddens, A. (1987): *Sociology: A Brief but Critical Introduction* (2nd ed.). New York: Harcourt Brace Jovanovich

Gramsci, A. (1971): *Selections from Prison Notebooks.* Q. Hoare/G. Nowell Smith (Trns./Eds.). New York: International Publishers

Horkheimer, M. and T. W. Adorno (1944): *Dialectic of Enlightenment.* J. Cumming (Trns.). New York: Continuum

Lefebvre, H. (1971): *Everyday Life in the Modern World.* London: Allen Lane

Markovic, M. (1974): *From Affluence to Praxis.* Ann Arbor, MI: University of Michigan Press

Markovic, M. (1982): *Democratic Socialism.* New York: St. Martin's Press

Marx, K. (1976): *Capital.* B. Fowkes (Trans.). New York: Vintage Books, Vol. 1

Perrow, C. (1986): *Complex Organizations* (3rd ed.). New York: Random House

Sjoberg, G. (1960): *The Preindustrial City.* Glencoe: Free Press

Venturi, R., D. S. Brown, and S. Izenour (1972): *Learning from Las Vegas: The Forgotten Symbolism of Architectural Form.* Cambridge, MA: MIT Press

Wirth, L. (1938): Urbanism as a Way of Life. *American Journal of Sociology* 44, pp. 1–23

Housing Modifications as Organizational Communication

Brian Rusted

1 Introduction

In the early 1970's, a small, coastal community on the Canadian island of Newfoundland petitioned its provincial minister of municipal affairs to install a water and sewer system. Some time later, officials appeared but from a federal government department involved in regional and economic development (DREE). They offered funds to restore traditional houses in this community. At the same time, another branch of the federal government, the Canadian Mortgage and Housing Corporation (CMHC) began offering funds so eligible homeowners could modernize their homes. A decade later both sources of government funding had disappeared, and the community still wonders if water and sewer services will be installed.

The centre of this situation is occupied by a particular class of artifacts: houses. They in turn are occupied, literally, by local residents, summer residents, and federal and provincial government officials. The significance of these houses is actively contested by the members of these groups through restoration, modernization, or demolition. "Preservation," "heritage," and so on are not part of a lexicon whose meanings are shared by all groups within this community. The meanings of the artifacts are also not fixed or absolute. They vary through time and across the memberships of these groups. The performances of construction, alteration, preservation, restoration, or demolition all contribute to the meaning houses have. Understanding these artifacts is to view them within the organizational contexts of these performances. From the vantage points of such performed acts of signification, the symbolism of inventing — possibly counterfeiting — cultural capital, or the symbolism of resisting — certainly opposing — elite distinctions can be identified.

Neither communication nor culture are foreign terms in the study of organizations (Pacanowsky/O'Donnel-Trujillo 1982, 1983, Smircich/Calas 1987). Combining them to study housing modifications extends their reach. The application of communication should not be limited to chirographic or interpersonal message systems. The use of culture should not be limited to its dominant or monolithic conceptions. The application of these perspectives should not be restricted to the study of formal organizations. Exporting them to research a particular community invites the subversion of research by loosely coupled or oppositional subgroups within the community. It prevents the researcher from viewing houses as inert, static goods, where specialists identify forgotten skills and the charm of obsolete economies. Organizationally, houses are sites of the ongoing performance of meaning, change, and opposition. Representing this process makes it apparent that knowledge and interpretation are as organizationally contingent and constructed as the community's houses.

A coastal community in Newfoundland is, to some, an exotic, organizational setting. To others, housing modifications are an unorthodox medium for exploring communication theory. Such a setting and such a medium, though, offer a case to explore symbolic and organizational qualities of these artifacts. Because this case involves the intervention of outside standards on a local system, it also provides an opportunity to consider the place of organizational ethnography in social change. Is there a critical moment in ethnography when action implies more than having the representational form embody the dialogic encounters of the field?

2 Artifacts and Communication

There appears to be three distinct but converging traditions in looking at material culture as communication. They can be characterized as semiotics, symbolism, and performance. In each, the weight of interpretation involves mapping material elements of a particular artifact or class of artifacts onto some larger conceptual context — language, history, social class, ideology, etc. Before considering the value of such an allegorical enterprise, let me characterize these approaches in more detail.

Semiotics is considered first because it traces its interest in artifacts as communication back through structural anthropology to linguistics at the turn of the century. As in much semiotic research, the goal here is to identify the structurally distinct elements in an artifact code in order to make comparison and analysis of the morphemic patterns in which they appear. Typically, the meaning inheres in the artifact and is distinct from the use by any particular individual (Agrest/Gandelsonas 1977). Glassie's study of house forms in Virginia is a classic of this approach (Glassie 1975). Individual detail is frequently submerged in the higher order attempt at formulating typological change through time.

In Mary Douglas's words, a symbolic approach to artifacts would see them "as signaling devices, transmitting from person to person information about the social system" (Douglas 1982: 31). Research here extends beyond typological and historical approaches (Ames 1980) to excavate tacit aspects of social relations (Bourdieu 1979, Douglas 1972, Lofland 1988), distinctions of social class (Appadurai 1986, Pratt 1981), and to establish boundaries between generations of residents or between local and non-local residents (Forrest 1988).

The performance approach to artifacts, as in other uses of performance (Conquergood 1989), is moving in two distinct directions. One of these is towards the construction process as a performance that relates social meanings to architectural choices in a particular context (Herman 1985, Upton 1979). The second direction of the performance approach moves away from a rigorous definition of an historical context to explore power and knowledge and to question representational form. The most vigorous discussion here has involved the display of material culture by museums (Clifford 1988, Dominguez 1986, Errington 1989), but has also involved analysis of heritage conservation and the restoration of housing (Cannizzo 1987, Galt 1987). The general trend is to see the meaning of architecture as polysemous and contested. Meaning is something shaped by the practical actions of particular groups of individuals and is not a reified property of a system (Foote 1983).

These approaches to housing are generally qualitative although quantitative studies certainly have their place (Csikszentmihalyi/Rochberg-Halton 1981). Each approach involves a research strategy that ranges from the detached to the participatory. Each tends to take the organizational contexts for granted or to leave them unexplored. Each also implies allegorical renderings of the material form, in some examples stressing structure while in others stressing the psychological or social. In discussing the implications of recognizing this trope in ethnography, Clifford suggests that "realistic portraits, to the extent that they are 'convincing' or 'rich,' are extended metaphors, patterns of associations that point to coherent (theoretical, esthetic, moral) additional meanings" (1986: 100). Seeing these "additional meanings" as allegorical makes it "difficult to view one of them as privileged" (1986: 103). He exposes the arrogance inherent in translating experience and practice into written form.

Clifford goes on to discuss Benjamin's notion of allegory and to suggest that, "The material analogue of allegory is thus the 'ruin' ... an always — disappearing structure that invites imaginative reconstruction" (1986: 119). In the case presented here, there are two implications: to consider whose allegory is being authored by the reconstruction of traditional houses, and to consider the further reconstruction in writing about modifications as organizational communication.

3 Setting and Modifications

This research[1] was set in Trinity Bay, on the northeast coast of Newfoundland. Although carried out along a section of the northwestern shore of this bay, the community of Trinity was the particular focus.[2] European settlement in this area dates back to the 1600's and it continues to be distinguished by mercantile and fishing communities. The populations of communities throughout this area peaked with their economic prosperity between 1775—1825. It has been in gradual decline ever since (Handcock 1985).

Although far from stable over the centuries, the population today is the same as it was 200 years ago — about 300 full-time residents (*Statistics Canada* 1982). The people who remain have resisted the strong trend of outward migration. They make the best of it in a marginal economy that is characterized by fishing, logging, boat building, and lately, tourism. And they seem to do a lot to their houses. To understand the labour expended on houses as organizational communication, it is necessary to gain a sense of the varieties of modifications and the architectural background of the built environment.

The houses in this part of Newfoundland carry traces of building traditions and styles from the earliest inhabitants. The oldest families here came from the west country area of England and from Ireland (Mannion 1977). Although people from these areas would not have built houses before 1600, and none now standing is older than 1800, it is not surprising to find medieval building techniques still in practice (Hewett 1969, O'Dea 1982). The housing stock displays an array of types from vernacular forms and folk transformations of elite forms, through to architecturally styled homes in Georgian, Second Empire, and Queen Anne traditions. The question that takes a researcher into the organizational context does not involve the origins of houses as much as the subsequent modifications to them. Who made the modifications, when, and most importantly, who regulates them?

The majority of homes are variants of one and a half or two storey structures with a central front door, central staircase with living room and kitchen off either side, and a chimney on each gable end (plate 1).[3] When this particular house was built in the 1860's, the front was without the vestibule and the large window flanked by the two smaller windows. The roof of the house also had a much steeper peak in profile and the rafters would have carried out over a one storey porch area in the rear (plate 2).

Known locally as a *long slope roof* house,[4] this type frequently had its roof line altered after the turn of the century. In some instances, the rear portion would be raised to a full two storey height, and the structure would be referred to as a *peak roof* house (plate 3, house on the right), while in

Plate 1

Plate 2

others, the angle of the roof would be altered altogether resulting in a form known as the *bawn box* (plate 3, house on left).[5]

Bawn box houses were being built and modified after the turn of this century when the salt cod trade was the mainstay of the economy and most of the male population was involved in catching cod, cleaning, splitting, salting, and then drying it for market. The part of the beach where the cod was set out to dry was known as the *bawn* (Story/Kirwin/Widdowson 1982). The houses look like the boxes used to carry fish from the beach or *bawn*.

Houses then were built in each of these vernacular types, yet were just as frequently modified from one type to another. The younger owners of many of these houses continue to modify their homes, "doing it up," as they say. The house in plate 1 has had its rear porch extension removed (plate 4).

At later stages, "doing up" this house might involve replacing windows, doors, or siding. The process may simply involve the replacement of traditional, double hung windows with horizontal sliding varieties (plate 5, window, lower right).

In some instances, the house is reclad with vinyl or aluminium siding that is placed over existing wooden siding (plate 6). Main doors are replaced with contemporary, insulated steel varieties (plate 7), and in the most extreme examples, the second storey is removed entirely (plate 8).

These modifications are not unique to Newfoundland. The use of mass-produced siding systems is a common practice (Forrest 1988), and the overall modernization process is often linked with social class (Hugill 1980). Modifications are neither random nor peculiar to individuals. Pattern and

Plate 3

Plate 4

Plate 5

order become visible when these practices are seen within networks of community relations, age grades, and residency.

The owner of the house in plates 1 and 4 is not alone in removing the porch from his house, but not everyone who modifies a traditional house removes the porch. Some who have houses with existing porches leave them on while others build new ones where none existed before. Front doors are rarely used in these communities (Szwed 1966), and often they have no steps because all traffic is through the back door. The factor in the modification process which might predict the treatment of a porch is whether or not the owner was born in the community. People do not knock to enter each other's houses — they walk right in. If you were born in a particular community and grew up there, this tradition would not take you unawares. If you have moved there, or married into the community, adding or keeping a porch provides a social buffer for people visiting.

Traditionally, houses were clustered according to kinship networks, "gardens" (Faris 1973), formed across generations from father to son, within one generation such as a group of brothers, or by marriage. The houses exhibit strong similarities because of the pooled resources and carpentry skills. This tight pattern of patrilocality does not continue today with the same strength as it did a generation ago due to the collapse of the traditional

Plate 6

Plate 7 (top) Plate 8 (bottom)

salt fish economy and outmigration, yet the reproduction of family organization is still evident.

The house in plate 7 "done up" soon after the owner's marriage is the only one of this type with large picture windows in the front. It might be thought an extravagant form of personal expression until seen in relation to his father's house (plate 9). His house was built from a contemporary plan approved by the Canadian Mortgage and Housing Corporation (CMHC). The choice of fenestration for both houses signals family affiliation despite the seventy-five years difference in the age of the houses and the generation separating their owners.

Many of these CMHC-inspired homes were built during the 1960's when the federal and provincial governments instituted programmes that attempted to centralize the population (Iverson and Matthews 1968). Whole communities living in parts of the island without roads or health care facilities were moved to larger centres that could be serviced more easily. This period of migration and transition helped revise the vocabulary of building and modification. In Trinity, the owners of these homes are distinguished from the long-standing residents of the community by their membership in voluntary organizations. They were frequently referred to as "the Lions crowd" because they had been the founding members of the local chapter of Lions International.

This pattern of migration and building is not without precedent. There are a number of architecturally styled houses that date from the turn of the century. They have strong Georgian, Queen Anne, or Second Empire features (see plate 10), and have frequent examples of the cross-gabled roof, decorative shingles under the eaves, palladian windows, projecting dormers set in a curved, mansard roof, and bay windows. Like the contemporary CMHC houses that followed in the 1950's and 1960's, these structures went up in response to resettlement. Between 1890 and 1920, there was a great deal of social and geographical movement in Newfoundland. A railway across the island was completed, papermills were opened, and a whaling factory started operation. New groups moved in, and older residents stayed in the flush economic changes prior to the depression. These buildings were a response of a professional middle class to the resettlement of displaced labour, or a new wage-earning working class. In the 1960's when resettlement again brought new residents, the local, long-standing families responded by founding the Trinity Historical Society.

In recent years, a new population segment has appeared: summer residents. Over a third of the houses in Trinity are summer homes owned by former residents or non-residents. The majority of the summer residents live in the older traditional houses, which remain vacant for a substantial portion of the year. Some of residents keep a morbid tally of the houses boarded up at the end of each summer season.

Plate 9

Plate 10

4 Organizing Modifications

These communities are segmented into multiple, interpenetrating, formal, and informal organizations: families, kinship networks, religious congregations, voluntary associations (Lions Club, Loyal Orange Lodge, Firettes, etc.), residents, summer residents, and so on (Davis 1983). Residents frequently hold multiple memberships, so at this level of analysis, it is not possible to distinguish modifications that might be specific to one membership. It has already been suggested that families exhibit pattern in their modifications to houses. Summer residents characterize themselves by removing interior partitions in older houses. With the traditional layout of rooms reflecting an understanding of hierarchy in the community (Pocius 1979), it is not surprising that residents might think of these modifications as leaving the house "all broke up inside."

The most obvious boundary across which modifications are not understood involves the restoration of the older styled and vernacular houses in the community. If houses are not only active products but the very sites of organizing, then there is little reason to expect a community to have an interest in inscribing its organizing in a static architectural form. Even buildings which we might expect to remain static in relation to particular organizations — sacred and ceremonial structures such as schools and churches — reflect the active spirit of organizing. Schools, community halls, and churches are "done up" with new windows, siding, and so on just as frequently as houses. Their roofs are raised or lowered, dormer windows added or removed, they are reclad, and older, handmade decoration is obscured with the new fashions of the machine age. The tradition of rebuilding from materials of older structures is so strong that the sacred buildings of abandoned communities frequently have their interior timbers removed for reuse in new structures. The exterior remains, a husk of its former self.

In this sense then, the community has no tradition of preserving or restoring a house to represent a static moment. Rather than expect a parallel with elite or urban practices, it is more likely that a parallel for preservation can be found in other community activities that involve the cultural processing of natural goods. In this environment, if preservation exists, it must take the form of change: otherwise things rot. The harshness of the process for housing is evident here: with over three hundred years of recorded European settlement, the oldest buildings are not half that age. Churches, rectories, and private homes follow a cycle of rebuilding that spans about 70 years.

Houses are "preserved" then, not in form but in process through modifications. In this sense, building performances (whether construction, alteration, or demolition) are analogous to the domestic performances involved in preserving food. Food was either "live" or "fresh," or it was bottled, pickled, or dry cured with salt (Gard 1981). Fresh fish was "green" until it was cleaned, split, salted, and dry cured, just as lumber was "green" until it had been sawn, dressed — that is planed and squared —, and allowed to dry (Story/Kirwin/Widdowson 1982). To not respect the proper stages of this process would be an abominable breech of socially sanctioned pollution rules (Douglas 1975).[6]

With this analogy between preservation of food and buildings in mind, it is possible to imagine the turmoil of residents when the community was given $ 1.5 million to preserve the historic character of their village. To stop the active organizing of modifications by which houses are kept habitable would result, almost by definition, in a collection of dwellings that were unpalatable and unhygienic.

5 Organizing Simulation

The project grant was the culmination of actions from inside and outside the community: lobbying by the Historical Society, the community council, and at least four consultants' reports commissioned at various times by Parks Canada, the provincial planning office, the Department of Municipal Affairs, and the Department of Tourism.

In 1973, the study commissioned by the provincial planning office assessed the area's resources and development potential. This study recommended "control" (Project Planning Associates 1973: 27) of buildings with historic or architectural merit, and offered various scenarios of federal grants and legislation to stabilize and improve the housing stock.

The consultants recognized that the goals of preservation were at odds with the needs of the community but suggested that modern services could be provided in a manner that kept demolition or alteration of exteriors to a minimum. The goal was to maintain the setting, character, and scale of the community, and they suggested "maxims" (Project Planning Associates 1973: 28) to control the use of materials, colours, alterations, etc. The goal was to heighten the visual experience of the community by removing various pollutions such as car wrecks and obscuring other distasteful views (e. g. trailer homes) by building traditional looking structures in front of them. The report suggested the council adopt heritage guidelines to control any new building in the area to have it conform with explicit architectural criteria. An area map detailed with all buildings was annotated by remarks such as: "This single storey new house is painted yellow and brown which is out of character" (Project Planning Associates 1973). It is a testament of the owner's stamina and the strength of local standards that 16 years later the house is still the same colour.

In 1977, while the council was still waiting to see the 1973 report, the Department of Municipal Affairs tabled another consultant's report. This updated the earlier report, and recommended that the community be designated an Historic Conservation Area, with the "comprehensive intention" being "to strictly preserve Trinity as an example of an early 19th century outport" (Edge 1977: 22).

By 1978, the Historic Resources Division of the Department of Tourism had pursued a heritage village plan with DREE. The $ 1.5 million was allocated for restoration in conjunction with DREE's plans for tourist development in the region. Certainly, government has always had a stake in promoting tourism (Overton 1984), and by the 1960's it was common for them to be active in the region designing what tourists would experience (McKay 1988, O'Hollaren 1987). The point and place at which this occurs is an opportunity to ask "whose culture is on display? Whose heritage is being simulated?"

A combined community council and Historical Society met with the federal and provincial government officials to discuss where they felt the money should be spent. In terms of priority, the first item on the list for local residents was to pave roads. Following that, they felt the Anglican cemetery should be cleaned up, and then, the Methodist cemetery. At the end of the list, the community expressed the desire to see the "Lester-Garland" home reconstructed (Minutes 1978, March 16).

The Lester-Garland house was built of brick in the 1770's for Benjamin Lester. It followed a Georgian plan, and was two and a half stories high. After it was inherited by George Garland, who continued to live in England, plans were made to rebuild in the second decade of the nineteenth century. Garland wrote to his nephew living in the house, suggesting that it was "too old and ill-contrived to make anything of without" (Garland 1817). He recommended demolition of the house and salvage of the interior fittings. In the end, the rear portion of the building's parallel gable roof was replaced with a long sloping roof reminiscent of vernacular practice.

Subsequent tenants wrote back and forth to the owners throughout the nineteenth century complaining about the building's condition, and it was still described as "fast going to decay" a century after Garland's observation (Lockyer 1921). It was lived in until the late 1940's and was finally demolished and many of its bricks sold during the 1960's after a federal heritage agency began documenting its heritage qualities.

The building was important to the residents because of its direct link with the merchant families of the 1800's and the period when Trinity was one of the province's major economic centres. The community petitioned at various times to have three different plaques placed on the site to commemorate historical activities of the residents and owners of the house.

After the community presented the government with its priorities for restoration, they were told that sites such as the Lester-Garland home were not feasible because of their ruined condition. Government officials stated that the project's main objective was to "retain the look of ... the houses outside, the same as when they were built" (Minutes 1978, 3 May). Their priority was to restore the commercial premises adjoining the ruined Lester-Garland house. The completion of this was stated as the goal for 1978, yet the building is neither completed nor yet open to the public. About thirty-five houses did receive work in the form of paint, siding, windows, and in some instances structural work on foundations. The churches received exterior maintenance, and the community hall was modernized to meet fire safety requirements.

The work undertaken was visual following the tone of the early consultants' reports. It is not surprising that local residents refer to the restoration project as the "alteration project." Certainly, the work done on the houses bore no relation to the culturally accepted process of modification, nor did it even return the houses to an earlier stage in that modification process. Given the local attitude towards organizing housing modifications, it is not surprising that the council would receive complaints about sewage leaks and rat infestations in the older houses owned by non-residents. Nor is it surprising that after the restoration project began the council issued permits

Plate 11

for the demolition of houses, though none were issued before. Residents considered the living conditions of these houses to be unhygienic and unsafe. Quite simply, if a house was not lived in, it was not a house. It was a resource for new building activity, it was firewood, but it was no longer a house. To leave it standing was a celebration of the community's decay and depopulation.

There were, then, two distinct ways of organizing the built environment of this community. Residents organized houses in terms of use or disuse, and non-residents organized houses in terms of the presence or absence of architectural merits.

The manager of the restoration project expressed an awareness of the local attitude but had evolved no strategy to compensate for it. "There was a lot of misinformation in terms of how people perceived the project and what our objectives were ... Our relationship with the community council was tenuous. Why that was, I was never really quite sure ... We did not feel that we had substantial rapport with the community council and we could not depend on them taking a positive attitude ... I think that meant the project suffered somewhat ..."

The centrepiece of the restoration project was the Hiscock house (plate 11), built in the late 1880's, but "restored" circa 1910. At its official opening, the last living member of the family the house was built for cut the ribbon over the threshold. When she lived in the house, it had been a store, the Royal Bank, and her home. No longer used in a traditional sense, she expressed what might have been said by anyone in the community: "you know, it never looked like this, like it does now."

6 Conclusion

The projects are mostly finished now. People still do things with their houses, and plaques are still unveiled so history can continue. The built environment is riddled with infractions of the building codes (see plate 5) that the government officials tried to see enforced. Houses that once made statements about the process and renewal of a built heritage can now be read as sites of opposition to imposed standards. Or can they?

There are certainly multiple stories, multiple allegories to be read in these houses. There are biographies, autobiographies, allegories of economic oppression, state domination, vernacular opposition, or regional renaissance. There is the story residents tell with their houses, the one the government officials would like to see told with these houses, and there is a version documented here.

Organizational interventions are sought when companies plan for or are surprised by change. More informal organizations such as communities also confront change, but with a crucial difference for the researcher. Change may be natural and environmental, or induced strategically by government. In the latter case, a consultant's report is often commissioned. Rarely would a consultant be invited by the community to diagnose the problem, evaluate it, or to suggest local strategies for coping. Developing a participatory research style invites a dialogic approach to fieldwork which facilitates the time spent documenting housing modifications, studying archival records, census data, council minutes, interviewing contractors and carpenters, bureaucrats and homeowners.

But others have been here and studied the same sources: building inspectors, census takers, health officials, insurance people, or government project officers. Nothing changed. No one knows their names or where their reports are filed. Whose knowledge is this? Whose action should it serve?

The projects are mostly finished now. At an earlier point, an organizational ethnographer could have helped demonstrate the local attitude to preservation. It may even have been possible to circumvent an invented past by simply interpreting the process of change. At a later point, interpretive research could valorize the community response, apologize for the official response. In either case, the researcher is locked into an oppositional dialectic. Whether a pastiche of modifications or an attempt at restoration, none of these houses have history right. They will never look the way they did, nor will they be pure simulation. Even my further allegorization of their oppositional moment is questionable.

In the end, no version is authoritative: participatory, collaborative, but never finally authoritative. Perhaps that is the point, to resist authoritative versions (Smircich/Calas 1987). The representation of organizational cultures at play, opposed, resisting, is not authoritative or fixed. Organizational ethnography too is modified: researched to change the process of fieldwork, written to change the process of representation. Parts structural and cosmetic are modified as taste, materials, and environment allow or demand.

Notes

1 Research for this paper was supported by grants from the Social Sciences and Humanities Research Council of Canada between 1984 and 1986 while I was a postdoctoral fellow with the Institute of Social and Economic Research at Memorial University of Newfoundland. The interest of Trinity's residents and their Historical Society, Museum and Archives was of equal support. The Faculty of General Studies at The University of Calgary offered me the time for further reflection on this material during the year I spent with them as a scholar-in-residence.

2 An effort was made to control generalizations by comparison with two other communities, English Harbour and the now resettled community of Kearly's Harbour. In contrast to Trinity, these communities were primarily fishing communities. Trinity was the trading and merchant centre for the region and has a tradition of housing that reflects an economy of stratified occupations.

3 Not all the photographs are of houses in Trinity. Plates 6, 7, 8, and 9 are of houses in English Harbour. Plate 2 is of a house in British Harbour, a resettled community south of Kearly's Harbour. Although there has been a great deal of discussion recently about making cultural representations more dialogic and polyphonic (Clifford/Marcus 1986, Marcus/Fischer 1986), practice has generally been restricted to chirographic representation. Indigenous photographic work, whether in the museum, in family albums, or in early tourist material, is an invaluable resource in learning to see a place or the artifacts that comprise it. Many residents in these communities had personal collections of photographs (their own snapshots, postcards, newspaper clippings, and other inherited photos) that were about how their village and its houses used to look. The role of photography in constructing local versions of the past is new research territory (Greenhill 1981, Motz 1989, Musello 1980). The collaborative use of photography and other imaging techniques is beginning to influence scholarly representational practices (Hammond 1988, 1989).

4 I have used local terms for distinguishing these varieties of houses although there are several excellent scholarly typologies which perform the same task with greater historical rigour (Mills 1982). For this project it was important to rely on indigenous discriminations.

5 See Pocius 1987, McAlester/McAlester 1984, and Mills 1982 for discussions about evolution and innovation of house types.

6 Over 90% of the houses in these communities were painted either white or yellow. This tacit rule of colour choice is exact enough to predict the resident/summer resident membership of homeowners. Following on this rule, it was a matter of local sense that houses would not be painted green: green would contribute to accelerated rot of the house siding. This rule may extend the linguistic analogies that connect building with culinary practice.

References

Agrest, D. and M. Gandelsonas (1977): Semiotics and the Limits of Architecture. *A Profusion of Signs*. T. A. Sebeok (Ed.). Bloomington, IN: Indiana University Press, pp. 90—120

Alexander, D. (1980): Newfoundland's Traditional Economy and Development to 1934. *Newfoundland in the Nineteenth and Twentieth Centuries: Essays in Interpretation*. J. Hiller/P. Neary (Eds.). Toronto: University of Toronto Press, pp. 17—39

Ames, K. L. (1980): Material Culture as Nonverbal Communication: A Historical Case Study. *Journal of American Culture* 3(4), pp. 619—641

Appadurai, A. (Ed.) (1986): *The Social Life of Things*. New York: Cambridge University Press

Bourdieu, P. (1979): The Kabyle House or the World Reversed. *Algeria 1960: Essays by Pierre Bourdieu.* R. Nice (Transl.). London: Cambridge University Press, pp. 133–153

Cannizzo, J. (1987): Living in the Past. *Ideas.* L. Sinclair (Produc.) Toronto: Canadian Broadcasting Corporation, January

Clifford, J. (1986): On Ethnographic Allegory. *Writing Culture: The Poetics and Politics of Ethnography.* J. Clifford/G. Marcus (Eds.). Los Angeles, CA: University of California Press, pp. 98–121

Clifford, J. (1988): On Collecting Art and Culture. *The Predicament of Culture: Twentieth-Century Ethnography, Literature, and Art.* Cambridge, MA: Harvard University Press, pp. 215–251

Clifford, J. and G. Marcus (Eds.) (1986): *Writing Culture: The Poetics and Politics of Ethnography.* Los Angeles, CA: University of California Press

Conquergood, D. (1989): Poetics, Play, Process and Power: The Performance Turn in Anthropology. *Text and Performance Quarterly* 9(1), January, pp. 82–88

Csikszentmihalyi, M. and E. Rochberg-Halton (1981): *The Meaning of Things: Domestic Symbols and the Self.* Cambridge: Cambridge University Press

Davis, D. L. (1983): *Blood and Nerves: An Ethnographic Focus on Menopause.* St. John's, Newfoundland: Institute of Social and Economic Research

Dominguez, V. R. (1986): The Marketing of Heritage. *American Ethnologist* 13(3), August, pp. 546–555

Douglas, M. (1972): Symbolic Orders in the Use of Domestic Space. *Man, Settlement and Urbanism.* P. J. Ucko/R. Tringham/G. W. Dimbleby (Eds.). London: Duckworth, pp. 513–521

Douglas, M. (1975): "Pollution"-and-"Deciphering a Meal." *Implicit Meanings: Essays in Anthropology.* London: Routledge and Kegan Paul, pp. 47–59, 249–275

Douglas, M. (1982): Goods as a System of Communication. *In the Active Voice.* London: Routledge and Kegan Paul, pp. 16–33

Edge, R. (1977): *Trinity Community Plan.* St. John's, Newfoundland: Provincial Planning Office

Errington, S. (1989): Fragile Traditions and Contested Meanings. *Public Culture* 1(2), Spring, pp. 49–59

Faris, J. (1973): *Cat Harbour: A Newfoundland Fishing Settlement.* St. John's, Newfoundland: Institute of Social and Economic Research

Foote, K. (1983): *Color in Public Spaces: Toward a Communication Based Theory of the Urban Built Environment.* Chicago: University of Chicago, Dept. of Geography Research Paper No. 205

Forrest, J. (1988): *Lord I'm Coming Home: Everyday Aesthetics in Tidewater North Carolina.* Ithaca, NY: Cornell University Press

Galt, G. (1987): Making History. *Saturday Night* January, pp. 130–134

Gard, P. (1981): Food. *Encyclopedia of Newfoundland and Labrador.* vol. II. J. R. Smallwood (Ed.). St. John's: Newfoundland Book Publishers, pp. 272–289

Garland, G. (1817): Letter to James Garland, Trinity, Trinity Bay 1817. *Walter White Papers.* St. John's, Newfoundland: Newfoundland Historical Society

Glassie, H. (1975): *Folk Housing in Middle Virginia: A Structural Analysis of Historic Artifacts.* Knoxville, TN: University of Tennessee Press

Greenhill, P. (1981): *So We Can Remember: Showing Family Photographs*. Ottawa: National Museum of Man

Hammond, J. (1988): Visualizing Themselves: Tongan Videography in Utah. *Visual Anthropology* 1(4), pp. 379—400

Hammond, J. (1989): Representation in a Collaborative Video Project. *Visual Sociology Review* 4(1), Spring, pp. 8—15

Handcock, G. (1985): The Poole Merchant Community and the Growth of Trinity 1700—1839. *Newfoundland Quarterly* Vol. LXXX(3), pp. 19—30

Herman, B. L. (1985): Time and Performance: Folk Houses in Delaware. *American Material Culture and Folklife*. S. Bronner (Ed.). Ann Arbor, MI: University of Michigan, pp. 155—175

Hewett, C. (1969): *The Development of Carpentry, 1200—1700. An Essex Study*. New York: Augustus Kelley

Hugill, P. J. (1980): Houses in Cazenovia: The Effects of Time and Class. *Landscape* 24(2), pp. 10—15

Iverson, N. and R. Matthews (1968): *Communities in Decline: An Examination of Household Resettlement in Newfoundland*. St. John's, Newfoundland: Institute of Social and Economic Research

Lockyer, C. (1921): Trinity. *The Evening Telegram* 24 December, p. 3

Lofland, L. (1988): Communication and Construction: The Built Environment as Message and Medium. *Communication and Social Structure*. D. R. Maines/C. J. Couch (Eds.). Springfield, IL: Charles C. Thomas, pp. 307—339

Mannion, J. (1977): *The Peopling of Newfoundland: Essays in Historical Geography*. St. John's, Newfoundland: Institute of Social and Economic Research

Marcus, G. and M. Fischer (1986): *Anthropology as Cultural Critique: An Experimental Moment in the Human Sciences*. Chicago, IL: University of Chicago Press

McAlester, V. and L. McAlester (1984): *A Field Guide to American Houses*. New York: Alfred Knopf

McKay, I. (1988): Twilight at Peggy's Cove: Towards a Genealogy of "Maritimicity" in Nova Scotia. *Border/lines* 12, Summer, pp. 28—37

Mills, D. (1982): *The Evolution of Folk House Forms in Trinity Bay, Newfoundland*. St. John's, Newfoundland: Technical Papers of the Newfoundland Museum

Minutes of the Community Council (1969—1986). Trinity: Trinity Bay Newfoundland

Motz, M. F. (1989): Visual Autobiography. Photograph Albums of Turn-of-the-Century Midwestern Women. *American Quarterly* 41(1), March, pp. 63—92

Musello, C. (1980): Studying the Home Mode: An Exploration of Family Photography and Visual Communication. *Studies in Visual Communication* 6(1), pp. 23—42

O'Dea, S. (1982): Simplicity and Survival: Vernacular Response in Newfoundland Architecture. *The Newfoundland Quarterly* Vol. LXXVIII (3), pp. 19—31

O'Hollaren, J. (1987): *Strangers in Our Midst: Tourism as a Development Strategy in Newfoundland*. Ottawa: National Library of Canada (Canadian Theses on Microfiche)

Overton, J. (1984): Coming Home: Nostalgia and Tourism in Newfoundland. *Acadiensis* 14(1), Autumn, pp. 84—97

Pacanowsky, M. and N. O'Donnell-Trujillo (1982): Communication and Organizational Cultures. *The Western Journal of Speech Communication* 46(2), Spring, pp. 115—130

Pacanowsky, M. and N. O'Donnell-Trujillo (1983): Organizational Communication as Cultural Performance. *Communication Monographs* 50(2), June, pp. 126–147

Pocius, G. (1979): Hooked Rugs in Newfoundland: The Representation of Social Structure in Design. *Journal of American Folklore* 92(365), pp. 273–284

Pocius, G. (1987): Raised Roofs and High Hopes: Rebuildings on Newfoundland's Southern Shore. *Material Culture* 19(2–3), pp. 67–83

Pratt, G. (1981): The House as Expression of Social Worlds. *Housing and Identity: Cross-Cultural Perspectives.* J. S. Duncan (Ed.). London: Croom Helm, pp. 135–180

Project Planning Associates (1973): *Trinity, Trinity Bay: A Townscape Study.* Bristol

Ryan, S. (1980): The Newfoundland Salt Cod Trade in the Nineteenth Century. *Newfoundland in the Nineteenth and Twentieth Centuries: Essays in Interpretation.* J. Hiller/P. Neary (Eds.). Toronto: University of Toronto Press, pp. 40–66

Smircich, L. and M. Calas (1987): Organizational Culture: A Critical Assessment. *Handbook of Organizational Communication: An Interdisciplinary Perspective.* F. M. Jablin/L. L. Putnam/K. H. Roberts/L. W. Porter (Eds.). London: Sage, pp. 228–263

Statistics Canada (1982): *1981 Census of Canada.* Ottawa: Minister of Supply and Services

Story, G. M., W. J. Kirwin, and J. D. A. Widdowson (Eds.) (1982): *Dictionary of Newfoundland English.* Toronto: University of Toronto Press

Szwed, J. (1966): *Private Cultures and Public Imagery: Interpersonal Relations in a Newfoundland Peasant Society.* St. John's, Newfoundland: Institute of Social and Economic Research

Upton, D. (1979): Towards a Performance Theory of Vernacular Architecture: Early Tidewater Virginia as a Case Study. *Folklore Forum* 12, pp. 173–196

Meaning of the Workplace: Using Ideas of Ritual Space in Design

Dennis Doxtater

1 Introduction

Wineman's excellent survey of existing literature on architecturally related behavioral aspects of work settings (1982) defines three areas of present research: (1) Physical comfort and task instrumentality; (2) Privacy and social interaction; and (3) Symbolic identification. While the human factors or task performance aspects of any work setting are critical, particularly at the ergonomics level, Wineman's second two categories are the primary initial interest here.

Within category (2), considerations of privacy or control form a sizable portion of the literature, frequently focusing on investigation of open vs. closed office spaces (e. g. Brookes/Kaplan 1972, Goodrich 1982, Hedge 1982, McCarrey et al. 1974, Sundstrom et al. 1982). Related issues of territoriality, power and crowding have also received attention, though here the causal contribution of the physical environment becomes more difficult to establish (e. g. Korda 1975, Lipman et al. 1978, Steele 1973, Szilagy/Holland 1980). Equally problematic in terms of the causality of built form are the less frequent, yet intuitively interesting vignettes of particular social relationships as in Whyte's description of a restaurant (1949) or the "manning" analysis of a supermarket by Lozar (1975).

Certainly these social issues have very important implications for any organization. Open office plans, for example, may at times actually inhibit communication (Hatch in this volume) and do not necessarily facilitate the work process; or the distinction between organizationally less mobile employees and those "on their way up" suggests numerous design considerations in reference to each; or linear layouts of executive office and window accessibility offer a positive alternative to power corners and enclosed office pools.

The third category of "Symbolic Identification," again in Wineman's reference to the environment and behavior litterature, largely represents the usage of "objects" to communicate identity and status in association with the territorial processes described in category (2). The attachment of meaningful objects to territories as "personalization" (Hensley 1982), whether by individuals or groups, provides identity. Sizes of desks and chairs, thickness of carpets, windows, etc., express the status of place (Campbell 1980, Konar et al. 1982, Korda 1975, McElroy/Morrow 1982).

The labeling of "territorial signage" as "symbolic" suggests certain limits to present theoretical perspectives within the environment and behavior literature. While it may be true that many of our contemporary workplaces are primarily territorial in essence, including signs of identity and status, still, our paradigms must also embrace other potentials for more clearly symbolic, spatially structured, "expressive" uses of the physical environment as occur in very traditional settings. The distinction between "cultural," "expressive," or "ritual" space and territoriality is only recently becoming topical and has yet to broaden our approaches to meaning in workplaces. My recent article arguing for a similar inclusion of such a distinction in studies of housing presents a much more fully detailed discussion of the issues than is possible here (Doxtater 1989).

Briefly, in traditional environments, the source of most of our examples of "ritual expression," it is quite clear that shared concepts of relatively formal spatial structure—axis or direction, threshold, center—are heavily laden with powerful symbolic meaning. These meanings inform virtually all scales of built and natural environments. Ritual performance, the movement through such space, is essentially a manipulation of this emotional energy primarily for purposes of social legitimacy, whatever its guise (Doxtater 1981b, 1984). The key to distinguishing these kinds of places from the territories and signs we see so often in our workplaces is understanding the different sources of affective or persuasive influence brought to bear in both instances.

In the briefly outlined case of traditional ritual, internalized spatial form provides a cognitive means of separating and making contact with symbolic content, as for example when one approaches the altar in a traditional church and is touched by the power of the spirit world. This highly affective experience, while always controlled by some social body, is at the same time largely independent from it. Here, power comes not so much from the association of social participants (the occupation of a priest notwithstanding), but from the dense symbolic associations, e. g. death and things of the spirit world, which are defined, held separate, and made ritually available through the structuring properties of space.

The influence of territorial space, on the other hand, is due to the more immediate occupation and manipulation of power by individuals and groups at hand. Signs of identity and status, while often conventional, are not arbitrary sources of affect which must be spatially manipulated in some relatively independent "system." They are relatively immediate signs, very closely associated with actual decision-making power and authority. The large desk of an executive, for example, in itself has no "independent" affective content as does the emotion of death in Christ on the cross. Larger offices and more affluent furnishings *communicate* the economic power of actual occupants of a territory, rather than contribute symbolic affect *per se* to some formally structured set of meanings in space.

Thus in traditional ritual space, power comes from the spatial manipulation of essentially arbitrary symbolic contents; in human territorial spaces, such as many work settings, the authority of the space comes from communication that the occupying individual or group has and may exercise real social, economic, or political power. It is this distinction which renders present environment and behavior thinking about workplaces incomplete. It immediately raises the question of whether these more independent, spatially structured, symbolic meanings of space exist or are possible in contemporary work environments.

One does find in white-collar settings occasional glimpses of spatial structures which begin to obtain at least formality and independent attached meaning, if not ritual manipulation. Korda, for example, speaks of "neutral zones" which make clear references to other places, here the "home turfs" of competing executives (1975). The symbolic meanings attached to these functionally distinct and structurally related places—an egalitarian place as the neutral focus of several hierarchical ones — should have formally opposite meanings according to ritual formula. In work by the symbolic interactionists, as well, one begins to sense these larger and more complex meanings, e. g. Holdaway's description of the opposed meanings and activities of "front" and "back" places of a police station (1980). In addition to these more ethnographic accounts, one finds philosophical essays which, though limited in theory and supportive detail, go beyond (territorial) "identification" by signs. The argument is for strong significance of symbolic space in abstract cultural themes or beliefs essential to the maintenance of complex, often hierarchical social organizations (Edelman 1978, Harris/ Lipman 1980).

Particularly interesting with regard to work environments, and more rigorous than the present essay format, is John Peponis' application of the ideas and methodology of "space syntax" (1983). It is claimed by the developers of this very influential, algebraic way of describing spatial forms and relationships, Hillier and Hanson (1983), that patterns which emerge from analysis can refer to many levels of meaning, including function, social organization, and even symbolic or ritual space. Yet in spite of the fact that Peponis speaks of "spatial culture" when discussing his analysis of factories, his work maps only task instrumentality and social territoriality.

The author's personal experience with work spaces began some ten years ago. When beginning to teach architectural design, after completing doctoral research on symbolism and ritual in traditional cultures, students were sent to "analyze" contemporary environments from such a point of view. Some results, particularly in office settings, were very suggestive of symbolic forms of space in traditional societies. As part of an actual programming and construction project for a new campus Facilities Planning Office at the time, the author interviewed employees and mapped the existing office setting.

The plan diagrams of Figure 1 are from a speculative article which interprets the formal "symbolic" and spatial aspects as something akin to ritual expression in traditional cultures (Doxtater 1981a). Beginning with a plan of the daylight basement office, the diagram of Figure 1b referred to two "cultural" themes the relationship of which seemed to go beyond territorial identity, "planner" (things dealing with process), and "architect" (things having to do with products). These appeared to be formally defined by the shape of the office space. The function of the office was to program the design and supervise building construction for major new projects on

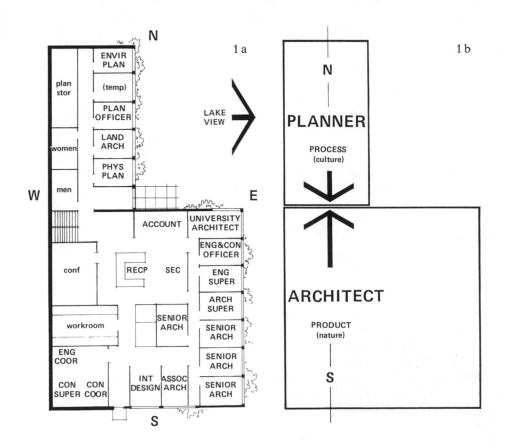

campus. Thus the distinction of process/product translated into acts and identities of employees who either spent their time in abstract planning or the opposite of producing much more immediate physical objects.

Figure 1c suggests that, not unlike traditional examples, these "north-south" meanings also occur at smaller scales within the Planning and Architectural departments. The issue of Figure 1d is the positions of supervisors at both scales, and the possibility that such formal spatial expression suggests ritually reminiscent, mediational functions between opposite areas, rather than just territorial control. The final Figure 1e includes the meanings of the east-west direction, dominance and subordinance, and how these combine with north-south content to define meanings of where employees sit.

This small and highly speculative study began to reveal the potential and also the difficulties of such work when approached methodologically from a social science perspective. While the author has continued to do research on traditional societies and only recently begun to methodologically investi-

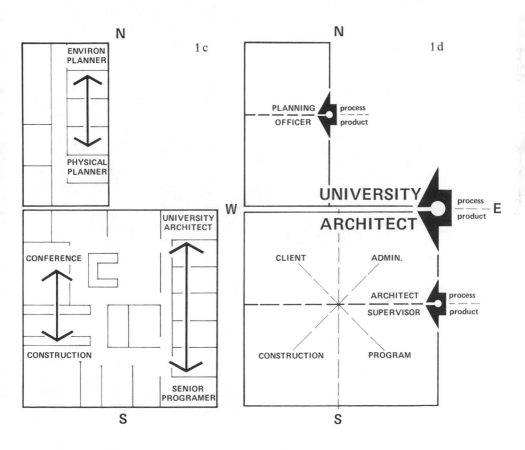

gate office environments from this point of view, much intuitive knowledge has been developed through a decade of using student office design projects for this kind of inquiry.

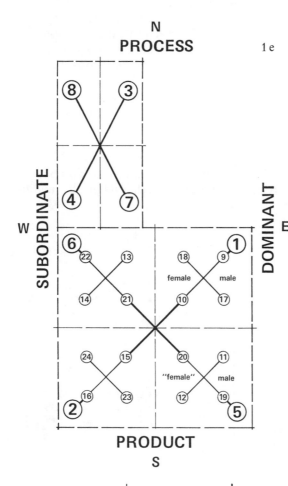

Figure 1: Diagrams of potential "ritual" space in an existing facilities planning office at a major university: 1a) architectural plan with labels of job descriptions; 1b) largest scale opposition between "process" and "product"; 1c) smaller scale oppositions between "process" and "product"; 1d) mediational positions of supervisors at both scales; 1e) meanings of employee work stations based on diagonal oppositions, composites of "process/product" and "dominant/subordinate."

process dominant	ne	sw	product subordinate	product dominant	se	nw	process subordinate
UNIV. ARCHITECT	①	②	CONST. SUPER.	SR. PROGRAMER	⑤	⑥	CLIENT ENTRY
ENVIRON. PLANNER	③	④	CLIENT ENTRY	PHYS. PLANNER	⑦	⑧	PLAN ARCHIVES
UNIV. ARCHITECT	⑨	⑩	SEC./RECP.	ENGIN. SUPER.	⑰	⑱	SECRETARY
ARCHITECT SUPER.	⑪	⑫	INT. DESIGNER	SR. PROGRAMER	⑲	⑳	PROGRAMER (2)
ACCOUNTANT	⑬	⑭	CONFERENCE	RECEPTION	㉑	㉒	CLIENT ENTRY
——	⑮	⑯	CONST. SUPER.	INT. DESIGNER	㉓	㉔	WORKROOM

2 Useful Assumptions in the Absence of Theoretical Distinctions

Without question, much theoretical and ethnographic work must be done to (1) further understand "ritual space" in traditional societies; (2) logically establish the distinction with the more territorial uses of space at the present; and (3) finally find ritual examples in contemporary environments if they exist. Given this lack, it is only in the role of client and designer, faced with the immediacy of creating a new work setting, that one dares consider the possibility of ritual content as briefly defined above. The following, then, amounts to a pragmatic, certainly interim way of thinking about design which at least begins to consider the potential of structured spatial symbolism in relation to some actual social or corporate purpose within. Application of these ideas in design is based upon three assumptions.

2.1 A Cross-Cultural Set of Spatial Structures

From traditional examples it is possible to derive a set of formal spatial patterns or structures which cognitively organize symbolic content and make it ritually available. These "structures" reoccur cross-culturally. The first assumption is that this set is useful in addressing *potential* "ritual" content in contemporary design processes, even though one cannot yet make definitive comparisons between these and traditional examples.

It may be useful to think of the structural set which will be briefly introduced as special kinds of "cognitive maps." In 1960, Kevin Lynch defined a limited set of cognitive spatial structures internalized from contemporary urban environments — paths, nodes, edges, landmarks, districts — the uses of which were primarily way-finding and territorial identification. As an appendix to this now classic piece, *The Image of the City*, Lynch compiled accounts of highly symbolic spaces in traditional societies which didn't seem to fit the mentioned purposes of the main portion of the book. Clearly, these particularly cultural kinds of cognitive maps served other "expressive" or "ritual" functions.

Again we see the researcher's attention on things obviously important to people in contemporary, often transient, particularly urban settings, i. e. knowing where we are in space, and knowing who exercises territorial control. Lynch did not find the highly symbolic kinds of maps to be evident in the way we internalized our environments; yet in small, very traditional societies, virtually *all* places — whether dwelling, settlement, or communally sacred place of worship — are symbolically defined and structurally related by forms of spatial cognition. In comparison to today's milieu, one certainly senses the greater importance of this particularly spatial aspect of culture in traditional societies. But one cannot assume that such meaning is presently even possible in our spatially and culturally diffuse experience, one only speaks of the cultural *potential* in all human environments. There are, however, certain places in our current milieu where this potential just might become possible.

2.2 The Need for Expressive Space in the Workplace as Society

The second assumption focuses our attention on the social and cultural similarities between smaller traditional societies and contemporary workplace organizations. While ritual use of space is potential in many other types of settings, we seek a contemporary situation (here the United States) where the need for expressive space will be the strongest. One would immediately think of churches as first candidates, particularly because of the obvious wealth of symbols and spatial organization. Yet one essential aspect of significant ritual is most often missing here. The experience is not usually critical to the maintenance of some active, purposeful, socio-economic group. Power relationships between individuals and groups, or one group and another group are only minimally influenced or legitimized, in spite of obvious historical successes in this regard. Even among the most traditional Catholic churches (such as in the earlier example of effective ritual), recent architectural modification has effectively "deritualized" the experience, creating less of a manipulation of spirit power than a place for a community meeting.

The potential in workplaces, however, exists in the much greater and immediate need to expressively manipulate active, purposeful relationships often between a multiplicity of social groups. Hierarchies must be effectively maintained, legitimized in part by communally shared values. Such is the case in traditional societies where one finds effective uses of expressive space.

In addition to the importance of purposeful social groups as the prime reason for expressive space, it is logical to assume that the time or permanence of occupation will also be important. Just as individuals must build adequate Lynchian maps through time and experience, so too will social groups require time to evolve spatial structures and meanings — supportive of their organizational form. In traditional societies individuals and groups live and die within a relatively constant, structurally defined environment. By contrast, it has been mentioned that contemporary environmental experience is often novel and transient, and shared symbolic structures may be hard to develop. Given the frequency of residential relocation, at least in the United States, the most permanently occupied places may be those where we work. This attribute becomes particularly salient when coupled with the social and economic purposefulness of these groups.

Finally, it is particularly "white-collar" or office settings, compared with service or industrial places, which might be the most likely candidates for both potential and possible "ritual" content. Again like traditional societies, the spatial forms of offices appear to be far less determined by systems engineering considerations of production than are manufacturing settings. Thus in spite of much conventional wisdom to the contrary, that physical adjacency, movement of goods, and flexibility are important in offices, by comparison, office building form may be far more "available" for the creation of social, primarily territorial purposes — particularly considering the effect of the personal computer on worker adjacency. It is this availability which may also make "ritual" space possible. Current work by the author, comparing the shapes of Swedish and U.S. offices, will begin to reveal the fallacy of thinking that Taylorism is the primary form giver. Individual territorial control and identity is paramount in most U.S. office settings, while in Sweden, most significant is a spatially based, cultural system of meaning which organizes social relationships between the individual and the group.

2.3 The Role of the Designer

This assumption deals with the evolution of structure. How do relatively short-term processes of individual designers differ from "vernacular" methods which evolve more slowly and indigenously through an ecological dialectic of social groups? In traditional societies, social groups rather than individuals *per se* are the causal factors. In workplace societies, even though individuals obviously will exert greater influence, it is assumed that where coherent structured organizations exist, there too the entire social group must be participant. Furthermore, individual way-finding relies on spatial, cognitive processes which, in their most complex, "map-like," states, are largely subconscious. The more expressive, ritually structured, socially produced "maps" are similar to these.

Part of the present assumption that designers might emulate or capture these socially based, subconscious meanings comes from the probability that some content will be found in the client's existing setting. Since these patterns most certainly are shared, discovery and hence incorporation in terms of some new design is possible. During most present design processes, however, the subconscious nature of spatial, structuralist relationships generally precludes their conscious consideration during design. In a sense, the process of graphic trial and error—the changing and laying over of drawings time and time again — is somewhat similar to the vernacular manipulation of real physically defined spaces by social actors. Perhaps this tool-using process allows the entry of subconscious content which the designer is largely unaware of.

Occasionally, the designer might have sufficient knowledge of, or might actually be a participant in, an organization's expressive culture so that this experience unconsciously guides the placement of spaces on paper — an influence every bit as persuasive as the conscious decisions of circulation, task performance, engineering, and the like. Also, a certain drawing board cosmology may exist at a similarly subconscious level. Often in our culture, North is associated with dominance or superiority; and in drawing convention, North on the board is "Up." Cursory analysis of office building designs suggests that powerful, executive positions may tend to be located toward the upper and often right-hand portion of the drawing. Other examples undoubtedly can be found.

In addition to the above assumptions lying behind a more conscious use of a ritual set of structures in offices, there exists the present necessity to define more specifically the actual forms of this set of structures. Moving to an example of a possible office, definitions of the set will serve to introduce the reader to issues of setting analysis and design application.

3 A Set of Spatial Structures

The fundamental unit of all ritual spatial structures, the "domain," consists of a spatially knowable area (edges, boundaries) whose attached symbolism contributes to a recognizable associational *theme*. Domains may be distinguished from territories primarily by this latter thematic consideration; territorial *identity* relates to signs of authority while the domain *theme* involves more arbitrary symbol-like associations. Socially purposeful territories, whether on the African savanna or in the workplace, may be marked by signs of occupation and dominance. Again, these signs of physical or economic power of the occupant seem to be inherently different from much more dense symbols which are woven into themes and associated with places. The more symbolic a place, the more artificial the sources of its persuasive emotions appear to be. This is an experience distant from the emotion of physical or economic force. Also, the greater the artificiality of the symbolic associations, probably the greater the time it takes for them to evolve. Thus, a possible continuum exists as organizations inhabit settings. Territories are fairly quickly formed by the use of signs of occupation, dominance, and hierarchy; with time these same places may become domains with their depth of thematic symbolic association.

In addition to its thematic meaning, a domain has formal, *positional* content, i. e. its ability to participate in structuring relational meaning between themes. Every domain whether large or small is, by traditional ethnographic definition at least, in opposition to some other domain or domains (Doxtater 1984). Again, part of our previous assumptions included the idea that a spatially cognitive component (relative to a known physical setting) was unique and perhaps fundamental to processes of expressive manipulation in traditional cultures. Questions about the effectiveness of other "media" more prominent in contemporary experience, e. g. television, remain beyond the scope of this paper.

When we consider the media of status signs used to establish territoriality — carpet thickness, size of office, finishes, artwork, presence of personal secretary, presence of couch, etc. — we find that even more extensive are the symbolic vehicles which will contribute to the much more developed, largely subconscious, thematic meanings. Most important, perhaps, will be formalized expressive behavioral acts which predictably recur in certain domains. An office conference, for example, might be as much a reference to or invocation of thematic meaning and structure as an exercise in task performance. Parties and other forms of celebrations may also manipulate thematic content. Certainly acts of work themselves may with time become laden with the thematic meaning of a particular kind or aspect of work, as opposed perhaps to another place and the special nature of work that is done there. The question may be raised of the example in Figure 1 of whether process/product meanings are more related to territorial identification or domain themes.

Besides expressive behaviors associated with certain domains, further contributions will be made by verbal labels, office gossip, stories, myths, memos, directives, charters. To these potentially symbolic "indexes" we must add the more visible physical artifacts, e. g. furniture, machines, plant materials, graphic arts, sculpture, and the like. Of course we cannot forget the architectural medium itself with its volumetric shapes, scale, details, colors, textures, proportions, lighting patterns, etc. (one speaks here of artificial, symbolic meanings in distinction to the more innate, universal, perceptual responses to these architectural stimuli).

Thematic, symbolic meaning is assumed to be generated not so much by individuals but by social processes in the workspace. Even though built-up meanings might in practice prove to be politically or economically oppressive, the outcomes may still be perceived as legitimate — as distinct from more territorial results which may be accepted but not legitimated. While individuals may initiate the attachment of themes to some object or act, to reinforce or perhaps even to contradict the meaning of a domain, still, such attachment will be understood and reacted to by the group according to the larger, shared, and still largely subconscious thematic structure of the place.

Finally, given the above definition of potential structure, one must emphasize the dynamic character of such seemingly static spatial definitions. In traditional situations, much of the ritual effect (the emotional impact of the performance) seems to be generated by the movement between domains. Given the incorporation of virtually all places into symbolic, spatial structure in these traditional societies, not just "calendrical" and "rite-of-passage" rituals were effective, but also repetitive everyday experiences as well. In the old Scandinavian farm societies, for example, churning butter, cooking, going to the sleeping area at night, leaving the house in the morning, the young maid sleeping in the loft during summer, taking the cows to the high summer pasture, all were expressive acts in that they involved movement or contact between domains (Doxtater 1981a). This spatial "belief system" is a primary way in which a traditional society makes legitimate its roles, statuses, hierarchical and egalitarian relationships.

Similar usages may be possible in contemporary work organizations where expressive spatial structures evolve or are designed. In spite of the fact that environment and behavior methodology requires extensive development of ethnographic technique, particularly in the area of distinguishing territoriality from "ritual" space, nevertheless, one can at least draw intuitive parallels between "ritual" acts in traditional societies and "cultural" activities in workplaces.

Provocative preliminary explorations of the culture of contemporary workplaces appear in Schein (1985) and Deal and Kennedy (1982), which use terms from symbolic anthropology such as "themes," "values," "cultural cores," "cultural heroes," "strong cultures," and the like. Useful as this work is, still, in terms of present purposes one must recognize that this research does not consider the potential or possible role of ritual space in expressing corporate themes, codes, or values. Deal and Kennedy do recommend studying the "physical setting" as the first step in learning to "read" corporate cultures — to them, however, this primarily involves territorial status in terms of either objects and images or sizes and locations of space.

Eventually it should be possible first to understand the meanings of domains and structure in a workplace, and then to document the movements of individuals and groups. Some or all aspects of these activities will be ritualistic in purpose, as for example in events like executive conferences, seminars, corporate initiations, visits to dominant or subordinate office spaces, movements between more complementary domains, gatherings for breaks, lunches, celebrations such as birthdays, entering the corporate domain (whether "front" or "back"): even the trip to the xerox machine, stock room, or restroom may have expressive implications.

The ritual use of structured domains will remain one of the most theoretically important, ethnographically difficult aspect of future research efforts in this area. More obtainable at present, considering the contingencies of architecture practice, is a rudimentary description of domain themes and structural disposition in some existing setting. This information can then be used to construct at least intuitively appropriate new designs.

4 Analysis and Design: A Hypothetical Example

Using the ideas about ritual structures described above, combined with some simple observation and interview field methods, it is possible to program existing or latent spatial expression in work settings. While such structures and their contents cannot be taken as conclusive social scientific evidence, from experience they make a great deal of "intuitive" sense to the designer, providing the ability to consciously examine the expressive potential which exists for all buildings, particularly those used as work settings. In an effort to develop this process, architecture graduate students have assumed the role of professional designers, first analyzing existing work organization and "place," and then using this information as the basis for the hypothetical design of a new building.

The first step in the analysis of the existing office building was to describe the physical setting, including plans of the building form and furnishings, and photographs of interior and exterior spaces. Observation of activities and interviews with employees followed. The initial description of the setting allowed observed activities to be recorded in plan or spatial context and also provided stimuli to interviewees when questioned about the meanings of things around them. We were not interested in "other," theoretically separate categories of user information which also can be important in office settings, e. g. visual aesthetics, way-finding, or task-performance. The primary interest was in establishing (1) the spatial positioning of authority, (2) the identity or theme of all recognizable territories or domains, and (3) the repetitive activities which might later be interpreted as ritualistic in effect.

As the reader will see in the example below, the assumptions about existing tendencies or potential for "ritual" space in an office emerge very speculatively from the actual analysis. While territorial identity and authority is relatively easy to establish by analysis of the setting, the reality of spatially defined oppositional themes and ritual manipulation is again extremely problematic. In traditional settings, spatial patterns of symbolic "objects," and the ritual movement through them, are repeated over and over — through long periods of time. All dwellings, for example, have the same culturally conditioned form. Any contemporary office setting, however, at least in the United States, is in effect a unique socio-cultural entity in itself. Thus the basic pattern of "symbolic" space will be difficult to establish via comparisons with others within the same culture.

Added to this difficulty is a problem common to any "structuralist" analysis, whether the society is contemporary or traditional. Unlike the much more believable and closer linkage between territorial signs and their intent or meaning, domain symbolism, at least by definition, remains arbitrary and therefore not immediately associated with some social phenomenon. How does one really prove that "separate" cognitive systems of association, i. e. cultural expression, do in fact make themselves felt in the legitimacy of social relationships? My previously mentioned article (Doxtater 1989) asserts that spatial forms of expression are more inherently connected to actual social realities — than for example myth or folklore. However, this article speaks primarily about traditional examples and might be inappropriate to relate to questions about office settings.

The problem of investigating associational schemata in the diffuse contemporary experience is nowhere better illustrated than in cognitive mapping research by environmental psychologists. While Lynch and others did establish initial ways to pull way-finding schemata out of the minds of informants, subsequent attempts to identify and explain other kinds of information, also organized spatially, has found little success. In truth, Lynch's appendix some thirty years ago remains an enigma for researchers in contemporary environments. For the much more intuitive designer, however, consideration of such content seems far easier.

4.1 The Design Example: A Geophysics Engineering and Research Corporation

(Site analysis and design by Elise Fett)

The existing office space, Figure 2, is a relatively recent building specifically designed for the Geophysics firm. The architectural concept was not unusual: a flexible open office space with a window wall along one side, surrounded by enclosed functions of conference, computer, bathrooms, storage, etc. What happens of course with open office spaces is the appropriation of territories. Typically, as in this case, areas along the windows will become prime territories, with less powerful or important functions and individuals located towards the interior of the open space. In addition to these and other obvious attributes of territoriality, and in spite of the designer's intentions of the flexible open plan, certain potential structural characteristics became evident in the course of the analysis.

Potential themes, beyond territoriality, existed in "Business," "Geophysics," and "Research and Development." Each theme seemed to be expressed by partially defined spatial oppositions, either hierarchical or complementary. "Business," for example, consisted of a *diagonal* opposition between the upper left-hand corner, labeled "business," (where bookkeeping, accounting, and general managerial activities occurred, including the hiring and firing of employees in the conference room) and the exterior "break" place, (where parties, lunches, and the like occurred, in clear preference to the interior small kitchen area at the entrance to the bathrooms which is under immediate surveillance by management). The thematic opposition here lies between the necessary self-interested and hierarchical aspects of the organization, and those aspects which speak to the social responsibilities of the office, first to the corporation as a communal whole, and second to the exterior society at large.

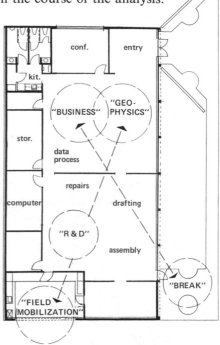

Figure 2: Architectural plan of existing geophysics engineering and research office, showing locations of task-performance activities and latent "ritual" oppositions.

We could define this opposition as a complementary one, in which the two principles of organization express necessary and ongoing aspects of human groups much as the relationship between "male" and "female" did traditionally. Yet compared to the other two, more clearly complementary opposed themes described below, the "Business" theme really contains an asymmetry of power. In most contemporary business cultures, at least, the ability to hire and fire, set wages, determine duties, etc. constitutes a vertical social structure where those higher up have greater decision-making rights of participation. The prevalence and power of the totally functional "managerial view" (Lipman et al. 1978) support this hierarchical definition of the "Business" theme.

Within the "Geophysics" and "Research and Development" themes, complementary opposition appears to exist between process and product, aspects of what these people do in the course in their work. This opposite diagonal from Business expresses these two complementary aspects of the geophysics portion of the organization, e. g. the process of geophysical engineering ("Geophysics") and actual work in the field or product ("Field Mobilization"). A similar opposition, though not expressed as strongly, exists in the spatial relationship between "Research and Development" as process, and its complementarily related "Workshop" (labeled "assembly" in the plan) where designed R & D products are built. Unlike the hierarchical axis of Business, where decision making is the issue, here expression relates more to necessarily different worldviews about the kind of work people do.

Given this oversimplified description of the existing organization, what is inappropriate about these partially defined spatial, structural expressions?

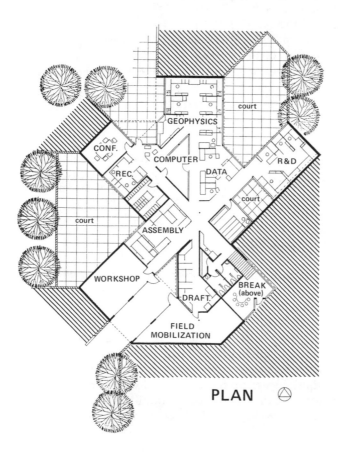

PLAN

How can a greater design consciousness lead to a new and better organization? First, it may be possible to moderate the territorial dominance exerted by management, "business," over the social aspects of the office. At present, no livable interior break space is provided and the exterior place is not well related to the building's interior territories/domains. Secondly, the territorial dominance which exists because of the open plan with windows on one side can be avoided entirely. Also in terms of territorial dominance there exists a certain confusion of domain between "Geophysics" and "Business." The organization's top executive, playing a management role, is most fundamentally a practicing geophysical engineer. His office is located in "Geophysics" but with visual and semantic overlap to "Business," where the office manager sits. At the level of ritual space, this situation can be clarified.

In the complementary oppositions, the possible "ritual" diagonal between "Geophysics" and "Field Mobilization" is quite strong; yet that between "R & D" and the "Workshop" is minimally expressed by comparison.

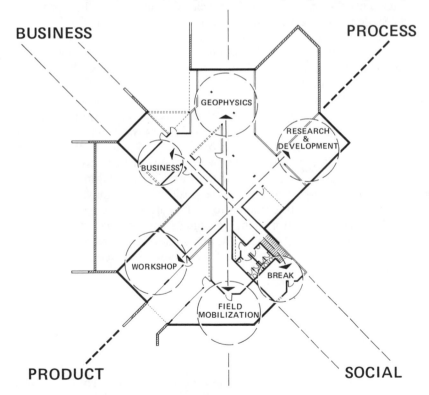

Figure 3: Architectural plan of newly designed office showing locations of task-performance activities; diagram of intended oppositional structure.

Highly important mediational or threshold domains such as the conference and computer rooms receive no symbolic emphasis in their location and are considered only at the level of task performance, like storage or even field mobilization. Finally, we would look for an obvious greater development of "expressive totality," a design which not only gives greater thematic distinction to specific domains, but better structures them into a whole.

The hypothetical new design of Figure 3 is an earth integrated structure, functional as well as symbolic of the largest scale of organizational theme, "Geophysics" in opposition to other organizations of the outside world. The courtyards provide an almost total accessibility to windows and some provision for building expansion. In terms of symbolic structure, each domain is individually defined and given strong axial relationship to its thematic opposite. The dominant "Business" theme is paired with the position of an interior and exterior "Break" room on the roof garden, associated with employee's parking and entrance; axially opposite, now, rather than an office manager and associated executive is the corporate conference room, a nice expression of communal rather than strictly managerial power in that still dominant domain. This business/social axis and domains form a mediational threshold between process and product aspects of the two complementary oppositions, "Geophysics/Field Mobilization," and "R & D/Workshop."

Thus the overall expression obtains greater unity. With the two clarified axial oppositions, process/product and business/society, we obtain a situation not unlike the diagonal composites one finds in traditional expression. Certainly the "R & D" domain is the most process-like, while "Workshop" is the most product-like. Similarly, the two domains of business and society are the greatest expression of that cardinal axis. The resulting diagonals, then, are consistent with their composite positions. "Geophysics" is both process and business in its combination of geophysical engineering and executive, managerial functions (the ambiguity between the executive and business is reduced in the process). Though somewhat more poetic, "Field Mobilization" uses the products of the "Workshop" in association with the external world or "society."

5 Conclusion

Can one conclusively say that the above design, if built, would actually produce a relatively independent, spatially structured set of thematic meanings? Would these in turn be ritually used to promote a more ideal form of work organization? And finally, do more "culturally" legitimate social relationships foster greater productivity? The graduate student designers of the experimental studio were certainly convinced; the process at least gave the opportunity to consider the *potential* which exists in any human environment, even though completed projects could not be taken as social science predictions of behavior.

I wish I could say that in the United States there was a great demand for more knowledge about the way architecture might contribute to social and cultural meaning of office settings. Due to our larger socio-economic, and perhaps our cultural predispositions, speculative office construction frequently lays primary emphasis on economically efficient building production and marketability as a consumer object. Architects "design" marketable shells, and interior designers satisfy basic ergonomic and status needs inside. The office users, most often distant from design decision making, are left to make do with a largely undesigned environment. The resulting territorial flux appears to negatively influence the social and economic well-being of the corporation as individuals incessantly seek to better their social position in the organization. Often this is mistaken as a cultural value of "American Individualism," in spite of the probability that similar examples can be found in England, Germany, Italy, etc.

Environmental researchers in the U.S. have understandably not yet developed strong interests in corporate culture in offices, in spite of the fact that one sees a strong shift toward "built form and culture" issues among interdisciplinary design/social science organizations. These newly emerging foci are either still on traditional societies, or on the "communicational" aspects of built form, something very compatible with the marketing of consumer objects. For Americans to become interested in the more spatially based cultural potential of place, we would somehow have to first become interested in fundamental social, territorial uses of our environments — anathema to our mistaken perceptions of individual control over our settings. Until we begin to appreciate the wider social importance of our environments, we will not develop strong interests in comparing this territoriality with the potential of cultural patterns of space.

The importance of understanding relationships between territoriality and "ritual" space has been reaffirmed by my current work with Swedish office settings. Looking for evidence of "ritual space" in contemporary offices, the research strategy here, rather than trying to find pattern in the multitude of unique situations in the U.S., is to examine a country which just might have maintained a nationally shared conception of "ritual space." The hypothesis is that Swedish "ritual space" strongly influences the form of office buildings and that it inhibits organizationally divisive territoriality.

The role of the designer as interpreter of cultural potential is less important in Sweden since these cultural values already exist and are always part of participatory design and construction processes. In the United States, by contrast, we have neither participatory control over our shared environments, nor a common set of conceptions about cultural themes and their spatial structure. These facts, taken together with the larger content of this chapter, suggest that designers in the U.S. at least may have a greater advocacy role to play in the creation of culturally possible settings.

References

Brookes, M. and A. Kaplan (1972): The Office Environment: Space, Planning, and Affective Behavior. *Human Factors* 14, pp. 373–391

Campbell, D. (1980): Professors and Their Office: A Survey of Person-Behavior-Environment Relationships. Proceedings of the 11th Annual Conference of EDRA

Deal, T. E. and A. A. Kennedy (1982): *Corporate Cultures: The Rites and Rituals of Corporate Life.* Reading, MA: Addison-Wesley

Doxtater, D. (1981a): Cosmos in the Corporation. *Environmental Design Research Association* (EDRA), vol. 12, pp. 36–45

Doxtater, D. (1981b): *Thursday at a Crossroads: The Symbolism, Structure and Politics of "Center" in the Old Scandinavian Farm Culture.* Dissertation: University of Michigan. Ann Arbor, MI: University Microfilms

Doxtater, D. (1984): Spacial Opposition in Non-Discursive Expression: Architecture as Ritual Process. *Canadian Journal of Anthropology* 4(1), Summer, pp. 1–17

Doxtater, D. (1989): "Cultural Space" as a Needed Research Concept of Housing Change: The White Pueblos of Andalusia. *Housing, Culture, and Design.* E. Chambers/S. Low (Eds.). Philadelphia, PA: University of Pennsylvania Press

Edelman, M. (1978): Space and the Social Order. *JAE* Vol. XXXII (2), pp. 2–7

Goodrich, R. (1982): Seven Office Evaluation: A Review. *Environment and Behavior* 14(3), pp. 553–578

Harris, H. and A. Lipman (1980): Social Symbolism and Space Usage in Daily Life. *Sociological Review* 28(2), pp. 415–428

Hedge, A. (1982): The Open-Plan Office: A Systematic Investigation of Employee Reactions to Their Work Environment. *Environment and Behavior* 14(5), pp. 519–542

Hensley, W. (1982): Professor Proxemics. Personality and Job Demand as Factors of Faculty Office Arrangement. *Environment and Behavior* 14(5), pp. 581–592

Hillier, B. and J. Hanson (1983): *The Social Logic of Space.* Cambridge, MA: Cambridge University Press

Holdaway, S. (1980): The Police Station. *Urban Life* 9(1), April, pp. 79–100

Konar, E. et al. (1982): Status Demarcation in the Office. *Environment and Behavior* 14(5), pp. 561–580

Korda, M. (1975): *Power: How to Get It, How to Use It.* New York: Random House

Lipman, A., I. Cooper, R. Harris, and R. Tranter (1978): Power, a Neglected Concept in Office Design? *JAB* 6(3), July, pp. 28–37

Lozar, C. (1975): Application of Behavior Setting Analysis and Undermanning Theory to Supermarket Design. *Environmental Design Research Association* 6, pp. 271–279

Lynch, K. (1960): *Image of the City*. Cambridge, MA: MIT Press

McCarrey, M., L. Peterson, S. Edwards, and P. von Kulmiz (1974): Landscape Office Attitude: Reflections of Perceived Degree to Control over Transactions with the Environment. *Journal of Applied Psychology* 59(3), pp. 401–403

McElroy, J. and P. Morrow (1982): Desk Placement in the Faculty Office: Effect of Camera Angle in Slide-Simulated Office Studies. *Psychological Reports* 50(2), pp. 675–678

Peponis, J. (1983): *Typology and Social Functions of Factory Space*. PhD Dissertation. University of London

Schein, E. H. (1985): *Organization Culture and Leadership*. London: Jossey-Bass

Steele, F. I. (1973): *Physical Settings and Organizational Development*. Reading, MA: Addison-Wesley

Sundstrom, E. et al. (1982): Physical Enclosure, Type of Job and Privacy in the Office. *Environment and Behavior* 14(5), pp. 543–559

Szilagy, A. and W. Holland (1980): Changes in Social Density: Relationships with Functional Interaction and Perceptions of Job Characteristics, Role Stress, and Work Satisfaction. *Journal of Applied Psychology* 65(1), pp. 28–33

Whyte, W. F. (1949): The Social Structure of the Restaurant. *American Journal of Sociology* 54, pp. 245–253

Wineman, J. (1982): Office Design and Evaluation: An Overview. *Environment and Behavior* 14(3), pp. 271–298

The Symbolics of Office Design: An Empirical Exploration*

Mary Jo Hatch

1 Introduction

In many American business organizations a strong and lasting value for private offices appears to exist. Dean (1977), for instance, reports that two-thirds of his sample of employees at the American Institute of Architect's (AIA) headquarters facility stated a preference for conventional office design four years after a move from conventional to open office facilities. This finding is particularly intriguing because the AIA represents the group primarily responsible for the corporate shift away from private offices — the architects who designed and promoted the open office concept.

The AIA case illustrates an anomaly that can be seen across corporate America: a value for privacy persists in the face of a pattern of migration to open office environments. Besides the AIA case, evidence of the value for office privacy can be found by visiting almost any American business executive. There you are likely to observe some combination of outer lobbies, receptionists, personal secretaries, floor to ceiling walls, doors, and remote locations.

Much empirical evidence indicating a widespread value for privacy has also been presented. For instance, in a two-panel survey of 389 employees in 25 firms that moved to open offices (Brill 1984), almost everyone surveyed reported that they did not have as much privacy as they wanted, either before or after moving. Oldham and Rotchford (1983) reported significant

* The author wishes to thank all of the participants at the Third International Conference on Organizational Symbolism and Corporate Culture for their stimulating and informative discussions of symbolism, and for comments on my presentation of an earlier version of this paper. In particular, I would like to recognize Pasquale Gagliardi, Per Olof Berg, Kristian Kreiner, and Ellee Koss. I would also like to thank Jai Ghorpade for his helpful comments on an earlier draft of this paper.

positive correlations between perceived privacy and work satisfaction, social satisfaction, and office satisfaction in their sample of clerical employees of a large university. Oldham and Fried (1987) found that the same clerical workers were most likely to withdraw from their offices and feel dissatisfied when density was high and barriers enclosing workspaces were few. Moves to open offices were found to be related to decreased work satisfaction, involvement, and work motivation (Dean 1977, Marans/Spreckelmeyer 1982, Oldham/Brass 1979) and to a decline in satisfaction with privacy (Sundstrom/Herbert/Brown 1982). Miller and Monge (1985) found that reported need for privacy had a significant effect on pre-move anxiety in a sample of state employees about to move to open offices.

The anomaly in the findings described above is that, in spite of demonstrations of the value for privacy, American corporations continue to use open offices. This is not to argue that preferences for private offices are necessarily universal. They are not. For example, some studies have reported positive reactions to open office moves (e. g., Boyce 1974). What *is* being argued is that the simultaneous expression of a value for private offices and widespread movement into open offices presents a phenomenon worthy of investigation.

Before proceeding, a popular explanation for the increasing use of open offices needs to be considered. That is, while employees may favor private offices, organizations cannot always afford them. The argument used to support this claim is that it is cheaper to build open offices because of savings in the square footage and materials required to construct interior walls. However, these cost savings are quickly offset by investments in expensive modular furnishings and sound masking systems (used to reduce the high level of noise experienced in some open office environments). Thus, it is unlikely that the question posed here can be resolved by mere reference to cost considerations. This study presents an exploration into employees' attitudes and behaviors in relation to their work environments in the hope of finding a more revealing explanation for the decreasing use of highly valued private offices in American business culture.

2 Office Privacy

Sundstrom, Burt, and Kamp (1980) recommend examining two different aspects of the relationship between privacy and work outcomes. One has to do with the ability to work alone; the other involves the symbolic significance of a private office. Sundstrom and his colleagues studied a sample of employees holding a variety of jobs and occupying a diversity of workspaces. They report a marked preference for private office space supported by a positive correlation between privacy and job satisfaction and conclude that:

... for all types of jobs studied, participants generally preferred privacy over accessibility. One obvious explanation concerns the noise and distraction experienced in nonprivate places ... Participants also liked their places enclosed and visually inaccessible, which suggests that they prefer areas in which they perhaps can tend less to maintaining appearances and more to getting the job done. Another explanation concerns the symbolic value of privacy (Steele 1973). People may prefer private workspaces because they often signify status or importance (p. 114).

Links between privacy and both communication and status, described by Sundstrom and his colleagues, have been examined by others as well. For instance, in the area of communication, Steele (1983) has suggested that the sacrifice of traditional private offices to open designs leads to greater teamwork, interpersonal familiarity, and spontaneous interaction among those who are mutually accessible. Related findings are reported by several researchers who have examined the effects of corporate moves from private to open office settings. For instance, Allen and Gerstberger (1973), Brookes and Kaplan (1972), and Szilagyi and Holland (1980) report increases in perceived ability to communicate easily with others accompanying moves to open offices.

Recently, Hatch (1987) reported that physical barriers associated with private offices (partitions and doors) were positively associated with amount of interaction and negatively associated with time spent working alone for a sample of technical and professional employees. Similarly, Zalesny and Farace (1987) found that significant decreases in information requests were reported by professionals and managers after a move to open offices (significant increases were reported by clerical workers but many of these had been moved from areas with no partitions to areas with partitions, thus increasing rather than decreasing their degree of enclosure). In that study, clericals and professionals also reported less perceived feedback about their work in the open plan environment.

In regard to status, several studies have identified privacy as a central issue. Louis Harris and Associates (1978) found that survey respondents listed style of furnishings, privacy, and floorspace as the three most prevalent signs of rank in their organizations. Similarly, the Buffalo Organization for Social and Technological Innovation (BOSTI 1981) asked survey respondents what they would prefer to use to indicate their new status in the event they were promoted. The status markers mentioned most often were: more office space, privileged location, more or higher quality office furnishings, and controlled access. Among the status markers Konar et al. (1982) found to be associated with status support (the degree to which survey respondents felt that their work spaces accurately reflected their status) were quality of furniture, floorspace, and privacy.

Both the BOSTI (1981) group and Konar et al. (1982) found positive relationships between satisfaction and status support. Zalesny and Farace's (1987) results show that low status individuals found their move from conventional to open offices to increase the perceived favorability of their environment (operationalized as work space adequacy, privacy, and positive interpersonal relationships) while high status individuals experienced a decrease in the perceived favorability of their environment. Zalesny and Farace also report a drop in satisfaction associated with the change in office design for all status levels in their sample.

The review supports Sundstrom/Burt/Kamp's (1980) claim that there are at least two different dimensions to be considered in comparing open and private office arrangements. On the one hand, office design appears to be related to communication activity, and on the other, the private office seems to symbolize status in American business culture. This dual role of office privacy suggests that examining both aspects simultaneously might lead to a better understanding of the significance of the private office. Thus, this study explores the relationships between work activities, satisfaction, and privacy. Work activities and outcomes to be considered include time spent working alone versus interacting with others, and frequency of interaction.

The study reported below is exploratory. The data were not collected to test the ideas presentend here and are not complete with respect to all of the dimensions identified as important. Therefore, the present study is reported in the most tentative terms. It is intended to clarify questions concerning private and open offices in business culture rather than to answer them. Additional research is needed before any conclusions are drawn.

3 Method

This study compares the attitudinal and behavioral responses of employees assigned to private offices with those of employees assigned to non-private offices. Privacy is assessed by two dichotomous variables: open vs. closed office design and shared vs. unshared office space (Figure 1). Closed office designs provide privacy via floor-to-ceiling walls and doors, while sharing an office reduces privacy by exposing the individual to the relatively continuous presence of others. In the data examined here, all styles of offices except the bullpen (shared, open offices) are represented.

OFFICE SHARING

		Shared	Unshared
	Open	Bullpen Office	Landscaped or Partitioned Office
OFFICE DESIGN			
	Closed	Conventional Nonprivate Office	Conventional Private Office

Figure 1: A Typology of Offices Based on Objective Indices of Privacy

Perceived privacy was not measured because it was believed that participants might be influenced by this direct reference to the central issue of the study — objective characteristics of the workplace. This should not prove a major problem since Sundstrom/Herbert/Brown (1982) demonstrated a strong relationship between perceived privacy and the amount of enclosure around an office space. However, in the Sundstrom et al. study the enclosure-perceived privacy relationship was moderated by position (secretary vs. bookkeepers vs. managers), so data on position is used to control for this effect.

3.1 Sample

Two large, high technology companies located in the San Francisco Bay Area served as research sites. One company (Firm 2, n = 22) provided all of its employees with open offices (having no doors and 3 to 5 foot partitions), the other (Firm 1, n = 101) used mostly closed offices (n = 88), but had one building in which only open offices were used (n = 13). Office space was shared with others only in Firm 1 (n = 13). Of 181 volunteers for the study, 147 provided full data (81%); of these, all technicians (n = 30), engineers (n = 16), and managers (n = 77) were selected because these were the only job categories for which variance on at least one of the office privacy measures was found (N = 123).

The sample from which data were collected was a sample of convenience. Although firms doing similar work in different types of offices were sought, a high technology company which used *only* closed offices was not found. This situation was unexpected since closed offices are often thought to be standard in American business firms. However, among high technology firms in the area where the study was conducted, open offices were much more typical.

3.2 Procedure

A questionnaire composed of seven point, Likert-type items was used to collect the satisfaction and position data. The scales selected were developed and validated as reported in Cammann et al. (1983). The questionnaires were completed by participants at an initial meeting after which participants logged their activities for one week. To record their activities, subjects used preprinted forms listing nine work activities selected in a pilot study: work alone, work together, meetings, interruptions, build relationships, socialize, phone or computer mail, breaks, and personal time (see below). Participants entered the time they began a new activity, making log entries under the appropriate category heading each time they changed from one activity to another. Data concerning privacy were collected by observation. This was done after the activity logs were completed so as to avoid unnecessary influence on the subjects through contact with the researcher.

In the appropriate column, please enter the time you begin in activity. Use a separate line for each entry.

WORK ALONE: read, write, think, compute	SOCIALIZE: shoot the breeze, discuss personal matters, make social plans	BUILD RELATIONSHIPS: greet other employees, make contacts, iron out differences	INTERRUPTIONS: answering questions, delivering messages	MEETINGS: meetings with more than one other person	WORK TOGETHER: meet with other to confer, discuss, receive or give directions	Use PHONE or COMPUTER MAIL	BREAKS: includes lunch, go home	PERSONAL: read newspaper, daydream, personal correspondence, any nonwork activity performed alone

3.3 Measures

3.3.1 Satisfaction

Participants provided data on their satisfaction with work in general, with the social aspects of work, and with extrinsic rewards. Social satisfaction was measured separately because advocates of open offices claim that open designs provide more desirable social environments than do conventional offices. Extrinsic reward satisfaction was included because status is a form of extrinsic reward.

Three questionnaire items measured work satisfaction. The items asked respondents to report how satisfied they were with their job, to what degree they disliked their job (reversed), and how much they enjoyed working for their company. The items were summed to form the work satisfaction scale (alpha = .78).

The social satisfaction scale used three items measuring desired levels of social satisfaction and three measuring perceived levels. These items referred to the friendliness of, the respect they receive from, and the way they are treated by the people subjects work with. Desired levels were subtracted from perceived levels and these discrepancy values were summed to form the social satisfaction scale (alpha = .87).

The extrinsic reward satisfaction scale was also based on a discrepancy measure. Items referred to fringe benefits, pay, and job security. Desired levels were subtracted from perceived levels and summed to form the scale (alpha = .65). Due to the low reliability for this measure, analysis of the single item directly measuring fringe benefits was also included since a private office is generally considered to be a fringe benefit.

3.3.2 Work activity

Three measures of work activity were derived from the activity log. Interaction frequency was measured by a tally of face-to-face interactions reported in the categories of building relationships, working together, meetings, and interruptions. Measures of working alone and interacting with others were calculated as percentages of total time logged which involved these activities. The amount of time reported in each column of the activity log was summed and divided by the total time reported in all activities. This calculation produced measures of the percent of time reported in each type of activity. Proportions of time reported in building relationships, working together, meetings, and interruptions were summed for the interaction measure. The summary measure was used because it matches the level of analysis inherent in the issue of whether or not privacy and interaction are related.

3.3.3 Privacy

Open versus closed office design was scored as a dichotomous variable (open = 1, closed = 2), as was the office sharing variable (shared = 1, unshared = 2).

4 Analysis and Results

Means, standard deviations, and inter-correlations for all variables are shown in Table 1. Analysis of variance (ANOVA) was performed for each behavior and each satisfaction measure using office design and office sharing as the independent variables of interest (Table 2). In order to control for the influences of position level, job type, and firm, these variables were also included in the analyses. However, since "manager" was one of the job type categories, position level was confounded with job type in the data. All management levels (including supervise others, manage others

Table 1: Means, Standard Deviations, and Correlations* for All Variables (N = 123)

Variables	Means	Standard Deviations	1	2	3	4	5	6	7	8	9
1. Office design	1.72	0.45									
2. Office sharing	1.89	0.31	−22								
3. Position	2.38	0.85	12	−06							
4. Work alone activity	0.45	0.18	−32	−19	−45						
5. Interaction activity	0.36	0.17	39	16	45	−89					
6. Interaction frequency	31.16	20.53	−22	13	15	45	50				
7. Job satisfaction	17.7	2.52	04	02	12	−25	20	07			
8. Social satisfaction	−.09	4.41	02	−01	−11	10	−05	02	45		
9. Extrinsic reward satisfaction	1.59	4.95	04	−06	03	−10	12	08	21	42	
10. Satisfaction with fringe benefits	0.94	1.94	01	−08	03	−13	13	05	06	31	81

* For $r > .15$, $p < .05$.

Table 2: Cell Means and F-Tests for Main Effects and Overall ANOVA Models Using Full Sample

	Design			Sharing			Position				Firm			Overall
	Open (n = 35)	Closed (n = 88)	F	Shared (n = 13)	Unshared (n = 110)	F	Tech (n = 30)	Engineer (n = 16)	Manager (n = 77)	F	Firm 1 (n = 101)	Firm 2 (n = 22)	F	Overall F
Working alone	.54	.41	16.6***	.55	.44	16.8***	.56	.55	.38	20.0***	.43	.53	n.s.	8.2***
Working with others	.25	.40	21.9***	.28	.37	13.8***	.24	.29	.42	17.5***	.38	.27	n.s.	8.1***
Interaction frequency	24	34	11.0***	23	32	5.1**	27	25	34	n.s.	32	29	4.6**	1.9*
Extrinsic satisfaction[+]	1.26	1.73	11.3***	2.38	1.50	n.s.	1.03	2.75	1.57	n.s.	1.12	3.77	16.3***	3.0***
Fringe benefits[++]	.91	.95	4.8*	1.38	.89	n.s.	.70	1.50	.92	n.s.	.79	1.64	7.7**	2.8**

* $p \leq .05$; ** $p \leq .01$; *** $p \leq .001$

[+] Significant interaction found for POSITION X DESIGN, F = 3.4*

[++] Significant interactions found for POSITION X DESIGN, F = 8.1*** and FIRM X POSITION 5.9**

who are supervisors, and manage others who are managers) were grouped
into the category of manager (following Zalesny/Farace 1987), and a single
variable for position was used to distinguish managers from technicians
and engineers.

Significant main effects for office design and sharing were found for
working alone, amount of interaction, and interaction frequency; office
design was also significant in the extrinsic reward satisfaction and satisfaction with fringe benefits analyses. A significant interaction between position
and office design was found for extrinsic reward satisfaction and for
satisfaction with fringe benefits indicating that the design effect is stronger
for technicians and engineers than for managers, and differs for engineers
and technicians (Figure 2a). A similar pattern of findings has been reported
for clericals, professionals, and managers (Zalesny/Farace 1987). ANOVAs
for job and social satisfaction failed to achieve significance.

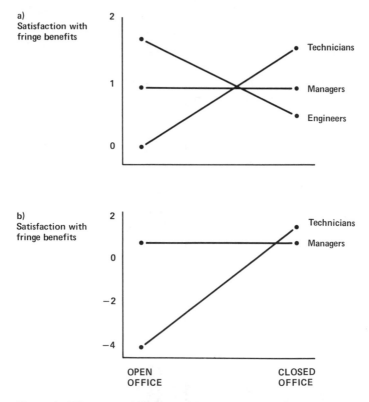

Figure 2: Diagrams of the Interaction Between Position and Office Design Variables
Found in Fringe Benefits ANOVA for: (a) Full Sample and (b) Firm 1 Subsample

As discussed above, there were empty cells in the ANOVAs due to a lack of private (closed or shared) offices in the Firm 2 sample and a lack of sharing among engineers in the closed offices of Firm 1. Two subsample analyses allow investigation of the effects of these empty cells on the relationships reported.

First, ANOVAs were run for all dependent variables by job type, office design, and sharing for Firm 1 data only (Table 3). This was done to eliminate the effects of empty cells in the Firm 2 sample. Also, engineers were dropped from this analysis because only one engineer occupied an open office in the Firm 1 data. A pattern of significant main effects and an interaction (Figure 2b) nearly identical with the first analysis indicates that the results are not strictly due to differences in the firms studied or to the empty cell for closed offices in Firm 2.

Second, ANOVAs were conducted for all dependent variables by technician and manager job types and office sharing within the Firm 1 subsample representing only closed offices (Table 4). This was done to eliminate any effects of having no subjects who shared open offices. Significant main effects for office sharing were found in the ANOVAs of working alone and working with others repeating the patterns observed in the data displayed in Tables 2 and 3. The ANOVAs for interaction frequency and the satisfaction measures failed to achieve significance. This pattern indicates that the results cannot be attributed to the effect of empty cells for shared open offices in the Firm 1 data.

Table 3: Cell Means and F-Tests for Overall and Main Effects in ANOVAs Using Firm 1 Subsample

	Design			Sharing			Position			Overall
	Open (n = 12)	Closed (n = 83)	F	Shared (n = 13)	Unshared (n = 82)	F	Tech (n = 25)	Manager (n = 70)	F	F (N = 95)
Working alone	.54	.41	13.2***	.55	.41	16.3***	.56	.38	33.5***	12.1***
Working with others	.24	.40	16.1***	.28	.39	11.9***	.25	.42	29.1***	10.7***
Interaction frequency	17	34	9.2**	23	34	4.9*	27	34	n. s.	3.0*
Extrinsic satisfaction	−3.58	1.88	15.6***	2.38	1.00	n. s.	.32	1.5	n. s.	4.8***
Fringe benefits[+]	−0.50	0.96	6.7**	1.38	0.68	n. s.	.48	.89	n. s.	5.1***

* $p \le .05$; ** $p \le .01$; *** $p \le .001$
[+]   A significant interaction between position and office design was found, $F = 16.0$***

Table 4: Cell Means and F-Tests for Overall and Main Effects in ANOVAs Using Firm 1, Closed Office Subsample

| | Sharing | | | Position | | | Overall |
	Shared (n = 13)	Unshared (n = 70)	F	Tech (n = 22)	Managers (n = 61)	F	F (N = 83)
Working alone	.55	.39	16.0***	.53	.37	23.0***	12.6***
Working with others	.28	.42	11.4***	.28	.44	20.2***	10.2***

*** $p \le .001$

Since one cell of the 2X2 representing firm by design type is missing (i.e., Firm 2, closed offices), one final analysis of the data collapsing this distinction was conducted. Using the full data set, ANOVAs were run for all dependent variables by sharing, position, and firm/design (Firm 1/closed = 1; Firm 1/open = 2; Firm 2/open = 3). The analyses indicated the same pattern of significant results reported in Table 2.

To aid in the interpretation of the results, differences between means for all combinations of the three firm/design possibilities are presented (Table 5). T-tests show an interesting difference in the patterns of the work activity

Table 5: t-Tests Comparing Firm/Design Differences for Work Behavior and Satisfaction Variables (Full Sample)

	Panel A: FIRM 1/OPEN VS. FIRM 1/CLOSED *Group Mean (Standard Deviation)*			
Variable	Open (n = 13)	Closed (n = 88)	t-Value	2-tail Probability
Working alone	.55 (.20)	.41 (.16)	2.9	.005
Working with others	.23 (.18)	.40 (.17)	3.4	.001
Interaction frequency	16.2 (12.9)	34.0 (21.3)	2.9	.004
Extrinsic satisfaction	−3.00 (6.1)	1.73 (4.5)	3.4	.001
Fringe benefits	-- .31 (3.1)	.95 (1.6)	2.26	.03

Table 5: continued

	Panel B: FIRM 1/CLOSED VS. FIRM 2/OPEN *Group Mean (Standard Deviation)*			
Variable	Closed (n = 88)	Open (n = 22)	t-Value	2-tail Probability
Working alone	.41 (.16)	.53 (.17)	2.9	.004
Working with others	.40 (.17)	.27 (.11)	3.6	.001
Interaction frequency	34.0 (21.3)	28.5 (17.0)	1.1 1.1	n. s. n. s.
Extrinsic satisfaction	1.73 (4.5)	3.77 (4.6)	1.9	n. s.
Fringe benefits	.95 (1.6)	1.64 (1.9)	1.7	n. s.

	Panel C: FIRM 1/OPEN VS. FIRM 2/OPEN *Group Mean (Standard Deviation)*			
Variable	Firm 1 (n = 13)	Firm 2 (n = 22)	t-Value	2-tail Probability
Working alone	.56 (.20)	.52 (.17)	.50	n. s.
Working with others	.23 (.18)	.27 (.11)	.70	n. s.
Interaction frequency	16.2 (12.9)	28.5 (17.0)	2.24	.03
Extrinsic satisfaction	−3.00 (6.1)	3.77 (4.6)	3.75	.001
Fringe benefits	−.31 (3.1)	1.64 (1.9)	2.28	.03

results and the results for satisfaction. No significant differences in working alone or working with others occur among occupants of open offices in the cross-firm comparisons (Panel C), but Firm 2 employees are significantly more satisfied than their Firm 1 open office counterparts. In contrast, within the Firm 1 sample (Panel A), open office occupants spend significantly more time working alone, do significantly less interacting with others, and are significantly less satisfied than their closed office colleagues. Finally, in comparing the closed office occupants of Firm 1 with the Firm 2 open office employees (Panel B), behavioral differences once again are associated with the two types of office designs, while no significant differences in satisfaction are found.

5 Discussion

In this study, employees' work behaviors were found to be significantly related to the design of their offices. Their reported levels of satisfaction with fringe benefits, however, were found to be significantly related to their office space design only when some people in the firm had privacy and others did not. The data suggest that satisfaction is associated with the amount of privacy one has relative to others, while the behavior – office design relationships are not moderated by this sort of comparison. These results indicate that at least two different domains represent the role of office design in organizations. These domains appear to be linked to communication behavior and status, just as Sundstrom/Burt/Kamp (1980) suggested they would be.

Within the communication domain this study suggests that privacy encourages communication while the absence of privacy limits communication. This is contradictory to a widespread belief that open offices stimulate communication (see Ornstein 1989, for documented evidence of this belief, or consider the case of open door policies). Thus, it would appear that open offices can bear a meaning quite dissimilar to their actual relationship with behavior.

Within the status domain, the satisfaction data indicate that if private offices are available in the firm, people will be relatively dissatisfied if they do not have one. However, if office space is homogeneous within a firm, not having privacy may not affect satisfaction. These results are consistent with the view that office designs symbolize status and that symbolic meanings (rather than behavioral effects) dictate the relationship between office design and satisfaction.

In spite of the limitations of the design of this study (described earlier), the findings reported here are consistent with those of earlier, better-designed studies, which enhances confidence in them. First, the negative relationship between open offices and interaction behavior replicates findings presented by Zalesny and Farace (1987). This behavioral side of office design is given close examination in Hatch (1987). Second, that satisfaction is related to privacy in comparative rather than absolute terms is not inconsistent with earlier studies reporting significant positive relationships between privacy and satisfaction. Most of these studies were conducted using single-organization samples involving private-to-open office moves (Dean 1977, Marans/Spreckelmeyer 1982, Miller/Monge 1985, Oldham/ Brass 1979, Sundstrom/Burt/Kamp 1980, Zalesny/Farace 1987). Thus, the comparative basis for relative dissatisfaction was present, although the comparisons were subjective-personal (satisfaction with my old private office versus satisfaction with my new open office) rather than subjective-social (my open office compared with the private office someone else has). (See Masters/Keil 1987, for a typology of social comparisons.) The subjective-social comparison intimated in this study replicates the privacy-satisfaction relationship reported by Oldham and Rotchford (1983). The consistency of the results across the two types of social comparisons enhances confidence that this process is important for explaining privacy-satisfaction relationships.

Weaknesses in the design of this research make it clear that these issues require further study. A replication including data from a firm employing all closed offices would be extremely useful. Also useful would be a study that examines the extent to which subjective-personal versus subjective-social comparisons explain links between privacy and satisfaction. This could be done by comparing the pre-post satisfaction of individuals who move between open offices, between private offices, from private to open offices, and from open to private offices.

6 The Symbolics of Office Design

Both the communication and the satisfaction findings discussed above point to the importance of considering the meaning individuals attach to offices within their work environments. These findings suggest that office designs might best be analyzed as symbols produced by organizational cultures. While the present study did not directly investigate the symbolic domain, it has suggested a need to develop methods for doing so. Toward this end, some suggestions for approaching office designs as key symbols representing organizational culture are offered.

Ortner (1973) suggests that the key symbols of a culture can be located along a continuum from summarizing to elaborating. Summarizing symbols (e. g., a national flag) synthesize experience by relating the respondent to the cultural system as a whole. Elaborating symbols, on the other hand, are analytic in nature. They organize experience by sorting out feelings and ideas. "... making them comprehensible ... communicable ... and translatable into orderly action" (Ortner 1973: 1340). It is not entirely clear where along Ortner's proposed continuum office design belongs. For this reason, her recommended methods for analyzing both types of symbols are each used to suggest future directions for research on the symbolic nature of offices.

The mode of analysis Ortner (1973) suggests for *summarizing symbols* lies in the discovery of a link between a relatively undifferentiated commitment to a worldview (e. g., a corporate culture) and the key symbol of interest (i. e., the private or the open office). Thus, one might examine the meanings associated with open and closed offices and determine their relationship to the central features of different organizational cultures. Many specific questions could be investigated from this analytical framework. For example: are office space designs significantly related to cultural values such as status equality versus status differences, participative versus authoritarian management practices, or humanitarian versus classical assumptions about the nature of man?

Two methods of analysis appropriate for interpreting *elaborating symbols* are recommended by Ortner (1973): schema and metaphor. In the case of schematic analysis, Ortner suggests that symbols be analyzed as schemas capable of organizing action within a culture. For instance, the private office could be viewed as a generator of deference behavior, supporting and maintaining hierarchical authority. Meanwhile the open office might be seen as a schema for the development of lateral relationships maintaining more organic structural forms.

In the case of metaphorical analysis, the symbol is analyzed as a root metaphor capable of organizing thought (see also Smircich 1983). For example, the private office could be analyzed as a metaphor for individualism (independent action) often assumed to be a core value of American business culture (e. g., Ouchi 1981). The open office, in contrast, might be analyzed as a metaphor for cooperative effort. Recent moves between the two types of offices might then be interpreted as a manifestation of a change in the core values of American business culture.

The above are, of course, only speculations offered as examples of what a symbolic analysis of the meaning of office design might produce. Ethnographic study is suggested as a means of moving further in this direction.

7 Conclusion

This study has suggested that private and open offices may best be understood as cultural artifacts of organization. Such an approach requires sensitivity to the symbolic significance of office design. Since the study has design limitations, further investigation is essential before conclusions are offered. However, the implications of replicating the findings presented here lead to more interesting research questions. These questions are posed within the context of social comparison theory (Festinger 1954), and also within the framework of the cultural analysis of key symbols (Ortner 1973). Recommendations for pursuing each of these avenues were presented.

References

Allen, T. J. and P. G. Gerstberger (1973): A Field Experiment to Improve Communications in a Product Engineering Department: The Nonterritorial Office. *Human Factors* 15, pp. 487–498

Boyce, P. R. (1974): Users' Assessment of a Landscaped Office. *Journal of Architectural Research* 3, pp. 44–62

Brill, M. (1984): *Using Office Design to Increase Productivity.* Vol. 1. Buffalo, NY: Workplace Design and Productivity, Inc.

Brookes, M. J. and A. Kaplan (1972): The Office Environment: Space Planning and Affective Behavior. *Human Factors* 14, pp. 373–391

Buffalo Organization for Social and Technological Innovation (BOSTI) (1981): *The Impact of Office Environment on Productivity and Quality of Working Life: Comprehensive Findings.* Buffalo, NY: Buffalo Organization for Social and Technological Innovation

Cammann, C., M. Fichman, G. D. Jenkins Jr., and J. R. Klesh (1983): Assessing the Attitudes and Perceptions of Organizational Members. *Assessing Organizational Change: A Guide to Methods, Measures and Practices.* Seashore/Lawler/Mirvis/Cammann (Eds.). New York: John Wiley & Sons, pp. 71–138

Dean, A. O. (1977): Evaluation of an Open Office Landscape: AIA Headquarters. *American Institute of Architects Journal* 66, pp. 32–39

Festinger, L. (1954): A Theory of Social Comparison Processes. *Human Relations* 7, pp. 117–140

Hatch, M. J. (1987): Physical Barriers, Task Characteristics, and Interaction Activity in Research and Development Firms. *Administrative Science Quarterly* 32, pp. 387–399

Konar, E., E. Sundstrom, C. Brady, D. Mandel, and R. Rice (1982): Status Markers in the Office. *Environment and Behavior* 14, pp. 561–580

Louis Harris and Associates, Inc. (1978): *The Steelcase National Study of Office Environments: Do They Work?* Grand Rapids, MI: Steelcase

Marans, R. W. and K. F. Spreckelmeyer (1982): Evaluating Open and Conventional Office Design. *Environment and Behavior* 14, pp. 333–351

Masters, J. C. and L. Keil (1987): Generic Comparison Processes in Human Judgement and Behavior. *Social Comparison, Social Justice, and Relative Deprivation: Theoretical, Empirical, and Policy Perspectives.* Masters/Smith (Eds.). Hillsdale, NJ: Erlbaum, pp. 11–54

Miller, K. I. and P. R. Monge (1985): Social Information and Employee Anxiety about Organizational Change. *Human Communication Research* 11, pp. 365–386

Oldham, G. R. and D. J. Brass (1979): Employee Reactions to an Open-Plan Office: A Naturally Occurring Quasi-Experiment. *Administrative Science Quarterly* 24, pp. 267 – 284

Oldham, G. R. and Y. Fried (1987): Employee Reactions to Workplace Characteristics. *Journal of Applied Psychology* 72, pp. 75 – 80

Oldham, G. R. and N. L. Rotchford (1983): Relationships between Office Characteristics and Employee Reactions: A Study of the Physical Environment. *Administrative Science Quarterly* 28, pp. 542 – 556

Ornstein, S. (1989): The Hidden Influences of Office Design. *The Academy of Management Executive* 3, pp. 144 – 147

Ortner, S. B. (1973): On Key Symbols. *American Anthropologist* 75, pp. 1338 – 1346

Ouchi, W. G. (1981): *Theory Z.* Reading, MA: Addison-Wesley

Smircich, L. (1983): Concepts of Culture and Organizational Analysis. *Administrative Science Quarterly* 28, pp. 339 – 358

Steele, F. I. (1973): *Physical Settings and Organization Development.* Reading, MA: Addison-Wesley

Steele, F. I. (1983): The Ecology of Executive Teams: A New View of the Top. *Organizational Dynamics*, Spring, pp. 65 – 78

Sundstrom, E., R. E. Burt, and D. Kamp (1980): Privacy at Work: Architectural Correlates of Job Satisfaction and Job Performance. *Academy of Management Journal* 23, pp. 101 – 117

Sundstrom, E., E. K. Herbert, and D. W. Brown (1982): Privacy and Communication in an Open Plan Office. A Case Study. *Environment and Behavior* 14, pp. 379 – 392

Szilagyi, A. D. and W. E. Holland (1980): Changes in Social Density: Relationships with Functional Interaction and Perceptions of Job Characteristics, Role Stress, and Work Satisfaction. *Journal of Applied Psychology* 65, pp. 28 – 33

Zalesny, M. D. and R. V. Farace (1987): Traditional Versus Open Offices: A Comparison of Sociotechnical, Social Relations, and Symbolic Meaning Perspectives. *Academy of Management Journal* 30, pp. 240 – 259

Designing Dynamic Artifacts: Computer Systems as Formative Contexts

Claudio U. Ciborra and Giovan Francesco Lanzara

1 Introduction

In the last thirty years the development of information technology has generated a whole variety of computer-based information systems that nowadays populate our workplaces and indeed our lifeworld. Though none of such systems is as ubiquitous as the telephone (maybe with the only exception of the pocket calculator), some of them are rapidly shaping our daily work routines in the office and on the shopfloor. Countless studies have looked at the impacts of automated systems on issues such as task execution and allocation, information flows, decision making, upgrading/ downgrading of skills and employment. Considering the basic premises of such studies, two main metaphors about the role of computers can be singled out:

— the computer as a *tool*, that supports the execution of existing routines in a more efficient way or the implementation of new ones (robotics; office automation). The computer is here seen as a neutral, docile, and passive device harnessed by management, the experts, or whatever coalition dominates the organization;
— the computer as a *control device*, or organizational technology, that automates control and coordination processes, centralizing or decentralizing decision making (management information systems).

Note how both metaphors refer to systems as artifacts designed and implemented by specialists for a given, usually by management, purpose.

Successes, failures, and power struggles around the design and usage of the innovation are also reported in the literature, together with explanations regarding the causal chains of events that lead to specific organizational outcomes: for example, user participation in systems development; or the application of structured systems design methods leading to a successful computerization; or the political skills required for the effective management of change, etc. (Keen 1981).

However, what characterizes all such stories of computerization is a sort of deterministic, linear explanation strategy, and specifically the "closed," instrumental role attributed to systems: they are "designed," embed "purposes" and accordingly provoke "impacts." It seems that despite their intrinsic complexity systems are artifacts that never show unexpected features and cannot influence the premises, the goals, and the frames adopted by the actors involved in the computerization process. In other words, each actor seems to have a clear view, and stance, with respect to what a system should or should not do, and the system behaves accordingly.

We argue that this genre of story telling is too coarse and misses the deeper, multiple realities and meanings of computerization (for an exception, see Zuboff [1988]). We submit that most recounts overlook the complex interactions between systems as *dynamic artifacts* and *organizational culture*: the lack of concepts and even a language to describe the interactions between computers and culture has not helped either. To be sure, artifacts have been looked at as part of organizational culture: they embody, define, or symbolize the physical contours of *organizational routines* and have been generally understood and implemented in relation to the execution of those routines.

On the other hand, we refer to dynamic artifacts when they are associated with *organizational change*, i. e. they trigger, symbolize, or play the role of plastic objects in processes of cultural change during an organizational transformation. They can be acted upon and symbolize revolutionary change (*la prise de la Bastille*), be the signposts of institutional deviations and *bricolage* (the French term for "tinkering" [Berry/Irvine 1986]) that lead to sharp twists in organizational routines (like the "banana time on the assembly line" [Roy 1960]), or be technological systems that occasion alternative structuring of patterns of social interaction (Barley 1986). Once that change has occurred, dynamic artifacts may turn static and become the *simulacra* of change past, monuments celebrating the revolutionary events in the life of an organization (like the conservative interior decor of the AT & T headquarters after the Ma Bell break up), unless they be plastic and open to continuous re-invention, so that their dynamic nature is kept alive and their potential for promoting change intact.

Despite the *prima facie* characteristics attributed to information technology, i. e. standardization, routinization of tasks, centralization, etc., systems are indeed dynamic artifacts, and they will be even more so in the future, when further miniaturization of components, decrease in production costs, advances in software, and digitalization of voice, images, and data will foster the diffusion of "active media," whereby a small device (the size of a book) will perform all the functions of a telephone, colour TV, personal computer, office desk, and fax.

In order to appreciate the role of systems as dynamic artifacts, the paper elaborates the following thesis: computer-based information systems are embodiments not of just data flows and work routines, but also of organizational cultures and archetypes (Greenwood/Hinings 1988). More specifically, we intend to show that computers are able to interact with *both* the structural and institutional arrangements associated with a given division of labour *and* the assumptions, frames, and mental images people have while enacting and practicing routinely that division of labour. To denote this complex mix of cognitive and institutional factors, we have introduced the term "formative context," borrowing it from Unger (1987).

Interactions unfold in both directions: systems are relatively open and plastic, no matter what their initial purposes and design may be. But once designed and introduced in the organization, they can affect in subtle ways the existing organizational formative context and make it evolve in ways that are irreversible, for this process is often unnoticed and taken for granted. Though participation, structured approaches, and even conflict can determine the actual shape of systems in an organization, there are often deeper changes that go largely unnoticed regarding the ways people:

— work and divide labour;
— reflect upon the costs and benefits of a given work organization and technical infrastructure that supports it;
— imagine alternative arrangements and systems;
— implement these alternative views and designs.

It turns out that systems can put the culture of an organization on a different track leading to the enactment of new routines, mental images, and conceptions: thus they become a part of the formative context of the organization where emerging routines and frames are continuously tried out, adopted, or discarded, often in unaware, but no less pervasive ways.

If our thesis holds true, the whole issue of computerization and its impacts should be looked at in a different light. A cultural, anthropological analysis will always be needed to identify the subtle deviations in actors' behaviours, routines, and cognitions: these "true stories" will be more telling about the underlying changes induced by the new technology than the monitoring of more apparent modifications, such as reduction in the number of jobs (Ciborra/Lanzara 1989). To wit, intervening on the latter type of changes is quite straightforward if resources and will are available, while being unaware of the former may cause the failure of any policy aimed at changing or redirecting the course of computerization altogether.

The next two sections (2 and 3) spell out our analysis of organizations as formative context and of computer systems as open and dynamic artifacts: a richer set of concepts is thus introduced to understand the processes by which organizations adopt and use systems, or fail to do so. In section 4 the open, pasted-up nature of systems and routines and the embedded quality of practical knowledge informing human skills are shown to be positive assets to be purposefully exploited rather than handicaps to be removed. Finally, in section 5, the main implications for a new vision of design based on intervention and on-line practical experiments are sketched. The outcome of such "designing-in-action" could be artifacts and routines that help organizational actors perform a perpetual activity of reflection and self-questioning while they are engaged in action.

2   Organizations as Formative Contexts

2.1 The Hypothesis of a Formative Context

Only a naive conception of technological change would consider the adoption of a new system in an organization as the result of a rational, straightforward process of planning, designing, and implementation, lubricated by appropriate techniques at each stage of the system life cycle: project management tools for planning, structured methodologies for systems development, software engineering for implementation, and user participation for organizational development. Also, the political analysis and management of the change process carried out according to the "power perspective" may add a Machiavellian flavour to the labour of computerization, but misses the *gusto* of the everyday reality of introducing and using a computer-based information system in an organization: methodologies and tools are soon abandoned; the rush for delivering the system becomes the paramount driving force; systems are thrown onto users' desks and ... nothing happens: productivity stays sluggish; level of use is moderate; success is mixed; political strategies and manoeuvres seem to lead nowhere; and little experience is gained, while the big rush for the next system is starting and new cries for "more structured" methodologies and "higher user participation" are being launched.

   Why do the various actors of computerization — managers, designers, users — remain so blind during change and show such a limited capability to learn? To address the issue of organizational change surrounding a technological innovation, we submit that a new way of looking at how people work and organize themselves needs to be introduced: the actors, when skillfully executing their routines, when implementing innovations and imagining alternatives to improve their effectiveness, are under the influence of a deep-seated structure, or *formative context*, which accounts for their skills, the inertia of their learning, and the unawareness of their actual practices.

The formative context is the set of the pre-existing institutional arrangements, cognitive frames, and imageries that actors bring and routinely enact in a situation of action (Unger 1987). A formative context comprises both an organizational and a cognitive dimension and has far-reaching, subtle influences: it constitutes a background condition for action, enforcing constraints, giving direction and meaning, and setting the range of opportunities for undertaking action. Though a formative context provides the ground for routine execution and influences the creation of new routines, actors are usually not aware of the formative contexts that inform their practical and argumentative routines. They tend to take them for granted, except in the case of major breakdowns (Bateson 1972, Garfinkel 1967, Schutz 1973).

The outcome of a formative context in a work setting is a texture of routines, roles, and tasks that come to possess an "aura of naturalness" for those who daily execute the routines in that context. For example, consider the hierarchy as a formative context. From an institutional point of view it is a special type of employment contract and authority relation (Williamson 1981). Furthermore, it is a way of splitting task execution and task definition. However, these institutional and organizational aspects do not dispose of the hierarchy as a formative context. The hierarchy is also a cognitive framework: think of the functional decomposition as a strategy for problem-solving and its drive toward structured formalization. And it is a social, emotional bundle of experiences and preconceptions: recall the usual conflicts between technical and bureaucratic roles, the informal organization of work seen as opaque and dysfunctional, or authority experienced as domination. What is characteristic is that the hierarchical formative context is retrieved and enacted by the actors in situations every time they need to make sense of their everyday routines and invent changes to achieve higher effectiveness.

2.2 A Specification of the Concept

Together with crucial differences, the notion of a formative context shares some similarities with a number of concepts, such as culture, frame, or schema. Such similarities might suggest that there is no need for introducing a new concept: after all, what does the formative context do that the other concepts don't? Only by comparing the idea of formative context to other related concepts, it is possible to spell out those special aspects that this concept is able to capture in the fields of organizational change and design.

To begin with, a formative context designates what binds, in a loosely connected texture, an individual or a collective (group, organization, etc.) to an established world of objects and relations, and to the associated cognitive imageries, presuppositions, and meanings of which that world is the embodied vehicle. It comprises what actors take for granted in their daily practical routines and transactions, what somehow they perceive as having an "institutional" valency for them. The context is "formative" in that it shapes the ways people perceive, understand, make meaning, perform, and get organized in a situation bounded in space and time. It is "formative" because it may help people see and do things in new ways, or, on the contrary, make them stick stubbornly to old ways. Following Bateson (1972), *context* is used here in its interactional or transactional meaning, rather than psychological. It is thus directly related to the manner in which individual or collective experience is organized, and to choices and actions that can variously punctuate and modify the flow of experience.

When enacted in a situation of action, formative contexts are expression of a social cognition that transcends the individual. Such cognition may well be embodied in material or symbolic artifacts, organizational structures and procedures, institutional settings, and, most crucially, in the relationships or "couplings" binding actors and their work tools in a sort of microecology of stable uses and shared meanings. Thus, by introducing the idea of a formative context in organizational analysis, we want to capture both the institutionally embedded quality of social cognition and the cognitive dimension of institutional and organizational arrangements. As institutions and organizations embody and "act out" established assumptions and cognitions, and pose different cognitive demands to their members, depending on how roles, ranks, and tasks are defined and assigned, so shared cognitive and learning processes, and the outcomes of them, feed and crystallize into established artifacts and repertoires of cognitions that work as "cognitive institutions" in their own right, and can only be modified or updated through complex social and institutional mechanisms. As Mary Douglas (1986) has nicely pointed out, institutions — social and political — are established systems of premises or programs for action that help people think and act, or prevent them from doing so when they want to do it differently. To borrow Seymour Papert's felicitous expression, they are — like the telephone or the computer — tools people use to think and act with (Papert 1980).

Even this brief account of the features of a formative context might shed some light on the differences with respect to purely cognitive concepts like frame, script, or schema as they have been developed in the cognitive sciences (Abelson 1976, Minsky 1975, 1977, Shank/Abelson 1977), in the psychology of choice under uncertainty (Tversky/Kahnemann 1981), or in policy analysis (Rein/Schon 1981, Schon 1979). These are too mentalistic. Being based on the pervasive idea of representation as an explicit symbol system, when applied to the analysis of organizational phenomena (Shrivastava/Schneider 1984, Sims/Gioia et al. 1986), they tend to lead to an excessive mentalization of organizational reality. Using purely cognitive constructs, like frames or schemata, misses the fact that many important human skills and organizational abilities need not be associated with a capacity for external symbolic expression. In other words, it may happen that individuals and organizations know how to *do* things that they cannot yet *say* or explicitly *represent*.

Furthermore, these notions apply more easily to individuals rather than collectives. Being conceived as structures or schemata that sit in the individual's mind, they are too individualistic. When transposed to the analysis of organizational phenomena, they lead to theorize, by analogy, a sort of organizational mind where all the representations are stored, waiting to be acted out in some behaviour or performance. What tends to get lost is the *social* dimension of organizational cognition, that is, the fact that all organizational cognition is produced within a social interaction. The difference, then, is clearly stated: underlying the idea of a frame there is a theory of representation, underlying the idea of a formative context there is a theory of social interaction and a theory of meaning. Thus, while one looks for a frame or script inside an individual's mind, one looks for a formative context in the interaction among the individuals. A formative context "runs across" the individuals' minds, connecting them to the outside world.

Secondly, a formative context is to be understood in the perspective of action science (Argyris/Putnam/McLain Smith 1985, Schon 1983). The idea that formative contexts are an action-oriented concept is not easy to grasp. When actors undertake action, they enact a context in a local, specific situation and respond to it. There must be an action going on in order to have a formative contexts. For example, cultural features, organizational arrangements, specific procedures, or even material artifacts can become "items" of a formative context, when they function as unquestioned grounds or "vehicles" for executing or designing routines in a situation of action.

Note how the focus on action makes it difficult to use the concept of culture for our purposes. Though the notion of formative context is naturally inscribed in the culture-oriented approach to organizational analysis, the study of organizational culture has dealt with the world of action only in a restricted way. Thus, for example, organizational culturalists such as Schein (1984), Van Maanen and Barley (1984), or Smircich (1983) who provide very perceptive and valuable insights on a variety of organizational phenomena, do not seem to have an agenda for organizational design and intervention. And those who have applied cultural analysis to the issue of change in institutional settings (Gagliardi 1986, Pfeffer 1981, Schein 1984) seem to concentrate their attention on the conscious mental levels, working on explicit representations and emotions, disregarding the taken-for-granted routines, assumptions, institutional arrangements, and artifacts that deeply affect conscious behaviours, imageries, and perceptions.

We claim instead that there is often an important gap between observable behaviour and background culture. That happens because people tend to design routines in response to a situationally determined context which has mediating and "filtering" (formative!) properties with respect to their culture, and of which they may not be aware. Consequently, it may happen that people, who hold the same "cultural" assumptions at a general level, design remarkably different routines and behaviours pointing to different contexts.

The distinction (and the connection) between organizational routines and their background formative context is of paramount importance when we come to the question of how to design and implement innovation, for, when designing a new system, the object of design and construction — be it deliberate or unintended — does not only consist of new routines, programs, and procedures but, more importantly, of a new formative context. Hence, strategies for change and design must be able to unfreeze and restructure cognitions and meanings that are hidden in the practical relations of people to their formative contexts.

This is not easy to do, because smooth functioning of organizational routines tends to disconnect individuals and organizations from their underlying contexts. In such conditions, effective change becomes problematic. Argyris and Schon (1978) rightly point to this problem in their analysis of limited learning cycles, based on the distinction between an espoused theory and a theory-in-use. To be sure, what Argyris and Schon call theories-in-use share with formative contexts the same tacit, embedded quality that makes them hard to access and change. But, unlike a theory-in-use, a formative context needs not have a causal structure. Rather, it has a *fabric* textured with associative relations linking a wide variety of materials. While theories-in-use inform individual or organizational capacity to produce behaviour in specific circumstances and tend to stay constant across situations, formative contexts express the engrained, sedimented cognitions and the enduring, "institutional" artifacts that those theories-in-use have yielded and stabilized in organizational history.

3 The Open and Dynamic Nature of Computer Systems

There are two features of computer-based systems that give them their dynamic character, i. e. almost a life of their own, which defies attempts by members of the organization to fully harness and govern systems for their own purposes. These features are in a way technical: thus they are often taken for granted by system designers, and overlooked or misunderstood by sociologists. As a result, the interaction between systems and their organizational, behavioural, and cognitive contexts remains largely *terra incognita*.

The first feature is that systems are becoming platforms for creating applications, routines, languages, communication modes, and simulated, virtual environments that go beyond the limited set of purposes and functions initially laid out by designers and sponsors. Systems are job shops where the more visible artifacts associated with the executions of everyday routines can be designed, engineered, and assembled. Think of the by-now familiar icons that fill the interface of any office application: menus, documents, file cabinets, the dustbin .... In any personal computer its operating system supports such a man—machine interface, consisting of a set of abstract software rules and objects that simulate an office desk and the actions one can perform in this environment. The operating system is a dynamic artifact: it stays in the background, is hidden and invisible but its influence is far-reaching, for it sets the constraints and opens up the possibilities to simulate a whole work environment, including its familiar objects, routines, and preconceptions.

In a way, it shares the qualities of a building or a physical office space: walls, furniture, desks, chairs define the pattern of possible interactions that form the fabric of office work. But it is more dynamic than an architectural artifact, for its appearance can be more easily dismantled and readapted to specific user requirements and idiosyncracies. Second, it makes of every user a potential architect, empowering him or her with tools (applications, abstract objects, etc.) to reinvent work routines and social relations occurring through the system. Contrast, for example, how a building establishes the office layout as a set of passive constraints to work-related and social interactions, symbolizes in a static way differences in status and hierarchy etc., and the way an operating system together with a generic office application can support a simulated environment open to:

— defining the execution of office tasks;
— defining the format and pattern of communications with co-workers;
— suggesting ways of how to reshape current tasks;
— tinkering with new, simulated routines to experiment the execution of jobs and communications according to alternative designs;
— looking at the office organization from different perspectives, for example, exploring situations whereby the work organization is not constrained by the physical proximity of people and machines or by a hierarchical structure of supervision.

The second feature is that systems at their boundaries brittle. Recall our previous observation of the realities of computerization: what everyone can experience in the everyday life of an organization is that systems and routines are subject to "shift and drift" phenomena. The ways they are implemented and used never fully correspond to the original plans and visions, and design processes more often than not take paths unthought of at the start, almost beyond the actors' will. Systems, and the processes that lead to their construction, possess an open nature and are subject to continuous reinvention, i.e. to an innovative adoption process carried out by the users themselves (Rice/Rogers 1980). In part, they are characterized by formalized components, such as hardware, software, rules, functions, etc., but these do not completely dispose of how systems and processes behave in everyday life. Surrounding these stylized components, usually laid down as a result of *ex ante* design, there are routines and interventions carried out by users who may take unplanned courses of action or by designers who happen to be temporarily with the project and may introduce quirky or irreversible design choices, and then leave. All such routines and interventions are continuously developed, tried out, retained or discarded, retrieved and combined, on a local, often tacit basis, outside or at the margins of the master plans and designs, in an endless process of *bricolage*. Still, they are not without implications for implementation. There is no way to avoid their influence on how a system or process will actually be and behave in its real-life operation. They are the outcome of an on-line design activity that we can call *designing-in-action* (Ciborra/Lanzara 1990).

4 Practical Knowledge and Organizational Change

The foregoing analysis suggests that the relationship between dynamic artifacts and formative contexts is one of mutual inclusion and isomorphism: it is this complex and intertwined relationship that makes the cognitive and behavioural dependencies of actors upon contexts and artifacts not amenable to explanations based on linear sequences of strategies, actions, and consequences. A further discussion is thus warranted of how contexts influence thought and action and what can be the actors' degrees of freedom when designing and applying any technical change.

In general, a pre-existing formative context is responsible for molding practical knowledge of people at work, perfectioning the learning skills, and biasing the imageries of those who engage in design and change. Individual skills and organizational routines supporting everyday practices are grounded on a knowledge base that is taken for granted when engaging in action. Established repertoires of experiences and frames that have proved successful on similar occasions enable the actors to smoothly and unreflectively perform their routines (Polanyi 1966). The formative context embeds such knowledge base which represents the hidden, background component of skilled performance, straightforward organizational routines, and quiet functioning of institutional arrangements.

Due to the embedded quality of practical knowledge that informs human skills, one tends to pay attention to the locus of performance, while *at the same time* becoming unaware of the formative contexts. Consequently, people exhibit poor capability at surfacing, questioning, eventually smashing them when we need to do so. A source of limited learning is to be found precisely in how knowledge for action is split in the two levels of ready-at-hand routines and underlying formative contexts: if the focus of attention is on the former and the performance is successful, the latter tend to fade in the shadows of unawareness, becoming pre-written and unquestioned social scripts. Failures and novelties threatening their stability will seldom trigger a learning process leading to their restructuring: formative contexts thus gain a semblance of "natural necessity" (Bateson 1972, Garfinkel 1967).

Knowledge and experience sealed in formative contexts are expression of what may be called the rationality of the obvious: they are, in a way, ready-at-hand cognitive resources that need not be questioned or tested every time one uses them. But the incapability of questioning the obviousness of contexts generates cognitive inertia in organizations, precisely when a high capability for change and innovation is required, for example when applying a new technology. This also means that whenever a knowledge-based system or even a bread-and-butter computer application such as a payroll system are designed and implemented in an organization, the basis for competence and the relevant formative context are affected in at least three ways (Hopwood 1987). First, the boundary is shifted between what is tacitly held as background knowledge and what we are aware of as foreground "situational" knowledge (*where* in a specific work situation the focus of attention is explicitly directed at). Second, the basis for the invention, test, and adoption of new forms of practical knowledge surrounding the use of the system in the work setting is altered. New practices, informal rules, and ways of circumventing routines are tried out and set in place within the constraints defined by the new infrastructure and its intrinsic requirements. Third, any invention of alternative practices or any radical departure from existing routines are deeply conditioned by the new mix of background and situational knowledge, the new set of formal and specialized tools required by the system, and the local practices and informal know-how developed around it.

5 Reframing Computer-Based Systems as Dynamic Artifacts: Implications for Design

5.1 Second-Order Constructs

A formative context, as for the case of dynamic artifacts, has not and cannot have a coherent and orderly structure: it results from a pasted-up combination of everyday practices and tinkering, a sedimentation of local and global arrangements. Thus formative contexts also "shift and drift." For example, the formative context underlying the routines of a given information system as it is concretely used may not coincide with the one that has governed the design and the development of the system. It may reflect instead the actual division of work as it emerges from the actors' daily interactions with the system (Weick 1977). In this loosely connected set of practices, routines, and frameworks, single components are always up for grabs, while the set shows strong resilience as a whole.

Formative contexts and dynamic artifacts thus share a double nature. On the one hand, they appear to be highly stable and inescapable, given their wishy-washy, sticky pervasiveness; on the other hand, they can be regarded as the culture bed, at the routine level, for experiments in organizational restructuring and innovation, within certain economic and technical constraints, themselves subject to local revision and manipulation. A regimen of permanent, ineliminable fluctuations characterizes such a culture bed (Ciborra/Migliarese/Romano 1984). Each fluctuation can "escalate," be amplified and become the new way of running and conceiving things, thus contributing to shape the emerging formative contexts. Whether local fluctuations in practices and routines can escape the pre-existing formative context, be intentionally tried out and developed by actors in everyday situations, depends heavily upon the degree of cognitive openness and vulnerability the actors, the artifacts, and the formative contexts allow for, or, in the words of the poet Keats, on the degree of *Negative Capability* they are equipped with, that is the capability "of being in uncertainties, mysteries, doubts, without any irritable reaching after fact and reason" (Keats 1962).

Our argument needs now to be pursued further by dealing directly with the issue of systems development, where the question of being able to restructure and invent organizational routines becomes crucial. According to a view in good currency information systems consist of routines, procedures, and technologies to process data electronically. Designing an information system means designing and implementing functional requirements and specifications leading to formal and rigorous encodings, software routines, data bases, and so on.

The implicit assumption is that information systems can be realistically and rigorously described and designed in terms of data flows, work routines, or economic transactions. In this perspective, knowledge necessary for the design and the implementation of the new system can be acquired by interviewing users about their current routines and activities within a given user/analyst interaction. Such interaction may indeed involve conflicting interests and visions vis-à-vis the technology or the organization, but is supposed to be *transparent* with respect to the meanings attributed to data flows, data bases, decisions, tasks, functions, etc. In other words, the conventional approaches limit their inquiries and methods to the explicitly visible patterns of activities, though segmented and grouped in different ways. They construct pictures of information systems based − each in its own way − on a distinctive kind of obviousness.

Taking a different perspective, we submit that the components of an information system − data flows, work procedures, or transactions − retain a more complex quality than what is currently assumed in these naively realistic pictures. These components are *second-order constructs* both from a cognitive and an institutional point of view. They are visible embodiments of ways of organizing reality, cognitively and institutionally, which are deeply entrenched in the formative contexts we bring to projects and organizational situations (Boland 1979, Weick 1986). What is considered to be the "natural necessity" of a data flow, a work routine, or a pattern of transactions is indeed *contingent* upon a formative context that may change as institutional arrangements and cognitive images evolve, shift, and break down. When that happens, what is taken to be data, routine, task, or organizational function may lose its habitual meaning, and be seen and "acted out" in a different way.

We can then restate our thesis in a way full of consequences for the design and the use of new technology. Any information system, and more generally any artifact or tool affecting the division of work and the practical knowledge of people at work, shows the features of a formative context. Indeed, formative contexts mold information systems. They do it cognitively: the use of information systems embodies forms of practical knowledge concerning the gathering, processing, and distribution of information. By introducing new modes and procedures by which individuals and organizations deal with knowledge, an information system may cause a shift and a restructuring of the cognitive frames and assumptions underlying human skills and governing human actions. In other words, the hardware and the software may convey a varied cognitive imagery through which people grasp their world, undertake action, and communicate in a specific situation. They do it institutionally: an information system can be regarded as supporting a set of contractual and institutional arrangements between individuals and organizations. By bringing about specific ways of organizing social relations and performing economic transactions, an information system embeds a set of rules, norms, constraints that partially come to govern the processing, the communication, and the use of information. Designing a system means to a large extent changing and restructuring the institutional bonds and background conditions upon which people establish and enact their practical dealings and relations.

Information systems, then, should always be treated and designed at two distinct levels: the one of the formed routines and the one of the formative contexts. It is unlikely that a routine, even a payroll application, can be designed without at the same time affecting its formative context, and it is difficult to restructure organizational practices if the underlying context is not restructured, too. In other words, the design of dynamics artifacts cannot escape the issue of how to inquire and design formative contexts.

Are we equipped theoretically and practically to conceive and design systems as formative contexts? If real-life systems are the outcome of "pasting-up" and *bricolage* activities, what criteria should govern their construction? How can we tap relevant knowledge embedded in formative contexts and connect it to effective system design and implementation? These questions lead us to propose a style of design, based on practical on-line experiments, exploiting rather than denying the qualities of systems and practical knowledge described above.

5.2 A New Agenda for Systems Design

Current system design practices, being mainly committed to designing data bases and procedures in a cost-effective way or according to some principle of economic or political equity, tend to overlook the institutional and cognitive frameworks within which routines are formed, and given legitimacy and meaning. To wit, no matter how formally rigorous or participation-oriented they are, these practices seem unable to question and affect the quality of the actors' relations to the institutional and cognitive frameworks that they establish and inhabit in organizations. On the contrary, by not distinguishing clearly between routines and formative contexts, they tend to obscure the knowledge necessary to relate routines' change or persistence to the restructuring of formative contexts, to track the complex feedback loops binding contexts and routines, and to analyze the quality and structure of the contexts.

While current design methods capture and emphasize the functional or problem-solving role of a routine, they fall short of understanding how the same routine may reproduce or break powerful imageries and institutional bonds at a deeper level.

Conventional methods are based on the assumption that people will "automatically" start out adopting novel patterns of behaviour and new ways of looking at things just because a new machinery has been cast into the organization; or, they claim not to disrupt the present organization, when in fact they do, again leaving the actors incapable of effectively handling technical change and becoming aware that a new formative context is emerging. Thus system designers keep reproducing the conditions for the recurrent discrepancy between theory and actual system performance.

In sum, if we are to face the challenge that the complexity of real-life systems in organizations is calling for, current design practices need to be redirected. We argue that these should amount to more than property determination and requirements specification, to more than exercises in routine problem solving or interest accommodation, for they should deal with the structures and frameworks within which such exercises take place, i.e. with shaping and restructuring formative contexts (Boland 1979, Boland/Day 1982, Weick 1986).

One can change formative contexts only by *intervening in situations*. Intervention, as we propose it, is a strategy of action to come to grips with the pasted-up nature of contexts both cognitively and institutionally. Practical intervention in a specific organizational setting challenges the institutional arrangements and the cognitive imageries on which the *status quo* is based. The issue here is to be able to gain insight into formative contexts, *while* actually designing or performing routines in situations.

To be sure, the logic of intervention is in many respects different from the logic of analysis: its epistemology draws on a theory of action (Argyris/Schon 1978, Argyris/Putnam/McLain Smith 1985). It is concerned with understanding and acting in situations by enacting practical experiments to test formative contexts, to surface conflicts and inconsistencies, to explore deviations from routines and frame the alternative contexts that they may lead to.

5.3 The Dynamic Artifacts of the Future: Systems for Self-Questioning

New sophisticated technologies and systems that keep invading our workplaces, organizations, and institutions are currently designed and implemented within the existing, hierarchical formative context determined by established models of design practice and computer-based organizations. However, if we take a closer look at their features and behaviours, as we tried to do in this chapter, we would see that they often point to emerging formative contexts. It is precisely because they are the outcome of design-

in-action and continuous reinvention that these systems are dynamic artifacts that exhibit emerging properties.

Thus, the making of formative contexts as one of the basic activities in
systems design could influence the outcome of design itself, i. e. the computer-based systems. The qualities that dynamic artifacts may come to possess
in this new perspective would entail:

— facilitating the process of reinvention, that any complex technological
  artifact undergoes when put to use;
— not concealing the relations between routines embedded in systems and
  formative contexts; on the contrary, making those relations explicit and
  questionable;
— acting as media for enhancing coordination and communication: problems and solutions shift all the time and systems, because of their open,
  pasted-together nature, would benefit from loosely coupled forms of
  organizing;
— providing real-time feedback to users on their current organization of
  work, and the emerging coordination and communication patterns when
  using the systems;
— performing as "expert," though in a quite different way from current
  conceptions: in addition to supporting or replacing the knowledge-based
  routines of professionals and managers in specific domains of expertise,
  they could support their capabilities for reflection and inquiry within
  the contexts in which they are embedded, helping people to build up,
  question, and modify practical knowledge according to the emergence
  and the shift of problematic situations and contexts;
— finally, behaving as proactive, dynamic mirrors of human action, supporting and enhancing perpetual individual and institutional self-questioning: in short, they could play the role of "reflectors," helping the
  users connect their practical and argumentative routines to the established or emerging formative contexts, rather than concealing that
  connection, as they normally do.

6 Concluding Remarks

What we have been claiming so far is that current ways of looking at
systems design fall short of understanding it as a phenomenon in the
domain of action and change. In our view, they all share two fundamental
flaws: first, they assume a direct consequentiality between conditions,
choices, and actions leading to change and innovation; second, they look
at systems as "closed" and "static" artifacts.

The open, pasted-up nature of systems and development processes defies many formalized and participative attempts at mastering and steering the computerization process toward specifically programmed objectives; on the other hand, such nature can be purposefully exploited to design-in-action, to make things change by intervening in situations and experimenting with makeshift artifacts, or to keep going when the situation seems to be hopelessly "blocked." The reframing we have proposed leads to a further outcome, which can shed a new light on the role of systems *per se*. Namely, dynamic artifacts share many of the qualities of formative contexts, and designing a system interferes, if not coincides, with creating or changing a formative context, i.e. a cognitive, institutional, and behavioural artifact, and a makeshift one. This dynamic artifact influences not only the routines that form the everyday world of people at work, but also, and most importantly, the ways people make sense of their routines and imagine future changes to their lifeworld. Our approach takes such everyday practice seriously for designing present and future dynamic artifacts, instead of exorcizing in the name of imperatives dictated by a misplaced notion of technical rationality and by an artificial split between knowledge and practice.

References

Abelson, R. P. (1976): Script Processing in Attitude Formation and Decisionmaking. *Cognition and Social Behavior*. R. Carroll/J. Payne (Eds.). Hillsdale, NJ: Erlbaum & Associates, chapter 3 pp. 33−45

Argyris, C. and D. A. Schon (1978): *Organizational Learning. A Theory of Action Perspective*. Reading, MA: Addison-Wesley

Argyris, C., R. Putnam, and D. McLain Smith (1985): *Action Science*. San Francisco, CA: Jossey-Bass

Barley, S. R. (1986): Technology as an Occasion for Structuring: Evidence from Observation of CT Scanners and the Social Order of Radiology Departments. *Administrative Science Quarterly* 31(1), March, pp. 78−108

Bateson, G. (1972): *Steps to an Ecology of Mind*. New York: Chandler Publishing Co.

Berry, J. W. and S. H. Irvine (1986): Bricolage: Savages Do it Daily. *Practical Intelligence − Nature and Origins of Competence in the Everyday World*. R. J. Stenberg/R. K. Wagner (Eds.). Cambridge, U. K.: Cambridge University Press, pp. 271−306

Boland, R. Jr. (1979): Control, Causality and Information Systems Requirements. *Accounting, Organizations and Society* 4(4), pp. 259−272

Boland, R. Jr. and W. Day (1982): The Process of System Design: A Phenomenological Approach. *Proceedings of the Third International Conference on Information Systems*. Ann Arbor, MI: December, pp. 31−45

Ciborra, C. and G. F. Lanzara (1989): Change and Formative Contexts in Information Systems Development. *Systems Development for Human Progress*. H. K. Klein/K. Kumar (Eds.). Amsterdam: North Holland, pp. 21 – 40

Ciborra, C. and G. F. Lanzara (1990): Designing Networks in Action. *Telematics and Work*. R. A. Roe/E. H. Andriessen (Eds.). New York: Wiley

Ciborra, C., P. Migliarese, and P. Romano (1984): A Methodological Inquiry into Organizational Noise in Socio-Technical Systems. *Human Relations* 37(8), pp. 565 – 588

Douglas, M. (1986): *How Institutions Think*. Syracuse, NY: Syracuse University Press

Gagliardi, P. (1986): The Creation and Change of Organizational Culture: A Conceptual Framework. *Organization Studies* 7(2), pp. 117 – 134

Garfinkel, H. (1967): *Studies in Ethnomethodology*. Englewood Cliffs, NJ: Prentice Hall

Greenwood, R. and C. R. Hinings (1988): Organizational Design Types, Tracks and the Dynamics of Strategic Change. *Organization Studies* 9(3), pp. 293 – 316

Herbst, P. G. (1974): *Socio-Technical Design: Strategies in Multidisciplinary Research*. London: Tavistock

Hopwood, A. G. (1987): The Archeology of Accounting Systems. *Accounting, Organizations and Society* 12(3), pp. 207 – 234

Keats, J. (1962): Letter to George and Tom Keats, 21, 27(?) December 1817. *Poems and Selected Letters of John Keats*. Carlos Baker (Ed.). New York: Bantham Books

Keen, P. G. W. (1981): Information Systems and Organizational Change. *Communications of the ACM* 24(1), January, pp. 24 – 33

Minsky, M. (1975): A Framework for Representing Knowledge. *The Psychology of Computer Vision*. P. H. Winston (Ed.). New York: McGraw-Hill, pp. 211 – 277

Minsky, M. (1977): Frame System Theory. *Thinking: Readings in Cognitive Science*. P. N. Johnson-Laird/P. C. Wason (Eds.). Cambridge, U. K.: Cambridge University Press, pp. 355 – 376

Papert, S. (1980): *Mindstorms*. New York: Basic Books

Pfeffer, J. (1981): Management as Symbolic Action: The Creation and Maintenance of Organizational Paradigms. *Research in Organizational Behavior*. B. M. Staw/ L. L. Cummings (Eds.). Greenwich, CT: Jai Press, Vol. 3, pp. 1 – 52

Polanyi, M. (1966): *The Tacit Dimension*. Garden City, NY: Doubleday

Rein, M. and D. A. Schon (1981): Problem Setting in Policy Research. *Using Social Research in Public Policy Making*. C. H. Weiss (Ed.). Lexington, MA: Lexington Books, pp. 233 – 265

Rice, R. E. and E. M. Rogers (1980): Reinvention in the Innovation Process. *Knowledge* 1(4), June, pp. 488 – 514

Roy, D. F. (1960): Banana Time: Job Satisfaction and Informal Interaction. *Human Organization* 18, pp. 156 – 168

Schein, E. H. (1984): Coming to a New Awareness of Organizational Culture. *Sloan Management Review* 25(4), Winter, pp. 3 – 16

Schon, D. A. (1979): Generative Metaphor: A Perspective on Problem Setting in Social Policy. *Metaphor and Thought*. A. Ortony (Ed.). Cambridge, U. K.: Cambridge University Press, pp. 254 – 283

Schon, D. A. (1983): *The Reflective Practitioner: How Professionals Think in Action.* New York: Basic Books

Schutz, A. (1973): *Collected Papers, Vol. 1: The Problem of Social Reality.* The Hague: Martinus Nijhoff

Shank, R. and R. P. Abelson (1977): *Scripts, Goals, Plans, and Understanding: An Inquiry into Human Knowledge Structures.* Hillsdale, NJ: Erlbaum Associates

Shrivastava, P. and S. Schneider (1984): Organizational Frames of Reference. *Human Relations* 37(10), pp. 795−809

Sims, H. P. and D. A. Gioia & Associates (1986): *The Thinking Organization: Dynamics of Organizational Social Cognition.* San Francisco, CA: Jossey-Bass

Smircich, L. (1983): Concepts of Culture and Organizational Analysis. *Administrative Science Quarterly* 28(3), pp. 339−358

Tversky, A. and D. Kahnemann (1981): The Framing of Decisions and the Psychology of Choice. *Science* 211, pp. 453−458

Unger, R. M. (1987): *False Necessity.* Cambridge, U. K.: Cambridge University Press

Van Maanen, J. and S. R. Barley (1984): Cultural Organization: Fragments of a Theory. *Organizational Culture.* P. J. Frost et al. (Eds.). Beverly Hills, CA: Sage, pp. 31−53

Weick, K. (1977): Organization Design: Organizations as Self-Designing Systems. *Organizational Dynamics* 6(2), Autumn, pp. 30−46

Weick, K. (1986): Cosmos versus Chaos: Sense and Nonsense in Electronic Contexts. *Organizational Dynamics* 14(2), pp. 50−64

Williamson, O. (1981): The Economics of Organization: The Transaction Costs Approach. *American Journal of Sociology* 87(3), November, pp. 548−577

Zuboff, S. (1988): *In the Age of the Smart Machine. The Future of Work and Power.* New York: Basic Books

Part II:
Disclosing Organizational Cultures Through Artifacts

Colors, Artifacts, and Ideologies*

Joseph Sassoon

1 Introduction

The relationship between colors and social matters is a theme that has been too little analyzed in sociological literature. It is easier to find considerations on the subject of an anthropological nature (about the role of specific colors in certain rituals) or psychological nature (on the emotional resonance and the symbolic significances generally attributed to colors). This is surprising, since there is no doubt that the impact of colors in social life is quite considerable. They permeate our experience with things — elements of nature or artifacts — and often reflect decisive symbolic discriminations, for example in the political world.

A theme even less studied is the relationship between colors and ideologies — the term "ideology" is used here in a wider (and not necessarily negative) sense, as a system of values and behaviors, based on common principles and having a certain continuity. On this subject, incidentally, observations about colors can be very illuminating. This essay therefore examines the connections between color codes and the formation of ideological thought, by way of colored artifacts.

The argumentation that follows is based on three assumptions:

1. The colors that identify the various social organizations, or certain artifacts, are often very revealing about the implicit categories of values.
2. The anchoring of a social organization or of an artifact to a single color is a strong clue as to the presence of an ideology. (Inversely, organizations and artifacts that are non-ideological tend to be polychromatic.)
3. Changes in the tonality or the saturation of a color translate into interesting changes in the ideological vectors and the social significance of the artifacts.

* First published in *Social Science Information* (1989), reprinted with kind permission of Sage Publications.

The method of analysis used is analogical and inductive. It does not aim to offer proofs, but only to indicate possible correlations and to construct hypotheses.

2 Semantic Relevance

Colors are not unrestricted signs. A long tradition ties them to ceremonial rules, customs, social roles, and largely determines their process of signification (Baudrillard 1968). Certainly, in the last decades the increased variability of color in clothing and furnishings — a delayed effect of the chromatic revolution in painting — has permitted the breaking of many bourgeois conventions. In certain spheres, as described later, a type of color liberation has been achieved (which coincides, among other things, with its substantial neutralization). Nonetheless, in general, the variability permitted is not without limit, and tends in fact to be easily repudiated in favor of adherence to a chromatic code perceived as conventional or semantically "branded" — in other words, normative and full of significance. The burden of values that weighs on colors is, after all, centuries old, and it would be illusory to think that we can rid ourselves of it in the space of a few generations.

2.1 The Fundamental Trichromaticism: Black, White, Red

The crucial colors, from a cultural and symbolic viewpoint, do not coincide with the base colors from an optical viewpoint. Black and white, strictly speaking non-colors, are at the origin of any classification of reality in chromatic terms: the classic intercultural study by Berlin and Kay (1970) conducted on 98 different languages shows that, in all cases where only two words exist to indicate color, these are always "black" and "white." If a third exists, it is always "red." The names of other colors come afterwards, among these blue and green — that is, the two colors which, together with red, constitute the triad of "primary colors" from an optical viewpoint (those by means of which it is possible to obtain all other colors).

This analysis converges with Turner's, for whom black, white, and red seem to be the three fundamental colors of primitive symbolism, of ancient symbolism, and presumably of the symbolic representations of all humanity (Turner 1967). Most importantly, this original trichromaticism — often experienced as sacred — assumes, in all periods and places, semantic values that are extremely similar, or which in any case lead back to isomorphic symbolic structures. The significance of these colors is so forceful that, for every cultural formation or ideological system, the elective relationship with any of them is rarely casual and is often very revealing.

Black is the color of obscurity and night. Traditionally, and for almost all populations, it is the color of shade, and therefore of shadows — the color of death. The symbolic phenomena which confirm this association throughout the most diverse cultures are so numerous that justification of eventual exceptions (mourning associated with white in China, the variegated funeral rites in Bali, Madagascar, etc.) is not required. Various factors of a historico-cultural nature can explain these inversions, and, in any case, the semantic field of colors is certainly not intended as a semiotic code in which the values of the terms are unequivocally fixed. The colors themselves are symbols and therefore necessarily plurisemantic (Jung 1912). However, the tendency to attribute significance to certain areas is very strong, and without doubt black inherently carries an ominous aura or, at any rate, connotations of decadence, limitation, and finality (Durand 1969). In many languages, the expression "black list," "black mass," "black market" are the translation into the negative of terms that are otherwise positive or neutral. A "black Friday" can indicate a particularly unfortunate day for the history of a country, or simply an unlucky day for a single individual. When it is ritualized, this color almost always symbolizes the dimension of authority (which follows from the possibility of setting limits) or of renouncement (which expresses the striving for self-limitation). In the world of artifacts, it is no coincidence that the uniforms of the police and guards of many countries, the robes of judges and university professors, the habits of priests and nuns, are black. Towards the end of the 1600s, the black clothing used by the religious upper class born of the Protestant Reform (so well represented in portrait galleries) chromatically expresses the values of a new moral order (Brusatin 1983). The black robes worn by Arab women have been, since the seventh century AD, a form of clothing signifying renouncement, which has been reimposed in Iran by Khomeini — after a transitory parenthesis of Westernized polychromatic fashions — as a necessary support of the Islamic order.

However, black tends to be most visibly the color of death in those social organizations that impose it in a maniacal and exaggerated way; most of all in Nazism. The black shirts, the black uniforms of the SS, the somber hangings of their oceanic parades, the whole collection of black artifacts of the period (including arms) were the warped mirror through which a regime dedicated to death expressed its ideology. Even today, the operations of the "Black International," turbid and deadly, once again suggest the inescapable relationship that exists between the extreme right's ideology and its color. Used in a more ironical and paradoxical key, on the other hand, the color black can certainly reduce its destructive range: this is the case with the punk movement, whose radical chromatic choice expresses the negation of a society whose values are rejected. But even among punks, the connection with death remains; nor is this a coincidence on an ideoligical level ("no future, no dream") or on a behavioral level (self-destructive use of drugs, suicidal tendencies, extreme marginalization).

Conversely, as Turner notes, the connection between white and the values of light, purity, and life is clearly predominant among both primitive and civilized peoples. In the population that he studied in particular, the Ndembu of northwest Zambia, it appears that the significance of white takes its origins from two primary references of an organic type — milk and semen — together with the obvious fundamental experience of daylight. According to Turner, this link with features of biological existence lies at the root of the primordial classification of colors: not only for white (black is tied to both the obscurity of the night and the catabolism of physical excrements, while red is above all the color of blood); and not only for the Ndembu, but for countless primitive populations (if not for all mankind). This thesis contrasts with the opinions that base the semantic values of colors on perceptive and analogical phenomena in a broad sense, in other words, beyond biological features. But even without entering into the merits of this discussion, one must agree that the symbolisms signified by white in the Ndembu rituals — freedom from contamination, vitality, health, good fortune, relations with the spirits — are most certainly representative of the semantic labels universally attributed to this color. White is, in effect, the color almost universally associated with birth and puberty: the Catholic confirmation, in which the children's white clothing manifestly symbolizes their purity, is the most indicative ritual in this sense (Birren 1963). The white bridal gown, which in many regions of the world expresses virginity, has an analogous value. The spirituality of the color white is evidenced in the priestly vestments of the highest religious authorities in both Christianity and Judaism (the Pope always wears white, but the garments worn by rabbis on particularly solemn occasions are also white). The purifying characteristics of white find, among other things, prosaic applications. In hospitals, whiteness is a guarantee (only mental) of asepsis. In private furnishings, hygienic white imposed itself, on an industrial scale, with the advent of kitchen appliances. For these artifacts, first and foremost functional, but with highly accentuated hygienic symbolism, the emancipation from white (due to factors of fashion and market competition) has come about after several decades of emblematic monochromatism. It is not surprising, after the preceding assumptions, that in the political world white is the color appropriated by the Christian-Democratic parties: in other terms, parties orientated towards a vision of the world in which the protection of life is paired with an ideology of spiritual and bodily purity. An orientation which translates, coherently, into taking position against abortion, divorce, and widespread sexual activity, and in favor of the right to life, virginity, religiosity, and morals. Elsewhere, when it takes aberrant forms — as in the robes of the Ku-Klux-Klan — it maintains, exalts even, the symbolic values of ("white") purity as compared to the highly feared risks of contamination ("black" as well as "red").

With regard to the third color of the triad, red, it is easy to find just as many convergences of significance. Traditionally, and following common sense, red is a warm, passionate, and aggressive color. These connotations are confirmed by clinical tests and validated by noted psychologists: exposure to red accelerates the heartbeat, alters arterial blood pressure, and increases the respiratory rate (Lüscher 1969, Steiner 1959). In Ndembu symbolism, red is above all associated with blood: the blood of slaughtered animals, the menstrual blood of women, the blood of witchcraft, the blood of murder or stabbing. In many other cultures, the sanguinary characteristic of red constitutes a semantic anchorage, even where that color is not particularly ritualized. In Chinese, the term "blood red" is more ancient than "red," and in some other languages there is a single term that signifies both. Since blood is indispensable for the existence of both men and animals, red also signifies life, but in a more dynamic and energetic sense than white. The emotions associated with red are those that "make the blood rush to your head" — desire, love, aggression, anger. In Puritan England, prostitutes were called "scarlets" and were branded by fire with a scarlet letter. In our times, too, "red light" locales and cinemas offer diverse opportunities to accelerate the heartbeat. So red stimulates passion, and not just through the floral message of roses. It is an impulse to move actively, to obtain results, a push towards vitality and power, on an instinctive and sexual level as well as in social life. The red uniforms used in armies have always had the capacity to fire up the spirits for combat and the practical advantage of not showing the blood shed on them, even if they did not offer any mimetic protection (*Color* 1980). Red, in other words, is the color of extroverted energy: the color of battle. That it was universally chosen as the standard color of revolutionary transformations by the world's Communist movements can certainly not be considered a coincidence, nor a circumstance justifiable simply in relation to some specific historical episode. No other color, in fact, turns out to be more pertinent to an ideology of struggle, social clashes, or violent changes in the course of history provoked by hot-blooded, passionate movements like those of the Communists, especially in the incandescent phases of a revolution. Used in its plural form, as in the title of a recent film, *Reds*, and also in street language, the term designated by this color acquires a very particular semantic density: deferring immediately, almost brutally, to images of a physical type and to socio-political stereotypes in which the characteristics of redness and the hypostatic characteristics of Communism become mingled.

2.2 Other Colors, Other Ideologies

Semantic coherence with ideological orientations is easily traceable in the case of other colors, too. The characteristics of blue as a color that transmits sensations of freshness, distance, calm, and peace were propounded by Goethe in his well-known *Theory of Colors* (1810). In nature, blue is quite rare in the animal and vegetable kingdoms, but the unbounded expanses of sea and sky are analogical terms of great evocative power, which orientate the significance of the color. The heights of the skies and the depths of the seas, the sense of the infinite that one feels when contemplating them, besides having a pacifying effect on the central nervous system, confer to blue values of a spiritual nature. When blue assumes greater chromatic fullness, as the sky does in the softness of the evening, it accentuates the values of tranquility, intimacy, and intensity of feelings (Arnheim 1974, Klee 1956). The negative aspects of this color emerge when some of its connotations are excessively accentuated: freshness becomes coldness, calm becomes isolation and solitude. The favoring of blue is always an indication of a preference for tranquil, orderly, and trouble-free environments in which events proceed softly, along more or less traditional lines. It is no coincidence that this color has always been connected with royalty and nobility. In ancient Greece and Rome blue represented Zeus and Jupiter. In more recent times, Western nobles professed to have "blue blood." The noble connotation of this color was further confirmed with the creation in 1348 of the Order of the Garter, the highest English knightly order, by Edward III, from which was born the use of the term "blue ribbon," as a badge of excellence in a specific field (*Color* 1980). Blue is, therefore, fundamentally a conservative color and, in fact, has been appropriated by the Monarchic political parties. In this context, it should not be surprising that in the present century blue has found an apparently contradictory diffusion in the "blue overalls" of the working class. Beyond functional considerations (resistance to dirt, etc.), it is easy to perceive how, in many cases, the providing of blue garments to the working class contributed through their stimulation of tendencies to a pacifying calmness, to the containment of conflictual inclinations — which would certainly have been exasperated by the use of red overalls.

Blue's complementary color, yellow, transmits very different and sometimes opposing values. Its closeness to the optical effects of daylight gives it stimulating qualities that produce feelings of warmth, radiation, optimism, and joy. Kandinsky observed that, contrary to blue, which seems to recede from the observer, yellow gives the impression of closing in, which is why a light-blue room seems larger, while a yellow room seems smaller than it really is (Kandinsky 1912). Yellow is associated with the pleasant warmth of the sun, and psychologically expresses the relaxation related to dilation. The thrust of the color yellow is, in any event, active, orientated optimistically towards the future. The positive values of yellow are to be found in the stimulating powers of many artifacts of this color. Nevertheless, yellow has a notable instability with respect to both its psychological effects and its chromatic values. Splendidly shiny when associated with gold, it becomes dull and "dirty" when it assumes greenish tones. The "yellowing" of white and other colors is often viewed as a form of degeneration, and the negative ideology of the "yellow race" is an indication of this sensation. The tendency to degeneration is probably at the root of the conventional way of representing Judas with yellow garments adopted in medieval paintings. As a treacherous color, yellow was imposed on the Jews, traitors to Christ, both in the Middle Ages and in the Nazi era. For many centuries, yellow has also been the color of sickness — epidemics of plague on board a ship are signaled by a yellow flag. These connotations of instability, perfidy, and pathology explain why, in the political world, yellow has seen very few forms of appropriation. Yellow (golden) was adopted as an auspicious and regal color in the Chinese Empire; but in the West those "yellow unions," sold out to the owners or, in any case, inclined to suspicious ideology, are a sufficiently eloquent example of the reasons for a distancing from this color.

On the other hand, the blending of yellow and red, in other words orange, seems to unite the energetic values of both colors. The analogical terms, provided mainly by the sun at sunset and by fire, induce perceptions of expansion, vitality, and extroversion, often connected with values of a sexual nature. In recent times, this color has been adopted as the emblem of the neo-religious movement of Bhagwan Rajneesh, whose followers for many years dressed only in the "colors of the sun," and whose ideology was founded to a great extent on the evolutive sense of very liberal sexual practices. It is noteworthy that the elimination, decreed by the guru at one point, of the obligation to wear orange coincided with a notable attenuation of the drive to find the path of spiritual elevation through sexuality. The abandonment of the color was, therefore, accompanied by a clear — and semantically significant — ideological turnaround.

Cases of equally telling semantic relevance can be found for any other color in practically every social environment. The social use of an "uncolorful" color such as grey, for example, is of remarkable interest. Psychologically, grey is a neutral color, totally lacking in energy, but which nonetheless represents a border, a demilitarized zone, a separation between interests and contrasting forces — like the symbolically grey Berlin wall. Grey implies non-involvement, non-participation, and the tendency to do what has to be done in a mechanical and artificial fashion (Lüscher 1969). It is therefore not surprising that this color is so often employed in banks and many other public institutions (post offices, ministries), for whom in fact it is more important to affirm values of neutrality and anonymity than to participate emotionally in the lives of the citizens. An "executive" propension for the correct but impersonal treatment of operations is therefore the principal representative content of grey, both in the chromatic codes of furnishing and in artifacts in general; it is no coincidence that this color is often preferred by managers and executives in their personal choice of clothing (the classic "grisaille"), accessories (grey umbrellas, briefcases, and suitcases), and cars (silver-grey cars).

2.3 In Particular: Green/The Greens

The color green merits special attention because of the fact that it gave its name to an important collective movement from the outset. The coherence between the color and the movement is evident to all on a basic level of significance: green is the color of vegetation, that is a large part of the world of nature; and the protection of nature is ideologically the principal anchoring of the Greens in all countries. But, if one enters more fully into the merits of the symbolic values of the color green, it is possible to find a much more complete and profound semantic pertinence to the ideology of this movement.

Like blue, which it contains, green determines a lowering of stimulations and produces a sense of peace. The relaxing qualities of this color, well known since antiquity ("the emerald delights the sight without tiring it," commented Pliny) are still exploited in clinics and all other situations in which there is a desire to create a calming environment. The psychological condition connected to green is not, however, devoid of energy; it is denoted specifically as a state of "elastic tension." That is, in psychological terms, a will to operate in a flexible manner but with perseverance, tenacity, and a notable propensity to resist changes (Lüscher 1969). Green, in other words, activates a tension that checks all forms of excitability, inducing reactivity to events in the name of immutable principles — an attenuated but stubborn form of reaction, symbolically isomorphic to the apparent pliability of plants. As such, it is not difficult to recognize in these prerogatives of the color the general ideological values and even some of the behavioral modes that characterize the Green movement. The grand pacifist option is, in fact, one of the basic ethical credentials of the entire range of the movement. The quest for spiritual tranquility or greater harmony in one's existence and in relations with other forms of life are other fundamental values that inspire the political objectives of protecting the environment. Beyond this, the movement's forms of action — passive resistance, bloodless manifestations, life options that favor models of traditional-style habitat, work, nutrition, and social life — express in a thousand ways the will to oppose the logic of socio-productive developments which appear aberrant through flexible but stubborn forms of strife. It is interesting to note that the negative values of the color may also have a relevant connection with the social role of the Green party. Many of the repulsive implications of green derive from the fact that this color is never found in the human body, unless it is covered with bruises, or infected, or dead. Moreover, in the animal kingdom, green is the color of reptiles — lizards, snakes, crocodiles — animals which inspire horror in many people. A proof of this is the universal tendency to imagine dragons, monsters, extraterrestrial aliens, and all forms of strange and foreign creatures with green, scaly skin: beings that are "out of this world," characterized by a total terrorizing unpredictability, which is also that of reptiles. Furthermore, in the political arena, examples of the anomaly and unpredictability of the Greens are not lacking. However, their capacity to instill terror is moderate. But more than a few politicians hesitate to form alliances with the Greens from fear of getting too near to a strange political animal that could turn out to be a "viper in one's bosom."

3 Monochromaticism and Ideological Thought

The more marked the tendency to a monochromatic option, the more apparent the ideological adherence to the semantic fields evoked by colors. In the political world, as we have seen, the anchoring to a single color is a rather significant indication of ideological orientation. In the world of artifacts, the same principle is valid in all cases where the choice of a single color is not transitory and is motivated not by technical-productive necessities but by symbolic or conventional factors.

3.1 The Ideological Power of Single Colors

The fact that the use of the reference color generally grows in proportion to the degree of ideological fervor tends to confirm what has been said. A notable and clear example is provided by the cultural revolution in China, and the coinciding manifestations of adhesion to Maoist ideology in Western societies. Red, as is well known, is the color of the flag of socialist countries of all orientations, and regimes with revolutionary ambitions of very different natures and weights are attracted by it. But the symbolic power of red is such that many of the regimes based on more pragmatic ideologies are careful not to over-use it. Conversely, in the cultural revolution, a movement characterized by extraordinary militancy and a very strong tendency to ideological extremism, red was subjected to hyperbolic use. Beyond the glorification of the "little red book," the propagandistic materials that came out of China in those years (in the form of illustrated magazines and booklets) offered images in which the spread of red was consistently the essential semantic key: in the agricultural communes, the factories, the schools, everywhere, there was a triumph of red flags, red banners, red scarves, red badges, red drapings. The ideological contagion of Maoism did not attenuate its monochromatic thrust when it passed to the West. In Italy, France, and England as well, those who shared doctrines and political principles of the cultural revolution draped themselves in red cloth, giving way to an iconography (but also a form of militant action) strongly immersed in redness. In successive phases, after the period of revolutionary rapture, the return to more moderate ideological positions, both in China and the West, brought about − in a perfectly consequential manner − a net redimensioning of the symbolic role of this color, subsequently used in more sober forms and quantities.

Another case, of another scope but equally exemplary, is the adoption of a clothing artifact with high symbolic power, like blue-jeans, by the masses of Western youth. The predominance of jeans − blue in color or, more exactly, blue denim, which is equivalent to indigo − was more or less the absolute in youth fashions for all of the 1960s and 70s. The reasons for such success were numerous and should be ascribed − beyond functional reasons (the garment's practicality) − to diverse motivations of a symbolic nature. There is, in fact, no doubt that jeans satisfied a need (common to the first hippies and to the protestors of the 68-generation, to the counterculture groups, and to the ecology groups) to adhere to a nonconformist fashion of simplicity, which was attested by both the raw, squared-off form and the hard and tough-to-manage material. But blue-jeans served as a symbolic reference from a color standpoint as well, and for years, from the belt down at least, they held a real chromatic monopoly. On a semantic level, the responsiveness of indigo to youth values can be seen in relation to traits common to differing ideologies: if one must identify a common ideological denominator for the 68 militants, the counterculture movements, the neo-religious groups, the ecologists, and all the other jeans wearers, it is probably to be found in a state of removal from the normal routine of existence, geared to a search for values and meanings that were, in the end, ethical or spiritual. In other terms, an ideal dimension, which is one of the principal semantic contents of blue (as the color of the sky and the sea), and which is even more enhanced in indigo (as the color of the infinite). The capacity of blue-jeans to signify chromatically these values has never been explicit, but this does not mean that it has not been effective. The blue denim of jeans has managed — and it is the only color to have done so (and in significant semantic terms) — to cross the lines between groups and experiences primarily marked by different colors (the psychedelic rainbow, the red of contestation, the green of ecologists, etc.). Worn as a "base" for diverse models of dress, jeans did not lose their symbolic power as long as they were worn en masse by young people, and as long as they retained their monochromatic hue.

The predilection for a single color tends to have precise meanings in the business world too. For decades, Coca-Cola used a flaming red as the fundamental color of their trademark and all their packaging to underline the dynamic, vital, and extrovert qualities of their product. The company philosophy fully reflected it, with its values of aggressive development and expansion on a planetary level. It was not by accident that, in the 1970s, the image of Coca-Cola in the perception of the European left was easily superimposed on that of violent, abusive Yankee imperialism, of which the drink became a symbol (to the point that many militants refused to consume it, for purely political reasons). If the aggressiveness of red strongly expressed the company's ideology, it is interesting to note that, more recently, there has been a net change which serves as a form of verification. The market launch of an energetically "deprived" product like Diet-Coke, intended to satisfy the new nutritional, dietary, and cultural needs of the consumer, brought about a desertion of the color red for the first time: the new product has a white packaging, which serves to distinguish it from the traditional one and at the same time confers a more aseptic, moderate image, which responds to a newly reacquired "virginity" on the part of the company.

3.2 Polychromatic Dispersions

Nothing evidences the particular relationship between single colors and ideology better than the inverse proof, which consists in noting the difficulties ideological thought has in maintaining coherence in a polychromatic context. For this reason, all social organizations with a strong ideological orientation have tended to repress expressive liberty on a chromatic level. And for this reason, too, many breaks with ideological, cultural, and social molds were manifested by the provocative and unexpected use of color. Starting with the scandal created by the Impressionists, with their desecration of the pictorial and chromatic conventions of their time, the world of art — and not it alone — was turned upside down numerous times by the artists' propensity for a freely creative and advanced use of color (Albers

1975, Gombrich 1966). In more recent times, the social norms of quiet living were suddenly sent into a state of crisis by the radical subversion of the color code practised by the psychedelic movement in the mid-1960s. The discovery of fantastic worlds of color encountered through the use of drugs, and the wave of Orientalism connected with the youthful fashion of "the trip to India," brought about marked polychromatic influences in ways of dressing, making oneself up, and furnishing one's home: the streets of Western cities were full of young people dressed in Afghan clothing, saris, kaftans, African and Indonesian skirts, or folk costumes in general; in many homes, vividly colored Indian cotton prints covered beds or hung on walls, while oriental carpets purchased abroad multiplied on floors. The impact of these tendencies on the existing social order, while fundamentally non-violent (at least in the attitude and intentions of the "flower children"), still had an inevitably disintegrating character — which the most conservative condemned as a degeneration of social customs or a symptom of moral depravation. In effect, the psychedelic revolution expressed considerable need for change at the level of freedom of behavior, and the unconventional use of color was its main vehicle in those years; no one could tell what a model employee would end up thinking or doing if he started to wear a fluorescent violet shirt instead of the classical white one. It should be noted that, even with its antibourgeois charge, the peculiar propensity to liberate colors typical of the psychedelic period did not translate into a new, recognizable ideology. The "alternative" ideologies solidified only towards the end of the decade, when each group had already chosen and adopted "its" color from the polychromatic kaleidoscope. The difficulty ideologies encountered in surviving in a polychromatic context is further confirmed if one considers what happens in other social environments where the variability of colors plays a crucial role. This is the case of advertising and fashion: inevitably highly colored worlds, but ones in which colors are not given the chance to deposit, become fixed, or to find a stable anchoring with regard to imagery. In advertising, horses can be white, black, or brown, but also pink, blue, or silver; and the same applies to any other image or symbol. In the fashion world, the rule of combinations imposes the continual alteration of colors in a game in which total reversibility is the rule — as long as this season's colors are not the same as last season's. Although it is certainly possible at any time to find in advertising and fashion the reflection of prevailing social models — Goffman (1979) demonstrated this prominently for advertising — nonetheless these are two structurally un-ideological systems in the sense that they are substantially indifferent as to what ideologies run through them: in advertising as in fashion, any value or idea (including "revolutionary" ones) finds a place, perhaps because they circulate in a weakened form, as a simulacrum of the original idea. For this reason these systems can accept, and carry to extremes, the total chromatic unpredictability for which they are noted. All colors are acceptable, and nothing stops their completely free circulation, certainly not ideology.

4 Changes in Tonality and Saturation

The capacity to transmit pertinent semantic values and contents can be found not only in the principal colors, but in the various chromatic graduations of a single color as well. In other words, the ideological vectors and social significance of artifacts tend to join up, in a notably coherent way, with the variations in tonality and saturation of colors. Naturally the chromatic code is quite complex and subject to methods of appropriation that depend in part on geographical and cultural contexts: it is well known, for example, that the more vivid colors are more widespread and appreciated in countries illuminated by the sun, while in the colder countries colors with dull tones are preferred. This does not prevent the translating of color graduations into densely significant forms of expression covering large cultural areas.

4.1 Pastel Hues or Shocking Pink

For a long time, the traditional bourgeois environment could not tolerate anything but pastels: beige, mauve, cream, light blue, and pale green, in an almost infinite range of tones, all linked by the discreetness of shades and nuances. This traditional stage, notes Baudrillard, is that where colors are rejected as full values: the stage of "pastelized" color — in clothing, wallpaper, curtains, bedclothes, cars — in other words, where a color is deprived of its violence and of its instinctive strength, to become instead a symbol for dignity, removal, and moral standing (Baudrillard 1968). As a matter of fact, it took decades and a world war to arrive at the social acceptance of a loud and "vulgar" color like shocking pink, which became popular in women's clothing at the beginning of the 1950s. Worn in dresses of taffeta or shiny satin, in solid colors or polka-dots, shocking pink was like a punch in the stomach for the conventions of elegance and sobriety that had reigned up until then. The exaggerated, aggressive tone of this color, its obvious exhibitionist intentions, made it very different from the tenuous pastel pink or peach considered so proper for young ladies' apparel at the start of the century and in the 1930s. In fact, shocking pink expressed precise values of breaking away from the bounds of a moralistic and misogynous society — even at the cost of an almost caricatural redesigning of women's image.

Starting in the 1950s, running parallel with the development of techniques in coloring plastic materials, bright colors began a progressive internal penetration of homes, and later of the workplace. Fire-red kitchens, sky-blue couches, canary-yellow chairs, bottle-green doors became the visible manifestations of the surpassing of a global order (bourgeois), which followed the affirmation of new social subjects without memories, without traditions, without style: the television generations. Pastel colors are now "old fashioned" and remain only in the homes of the elderly or in the furnishings of traditionalist institutions — public offices, universities, banks, insurance companies, restaurants, major hotels, etc. — or are recuperated by young couples as a distinction, but in a "retro" key. Conversely, bright colors seem designed to express the modern first of all. The technical perfection of the new synthetic colors makes them not very evocative of the authentic colors present in nature, and, in any case, their insistent use often produces hyper-realistic effects. As such, in the environments where their use is more or less obligatory — as, for example, in the furnishings of advertising agencies — their ideological intent is obvious: to signify the vitality, creativity, anticonformism, and the disenchanted pragmatism of the institution and those who work for it.

4.2 Desaturated Ideologies

To deepen or lighten the intensity of a color is a choice full of consequences in the political arena as well. The most evident verification again concerns red: adding white accentuates its lightness, but the resulting color — pink — is tied to another ideology: social democracy. It is a desaturated ideology, in relation to communism as pink is to red — in other words, one which is in attenuated, softened terms. From another viewpoint, it could be said that social democracy combines red values (recalling the traditions of struggle of the worker's movement) with white values (protection of the right to life and morality), giving birth to a system of intermediate pink values (protection of civil rights of those who live and work).

The lightening of other colors tends to produce equally determining effects. The addition of white to black, giving grey, seems inadmissable to those who identify themselves with the funereal values of the extreme right. In fact, that many para-fascist parties in Western countries have become bourgeois has caused, in the last decades, their descent into greyness. But the beginning of every extreme type tends to be accompanied by a return to the liturgy of blackness (experienced with some pleasures but also with embarassment by the grey representatives of the official right).

In the case of green, there have been no attempts yet to deviate ideologically in a way which relates to color alterations. The green of the Greens is a single color, or at least we imagine it this way: well saturated, neither too light nor too dark. One of the reasons for this is that, if it were too light, its power to evoke the splendor of nature would be weakened; and, if it were too dark, it would inevitably tend towards "poison green," no longer recalling the solution of hope but the solution of suicide.

5 Conclusions

With respect to the thesis put forward in this paper, the many examples mentioned do not have the benefit of proof. Nonetheless, they converge in a sufficiently marked way so as to render the connection between colors, artifacts, and ideologies non-aleatory. The capacity of colors to "signify" is not in question: most authors concur on this point. The problem is whether their significances correlate to an appreciable extent with the ideological vectors and the social sense of the artifacts. The aim of this paper was to point out that this correlation — without being truly systematic — is strong, and has varied explanations. Doubtless it is possible, and even easy, to find examples to the contrary — but they are fewer in number. Moreover, if, as was mentioned, colors are symbols, they escape the non-contradiction principle. What is essential is to verify the presence of important elements of analogy or isomorphism between colors and ideological phenomena. These elements seem to exist, and to deny this would require providing reasons for a surprising series of semantic parallels.

If one agrees that the observed correlation has a value, it follows that it may be possible to use a chromatic code as an instrument for analyzing social matters. In both the political field and in the world of production, preference for a certain color then becomes a densely informative signal, permitting us — eventually — to predict the value connotations of yet non-existent social subjects, or of those taking their first steps. The Grey, Yellow, or Violet parties, in other words, if they existed, would find it difficult to elude the significances that go deep down to the distant roots of each color.

References

Albers, J. (1975): *Interaction of Color*. New Haven, CT: Yale University Press
Arnheim, R. (1974): *Art and Visual Perception*. Berkeley, CA: University of California Press
Baudrillard, J. (1968): *Le système des objets*. Paris: Gallimard
Berlin, B. and P. Kay (1970): *Basic Color Terms: Their Universality and Evolution*. Berkeley, CA: University of California Press
Birren, F. (1963): *Color. A Survey in Words and Pictures*. New York: University Books
Brusatin, M. (1983): *Storia dei Colori*. Torino: Einaudi
Color (1980): Marshall Editions
Durand, G. (1969): *Les structures anthropologiques de l'imaginaire*. Paris: Bordas
Goethe, J. W. (1810): *Die Farbenlehre*. Tübingen
Goffman, E. (1979): *Gender Advertisements*. Cambridge, MA: Harvard University Press
Gombrich, E. H. (1966): *The Story of Art*. London: Phaidon Press
Jung, C. G. (1912): *Wandlungen und Symbole der Libido*. Leipzig—Wien: F. Deuticke
Kandinsky, W. (1912): *Über das Geistige in der Kunst*. München: R. Piper
Klee, P. (1956): *Das bildnerische Denken*. Basel: B. Schwabe
Lüscher, M. (1969): *The Lüscher Color Test*. New York: Random House
Steiner, R. (1959): *Das Wesen der Farben*. Stuttgart
Turner, V. (1967): *The Forest of Symbols: Aspects of Ndembu Ritual*. Ithaca—London: Cornell University Press

Photograph Analysis: A Method to Capture Organizational Belief Systems

Deborah Dougherty and Gideon Kunda

The survival of many organizations depends on how well they satisfy current customers and anticipate the needs of new markets. An important process for these organizations is how they perceive and make sense of information about customers, present and potential. Organization theorists are increasingly focusing on the cognitive and ideational aspects of this process. It seems that perception of environmental information departs from optimality and rationality. Limits to rationality constrain the breadth of perception (March/Simon 1958); social and cultural rationality guide comprehension (Perrow 1984); processes of social construction define both (Berger/Luckman 1966, Van Maanen 1979 b).

We propose that theories of customers arise in organizations and are used over time to systematically make sense of customer needs. These theories are sets of propositions used to select information about customers and interpret the data within an established framework of explanation (Kuhn 1962). Theories of customers also guide action (Argyris/Schon 1978, Beyer 1981) and determine in part how organizations respond to market changes or develop new strategies. Organizations do not simply adapt to new markets. They also act out their theories of customers, so the theories can play a significant role in their survival.

1 Conceptual Background

Concepts similar to theories of customers concentrate on organization members' views of their own organization (Sproull 1981), or on overarching interpretive schemes that order all aspects of members' lives within the organization (Bartunek 1984), or on unconfigured beliefs about individual clients or ideologies of treatment in people processing organizations (Strauss et al. 1964, Kunda 1986). So, while the general idea of theories of action is not new, few studies concern how one organization views others, in particular customer organizations.

These studies suggest two main properties for our construct. First, the theories of customers are like causal maps or sets of decision rules that are developed socially over time (March/Olsen 1976, Weick 1979). Hedberg (1981) suggests that the real world provides the raw material of stimuli, but the environment is born only when the stimuli are processed through perceptual filters. Child (1972) points to the strategic choice organization members exercize over environmental conditions based on their interpretation of them. Second, the theories of customers are relatively enduring configurations of values and assumptions (Miles 1982, Schein 1985). According to Schein, cultural assumptions are so thoroughly learned that they come to be a stable element in group life, guiding perceptions, thoughts, feelings, and actions. These properties imply that theories of customers are facets of the organization's culture that both persist over time and reflect other aspects of that culture.

In this paper we explore some empirical evidence about theories of customers, and use these data to describe the theories in a sample of existing organizations. By comparing theories of similar customers held by competing manufacturers of the same products, we illustrate the unique emphases of each. Drawing from this evidence, we suggest some implications and additional research to extend our understanding of customer theories.

2 Methods

There are no clear guidelines on how to identify such tacit belief systems in organizations. Most of the techniques proposed by students of organizational culture involve lengthy interviews with organizational members, or participant observation, or extended contact with them in a clinical mode (Schein 1985, Van Maanen 1979 a). Theories of customers operate at an ephemeral, complex level of organizational life, requiring these more qualitative and natural language research techniques (Boulding 1956, Daft/ Wiginton 1979). However, the idiosyncratic yet enduring nature of these theories suggests that, for our exploratory purposes, theories should be compared over time and across organizations. A longitudinal and comparative design makes these intensive strategies prohibitive.

Theories are cultural in nature, so aspects of them would be embodied in cultural artifacts such as stories, documents, and tools (Martin/Siehl 1983, Trice/Beyer 1984). Content analysis of a cultural artifact that is similar across a sample of organizations over time would be an efficient yet valid research strategy (Holsti 1968). We chose annual reports as the texts to analyze since they have been useful in other studies (Bettman/Weitz 1983, Bowman 1976). They are comparable across organization because they are governed by Security and Exchange Commission regulations in the United States, and serve a common purpose, at least within an industry. Dougherty (1984) reviews the process by which annual reports are put together and concludes that managerial culture at least in part infuses their content, making them a valid data source for our construct. While the mission of annual reports is to present the organization in the best possible light to investors, there are fairly strict rules about proper disclosure, and organization members deliberately choose and carefully review their specific contents (Foote 1983, Graves 1982). These choices in turn are guided to some degree by the tacit organizational beliefs about the subject matter. It is this roundabout process of cultural infusion that makes an artifact an apt source of data about cultural phenomena. The results of this artifact analysis will point to cultural assumptions that can be explored more thoroughly with intensive strategies.

Most analyses of organizational cultural artifacts use written or verbal content as units of analysis (Martin/Siehl 1983). Annual reports typically contain several kinds of content, among them photographs of customers. These photographs, we think, reveal aspects of an organization's theory of its customers in a nonverbalized yet substantive way. Analysis of photographs is a small but growing approach to social research (Becker 1978). Goffman (1979), for example, uses commercial photographs from advertisements to decipher social meanings. He suggests that photographs are a powerful and condensed rendition of important social relationships. As meaning bearing narratives they are different, he says, yet no more contrived than many other communications. Organizations self-consciously display themselves and their relationships in their annual reports; they deliberately select photographs of customers to complement this display. The photographs tell a story about the meanings and assumptions of customers shared among organization members. In this study we examine the self-conscious displays of customer activities for the tacit theories of customers underlying them.

Because both our construct and our data source may be affected by organizational attributes and industry, we limited our study to similar firms in the same industry — computer equipment manufacturers. This industry has evolved rapidly through different eras of customers in the past ten years and provides considerable variation in just a short period of time. Customer needs for the immediate future are just emerging — "office automation" is the projected huge new market for all the manufacturers of computing equipment, but neither customers nor providers fully comprehend its meanings and ramifications. The new market for this industry is now in the process of enactment, and there is no "accurate" theory of customers at the moment which can be used as a standard to judge the theories we find.

The five largest computer equipment manufacturers who also have the most similar market mix comprise the sample. Within the sample we match on era of birth (Stinchcombe 1965) and on technology (Perrow 1970). Two older mainframe manufacturers — IBM and Burroughs — have been around for 70 and 100 years, respectively. Two minicomputers makers — Digital (DEC) and Data General (DG) — emerged in the last 30 to 20 years, respectively, initially to serve the highly technical and scientific niches. Now both also compete with all other firms in the industry for the new market. The fifth firm, Honeywell, combines the mainframe roots of the first pair with the engineering orientation of the second, and provides another lever of contrast for the data analysis.

Our sample limits the generalizability of results. The matched pairs, however, allow us to check some of the presumptions of our proposal. If the photographs in the annual reports reflect just style or "PR," we should expect only idiosyncratic variation among the five firms. If the photos reflect theories of customer organizations then, on the one hand, similar ecological conditions and technologies should generate structural similarities in theories of customers; we should find systematic similarities within the pairs of firms. On the other hand, unique cultural solutions should generate idiosyncratic theories; we should also find some differences within the pairs.

The data set comprises the 425 photographs of customers in the available annual reports of these five firms between 1975 and 1984. Table 1 contains details on the number of customer photographs from each organization in each year. It should be noted that these documents also contain photographs of the organization members, buildings, and emblems, which would be interesting data for other analyses. The annual reports from DG for 1975, DEC for 1977, and IBM for 1979 and 1984 were unavailable and so àre not included.

3 Data Analysis

The major analytical task was to develop a scheme for categorizing the data, one which would capture the essence of customer representations and also allow us to compare the organizations. We spent several weeks scrutinizing and discussing the photographs. Among the categories initially proposed are: concrete vs. symbolic nature of the photo; nature of the activity portrayed (complex, simple, craftsmanlike); where and how the computer is shown (at a work station, with customer's customer, all over the room, not shown); what is the customer employee's status and sex; what does the customer do; what is the nature of the product. In an iterative process (Bailyn 1977) these categories were tested to see if they clarified essential qualities across organization and across time. We finally settled on two broad descriptive dimensions for theories of customers, and nested within them themes and then quantifiable indicators. The two broad dimensions are: (1) the nature of the customer organization, and (2) the nature of the relationship with customers.

Themes (and indicators) for the nature of the customer organization dimension are:

tasks: what the customers' tasks are like (scope and enormity, social importance, technological complexity);

Table 1: Number of Photographs by Year and by Market Era

	DEC[1]	DG[2]	IBM	Burroughs	Honeywell	
1975	8	—	12	5	8	
1976	—	8	15	12	6	
1977	9	13	9	14	7	
1978	11	11	—	38	6	
1979	12	10	8	9	12	
1980	8	6	10	4	10	
1981	9	10	11	2	3	
1982	5	16	4	4	3	
1983	8	10	7	2	18	
1984	—	10	—	8	14	
TOTAL	70	94	76	98	87	425

[1] DEC's fiscal year runs from July 1 to June 30. Their 1975/76 (FY 76) annual report is listed in the 1975 row above, and so on for the rest of their reports.

[2] DG's fiscal year runs from October 1 to September 30. Their FY 76 (ending Sept. 76) is listed in the 1976 row above, and so on.

Market eras: 1975 – 1977 waning days of the mainframe era
                 1978 – 1980 minicomputer era, start of Japanese competition
                 1981 – 1982 microcomputer era
                 1983 – 1984 turmoil in market started in mid-1983

people: what the customers' employees are like (their hierarchical position, sex, functional location);

organization: how the customers organize themselves (networked, number of people shown, interaction).

Themes (and indicators) for the relationship dimension are:

mode: how the product fits in with the customer organization (customer's activity level, product's activities, does the product help);

location: where the product fits in (at work station, in control room).

Our category scheme possesses, we feel, face validity — an assertion that can be checked by examining our descriptions and our exhibits. Results of the indicators and themes corroborate one another in an expected manner, lending some construct validity. The indicators are straightforward categories for counting the photos and can be implemented in a reliable way. Each photograph was categorized two times for each of the 20 indicators, and any discrepancies were analyzed.

To provide a more complete synopsis of the persistent aspects of each company's theory, we contrast descriptive summaries around the dimensions and themes. The descriptions are complemented with sets of photographs that compare portrayals of the same kind of customer. These comparisons in effect hold the customer constant, and highlight the unique views across the firms. These descriptive summaries are supplemented with quantified indicators, which provide a summary of the organizations' theories and are used to consider similarities and differences. Tables 2 through 6 show the proportion of the total number of customer photographs over the 10 years of annual reports that fit the particular indicator. We also performed Friedman's tests (nonparametric analyses of variance) on all of the indicators to examine the stability of the firms' relative ranks over time. Because one càn expect some variation from year to year in the indicators for each firm due solely to shifts in style, we blocked the 10 years into 4 market eras for the analysis. The market eras were established independently of the data from industry analyses in Value Line's *Surveys and Reports* and reflect the preeminence of different kinds of customer needs. Data from the two or three years of each era were averaged together, and then the firms' relative ranks within each era were determined. The Friedman's test assesses the stability of these ranks over time, and results are noted in each of the tables. Following discussion of the persistent aspects of each company's theory of customers, we analyze the changes over time in the way customers are perceived.

3.1 The Nature of the Customer Organization

Task: The task theme conveys what the organizations believe their customers do. Since the products are intended to facilitate the customers' work, this theme captures the most important aspect of the theories of customers in this sample. Our analysis of this theme is the most extensive. The other analyses then amplify particular facets of the task and illustrate how the themes come together for each organization.

In their photos of customers, DEC emphasizes the enormity and difficulty of customer tasks. The large, sweeping scope of the tasks is played up, almost celebrated. The tasks' importance and social contributions are prominent and the technological sophistication they require is highlighted. For DEC it seems that the customers' tasks consist of often enormous transformational processes. In the contrasting images of hospitals (Exhibit 1), for example, DEC shows a tense, dramatic moment in the operating room, and suggests a highly technical yet impersonal surgical process. Their portrayal of aircraft manufacturing (Exhibit 2) emphasizes the mammoth process of building the airplane and the anthill-like complexity that surrounds it. The semi-built plane in its entirety takes center stage while individuals seem to scurry about. And DEC's version of banking (Exhibit

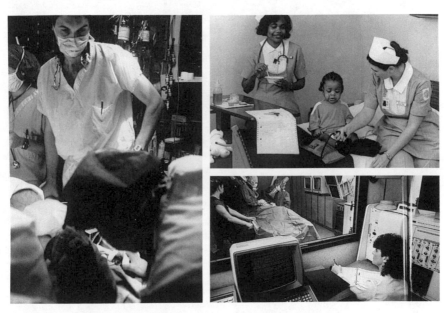

Exhibit 1: The Hospital Customer
Digital (DEC) — left, IBM — top right, Burroughs — bottom right

3) is an enormous panorama of presumably the entire banking process; the photo shows scores of people and suggests almost frenetic activity.

Like DEC, Data General features intricate technology, but they portray smaller pieces of a big job. A discrete step in the flow of action is emphasized in the DG photos, which generally suggest an array of inputs rather than a complex whole. DG's representation of aircraft manufacturing (Exhibit 2) at first glance looks much like DEC's. But note that the focus is on part of the job, on the wing rather than the whole plane, and the colossal complexity of DEC's photo is not here.

Exhibit 2: The Aircraft Manufacturing Customer
Digital (DEC) — top, IBM — bottom left, Data General (DG) — right

Exhibit 3 p. 193: The Bank Customer
Digital (DEC) — top,
Burroughs — bottom left, IBM — right

In contrast to the technological focus, both IBM and Burroughs capture the more ordinary, repetitive aspects of working. For IBM, people, their every day work, and their individual contributions dominate. The customers' tasks consist of people doing their often mundane work; the computing equipment is minimized. To illustrate, IBM portrays the hospital setting (Exhibit 1) by choosing a relaxed, simple check-up. Smiling nurses comforting a child replace DEC's awesome medical team. They highlight the service aspects and the human dimensions of hospital care. IBM's view of aircraft manufacturing (Exhibit 2) also differs notably, and it also exemplifies their focus on workers rather than on work. Here they show the plane partially hidden in the background and out of focus, an apparently finished product. The two people engaged in unspecified work dominate the view, and the task complexity is deemphasized. Again in Exhibit 3, IBM represents banking from the internal support perspective by focusing on a smiling teller discussing a bank book with a coworker.

For Burroughs, the computing equipment itself is central. The people are adjuncts to the task of information processing; data going into or coming out of the equipment dominate the scene. For example, in their image of the hospital (Exhibit 1) Burroughs closes in on the routine like IBM, but they feature information processing rather than service or people. We see medical records being stored in the foreground; the surgery in the background seems to be an afterthought. Also like IBM, Burroughs represents banking from the inside. But for Burroughs banking (Exhibit 3) occurs deep within the bowels of the Data Processing room, where we see a lone administrative worker almost engulfed by the computing machinery.

Indicators for the nature of the customer task in Table 2 support the qualitative description of the task theme of the five firms' customer theories. The proportion of photos taken outside conveys some sense of the enormity or scope of the customer's task. And the proportion of photographic space devoted to equipment versus people along with the number of words used to describe the customer's task suggests the technological orientation of the customer theory. The measures for all five remain fairly stable relative to one another over the ten year period on two of the three indicators, suggesting that at least these aspects of their customer theories have endured.

DEC depicts the out-of-doors most often of the five firms and they measure high on the two indicators of technological orientation. These data support our summary of their photographic emphasis on tasks which are large and technological in nature. Like DEC, DG discusses the customer's problems at some length in their captions, which implies that technical detail around the task is important to both (DEC's average dropped in their last annual report). But DG's more moderate measures elsewhere bear out their view of the customer task as a smaller technological step, and suggest that the scope and technology of the customer tasks are notable for them but not stressed. DG seems to view customer tasks as no nonsense, instrumentally focused activities.

Table 2: Nature of Customers Task[1]

	Scope	Technological Emphasis	
	photos showing out-of-doors**	equipment/ person ratio of 1 or more***	number of words in caption
DEC (n = 70)	36%	60%	66
DG (n = 94)	21	42	66
IBM (n = 76)	13	23	34
Burroughs (n = 98)	9	57	48
Honeywell (n = 87)	26	54	45

[1] Figures in the first two columns are the proportions of photos that fit the category of the column. The figure in the last column is the average of the annual averages of words per photograph in the caption.

** The Friedman's test (nonparametric analysis of variance) is significant at **$p = .05$ or ***$p = .01$. For those indicators noted, the relative rank of each company's measure was stable over the four market periods used — see Table 1 for details.

IBM and Burroughs' measures on the indicators in Table 1 also complement their photographic emphases. In keeping with their focus on the immediate aspects of the task, both show the out-of-doors in a low proportion of their photos (13% and 9% vs. 36% for DEC). But IBM is distinguished both from Burroughs and the rest of the sample by the technological indicators. The company plays down technology: only 23% of their photos display a high equipment ratio vs. 42% to 60% for the others. By averaging just 34 words (vs. 45 to 66 for the others), their captions provide only a layman's notion of the customer's activities. The routine, nontechnical tasks of everyday working that are also somehow vital to the organization fill IBM's photos. On the other hand, Burrough's high equipment focus illustrates their emphasis on the hulking, boxlike mainframes and data storage devices over the people who operate them.

Honeywell's measures on the task indicators all fall roughly into the middle of the ranges for the sample. Their proportions of photos of the outside and with high equipment ratios both are relatively high.

People: Table 3 summarizes indicators of the customers' worker characteristics and their functional location within the organization. These provide some sense for who the customers' workers are seen to be and for what they do. Two of the three location indicators are stable over time, but the companies' relative emphasis on the office setting is shifting. Neither of the two worker characteristics remains statistically significantly stable for all five firms because Burroughs and Honeywell have shifted in the recent market era — Burroughs away from the office setting and Honeywell into it. Both indicators of worker characteristics, however, highlight the firms with extreme measures.

Consistent with their focus on the transformational processes, DEC portrays customers' workers as part of the technological core of the organization. They are predominantly male, usually very masculine, casually dressed outdoors types, and often professionals. DG likewise emphasizes males, but for them the customers' workers are more often nonprofessional skilled laborers or office workers.

IBM portrays males only and the professional level the least of the 5 firms. Rather, they emphasize customers' workers who serve their customers — the workaday boundary spanners of salespersons, retail clerks, and service workers. These kinds of workers match IBM's presentation of the customer's task as a simple yet important part of a larger whole. Burroughs stands out in its office emphasis — a natural habitat for the predominant task of administrative information processing. The apparently happy female workers of IBM's hospital and banking images (Exhibit 1 and Exhibit 3) epitomize their depiction of customers' workers. The data handlers of Burroughs' photos in the same exhibits typify their view of customers' workers. Honeywell again falls in between with a moderate to high emphasis on males and a high emphasis on professionals.

Organization: Table 4 summarizes indicators of work organization in terms of task complexity, number of people, and degree of interaction. The five organizations do not hold their relative ranks on any of these indicators. To the degree that the indicators adequately capture the theme of customers' organization of work, it seems that this theme has changed the most in the theories of customers for this sample. But the company with the extreme score stands out so these indicators contribute some additional understanding.

DEC typically shows complex networks of activities, featuring the linked interdependencies of man and machine. A majority of their photos portray

Table 3: Nature of Customer's Workers[1]

	Worker's Characteristics		Functional Location		
	only male in photo	only managers/ professionals in photo	serving their customers**	in the factory*	in the office
DEC (n = 70)	51%	41%	10%	16%	13%
DG (n = 94)	44	24	7	18	22
IBM (n = 76)	29	16	36	11	24
Burroughs (n = 98)	34	23	8	4	37
Honeywell (n = 87)	39	39	7	15	14

[1] Figures in all columns are the proportion of photos that fit the category of the column.
 * Friedman's test p = .1
** Friedman's test p = .05

Table 4: How Customers Organize their Work[1]

	Complex[2]	Number of People Shown			Interaction Between Workers
		1	2−4	5 or more	
DEC (n = 70)	53%	17%	41%	37%	26%
DG (n = 94)	7	24	42	13	21
IBM (n = 76)	7	33	53	10	41
Burroughs (n = 98)	8	36	45	11	29
Honeywell (n = 87)	5	18	61	9	43

[1] Figures are the proportion of all photos that fit the category of the column.
[2] Defined as 3 or more people doing 2 or more separate but related tasks.

complexity. DG portrays a smaller piece of the work than DEC and suggests that the customers are organized in a linear sequence rather than a complex network. IBM and Burroughs both depict customers as single workers more often than the technologically oriented firms. IBM, however, also features interaction among dyads of workers as they carry out their seemingly well defined, craftsmanlike share of a larger unspecified task. In table 4, 53% of IBM's customers are portrayed as dyads or small groups, and 41% of them interact. In the contrasts of aircraft manufacturing (Exhibit 2), for example, the task complexity in the other firms' photos is replaced in IBM's by the interaction of two workers. For Burroughs, on the other hand, it seems that the equipment is first ponderously organized, and then the people are added, to work separately. For example, in Burroughs banking image (Exhibit 3) the array of machinery looks almost artful, but there is no hint that the lone worker is anything but an attendant.

Honeywell's customers are organized into small work teams who interact around the task. Their photos are proportionately higher than the rest in interaction and in 2 to 4 people. But few photos portray the workers interacting. Honeywell views its customers as independent, discrete projects rather than as a complex network or as sets of workers doing their jobs.

3.2 The Nature of the Relationship with the Customer Organization

We conceptualize "relationship" as the projected fit between the company's products and the customer organization. The two themes are mode — how the product fits, and location — where it fits.

First, on mode of fit, DEC's products seem to fit with the customers in an active mode. In the contrasting images of the industrial setting (Exhibit 4) we see DEC's computer participating directly in the production of automobiles. The terminal is right on the assembly line, a dirty blue-collar computer, one of the guys. This high level of activity on the part of both DEC products and customers suggests an engineering partnership between hands-on, busily working equipment and people. The location of fit complements the active mode of fit. A majority of DEC's computers are in complex data processing or futuristic control rooms, lined with large intricate machines and dotted with terminals. DEC sees itself at the technical core of the organization where the productive processes take place. DEC's image of the manager's office (Exhibit 5) indirectly corroborates this summary. The computer looks forlornly out of place in the otherwise machine bare office. The manager is bent over his desk while the machine sits alone on another table in the foreground, the screen facing away.

Exhibit 4: The Factory Setting
Digital (DEC) — left, IBM — top,
Burroughs — bottom right

DG, on the other hand, projects descriptions of what the customers do
rather than illustrations of their computer working with them to do it.
Their portrayal of the manager's office (Exhibit 5) shows the manager
intently engaged with the computer, but it is unclear what the computer is
doing. DG sees itself fitting into the flow of the task rather than doing the
job itself. DG much more often than DEC locates itself at a worker's
station, showing a much less imposing computer being used in part of a
larger task. They are not at the technological heart of the customer's
enterprise like DEC.

IBM suggests that they support the customers to perform their more
sedentary tasks on their own. In the manager's office setting (Exhibit 5)
IBM's manager smiles as he works in a relaxed manner. The caption
suggests he is carrying out easy-to-use accounting applications, and it is
vividly clear what the computer does for him. However, in the industrial
setting images (Exhibit 4) where physical activity would be expected, IBM's
representation seems awkward. The smiling female factory worker dominates the view and the computer is not in the picture. IBM has a helping,

facilitating relationship in contrast to the actively participating or task oriented ones of the minimakers. As both Exhibits 4 and 5 imply, they see themselves fitting in at the manager's or clerk's simple work station, carrying out administrative or support activities. To IBM this is the heart of the customer's enterprise.

Burroughs' customers and equipment lack almost all movement. Their image of the industrial setting (Exhibit 4) illustrates this. The computer is adjacent to the factory floor with no one operating it. The screen seems to display administrative applications rather than anything relating to production. Very little sense of a working relationship is projected; Burroughs simply provides an information processing installation. Burroughs locates its products at the computer's location, not the worker's. In their portrayal of the manager's office (Exhibit 5), we see a modeled display of the "office environment," with the bright green output on the computer

Exhibit 5: The Manager's Office Setting
Digital (DEC) — top left
Data General (DG) — top right
IBM — left
Burroughs — right

monitors dominating the posed managers. In fact, the managers look out of place.

Table 5 summarizes indicators of the mode of fit: it includes a measure of the customers' physical activity, and several measures of what the computer does for the customers. DEC's customers physically manipulate objects more than twice as often as any other firms' customers — in 43% of their photos vs. 4% to 18% of the others. Their computers are described in the captions as actually doing the work themselves over half the time. Like DEC, DG suggests that their products perform a high number of tasks in the captions — 2.3 tasks per caption on the average vs. 1.7 for the

Table 5: Relations with Customers: Mode of Fit[1]

	Customers actively manipulate objects***	What Product Does For Customer			
		computer does the work directly (in caption)**	number of different tasks (in caption)***	use of "help" (in caption)	computer output shown
DEC (n = 70)	43%	56%	2.7	10%	63%
DG (n = 94)	14	14	2.3	15	40
IBM (n = 76)	18	15	1.7	23	55
Burroughs (n = 98)	4	14	1.7	5	70
Honeywell (n = 87)	8	29	2.0	7	48

[1] Figures in columns 1 and 5 are the proportion of all photos that fit the category; in columns 2 and 4 the proportion of all captions; in column 3 the average of the yearly averages of separate tasks ascribed to the computer.
*** Friedman's test p = .01
** Friedman's test p = .05

Table 6: Relations with Customers: Location of Fit[1]

	At the Workstation**	In a Control or DP Room**	Office is Posed**
DEC (n = 70)	23%	51%	2%
DG (n = 94)	40	14	2
IBM (n = 76)	61	5	5
Burroughs (n = 98)	46	30	16
Honeywell (n = 87)	31	34	14

[1] Figures are the proportion of photos that fit the category.
** Friedman's test p = .05

two mainframers. But this figure is not complemented by high measures of activity in the other indicators. IBM uses the word "help" in their captions more often (23% vs. 15% to 5% for the other four) but measures relatively low in the indicators of how active the computer itself is. These figures bear out their facilitating rather than doing relationship. Burroughs' inactive or unmoving relationship with customers is demonstrated in their low measures on both the activity and the help indicators.

Table 6 summarizes three indicators of location of fit. DEC has the highest proportion of photos that show a control room or data processing room (51% vs. 34% to 5% for the others), and the lowest that show a simple work station (23% vs. 31% to 61%). The large proportion of fairly simple terminals at the worker's station (61%) characterizes IBM's relationship as a helper to the administrative and service personnel. Honeywell represent the office environment in modeled or posed form more often than the other three firms (Table 6: 16% and 14% respectively vs. 2% to 5%). Honeywell's fit is more indeterminable than the others — they show work stations and control rooms equally.

3.3 Configurations and Changes: Summary and Discussion

Each of the five organizations projects a distinct theory of their customer organizations that reflect both sub-industry niches as well as the unique character of each firm. The two pairs of matched organizations, DEC and DG, and IBM and Burroughs, are similar in many ways within the pair and distinct between the pair. There are changes in these theories, as one might expect from the changed products, customers, and uses in this industry in the short period of this study. However, the companies for the most part project stable views around at least several of the five themes.

DEC's customers are portrayed as complex networks, and as engineering oriented problem solvers. The customers' workers tend to be active, hard working males, professionals and technicians. Their tasks are large, socially important, and heavily technological. In just the most recent annual report some of the enormity has been replaced by equally formidable close-ups of laser beams and ore fusion apparatus. DEC may be closing in but the content of the work remains equipment/technology laden. Customers continue to be predominantly male (although this figure dropped for the most recent report). DEC continues to energetically contribute technical power and prowess to their customers' processes.

There are some changes in DEC's projection of how the customers organize their work and, relatedly, in where DEC fits into the customer organization. While the task complexity remains, the networking of separately related activities is gone from the past two annual reports. Fewer words are used to describe tasks, and the number of lone workers is up. And DEC shows their products less often in the control room, or at the work station, office or factory. So, while their task is fundamentally the same, DEC's theory of customers seems to be in flux around the themes of how their task is organized and how DEC's products relate to that task. DEC accentuates the overtly physical, technical, and active tasks, and underplays sedentary, people intense office type tasks. However, their rather strongly configured theory of customers is apparently loosening up in two of the five themes.

DG's customers have tasks which can be broken down into sequential steps. The work done by their customers continues to be technical but not as complex as that done by DEC's customers. The customers' workforce is, like DEC's, more male, but to DG they are skilled laborers and technicians, more plain folks, rather than professionals. Because DG's customers organize their work in discernable steps little interaction is necessary. DG's products fit right into a part of the process. There is little evidence of a major change in their theory of customers, but some aspects of the customers are shifting. Fewer panoramic outside views of cities and buildings are displayed, and more views of individuals at work stations. The indoors, work station types of settings are replacing the technological and industrial ones. Indoors versions of the skilled factory worker — more males in ties and fewer in hard hats — appear so the level of manager types has gone up. DG continues its emphasis on parts of a task, linear flows of work, on males, and on lone, noninteracting workers.

IBM persistently portrays its customers as service providers — clerical and secretarial workers, librarians, salespeople, policemen, and middle managers. IBM emphasizes individual performance and interaction around the immediate task. Rather than celebrate the enormous task like DEC, IBM celebrates ordinary people doing ordinary work. Their product is a friendly terminal and easy to operate, one that helps the workers get their jobs done. IBM fits into the "lo-tech" environment of service to customers, maintenance, and administration. Over the years IBM has steadily intensified its representation of certain facets of customers rather than abruptly change. They have increased their outside views and decreased their office shots, which suggests a broadening in their theory on scope and nature of the customers' tasks. More managers or professionals are portrayed, although 1983 returned to usual levels. Customers serve their customers even more. The most interesting shift is in organization of work. Fewer lone workers but more small groups appear, and interaction is shown more often. IBM seems to represent increased complexity by showing more workers interacting more often rather than by adding a backdrop of equipment.

Burroughs customers are processors of information — in the office, at the hospital, and increasingly at the military installation. The customers' workers are lower level administrators who don't interact much over their work. Their primary task remains data processing. It occurs much less often in the office setting since 1981 and more often in technologically oriented settings such as airport radar rooms. The proportion of all males has jumped while the proportion of professional level customers has declined — like DG these kinds of people match the same task in the new setting. Despite their new "working man" nature, the customers also remain inactive, perched at their work stations or in their control rooms reading output from the computers. Burroughs does discuss helping more often in their captions. Their portrayal of customers also focuses more on individual workers in the last several years. These shifts imply that their theory of customers has changed to include a more personal fit with the customer organization. Burroughs' transfer from a data processing room to new, more technological settings may mean that their theory is broadening its scope of customer applications. But they accentuate heavy information processing in these new settings.

Honeywell's customers monitor processes or control huge entities. Their tasks remain technological in nature, carried out by a relatively moderate amount of males. But the proportion of professional level workers has increased in recent years, and with it a sharp increase in small work groups interacting over the task. Honeywell represents itself as consultants to the customers' various and sundry discrete projects more often in recent years — thus the growing number of small groups of interacting professionals. However, the customers continue to be rather inactive physically despite the equipment laden nature of their work. Perhaps Honeywell's diversity in product lines across industries has limited any intense representation of particular customers' needs.

4 Concluding Comments

The photos of customers in these annual reports tell a fairly consistent story. Our data indicate that each of the five companies has a particular theory of their customer organizations which makes salient certain kinds of tasks, technologies, people, and relationships. We showed that many of the organizationally unique views have persisted over ten years, despite changes in both users of and uses for the computing products. As suggested in the introduction these theories can affect an organization's adaptation to environmental change. Organizations have been found by others to have strategic predispositions (Miles 1982), distinctive competencies (Schein 1985), and, from economics, comparative advantages that do not depend solely on marginal costs of production. To change effectively is to take advantage of the distinct competencies and to overcome any constraining predispositions. To do either of these, it is first necessary to know what the competencies and predispositions are. The theories of customers elaborated here represent one view of what these might be for the five firms of this study.

However, this discussion has only introduced the possibilities of theories of customers and of photographic analyses to find them. These findings must first be corroborated through additional research; intensive interviews, participant observation, and/or clinical analyses in these firms are necessary to support and clarify these preliminary results. Whether and how the theories filter information must also be established explicitly. The strength of such filtering relative to other organizational decision routines is an empirical question. It is also necessary to locate these theories in the organization. Do people throughout the firm operate with these theories? How strongly are they held? Such issues probably vary by organization. If so, perhaps there are structural constraints and contingencies that might help predict the differences. Beliefs about other aspects of the task environment should also be compared. Since the theories are part of the organization's culture, relations between them and other cultural manifestations should be explored.

A final note concerns our methodology. Analysis of these photographs has generated a rich initial understanding of these companies' theories of their customers. Such public representations are the essence of culture according to Geertz (1973). How other linguistic and graphic media portray patterned understandings, and how these patterns relate to the tacit knowledge of organization members, is an empirical question of particular importance to students of organizational culture. Content analysis in general is designed for the systematic analysis of communicative and symbolic behavior, and thus can be especially useful to the study of this underanalysed domain of organizing. We hope our findings at least suggest that much can be learned from the contrast of seemingly innocent photographs and the self conscious tales they tell.

References

Argyris, C. and D. A. Schon (1978): *Organizational Learning: A Theory of Action Perspective*. Reading, MA: Addison-Wesley
Bailyn, L. (1977): Research as a Cognitive Process. *Quality and Quantity* 11, pp. 97–117

Bartunek, J. (1984): Changing Interpretive Schemes and Organizational Restructuring: The Example of a Religious Order. *Administrative Science Quarterly* 29(3), pp. 355–373

Becker, H. S. (1978): Do Photographs Tell the Truth? *Afterimage* 5, February, pp. 9–13

Berger, P. L. and T. Luckmann (1966): *The Social Construction of Reality.* Garden City, NY: Doubleday

Bettman, J. and B. Weitz (1983): Attributes in the Boardroom: Causal Reasoning in Corporate Annual Reports. *Administrative Science Quarterly* 28(2), pp. 165–183

Beyer, J. M. (1981): Ideologies, Values and Decision Making in Organizations. *Handbook of Organizational Design.* P. C. Nystrom/W. H. Starbuck (Eds.). Oxford: Oxford University Press, Vol. 2, pp. 166–202

Boulding, K. (1956): General Systems Theory: The Skeleton of Science. *Management Science* 2, pp. 197–207

Bowman, E. H. (1976): Strategy and the Weathers. *Sloan Management Review,* Winter, 7, pp. 49–62

Child, J. (1972): Organizational Structure, Environment, and Performance: The Role of Strategic Choice. *Sociology* 6, pp. 2–22

Daft, R. L. and J. C. Wiginton (1979): Language and Organization. *Academy of Management Review* 4, pp. 179–191

Dougherty, D. (1984): Shared Comprehension and Organizational Viability. Paper presented at the Academy of Management, Boston, August

Foote, C. (1983): Put More Muscle in Your Annual Report. *Financial Executive* 49, March, p. 34

Galbraith, J. (1973): *Organizational Design.* Reading, MA: Addison-Wesley

Geertz, C. (1973): *The Interpretation of Cultures.* New York: Basic Books

Goffman, E. (1979): *Gender Advertisements.* Cambridge, MA: Harvard University Press

Graves, J. (1982): *Managing Investor Relations.* Homewood, IL: Dow-Jones-Irwin

Hedberg, B. (1981): How Organizations Learn and Unlearn. *Handbook of Organizational Design.* P. C. Nystrom/W. H. Starbuck (Eds.). Oxford: Oxford University Press, Vol. 1, pp. 3–77

Holsti, O. (1968): *Content Analysis for the Social Sciences and Humanities.* Reading, MA: Addison-Wesley

Kuhn, T. (1962): *The Structure of Scientific Revolutions.* Chicago: University of Chicago Press

Kunda, G. (1986): Ideology as a System of Meaning: The Case of the Israeli Probation Service. *International Studies of Management and Organization* 16, pp. 54–79

March, J. and J. Olsen (1976): *Ambiguity and Choice in Organizations.* Bergen: Universitetsforlaget

March, J. and H. Simon (1958): *Organizations.* New York: Wiley

Martin, J. and C. Siehl (1983): Organizational Culture and Counterculture: An Uneasy Symbiosis. *Organizational Dynamics* 12(2), Autumn, pp. 52–64

Miles, R. (1982): *Coffin Nails and Corporate Strategies.* Englewood Cliffs, NJ: Prentice-Hall

Mintzberg, H., D. Raisinghani, and A. Theoret (1976): The Structure of "Unstructured" Decision Processes. *Administrative Science Quarterly* 21, pp. 246–275

Perrow, C. (1970): *Organizational Analysis: A Sociological View.* Belmont, CA: Brooks-Cole

Perrow, C. (1984): *Normal Accidents: Living With High Risk Technology.* New York: Basic Books

Pfeffer, J. and G. Salancik (1978): *The External Control of Organizations: A Resource Dependence Perspective.* New York: Harper and Row

Sanday, P. (1979): The Ethnographic Paradigm(s). *Administrative Science Quarterly* 24(4), pp. 527—538

Schein, E. H. (1985): *Organizational Culture and Leadership.* San Francisco: Jossey-Bass

Sproull, L. S. (1981): Beliefs in Organizations. *Handbook of Organizational Design.* P. C. Nystrom/W. H. Starbuck (Eds.). Oxford: Oxford University Press, Vol. 2, pp. 203—224

Stinchcombe, A. (1965): Social Structure and Organizations. *Handbook of Organizations.* J. March (Ed.). Chicago: Rand McNally, pp. 142—193

Strauss, A. L. et al. (1964): *Psychiatric Ideologies and Institutions.* Glencoe, IL: Free Press

Thompson, J. (1967): *Organizations in Action.* New York: McGraw-Hill

Trice, H. M. and J. M. Beyer (1984): Studying Organization Cultures through Rites and Ceremonials. *Academy of Management Review* 9(4), pp. 653—669

Van Maanen, J. (1979 a): Qualitative Methods Reclaimed. *Administrative Science Quarterly* 24(4), pp. 511—526

Van Maanen, J. (1979 b): The Self, the Situation, and the Rules of Interpersonal Relations. *Essays in Interpersonal Dynamics.* Bennis et al. (Eds.). Homewood, IL: Dorsey Press

Weick, C. (1979): *The Social Psychology of Organizing.* Reading, MA: Addison-Wesley

Curing the Monster: Some Images of and Considerations About the Dragon

Burkard Sievers

> "The dragon was evolved along with civilization itself" (Smith 1919: 76).
>
> "The artefacts of culture can be understood as defense systems that help to create the illusion that we are greater and more powerful than we actually are" (Morgan 1986: 213).

1 On the Way into the Dragon's Cave

riting about and reflecting upon the dragon has become an ongoing venture for me since I decided to choose it as the object of my presentation at the Milano conference on corporate artifacts in 1987. Once I had allowed this creature to enter into my mind and had given it some space in my office it somehow began to crawl all over the place: dragons eventually were everywhere, in cartoons, in fairy-tales, legends, in advertisements, in churches, in mythology, in children's books. And the more I let my friends know what a curious creature I had in my mind, I received post-cards, newspaper articles and even a record with the famous song from Peter, Paul, and Mary: "Puff, the magic dragon." It is the story of little Jackie Paper who shared part of his childhood with Puff, the gigantic dragon, till he eventually left the dragon when it made way for other toys.

No later than when I first had listened to this song, I decided to play it at the beginning of my presentation which I was going to prepare. But when I did so, it happened that the sound of the small tape recorder was by far not loud enough for the auditorium. Then, to my big surprise, when I nearly had switched the music off, the people in the room suddenly began to sing the song of Puff, the magic dragon; first softly as if they didn't dare to trust themselves and then, the more they began to enjoy it, rather loud. Can you imagine, some hundred colleagues gathered in an auditorium of a famous Catholic University singing a song about the dragon like children? There it was, in the middle of the audience, the dragon!

The more I allowed the dragon to enter into my space, the more I made the experience that this creature allowed me to cross boundaries, time boundaries as well as cultural ones. Not only did I rediscover that previously in my life, as a boy-scout, there had been a time in which the dragon already had quite some significance for me as I identified myself with St. George, the hero. Very soon it also became obvious to me that the dragon not only is as old as mankind but more or less a universal creature which, despite its various meanings, can be found in nearly all cultures. Like the chimera, the centaur, or the sphinx, the dragon is a creature of the imagination. The question whether such an imaginary creature will be regarded as unreal or as real soon leads one into deeper areas of philosophy and of epistemology, in particular. Although at present there can be no doubt that the dragon is an artifact, created and brought into life through art, during previous millenia it often had the same reality as gods, angels, devils, ghosts, fairies, and other beings. Today we may be convinced that there is no such a thing as a dragon and that dragons never really existed, but nevertheless we are surrounded by countless symbolic representations which prove that there were times in which our predecessors considered dragons to be as real as either the particular hero who attempted to kill it or the horse he rode upon.

Over time, the more I tried to take the dragon seriously, the more I became confused with images and perceptions, previously taken for granted, of what reality was supposed to be. If, for example, according to contemporary Christian belief, the existence of God, the saints, and the angels is supposed to be real but not the existence of the great red dragon with seven heads and ten horns which is described in the Revelation of John (cf. Rosenberg 1956: 207 ff.), what are then the "criteria" to discriminate the real from the unreal? Similar is the case of St. George whose historic existence eventually was negated by the Church. What about all the good works which have been accomplished by thousands of Christians for his glory; are they less real after the annihilation of this saint? And if, on the other hand, the dragon will be regarded as a symbolization of a part of human reality which otherwise cannot be grasped or described, what then is that reality about? Is it a real reality, an unreal or even a false one?

But before I go further into what I came up with on my attempt to cure the monster it seems to be important to illustrate what I had in mind when, on the occasion of that conference, I decided to approach the dragon. This choice had to do with the fact that this was a SCOS-Conference in at least two ways. On the one hand, at the First International Conference of SCOS (Standing Conference on Organizational Symbolism) which I attended at Lund in 1984, the conference poster showed a beautiful fascinating dragon coming through the strong lines of an organigram.

Since then the dragon has become the "logo" of this network of social scientists, an autonomous work-group within EGOS, the European Group of Organization Studies; from 1985 to 1987 Dragon was the title of the

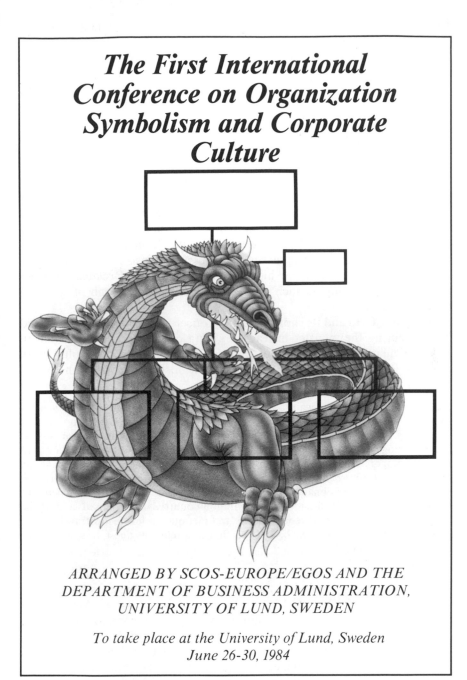

Figure 1: SCOS Poster, The First International Conference on Organization Symbolism and Corporate Culture

journal of SCOS. At the same time, my wish to become more concerned with the dragon was guided by the "slogan" of SCOS: "We do it for fun!" And as a matter of fact, quite some fun it was both searching for dragons as well as presenting part of my results on the occasion of the Milano conference.

It seems that what I came up with out of this particular search is twofold: it is a piece of research on the logo of a particular organization, but it also is the expression of how an organization member acts within the process of intersubjective constructions of reality and its meaning. As I cannot hide that I am a member of this particular institution the following results and reflections may also show how a particular SCOS-member used his own impact and authority to explain and describe what appears to him as a pursuable interpretation of organizational reality. As in any other organization such an individual interpretation seldom is a solipsistic one; it normally is rooted in the institutional history and tradition and related to other members representing as such either a mainstream approach of thinking or a more deviant one.

So far as SCOS and its short history is concerned, the notion propagated here of curing the monster instead of killing or taming it in itself and in this particular institutional context never was a prominent or revolutionary one. As Rein Nauta (1986: 6) states, in the history of SCOS there is a reversal of the ancient hero myth in which

the hero fights a struggle against a reality which is different from what he wants it to be ... . Reminding one of that fairy-tale written down by the Grimm brothers of the young man who travelled into the world in order to learn what horror was, at the beginning of SCOS some young and daring scholars went into academia not to fight the dragon, but to find him. Researching the dragon they enacted a revaluing of values (an 'Umwertung aller Werte' – a paradigm change), because they tried to use the treasure of rationality, of choice, of consciousness as an instrument for finding the dragon. On the road to the dragon-country, the promised land of life and understanding, we made some friends and met quite a few fellow-travellers ... . One interpretation of the ways of SCOS is that of a religious quest, in search of the truth of organization life.

"It is generally assumed," as P. O. Berg (1984: 4), the first chairman, put it, "that SCOS was created in the bar of Strathclyde Business School, the last evening of the EGOS 1981 Colloquium" in Glasgow. As a matter of fact, it was only a small group expressing their common interest in "organizational symbolism," using it somehow as a container for a possible broader methodological and interdisciplinary variety of organizational research. When after two smaller conferences in Exeter and Groningen the First International Conference was set up at Lund University in 1984, already more than 200 people from a whole variety of countries attended. Despite its increasing membership, SCOS has succeeded in remaining a network in its true sense over the years; it only has a very minimal organizational infrastructure and is primarily carried by its members' initiatives; it emphasizes "the importance of personal interactions in an open and nonevaluative atmosphere" (Nauta 1984: 7). Quite unusual or even superfluous for normal scientific associations, in SCOS "the shared attitudes of support and tolerance ... have left room for the individual, the spontaneous and the unpredictable performance" (Kreiner 1987: 17).

2 Draconology or the Science of Dragons: Some Facts and Figures

Before we begin the journey into the mythology of the dragon, its various images, and their symbolism, it appears appropriate to inspect some facts and figures through which the existence, quality, and dissemination of dragons may be proved. From such a "scientific" perspective enough evidence must be provided in order to confirm the truth that the dragon is a primeval, universal, and real phenomenon.

The dragon belongs to the wider family of snakes and serpents, as such it is much older than mankind. Contrary to men, dragons are creatures of chaos (*Redaktion...* 1985: 13). As can be learned from various accounts of the creation of the world, dragons have existed since the first days of the genesis.

Dragons are born from eggs which usually have the size of two man's fists. Especially during infancy their predominant living space is water; different species prefer lakes, swamps, rivers, or the seaside. At least for the Chinese version of the dragon, it can be proved that dragons take about 1500 years to grow up to their full length, another 500 years till their characteristic horns develop, and again another 1000 years till their wings are formed (*Redaktion...* 1985: 44). Descriptions of dragons were seldom accurate, because those who happened to meet a dragon were so scared that they could only remember one or the other of its horrible parts without any further perception of its gestalt (*Redaktion...* 1985: 95). Although it seems to be true that no one dragon equals the other (Mode 1983: 120), dragons predominantly consist of the following elements: the jawbones of a crocodile, the teeth of a lion, the wings of a bat, the legs of a lizard, the claws of an eagle, the body of a python, and the horns of a bull (*Redaktion...* 1985: 14).

Dragons are disseminated all over the world; detailed maps prove, for example, the dragon places in Middle Europe (*Redaktion...* 1985: 78 f., Vinycomb 1906: 79 ff.).

As Dickinson (1981: 75), for instance, indicates, there are at least 60 places in Europe which derive their names from the dragon, such as Drakenburg (Dragonburgh), Wurmlingen (named after a big worm which was the original Germanic word for dragon, as in *Lindwurm*), or Klagenfurt (a town in Austria which derives its name from the wailing which was heard when the town was destroyed by a dragon, a tragedy which is depicted by the huge monument in the town center).

From their historical evolution dragons can be classified into two main categories: the cosmic and the mythological dragons; the latter are often then subdivided into modern and psychic ones. Cosmic dragons cannot be regarded as animals in the literal sense, they were incarnations of the chaos, they are direct descendents of the Titanes who lived before time. Contrary to their predecessors, the modern mythodragons were natural creatures; they housed in caverns and canyons, curled around mountains and ancient mounds, leaving behind them stink and slime; they crawled through the woods and mixed with the ghosts of sources and rivers (*Redaktion...* 1985: 76). The psychic mythodragons, which seem to be the most interesting ones in the context of the symbolics of artifacts are inhabitants of the human inner world. As they often cannot be acknowledged as such, they have to

Figure 2: Matthäus Merian, sen.,
Merians Welt der Tiere, Nördlingen
(Greno) 1985

be projected into objects of the outer world (Steffen 1984: 7). — It seems to me that post-modern mythodragons can be neglected so far because they only are allusions to certain elements deriving from ancient styles.

As dragons nowadays are becoming more and more rare, the fact that SCOS has chosen the dragon as its emblem can be regarded as akin to the panda of the World Wildlife Fund. As for the panda, the days of the dragons are numbered; as it has no chance to survive in normal hunting-grounds, it not only has to be protected, but eventually will be bred in special zoological gardens. Perhaps one could even gain the Queen's husband, the Duke of Edinburgh, as honorary president of SCOS. As England has had St. George, who obviously was one of the predominant instigators of dragon killing, as its national saint for so many centuries, this could be an important act of reparation.

3 How to Cope with a Dragon?
Five Pragmatic Ways

Whereas the proof of the dragon's existence is more a matter for scientists or researchers, the question of how to handle a dragon leads us into the fields of scholars. As Cooper states, "the scholar cultivates the critical spirit of the 'humanistic sciences' " (Cooper 1983: 721) which "answer the central question of men's collective existence and of individual life history. Their themes are justice and freedom, violence and oppression, happiness and gratification, poverty, illness, and death. Their categories are victory and defeat, love and hate, salvation and damnation" (Habermas 1971: 96).

From such a broader perspective there are at least five predominant ways of treating a dragon:

1. The *heroic way:* "You have to kill him!"
2. The *magic solution:* "Kiss him!"
3. The *Chinese version:* "It is the emperor of wisdom and rain!"
4. The *science fiction approach:* "Ride him!"
5. The *lonely child solution:* "Let's be friends!"

Out of these five versions, the *heroic solution* of killing the dragon obviously is the predominant one in our western tradition. The magic creators of the SCOS logo around P. O. Berg have deliberately not chosen the image of the knight fighting the dragon because that would have given "too much power to the knight as being a symbol of the victory of the modern technocratic society over the primitive and instinctive dimensions of life" (Berg 1987 a). Another, obviously unconscious reason for their choice could have been that e. g. the image of St. George would have been too reminiscent of the Order of the Garter which then probably would have been in collusion with SCOS' predominant myth of an open network.

Although I favour such a creative attempt at organizational mythmaking, it appears to be important to elucidate a bit further the image of the dragon fight which as such is as old as mankind. The legend of St. George seems to be a good example to begin with because the history of his relation to the dragon not only has a relatively clear origin but also a significant relevance as a symbol of many European nations. As he was the patron saint of all those who had devoted their lives to fighting, St. George was also the patron of the crusaders. They obviously were the ones who brought the image of St. George as the dragon fighter back. It then ultimately became a constituent part of his iconography through Jacobus de Voragine, a dominican and archbishop of Genua, who, in the 13th century, included this legend into his "Legenda Aurea" (Golden Legend) which was of great influence on folkloristic piety (Braunfels-Esche 1976: 21 ff., Egli 1982: 223 ff.). Although St. George did not officially become the national patron of England until 1347, his feast, the 23rd of April, received the same rank as the great feasts of the ecclesiastical year through a synod at Oxford in 1222. Around that time he also became the national patron of Georgia, Greece, Russia, Hungary, Poland, and Sweden; in Germany he was the patron of the nobility.

That the dragon became the incarnation of evil, the enemy, and often enough the devil in Christian mythology during the last millenium not only became evident through thousands of churches which were dedicated to St. George all over Europe but also through the fact that the legends of nearly 60 saints are based, one way or the other, on dragon killing (Aufhauser 1911: 239); among them are also women who like St. Martha vanquished the dragon with holy water, or St. Margaretha who became the patron of pregnant women, because, when she was swallowed by the dragon, the cross which she was wearing grew till it finally burst the monster (*Redaktion...* 1985: 95, cf. Roheim 1972: 299).

That the dragon also has a long tradition in our western military history is, for example, indicated by the "dragons," the French cavalrymen in the Thirty Years War, who were equipped with small-arms called "fire-spitting dragons"; it seems that the fact that, for example, the English, French, German, and the Swedish language have incorporated the Latin "draco" (which was taken from the Greek "drakon"), originates from the dragon as a cohort sign of the Romans which they themselves had adopted from their Teutonic enemies (Höfler 1961: 99). The self-identification with the dragon in order to put one's enemies to flight is in itself a symbolic act which e. g. can be found among the ancient Persians, who wore dragon helmets, or among the Vikings, whose ship bows were shaped like a dragon,

Figure 3: Albrecht Dürer, St. George killing the Dragon. Woodcut ca. 1501/04

a symbol which was later put on the church roof as protection against the demons. "In the sign of the dragon they were conquering the dragon" (Steffen 1984: 30).

In addition to St. George, some further names and images may indicate how primeval and universal the heroic way of coping with a dragon is. There is, for example, the mythical story of the nordic hero Sigurd who when he killed the dragon on behalf of a dwarf realized only by chance that one single drop of the dragon's blood gave man the knowledge about the primeval things on earth. One also may be reminded what happened to Siegfried, his Germanic namesake, who took a bath in the dragon's blood in order to get the strength of the dragon himself. The epos of Beowulf and Wiglaf (*Redaktion...* 1985: 7 ff.) or that of the Golden Fleece are other examples that the dragon had to be slaughtered in order to receive the enormous treasure which he kept in custody. Ancient Egyptian mythology contains a further image of the dragon fight. It is the sun-god Re who, accompanied by his hyena-faced guard Seth, moved across the Egyptian sky in his shining barque, keeping away the dragon Apep who reigned over darkness striving to annihilate the god of light.

Out of all the stories and legends on dragon fighting I, however, prefer most the one of Sire Eglamour and Lady Chrytobel, two French lovers who had to suffer long and painfully because of their affection (*Time-Life* 1987: 128 ff.). Like the ancient hero Hercules, Eglamour had to accomplish a variety of works before he was allowed to marry Chrytobel. Before the hero had come back from the dragon fight, his love expected a child from him. And as her father had decided to kill her together with the infant, she escaped into the magic empire. It was a long odyssee till Eglamour and

Figure 4: Seth, the guard of the sun-god Re, fighting at the bow of the shining barque against the giant-serpent Apophis. Papyros 21. Dynasty (1085−950 B. C.); from: Steffen 1984: 48

Chrytobel eventually became united again: it was only after Eglamour unknowingly had fought his own son, thus preventing him, like the ancient Oedipus, from marrying his own mother, that the double marriage of Eglamour and Chrytobel as well as their son and his wife could be celebrated in the far Orient.

That a women or a virgin is part of the dragon fight myth, as in St. George's legend or in fairy tales (Rank 1922), is also a constituent dimension of many of the dragon images of ancient Greek mythology. There is, for instance, the Greek god of light, Apollo, a son of Zeus, who killed Python, the dragon who had tried to kill Apollo's mother Leto (Steffen 1984: 44). Perseus, another son of Zeus (together with Danae), fought the dragon at the seashore of the Red Sea and thus gained Andromeda as his wife (Egli 1982: 218 f., *Redaktion*... 1985: 120 f.), akin to Cadmus, a hero from Thebes, who liberated Harmonia, a double of Aphrodite, by slaying the dragon (Roheim 1972: 301). And most famous of all is the myth of Amor and Psyche. Amor, the son of Venus and Jupiter, liberated Psyche, the king's daughter, chained to the rocks for the monster. He hurt himself with one of his arrows. Thus he fell in love with her in order to save her.

In my attempt to understand especially these latter myths of the dragon fight, I found a contribution which Roheim (1972: 297 ff.) made quite challenging. As this author demonstrates a variety of connections between the ancient Apollo myth and that of Cadmus, it becomes evident that both these dragon- or serpent-slayers are serpents themselves. From such a reading of these myths it becomes evident that "Apollo or Cadmus, the young serpent, killed the old serpent at springtime and married the old serpent's daughter" (Roheim 1972: 307). As such "the idea of death (is) associated with that of a new life" (ibid: 304), thus the dragon or the serpent turns into a symbol of fertility and initiation (cf. Drewermann 1984: 397 ff.). − From another psychoanalytic perspective, i. e. from the Jungian tradition, Erich Neumann (1953: 83, 162) makes the point that the serpent or the dragon represents the archetype of the "great mother" which has to be conquered in adolescence in order to integrate the anima. Whereas the serpent or the dragon in these ancient myths, no matter whether they were Greek, Egyptian, or Judaic, originally symbolized the relation between man and his cosmos or the universe, it seems that particularly in the legends about various saints since the Middle Ages the dragon became a container for the often unconscious anxieties related to sexuality, marriage, and the loss of virginity. What originally had been a symbol of mankind was more and more converted into an episode of certain individuals. As such the dragon also became a symbol of the pleasure of the flesh and lasciviousness which then had to be projected by men into women.

I am quite aware that what I have stated so far about the dragon fight as the predominant mythological way of coping with a dragon has to be left as nothing more than a brief sketch. Before I try to refer to the SCOS-dragon, I would like to offer at least some further imaginations of how to cope with a dragon.

The above-mentioned *magic solution* is a proof that the relationship among virgins and dragons was more complex than just being a city's sacrifice to prevent the annihilation of the town through the monster. Some women, who had fairy-like magic power, kept these monstrous creatures as slaves in order to use their strength for bad purposes or just to tame these beasts (*Redaktion...* 1985: 83). The Russian sorceress Marina in the palace of Kiew used to seduce the dragon fighters and turned them into harmless magpies, pigs, or oxen. The French ghost-lady Succube rode a dragon and seduced her young adventurers through vampire-like kisses which ultimately made them die. As Neumann (1953: 121 f.) states it, the image of the madonna standing on the dragon is a symbol of the wholeness of the female self; in its Christian version it has been converted into the virgin (Mary), who tramples the head of the serpent.

The *Chinese version* of the dragon, however, has quite a different mytho-logical connotation than the traditional western one. Akin to the western dragons, the Chinese dragons are of cosmic origin but they were much more the friends of the mortals. As the dragon represented ultimate wisdom and was the source of blessings, he became the symbol of the emperor who thus was regarded as a descendant of the dragons. The dragons were the masters of the rain; they often had god-like qualities (*Redaktion...* 1985: 41 ff.).

It seems that the dragon in *science fiction* literature has for the most part lost its magic and threatening character; it occasionally has been converted into a domesticated animal which, as it is tamed and controlled, can be utilized like a flying horse due to its enormous power and its ability to fly attacks against one's enemies (e. g. McCaffrey 1981, Vance 1986). The degeneration of the dragon in science fiction stories in comparison to the ancient mythological figure seems to parallel the discrepancy between the horses of the horsemen of the apocalypse and brewery horses to quite an extent; like horses, dragons are tamed and bred; the passion is gone.

The dragon has also become an increasingly prominent figure in children books. Although in some cases (e. g. Lindgren 1986) the dragon seems to keep his magic notion, it predominantly seems to be turned into a pet or a friend for the *lonely child*. Quite often the dragon is trivialized into a child-like little creature who either is full of inferiority feelings himself (Korschunow 1984, Schmögner 1975) or becomes an ally against the child's parents or his comrades (Kent 1986, Nerev 1986). As such the dragon occasionally has become a substitute for the split-off double which, as, for example, in R. L. Stevenson's "Dr. Jekyll and Mr. Hyde," was a well-known pattern in the fictions and novels at the turn of the last century (cf.

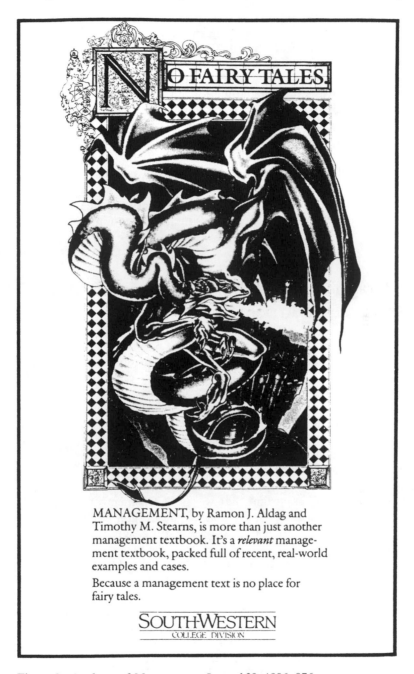

MANAGEMENT, by Ramon J. Aldag and Timothy M. Stearns, is more than just another management textbook. It's a *relevant* management textbook, packed full of recent, real-world examples and cases.

Because a management text is no place for fairy tales.

Figure 5: *Academy of Management Journal* 29, 1986: 876

McWhinney 1987, Rank 1971). The dragon in recent children books thus sometimes carries the notion of the Jungian shadow, the unaccepted split-off part of oneself which has to be integrated during the process of further maturation (Jung et al. 1986: 118 f., Neumann 1984: 69 ff.). However, from my own limited impression of children's books about dragons I hesitate to confirm their positive educational function (cf. Burkolter-Trachsel 1981: 168); these books rather often seem to favour their authors' point of view, as if the fascinating, frightening, magic part of reality did not exist. To quite an extent these books appear to me to be trivializations of the numinous, i. e. they seem to reconfirm a metamyth that there is nothing beyond the rational and the obvious, that it all can be handled (cf. Ingersoll/ Adams 1986: 362) and that not only "a management text" but also management itself "is no place for fairy tales" (cf. the advertisement for a recent book on management by South-Western using the dragon image).

4 The Dragon as a Symbol for Corporate Identity: Avantgarde or Arrièregarde?

As already mentioned above, it was a deliberate decision to take the image of the dragon for the SCOS-logo without the often related image of the hero or the knight. The designer actually was asked by P. O. Berg "to let the dragon tear down the organization chart that was trapping it" (Berg 1987 a). Underlying this image is obviously quite a different notion of corporate culture than the one propagated e. g. by Deal and Kennedy (1982): "For an organization you'll need heros; if you don't have them, create them!" Such a trivialization of the hero would, as I assume, ultimately lead to a trivialization of the dragon − and the concept of culture.

It seems to me to be important that we as SCOS-members collectively try to find out what such a new version of the dragon could mean and represent for us if we were prepared to give it more significance than just a trademark − which some people wear on their shirts in form of a crocodile. As the SCOS-dragon obviously is supposed to have another relevance than just to discriminate its members from those who in their respective organizations wear a lion or an eagle on their ties or banners, it seems important to discover its particular meaning through a comparison of its similarities and differences with other dragon images.

In my own first attempt to relate the SCOS-logo to other more traditional dragon images, I found the considerations about avantgarde and tradition/ arrièregarde quite helpful which Bazon Brock (1986: 102 ff.), a colleague of mine, developed in his theory of art. The widespread understanding of avantgarde is that of a total break with every tradition and the creation of the absolutely new, alternative, and unfamiliar, which then often enough either leads to the consequence that such a piece of art is either regarded as meaningless and gimmick or that the artist himself becomes the object of irony and aggression. Brock's perspective, however, is quite different; he is convinced that we only recognize something as avantgarde which forces us to build new traditions. "Traditions," as he states it, "are nothing other than those comprehensions about the relationship of historical events which result from the respective contemporaries' attempts to look backwards" (Brock 1986: 105). Unlike the usual understanding of tradition as a force coming out of history which then influences the respective present, Brock regards as tradition that which influences the social construction of historical events in the present insofar as these historical events are united as "history" through a new tradition. Without such a (re)integration of the new into history which — at least so far as the history of art is concerned — especially during the last centuries has been a history of the previously new or avantgarde, the avantgarde remains meaningless and falls into oblivion as soon as it is antiquated by the very next avantgarde.

As in art, the function of the avantgarde in mythology or symbolism could be to look at the apparently assured interpretations of our ancestors from a different perspective, i. e. to recognize again as unknown and surprising what has been regarded as evident and familiar. To the extent that traditional myths and images have to be rediscovered or reinterpreted from newly created or shaped images, the new myth may also appear in another light.

To create such a new tradition often enough means recognizing the social as well as the unconscious dimensions these images refer to and are built upon as parts of a common culture. This, for example, means that ancient images often carry latently, so to speak, more crystallized meaning than we are able to reactivate contemporarily or that we, in a non-conscious manner, are referring to earlier images; we may even quote from them without being aware of the fact or of its sources.

In order to demonstrate more explicitly what I mean by it, I would like to start with an example which, in the present context, appears to be interesting, because it might contribute towards a better understanding of the SCOS-dragon. On my hunt for the dragon I found a picture of one of the adventures of Baron Münchhausen fighting the dragon in what appeared to me at first sight as quite a curious way of dragon slaughtering. Münchhausen, a German army officer of the 18th century, well known for his countless adventurous journeys, once killed a dragon in Nubia by sticking a cake made of pitch and poison on a long stick into the dragon's throat. As soon as the monster had swallowed it, it burst into pieces with a terrible bang.

Well, I thought, just another of those curious stories of Münchhausen like the one in which he pulled himself up by his own hair out of the swamp (cf. Watzlawick 1979) or akin to the one in which he rode on a cannon-ball. But only later, when I discovered another picture showing the ancient prophet Daniel killing a dragon in Babylon in the same manner, was I able to realize that the Münchhausen episode was a quotation which, as it may be assumed, may be even older than the dragon fight in the Daniel-Apocrypha. Referring to the biblical context (Dan. 14, 23—27, cf. Schmidt/Schmidt 1982: 41), the Münchhausen story received quite another meaning: stick into the dragon what it normally is supposed to spit out.

And I made two similar discoveries in my attempt to look back on previous dragon images with the SCOS-logo in mind. One refers to the use of the dragon as a symbol for corporate identity, the other one is related to the combination of the dragon and the organization chart.

As it was stated before, the fact that the dragon became a symbol of corporate identity is not new. During previous centuries countless churches

Figure 6: Daniel, the prophet, killing the dragon. Matthäus Merian, *Die Bibel*, p. 787

and many nations as well as cities have chosen either St. George or St. Michael, the dragon-fighters, as their patrons. And even earlier, the Romans and the Vikings, among others, had chosen the dragon as a symbol which they carried in front of them on their various military and exploratory expeditions in order to scare their enemies as well as unknown demons. It seems that what later became a slogan of the crusaders referring to their cross, the "In this sign we shall conquer!," originally referred to the dragon; for the Roman legionaries, for instance, the preservation of their dragon's banner literally meant the survival of the legion.

According to my understanding, we at SCOS, unlike the ancient Romans or the crusaders of the Middle Ages, are not preparing a military campaign; we are not propagating the endless war of growing economic and managerial successes. What the SCOS-logo in comparison to these contemporary myths seems to represent is an anti-myth. This anti-myth is based on the assumption that "the dragon is to symbolize the underlying, powerful, restless, collective aspects of the organization which, although we try to imprison them ..., tend to break through, break out and 'disturb' the smooth machinelike functioning of the corporate machine" (Berg 1987 a). There can be no doubt that "the dragon itself is powerful, ruthless, determined — but not necessarily evil. It is people, who cannot stand things they cannot control, who see cruelty and viciousness in him" (ibid.).

What the dragon in the SCOS-logo is supposed to symbolize for our contemporary institutions and our work enterprises, in particular, is a different metamyth from the glittering and sterile pseudo-reality as it is expressed in the bestselling soap operas on corporate culture and the related search for excellence. The dragon in this newly created version may get the previously explored function of the avantgarde in order to help us to create a new tradition of looking backwards to previous dragon myths and images in order to (re)discover that there may be other ways to cope with a dragon than just to annihilate it. It may even be the case that, by referring to the Chinese version of the dragon, we may discover new ways to help wisdom out of the wheel-chairs where it has been dislocated societally, in order to incorporate it in our organizations again (cf. Sievers 1986 a, b, 1990 a, b). The dragon tearing down the organization-chart may thus, e. g. help us to perceive our history of industrialization from a new tradition, i. e. the repression and imprisonment of that part of reality which cannot be counted and measured.

So far as the image of the "dragon breaking out of the corporate psychic prison" (Berg 1987 a) in the SCOS-logo is concerned, I found two pictures which caught my thoughts and which may help on further attempts to perceive the mythology of this logo. The first one obviously is well known; it is the front page of the first English edition of Thomas Hobbes' "Leviathan," which appeared in London in 1651.

Figure 7: Front page of the first English edition of Thomas Hobbes' "Leviathan" (1651); ill. by Wenceslaus Hollar, Mansell Collection, London; from: Brandt 1987

The Leviathan, in the Judaic tradition, is the cosmic dragon which along with his counterpart Behemot was created at the beginning of the world (cf. Steffen 1984: 83 f., 112 ff., 142 ff.). Although this cannot be the occasion to argue about the meaning and the possible failure of the Leviathan as a political symbol — a point which was extensively made by the German political philosopher Carl Schmitt (1982) in his book which first appeared in 1938 — what strikes me, when I compare the composition of this picture with that of the SCOS-logo, is the combination of the chaos-symbolizing creature on the one and the hierarchical order of the state and the church on the other side. The similarity of the organigram and the dragon in the SCOS-logo is quite obvious!

Whether Hobbes himself or Wenceslaus Hollar, the artist who produced the engraving of the Leviathan in his commission, knew the other picture I found, probably cannot be proved. It is a page from a Middle Ages codex of the rules of St. Benedict and shows God, the father, fishing for the Leviathan.

So far as its one central image is concerned, it is based on Job's discourses with God in the Old Testament (Job 40, 25 ff.). On its left side it shows a ladder on which the angels are climbing up and down. Realizing that much of the rational structure in our contemporary industrial enterprises ultimately originated in monasteries and in those under the rules of St. Benedict, in particular (cf. Kieser 1986), may not only help us to perceive the dragon differently than as the traditional Christian image of the devil; it may also remind us that, particularly during the Middle Ages, the daily life in a monastery often enough was determined by other realities than just prayers and work (cf. Burrell 1984, Morgan 1986: 208). Brandt (1987), in an article about the front page of Hobbes' first edition of the Leviathan, adds some further interesting insights. As this author states it, "the Leviathan is his citizens" (ibid.: 168) — an expression which leads to the idea of looking at the SCOS-dragon's scales as being built by the members of an organization.

5 SCOS, the Magic Dragon: Pet or Fundamental?

The further exploration of the two Leviathan images which I happened to find on my way to the cave of the dragon may throw a new light on the SCOS-logo — probably not primarily through analogy but hopefully through a kind of playful creative exploration of our own cultural experience.

In revitalizing the dragon for our organizational world, we may discover
through this image a myth of the dragon which differs both from the pet

Figure 8: Illustrated page of the Regula Benedicti, Stuttgart; Code hist. fol. 415,
p. 87ᵛ; from Paulsen 1966

notion of the lonely child as well as from the cosmic creature, which filled up the emptiness and exceeded the universe. If we allow the dragon to be a symbol for the unconscious similar to the serpent from which it descended, we may find ways to perceive, to understand, and ultimately to live in our organizations which lead further than those which are offered by the mainstream approaches of our organizational and managerial theories. Curing the monster instead of killing it may help us to integrate into our own individual and collective lives those dimensions which traditionally are considered typhonic, named after Typhon (whom Zeus, in his attempt to annihilate him, imprisoned in the volcano Aetna), i.e. our "animalistic" nature which — when we discover it in ourselves or in others — often scares us so much that it has to be neglected. (As Typhon occasionally is regarded as the father of other monsters such as Cerberus, Hydra, or Lerna (Steffen 1984: 43 f.), the acquaintance with the dragon ultimately may lead us to further discoveries.)

Although I find it very encouraging that SCOS, with P. O. Berg's help, has rediscovered the dragon and chosen it as its logo, I would like to repeat on this occasion a warning which P. O. Berg already expressed: "You cannot fool a dragon — he senses tricksters miles away. Dragons are not calmed or fooled by smooth talk or manipulation but cut right through the most essential (power) relationships and (emotional) experiences" (Berg 1987 a).

This warning in mind, it seems to me that, so far as the presentations to our SCOS conferences as well as the contributions to our journal are concerned, we have not seriously enough started not to fool the dragon; on occasion it appears to me that there are just still too many tricksters around and that the stories and images which are presented about the dragon, i.e. about "the ugly face" of our contemporary organizations, are far away from an attempt to elucidate where, how, and to what an extent "our organizations are killing us" (Morgan 1986: 273). Much too often these contributions seem to repeat the title of one of the children books "There's no such thing as a dragon" (Kent 1986).

In order to let the dragon escape from the corporate psychic prison of our organizations, as it is indicated by the dragon tearing down the organization chart, a first step could be to indicate and to describe the traps and chains in which the dragon traditionally is caught in our organizations. What we as SCOS-members have been able to contribute so far to a further understanding and conceptualization of culture, in general, and of corporate culture, in particular, reminds me in its predominant part of a comment George Steiner (1971: 34) once made referring to T. S. Eliot's "*Notes towards a definition of culture*" which appeared shortly after the Second World War: "How, only three years after the event, after the publication to the world of facts and pictures that have, surely, altered our sense of the limits of human behaviour, was it possible to write a book on culture and say nothing." — If we are, however, prepared to discover in our "exercise in contemporary archaeology" (Berg 1987 b: 25) the dragon traps as corporate artifacts, we have to acknowledge that the dragon, whose image we are projecting on others, lives in us (cf. Steffen 1984: 253 f.). It has to be recognized, accepted, and cured by us before we will be able to discover it in the outer world of our organizations.

Don't let us forget that "a core element in the drawing," as Berg (1987 a) states it, is "that the dragon should be fearful, i. e. scare the people experiencing him. Fear (of the uncertain, of lack of control, of the unknown, of death, of love — that could be lost —, of pain, etc.) is probably one of the key emotions that build up the collective."

I would like to finish these thoughts with a Chinese fairy-tale which was given to me by one of my students. It is based on the Chinese idea that the dragon sleeps during wintertime. At this time it is very tiny. In the flash of the first thunderstorm at springtime it rises again towards the clouds. And thus it is expressing the nature of the dragon as a cosmic appearance.

6 The Dragon After Hibernation

Once upon a time there was a scholar reading in the upper floor of his house. It was a cloudy and rainy day and the weather was gloomy. Then he saw a little thing which was shining like a glow-worm. It was crawling on his desk. There, where it had been, it left behind burning tracks curved like the tracks of a rain-worm. It gradually twisted on to the book and the book, too, became black. He then realized that this could be a dragon. Therefore, he carried it on the book outside the door. He stood there for quite a while; but it remained seated, rolled up, and did not move at all.

Then the scholar said: "One shall not say of me that I was wanting in respect." With these words he carried the book back and laid it down again on the desk. Then he put on festive raiment, made a deep bow and escorted it outside. He was no sooner out of the door than he noticed that it raised its head and suddenly it extended. With a hissing sound it flew up from the book forming a shining stripe. It once again turned back to the scholar; by then its head was already as big as a barrel, and the size of its body measured nearly a cord. After another meandering a terrible thunder-clap crashed and the dragon went up into the air.

Then the scholar went back and investigated which way the little creature had come. The tracks went to and from as far as the bookcase (*Chinesische Märchen* 1961: 135 f.).

Don't let us be too afraid to have a look in our bookcases; we may discover a dragon in hibernation! We also may be reminded that it behoves a scholar, not a mere scientist, to become aware of what a dragon stands for.

References

Aufhauser, B. (1911): *Das Drachenwunder des hl. Georg*. Byzantinisches Archiv 5

Berg, P. O. (1984): The Retiring Chairman's Saga. *SCOS Note-Work* 3(2), Autumn, pp. 4–6

Berg, P. O. (1987a): Letter to the Author

Berg, P. O. (1987b): Some Notes on Corporate Artifacts. *SCOS Note-Work* 6(1), pp. 24–28

Brandt, R. (1987): Das Titelblatt des Leviathan. *Leviathan* 15(1), pp. 163–186

Braunfels-Esche, S. (1976): *Sankt Georg. Legende, Verehrung, Symbol*. München: Georg D. W. Callwey

Brock, B. (1986): *Ästhetik gegen erzwungene Unmittelbarkeit. Die Gottsucherbande. Schriften 1978–1986*. Köln: DuMont

Burkolter-Trachsel, M. (1981): *Der Drache. Das Symbol und der Mensch*. Bern: Paul Haupt

Burrell, G. (1984): Sex and Organizational Analysis. *Organization Studies* 5, pp. 97–118

Chinesische Märchen (1961): Düsseldorf: Eugen Diederichs

Cooper, R. (1983): Some Remarks of Theoretical, Individualism, Alienation, and Work. *Human Relations* 36, pp. 717–723

Deal, T. E. and A. A. Kennedy (1982): *Corporate Cultures. The Rites and Rituals of Corporate Life*. Reading, MA: Addison-Wesley

Dickinson, P. (1981): *Das große Buch der Drachen. Die fliegenden Ungetüme*. Oldenburg: Stalling. (English ed., 1979: *The Flight of the Dragons*. London: Pierroth)

Drewermann, E. (1984): *Tiefenpsychologie und Exegese. Die Wahrheit der Formen. Traum, Mythos, Märchen, Sage und Legende*. Vol. 1. Olten–Freiburg: Walter-Verlag

Egli, H. (1982): *Das Schlangensymbol. Geschichte, Märchen, Mythos*. Olten: Walter-Verlag

Fontenrose, J. (1959): *Python. A Study of Delphic Myth and its Origin*. Berkeley, CA: University of California Press

Habermas, J. (1971): *Toward a Rational Society*. London: Heinemann

Höfler, O. (1961): *Siegfried, Arminius und die Symbolik*. Heidelberg: Carl Winter, Universitätsverlag

Hogarth, P. and V. Clery (1979): *Dragons*. New York: The Viking Press

Ingersoll, V. H. and G. B. Adams (1986): Beyond Organizational Boundaries. Exploring the Managerial Myth. *Administration & Society* 18, pp. 360–381

Johnsgard, P. and K. Johnsgard (1982): *Dragons and Unicorns. A Natural History*. New York: St. Martin's Press

Jung, C. G. et al. (1986): *Der Mensch und seine Symbole*. Olten: Walter-Verlag

Kent, J. (1986): *Drachen gibt's doch gar nicht*. Ravensburg: Otto Maier

Kieser, A. (1986): Von asketischen zu industriellen Bravourstücken. Die Organisation der Wirtschaft im Kloster des Mittelalters. *Mannheimer Berichte aus Forschung und Lehre* 30, pp. 3–16

Korschunow, I. (1984): *Hanno malt sich einen Drachen*. München: Deutscher Taschenbuch Verlag

Kreiner, K. (1987): The Lost Innocence of SCOS. *SCOS Note-Work* 6(2−3), Autumn, pp. 16−18

Lindgren, A. (1986): *Der Drache mit den roten Augen.* Hamburg: Friedrich Oetinger

McCaffrey, A. (1981): *Die Welt der Drachen. Science Fiction Roman.* München: Wilhelm Heyne

McWhinney, W. (1987): Organizational Evil: Faust, Professionals, and Bureaucrats. Manuscript. Venice, CA

Mode, H. (1983): *Fabeltiere und Dämonen in der Kunst. Die fantastische Welt der Mischwesen.* Stuttgart: W. Kohlhammer

Morgan, G. (1986): *Images of Organization.* Beverly Hills, CA: Sage

Nauta, R. (1984): ... And the Chairman Elect's Saga. *SCOS Note-Work* 3(2), Autumn, p. 7

Nauta, R. (1986): Change and Myths. *SCOS Note-Work* 5(3), Autumn, pp. 6−7

Nerev, A. (1986): Der Drache hinter den Spiegeln. *Der Drache hinter den Spiegeln. Fantasygeschichten.* V. C. Harksen (Ed.). Frankfurt: Fischer, pp. 94−100

Neumann, E. (1953): *Kulturentwicklung und Religion.* Zürich: Rascher

Neumann, E. (1984): *Tiefenpsychologie und neue Ethik.* Frankfurt: Fischer

Paulsen, P. (1966): *Drachenkämpfe, Löwenritter und die Heinrichssage. Eine Studie über die Kirchentür von Valthjofsad auf Island.* Köln: Böhlau

Rank, O. (1922): Das Brüdermärchen. *Psycho-analytische Beiträge zur Mythenforschung aus den Jahren 1912−1914.* O. Rank (Ed.), Leipzig: Internationaler Psychoanalytischer Verlag, pp. 119−145

Rank, O. (1971): *The Double. A Psychoanalytic Study.* Chapel Hill, NC: The University of North Carolina Press

Redaktion der Time-Life-Bücher (Ed.) (1985): *Verzauberte Welten. Drachen.* Time-Life-Books B. V.

Roheim, G. (1972): *Animism, Magic and the Divine King.* New York: International University Press

Rosenberg, A. (1956): *Michael und der Drache. Urgestalten von Licht und Finsternis.* Olten−Freiburg: Walter-Verlag

Schmidt, H., and M. Schmidt (1982): *Die vergessene Bildersprache christlicher Kunst. Ein Führer zum Verständnis der Tier-, Engel- und Mariensymbolik.* München: C. H. Beck

Schmitt, C. (1982): *Der Leviathan in der Staatslehre des Thomas Hobbes. Sinn und Fehlschlag eines politischen Symbols.* Köln: Hohenheim (1st ed. 1938)

Schmögner, W. (1975): *Das Drachenbuch.* Frankfurt: Insel

Sievers, B. (1986a): Beyond the Surrogate of Motivation. *Organization Studies* 7, pp. 335−351

Sievers, B. (1986b): Work, Death, and Life Itself. *Dragon* 1(8), pp. 82−93

Sievers, B. (1990a): Zombies or People − What is the Product of Work? Some Considerations About the Relation Between Human and Nonhuman Systems in Regard to the Socio-Technical-Systems Paradigm. *Organizational Symbolism.* B. Turner (Ed.). Berlin: de Gruyter, pp. 83−93

Sievers, B. (1990b): The Diabolization of Death: Some Thoughts on the Obsolescence of Mortality in Organization Theory and Practice. *The Theory and Philosophy of Organizations. Critical Issues and New Perspectives.* J. Hassard and D. Pym (Eds.). London: Routledge

Smith, E. (1919): *The Evolution of the Dragon*. Manchester: University Press

Steffen, U. (1984): *Drakenkampf. Der Mythos vom Bösen*. Stuttgart: Kreuz

Steiner, G. (1971): *In Bluebeard's Castle. Some Notes towards the Re-definition of Culture*. London: Faber & Faber

Time-Life-Bücher (1987): *Verzauberte Welten. Liebesglück und Liebesleid*. Time-Life-Books, Inc.

Vance, J. (1986): Die Drachenreiter. *Drachenbrut*. J. Vance (Ed.). Bergisch-Gladbach: Bastei, pp. 89–205

Vinycomb, J. (1906): *Fictious and Symbolic Creatures in Art. With Special Reference to Their Use in British Heraldry*. London: Chapman and Hall

de Visser, M. W. (1913): *The Dragon in China and Japan*. Verhandlingen der koninklijke Akademie van Wetenschappen te Amsterdam, Afdeeling Letterkunde Deel XIII No. 2

Watzlawick, P. (1979): Münchhausens Zopf und Wittgensteins Leiter. Zum Problem der Rückbezüglichkeit. *Der Mensch und seine Sprache*. A. Peisl/A. Mohler (Eds.). Frankfurt: Oldenburg, Propyläen, Vol. 1, pp. 243–264

Williams, C. A. S. (1975): *Outlines of Chinese Symbolism and Art Motives*. Rutland: Charles E. Tuttle

The Symbolic Value of Computerized Information Systems

Christian Scholz

1 The Problem

Until recently, the choice of a *Computerized Information System* ("CIS") was basically a problem technical experts had to deal with. The selection of a particular mainframe did not concern the end user, who was not affected by the differences between alternative systems. Except perhaps for the problem of "who gets a computer terminal on his/her desk" most people did not become involved with decisions concerning CIS.

Ten years ago, the physical attributes of the old mainframes visible to the end-user were rather similar. Therefore, the statement "a CIS is invariant to all possible cultures of an organization" could not be challenged.

This situation has changed, drastically, in the last few years: with the emergence of personal computers, local area networks, telecommunications, intelligent workstations, and mainframe-PC connections, suddenly a wide range of alternatives is available. And it makes a difference whether one has an intelligent PC on his or her desk with the option of activating the network to the mainframe or whether one is, through the terminal, a "slave" to the company's central EDP department. Also, a choice between different personal computers (such as IBM's PS/2 or Apple's Macinthosh) is now more than just a comparison of technical details.

Still, both in the "old" and the "new" days, there has been a significant lack of acceptance of CIS. This holds true for working on the mainframe as well as for "Personal Computing" on the PC: even though computers have reached many new users and allow for many new applications, compared to their possibilities, we still have a rather low usage-rate.

This article discusses these problems from the viewpoint of *organizational culture*. It raises the question of the cultural consequences of the "new" computer wave coming into offices and shop floors. It also tries to answer the question as to whether some of the problems associated with a CIS may be attributed to cultural consequences of CIS working. In particular, this article focuses on the symbolic aspects of a CIS. These answers would be helpful in supporting the process of CIS implementation. They might also help us in dealing with another major problem: constructing a CIS which has desired cultural characteristics.

Even though there is a lot of literature on various topics in the field of organizational culture and, of course, an overwhelming amount of material on computers, our knowledge of the relationship between organizational culture and computers is still limited. Therefore, the main intention of this article is not to provide final answers, but to raise some new questions, to present a specific methodology, and to point to practical applications.

2 The Framework

In order to trace the characteristic symbolics of a CIS, we first have to position this research approach in the broad context of organizational research. Figure 1 displays the stepwise focusing on CIS symbolics: starting from organizational behaviour, we pass through organizational culture and information culture, and finally reach the CIS culture with its own distinctive CIS symbolics.

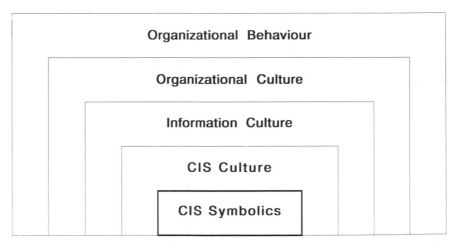

Figure 1: Focus of research

2.1 Organizational Behaviour

There are many ways to describe organizations as well as what can be termed organizational behaviour (e. g. Argyris 1964, Cyert/March 1963, Porter/Lawler/Hackmann 1975, Scholz 1989, Shull/Delbecq/Cummings 1970). Basically, there is a combination of a technological system and a social system: this social system consists of individuals with their specific interests, capabilities, and values. The behaviour of the individuals depends upon their particular characteristics and upon the context set by the technological system.

This individual behaviour, in combination with the performance of the technological system, aggregates into what can be labelled "organizational behaviour." It can be observed on the *visible* level by planning modes, decision processes, goal setting, communication rules, negotiation and bargaining processes, as well as rites and rituals, and by organizational hierarchies; it can also be detected by studying buildings, floor layouts, and furnitures. On a *less visible* level, organizational behaviour is based upon the individual's values, preferences, and on the built-in limitations of the technological/organizational system.

All these and many more aspects influence the social construction of organizational reality, as intensively discussed from various academic viewpoints (e. g. Berger/Luckmann 1966, Morgan/Smircich 1980, Pfeffer 1981, Sathe 1985, Schein 1980, Smircich 1983).

2.2 Organizational Culture

Organizational culture establishes itself from individually and collectively performed behaviour as a pattern of basic assumptions that has worked well enough to be considered valid and to be taught new members as the correct way to perceive, think, and feel (Schein 1985: 9). Organizational culture, therefore, results from those organizational attributes which are commonly accepted and have (or produce) shared meanings among the organization's members. There has been a basic consensus in the literature of both practitioners and academics (see summary in Scholz 1988) that this organizational culture is an important aspect of each organization (Frost et al. 1985, Pondy et al. 1983, Schein 1985, Turner 1990).

In order to trace in more detail the causes and the effects of organizational culture, we must explicitly establish the connection between organizational behaviour and organizational culture. Organizational culture must be understood as the implicit consciousness of an organization, which develops out of its members' behaviour, and which influences their behaviour. This *dualistic model* of organizational culture (Scholz 1987a, Scholz 1987b,

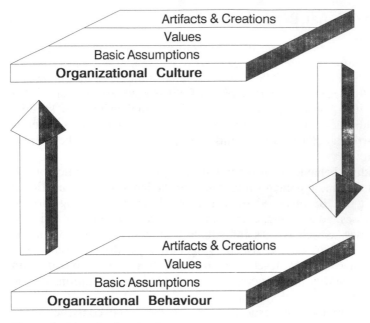

Figure 2: Organizational culture

Scholz/Hofbauer 1990: 56–61), therefore, calls for two directional influences (Figure 2).

On one hand, we have individual assumptions and values of the organization's members as a basis for individual behaviour. On all this a selective aggregation process builds up into what is to be labelled the "organizational culture," the commonly accepted patterns of behaviour in the organization. These patterns usually display behaviour, which has proved to work efficiently and effectively in that particular organization. In this sense, organizational culture *results from* organizational behaviour.

On the other hand, organizational culture acts as a steering device for individuals' behaviour. All three levels of organizational culture, namely basic assumptions, values, as well as artefacts and creations (Schein 1985: 13–21) have — to different degrees — the power of leading individuals into the desired cultural direction. If this culture is visible and communicated to the members of the organization, then organizational culture *directs* the individuals' behaviour.

This leads us to a dualistic control model, as it is known from cybernetics. It consists of the behavioural layer and the cultural layer, each made up out of three levels (assumptions, values, artifacts, and creations). Over the course of time, organizational culture builds itself out of individual behaviour, making it a controlled variable. When a strong culture originates, it becomes the control unit itself, which in turn controls the behaviour of the organization's individual members. Then, again, new patterns of behaviour may originate, repeating the complete cycle.

This dualistic model of organizational culture is an extremely powerful tool, not only to explain the creation of culture, but also to deal with complicated issues such as the problem of subcultures and the problem of cultural change over time. In the following, we will use this model to investigate the phenomenon of "information culture" and will return to it in section 6, for a more detailed example.

2.3 Information Culture

One specific aspect of organizational behaviour is the way in which individuals deal with information (e. g. McFarlan/McKenney 1983, Simon 1986): it is of particular interest how members of an organization collect and

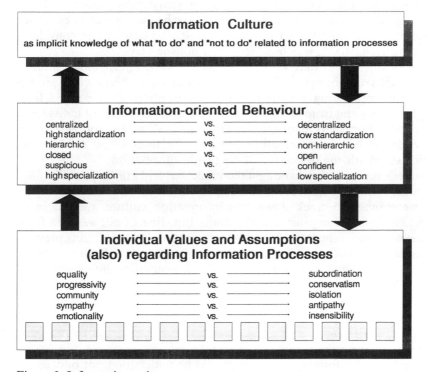

Figure 3: Information culture

process data, communicate information and knowledge, determine the importance of data items, protect assembled data, and destroy existing data.

On the layer of *organizational behaviour*, we have the basic assumptions of individuals, their specific value systems, and the derived artifacts. Basic assumptions of individuals relate to aspects such as conservatism vs. progressivity, specific values to, for example, privacy vs. openness. All these assumptions and values determine their holder's behaviour at any time. In fact, they influence the steering system for individuals' behaviour: if an individual strictly believes in subordination and hierarchy, he or she will accept mechanisms which lead to inequalities of information supply on different organizational levels and to emphasis on formal patterns of interaction. We therefore get information-oriented activities of individuals, to be characterized again by dichotomous variables such as centralization vs. decentralization.

A huge problem derives from the fact that there is almost an indefinite list of variables, which describe individual behaviour. On the other hand, the organization's members obviously have less problems in deciphering intuitively the "rules of the game" than do analytical researchers. From the viewpoint of organizational culture research, the answer is clear: the organization's members react to the organizational culture and consider it a composite construct, which is "felt" in a holistic way.

This means, again, that we have a second layer: *information culture* is the implicit consciousness of the organization's members, which directs information processing activities in the organization. It is derived from accepted values and from dominant and successful behaviour of individuals. The information culture originates from individual and organizational behaviour related to information processing activities and leads to an implicit standardizing device for dealing with information.

Figure 3 sums up this paradigmatic model, which will be partially filled out in the following sections.

If we manage to track down this information culture, we obtain an important aspect of organizational culture. But, first of all, we must focus our research, since the huge variety of information-related objects prevents a simultaneous analysis. We will therefore deal in the following sections with the information culture related to the computerized information systems (CIS).

2.4 CIS Culture

A computerized information system should be understood not only as the hardware and software of a particular computer, but also as the connections between computers. In this sense, for instance, not only the PC on the desk is to be considered a CIS, but also the complete office communication structure of a local area network including the link to a host-computer.

Being confronted with a CIS and searching for cultural consequences, we, firstly, must make use of the distinction between objective and subjective reality (Pondy 1983): *objective reality* is a set of empirical objects and events that constitutes organizational action; for an objective analysis only one reality can exist in a given situation; *subjective* (or symbolic) *reality*, on the other hand, constitutes a set of meanings and is a "social construction" (Berger/Luckmann 1966) of organizational members in a given situation.

Objective and subjective realities are of course connected: a specific objective reality can support a number of symbolic realities (Pondy 1983). The organizational members' perception of the objective reality (their "model" of the real system) is the critical fact. Hence objective reality is differentiated into the real "system" as it exists with all its elements and interactions and the "model" as particular image made by members of the organization. This model which reflects some of the attributes of the objective reality may be connected with functional and symbolic meanings.

A CIS, therefore, constitutes *objective reality*. It consists of all elements of the computer system and all their existing connections. In this aspect, we have to deal with processors, co-processors, erasable programmable memories (EPROMS), random access memories (RAMS), read-only-memories (ROMS), bus systems, micro-channels, disc controllers, hard discs, floppy discs, screens, graphic cards, network controllers, and so on. All these components and their connections constitute the objective reality, to be investigated as intra-systemic hierarchy (Scholz 1982) down to the atomic level.

Users create *particular models* of objective reality. They take some elements and some interactions. For an end-user these attributes may be size, speed, or compatibility. These attributes are derived from the specific functional utility the CIS provides. This depends not only upon the attributes of the objective reality, but also on the user's goals and on the general context in which the CIS is used.

These functional attributes are important, but they are not the only ones which count for the cultural analysis. Even more important are the individual meanings attached to the CIS. We therefore do not only focus on subjective reality, we go even further into the details of *symbolic reality*. The physical CIS attributes always have distinct symbolic values, even if we are not aware of them. Examples of those symbolic meanings are "status indicator," "instrument of power," and "being part of a network."

Figure 4 illustrates these three types of reality: it also shows that the choice of the CIS is influenced by the current organizational culture and that culture is reinforced by CIS according to the dualistic model.

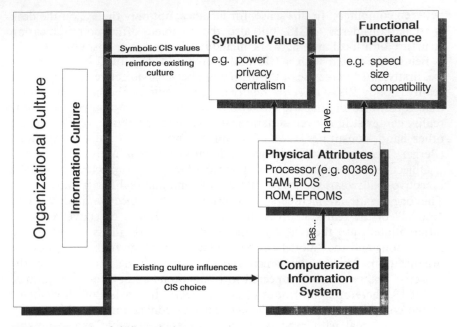

Figure 4: Levels of CIS analysis

3 CIS Symbolics

Narrowing down, we finally get to the subjective reality and to the CIS symbolics: symbols are "objects, acts, components, or linguistic formations, which stand ambiguously for a multiplicity of meanings, evoke emotions, and impel man to action" (Cohen 1976).

We need, though, a more detailed instrument to deal with cultural symbols. Using and combining important suggestions from the literature (Dandridge/Mitroff/Joyce 1980), we get *three types* of symbols:

— verbal symbols are oriented towards the communication of meanings,
— action symbols reflect specific behaviours,
— material symbols refer to the objects themselves;

as well as *three functions* of symbols:

— the descriptive function regards symbols as tools (indicators) to recognize culture,

- the system maintaining function of symbols protects a system and stabilizes it (even during periods of change and transition),
- the energy controlling function serves as mechanism to direct the behaviour of old and new organizational members into a desired direction.

The three types and three functions of symbols lead to a matrix of nine symbolic meanings.

Moving one step further, it is important to notice various procedures in dealing with symbols: taking the company's logo, it makes a difference whether we talk and discuss what the logo should look like, whether we introduce the logo, or see the logo as a physically existing object on the walls and the stationary.

Therefore, a differentiation between the three *procedures* in dealing with symbols shall be introduced, namely

- talking about symbols,
- introducing symbols, and
- having symbols.

Symbolic management therefore involves "talking" about verbal symbols and "having" material symbols, but also talking about material symbols and having verbal symbols.

A CIS is basically a material symbol making especially the last three columns of Table 1 suitable for further analysis. Still it should be mentioned that in connection with CIS the other types of symbols also do exist: there

Table 1: Organizational symbols

Types of symbols	Verbal Myths Stories Slogans Jokes			Action Rituals Ceremonies Planning procedures Luncheons			Material Status symbols Logos Architecture Computers		
	Symbolic approaches	Talking	Introducing	Experiencing	Talking	Introducing	Experiencing	Talking	Introducing	Experiencing
Descriptive									
System maintenance									
Energy controlling									

Functions

are stories about a CIS, heroes, and rituals in dealing with systems, as well as jokes about computers and symbolic planning procedures. Still, in the following we will concentrate only on the material aspect.

Applying the 3 × 3-matrix of symbolic meanings from Table 2 to a CIS, we get the following symbolic potentials of a CIS:

"*Talking* for *description*" (1) concerns discussions about the CIS. The computer is not important because of its functional attributes, but because of the discussions about these attributes. By discussing attributes of the CIS, the cultural analyst gets a picture of the existing information culture. Or from another point of view: the CIS is just a medium to stimulate discussion and to collect culture-related information. If a user emphasizes the ability of a PC to be locked up with a key, then this is a clue for the desire for privacy and the lack of openness.

"*Talking* for *system maintenance*" (2) uses conversations about an existing or an impending CIS as a tool in order to strengthen the existing organizational culture. In contrast to (1), the purpose of this "symbolic discussion" is not to collect information, but to give information about the existing culture to the organization's members. The addressees of these "symbolic talks," therefore, are the organization's members. For instance, by pointing out the boundaries of an existing local area network, the cultural promotor can point out the existing boundaries of local subcultures.

"*Talking* for *energy controlling*" (3) relates to changes. These changes do not necessarily involve the CIS. Just talking about the CIS is supposed to support changes in the organizational culture. If we discuss the introduction of a data base to be shared by two currently hostile departments, the discussion may in fact initiate a (small) cultural change.

The cases (1) through (3) all focus on the *talking* about a CIS in order to understand, strengthen, or change culture. The next group of symbolic alternatives deals with definite *actions*: creating a new CIS, modifying an old CIS, or explicitly rejecting another CIS may also constitute a symbolic action able to (4) locate specific characteristics of the culture (*descriptive*), (5) strengthen the existing culture (*system maintenance*), or (6) support cultural changes (*energy controlling*).

Except for the explicit rejection of a CIS, the symbolic introduction focuses on the process of CIS design and CIS implementation: the attributes of the CIS become important, since they deliver a certain message. If a controller in a subsidiary company gets an online connection with the data base of the headquarters, this connection has a symbolic meaning even before he uses it for the first time.

Finally, *experiencing* the CIS symbolism relates to the physical existence of the CIS and the meanings the organization's members connect with it. In contrast to the talking-symbolism and the introducing-symbolism, it is not "discussing" or "doing" that is important, but "having".

Table 2: CIS as material symbol

	Talking	Introducing	Experiencing
Descriptive	1	4	7
System maintenance	2	5	8
Energy controlling	3	6	9

In that case (7) the organizational culture can be derived from the observation who is equipped with which kind of computer (*descriptive*). Corresponding to the symbolics of office space, hierarchic solutions may exist: for instance, in the IBM world one may expect a PS/2-80 on the desk of the team leader, while the others have to work with PS/2-30 or PS/2-50.

Or the CIS may be used to reinforce the existing culture (8). This form of *system maintenance* is intended to stabilize the culture by means of a CIS. Local area networks are an excellent tool to keep system boundaries. Access to a data bank has both functional and symbolic value in determining who or what is important.

And finally even an existing CIS may turn out to be supportive for a cultural change. This type of *energy controlling* relates to situations in which we try to change the culture by means of changing the CIS (9). For instance, by experiencing the properties of a computer-integrated manufacturing system, the culture in that particular organization may eventually start to change — not only because of the functional attributes of that new CIS, but also because of the actual existence of that system.

But, these nine alternatives for CIS symbolics all rest upon some severe assumptions:

The *descriptive* usage assumes that the particular existing or planned CIS has enough attributes to reflect the culture of the organization, and that the CIS has been constructed implicitly or explicitly according to the organization's culture. If the decision on a specific CIS was taken on the fact that this system was available as a package-turnkey solution at extremely low cost, clues from this CIS on the nature of the organization's culture are not feasible. *System maintenance* is based upon the same assumption. Additionally, it requires the cultural expert to have knowledge of the organizational culture, which is supposed to be delivered by the CIS. *Energy controlling* requires even further precise knowledge of the old and the new culture.

Talking about a CIS and seeking to understand CIS symbolics calls for discussions of the new CIS, which do not only focus on technical data, but also on psychological aspects. This requires a situation free of stress and fear. An *introduction* of a CIS is only in that case a symbolic one, if the implementation process purposely considers the symbolic meanings of the CIS and communicates them to the people involved. *Experiencing* CIS symbolics relies on the assumption that the specific environment in the organization supports the idea of CIS decisions to be made not only by EDP experts, but also by cultural experts.

It is important to note that CIS symbolics exist even when no explicit concerns is taken of them by the managers: a CIS always has physical attributes and they always have symbolic meanings (not at least) to some organization's members.

It is the same matter as the two executives who got — without purpose, just "by accident" — offices of a different size. This fact has a (wrong, but still existing) symbolic meaning to the organization's members who are not familiar with the specific circumstances. Only if one is aware of the possibility of unwanted and undirected symbolic meanings, one can redirect the symbolic consequences.

Therefore, we have to investigate the CIS symbolics: the nine symbolic alternatives stated in Table 3 give us some direction of where to look.

4 CIS: What It Communicates

Still, we have to find a way to depict the symbolic meanings of a CIS. For this task, no general procedure seems possible. As a consequence, the next section is to be understood as one particular suggestion out of a larger set of symbolic contents.

4.1 An Adaptation from McClelland

McClelland (1975, 1985) has proposed an interesting and broadly accepted theory of motivation. He believes that some basic needs are acquired from the culture the individual is exposed to. In particular, McClelland discusses the following four needs:

— need for achievement,
— need for power,
— need for affiliation, and
— need for avoidance.

If an individual can "learn" these needs from culture, they must reflect basic values of the culture.

Table 3: Summary of symbolic alternatives

	Talking	Introducing	Experiencing
Descriptive	Discussions of CIS attributes in order to get an integrative interpretation by collecting data	Locating the culture – CIS relations in symbolic management	Counting and specifying the existing computers and their physical attributes to understand culture
System maintenance	Discussions to get a common interpretation by providing data	Enhancing the culture – CIS fit by symbolic management	Creating system boundaries by specific CIS features
Energy controlling	Discussions to change the interpretation by providing new data	Supporting cultural change by symbolic CIS management	Supporting cultural change by changing the CIS

Table 4: Guiding beliefs as part of the information culture

Basis		Individual	Group	Organization
Guiding beliefs	Need for power	The pursuit of individual power is o.k. for us	Power to all my friends (only to them!)	Only the power of the whole organization counts
	Need for achievement	Individual search for excellence has top priority	Performance of the department counts	Success of the whole organization is what we all need
	Need for affiliation	I belong "to myself" and to nothing else	Belonging to this group is really important	Be part of the whole organization!
	Need for avoidance	Anybody else should do it, but not me	Only our team has worked hard enough	All this should not be our business

We will use the McClelland idea and apply it in a modified way to information systems: in order to do so, we first interpret these four needs as *guiding beliefs* of the organization's members. Then we have to define the *conceptual basis* these values focus on: the two extreme alternatives would be the individual (as McClelland sees it), or the organization as a whole. As a position in between, guiding beliefs may be established for subgroups of the organization.

The four needs and the three corresponding bases lead to a 3×4-framework (Table 4), suitable for analyzing the belief systems connected with a CIS.

Related to a CIS, the two extreme bases have distinct different consequences: if a CIS is connected with *individual* achievement and individual power, the rules of the games tell us to construct barriers against others to protect our secret data; information becomes a tool to increase individual power and success. If, on the other hand, achievement and power are seen as being bound to the whole *organization*, we get a completely different behaviour: in that case, no information barriers hinder the free flow of information within the organization, since everyone agrees on using information as a strategic fact or to increase the overall success.

4.2 A Modified List of Variables

In order to get an efficient instrument able to capture information culture, these 12 guiding beliefs shall be reduced to decrease complexity and to make space for some other variables. Needless to say: all 12 variables stated in Table 5 are of empirical relevance. But not all of them relate to CIS in the same direct way.

Communication means two or more persons exchanging relevant data. But it is a problem whether information flows freely just within the working group or even further within the whole organization. The key answer to this question is the way in which the need for achievement has been established: if it is bound to the group, the emergence of subgroups and subcultures can be observed; if it is bound to the whole organization, these tendencies diminish. The same holds true for other activities, such as searching for new information or destroying old ones. Therefore, the need for *achievement* related to the *group* as well as the one related to the *organization* are two important variables.

On the other hand, the role of the individual is of extreme importance. Dealing with a CIS, he or she either takes it as an instrument to strengthen individual power or tries to avoid any contact with the CIS. Therefore, the *individual*-related needs for *power* and for *avoidance* must be added to the list of relevant variables.

Theories on organizations stress the importance of belonging to a group: this holds true basically for all members of an organization and is one of the explanations for the existence of organizations. With respect to a CIS, this desire leads to joint working procedures and shared data bases. It also may be associated with various other aspects such as commonly accepted rituals of dealing with computerized information. Therefore, the need for *affiliation* to the *group* is the next key variable to be considered.

All these variables mentioned above have a strong impact on the information-processing activities within the organization. Still, they only cover a small portion of the large spectrum of CIS phenomenons. Therefore, additional variables are needed.

Trying to implement or to change a CIS, everyone runs into the problem of *safety* in the sense of reliability and protection. If an information culture has safety as a dominant value, various procedures will be established to ensure uncomplicated system performance. The risk of wasting time for back-up rituals is considered to be less negative than to be surprised by the system. In the opposite culture, *ad hoc* repairs are accepted as rules of the game.

Each system has boundaries. Therefore, a variable is needed to describe the degree in which the organization considers free and unlimited exchange of information to be appropriate. *Frankness* describes the degree to which the communication within the organization or within the group takes place without any restrictions imposed by the organization or by members of the organization. A consequence of this frankness is the degree to which individuals get access to shared data bases.

Any organization has certain tendencies towards organizational structures. These structures relate to information culture in a way that it is considered to be common practice in the organization to accept or to enforce certain structural determinants. In this sense, *order* within the organization and *centralism* are important indicators for information culture. While centralism relates to structure, order focuses on processes. Order and centralism are independent of each other: for instance, a centralized CIS may display a fascinating chaos (loved by everyone). But it is important to note that not the mere existence of these structures is of cultural relevance, but their broad acceptance.

Speaking to developers and users of a CIS, one soon finds various degrees to which the technology by itself is regarded as a core value. "Computer freaks" need the most advanced hard- and software available to cope with their own standards. This tendency to try and use new technologies not for their particular functions but for pure delight shall be taken into account by *technology orientation*.

Finally, CIS cultures differ with respect to the degree of *flexibility* and *standardization* wanted by the CIS users. Again, not the actual flexibility and standardization turn out to be cultural components but the commonly accepted pursuit of flexibility and standardization.

Table 5 sums up these 12 variables which describe information cultures: even though they are currently based on isolated experiences by the author and not on broad empirical research, they still show enough face validity to be used in the following sections.

Table 5: Variables characterizing information cultures

Criterion	Definition	Evaluation
1 Achievement/group	Strive for success and for the group's goal attainment	Modified TAT In-depth interviews
2 Achievement/organization	Organization's pursuit for success and performance	
3 Avoidance/individual	Individual need for avoidance of certain things	
4 Power/individual	Individual need for power and dominance	
5 Affiliation/group	Searching for social contacts within the working group	
6 Safety	Protection against discontinuities	Questionnaire Interview
7 Frankness	Unrestricted communication within the whole organization	
8 Order	Degree of process harmonization	Document analysis, expert reasoning, interviews
9 Centralism	Distribution of competences within the organization	
10 Technology orientation	Tendency to try and use new technologies	Assessment of used technologies
11 Flexibility	Adaptability to changing situations	Document analysis, expert reasoning, interviews
12 Standardization	Unification of task processes	

4.3 Radar Chart as an Illustrative Tool

To make the results of the CIS-Culture-analysis more visible, the *radar chart technique* shall be used, which has proven to be effective in industry analysis (Scholz 1987b, Scholz/Josephy 1984).

By constructing a closed curve to represent a given set of data, the radar chart takes advantage of the human mind's ability to discern similarities and differences in (closed) visual images: the radar chart allows to comprehend simultaneously several variables as one whole figure. Instead of plotting the values above a horizontal axis — as usually done in regular line diagram —, a closed figure is constructed by plotting and connecting points along the radii of a circle. Using standardized scales, the centre represents the value of 0, the circumference the value of 100.

Figure 5 displays an example of a real information culture: in this case, we find *high* scores for avoidance/individual, affiliation/group, order; in contrast to this, variables such as centralism and technology orientation display rather *low* values. For other variables, e. g., for achievement/group and safety, we see *medium* scores. Because of the standardization procedure, the labels "low" through "high" are always to be seen in the particular context of the sample under investigation.

It is important to note that this particular culture in Figure 5 does not reflect the behaviour or the values of an individual, but the information culture of a group or of a whole organization.

Of course, there might be various *subcultures* within the organization, each having its own information culture: the probability of those subcultures to exist is always high in cases in which

— the affiliation to the group is high, and/or
— the achievement of the group is high, and/or
— the need for individual power is low, and/or
— the achievement of the organization is high, and/or
— centralism and standardization are low.

If the information culture of the organization displays these values, a variety of different information cultures is to be expected, which have their common cultural basis in similar values for those five variables.

Information Culture Radar Chart

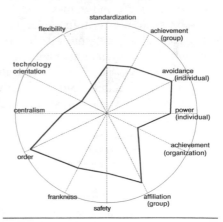

Figure 5: Information culture radar chart

5 CIS Culture: Illustrations

Attributes of a CIS, such as access to the computer and to data banks, size, and speed, as well as compatibility, always have functional and symbolic meanings. This holds true especially for a CIS as a *symbol of power*. Some years ago, the powerful managers usually made others work on the computer. Now the trend is changing: the existence and the control of a CIS signals power! Therefore, some people measure the power of an institute or a department by counting PCs, laser printers, and network accesses. Again, we see the symbolic meaning: it is not only important to use computers, but also to simply have them.

In summary, symbolic meanings are associated with the type of CIS (affiliation), with the strict non-acceptance of a CIS (avoidance), and/or with the technical data of the systems (achievement).

Especially *local area networks* (LANs) become increasingly important because of their symbolic value. Such a LAN is based upon guiding beliefs, especially the needs for

— individual/collective power,
— individual/collective achievement,
— individual/collective affiliation, and
— individual/collective avoidance.

The specific symbolic meanings depend on the specific type of LAN structure, its content, and its design process. Only to a certain degree it depends on functional attributes: one system may be seen to support individual power and achievement, connected with collective affiliation and avoidance, while a physically identical system may be seen to support exactly the opposite beliefs and values.

The symbolic meaning of a CIS, therefore, depends not only on the technical and functional attributes, but also on the organizational context in which the system is planned, constructed, or used. It also depends on the *ad hoc* psychological context of the individuals involved. Also psychological details contribute to CIS symbolics, such as how the system is drawn in the manual, in particular, with or without users, or with or without organizational hierarchies.

Many of these systems are just in the process of construction, making the energy-controlling aspects really important. Discussing where and why and how these LANs should be installed is, therefore, not only useful to detect culture, but is also a tool to change organizational culture. Since we usually are short of tools which foster cultural change, designing, implementing, and experiencing a CIS may be of substantial value to the cultural agent.

6 CIS Culture: A Dynamic Example

CIS culture is, by no means, a static construct: it changes over time as a *dynamic system*. Especially the dualistic exchange between organizational culture and organizational behaviour, discussed already in Figure 2, leads to various changes in culture as well as in behaviour.

The following development of a CIS culture (based on a real case) shows an extreme example with four different types of culture manifesting themselves along the time axis (Figure 6):

1 The organization starts out with a strong *bureaucracy culture*, characterized by high values for standardization, security, centralism, order, and individual avoidance.
2 Derived from the corporate strategy, the organization aims at an *innovative culture* with high marks on flexibility, affiliation, achievement (group), and openness. While (1) has been an existing culture, (2) is, at this stage, just a goal: it shows how the culture should look like.
3 Due to the influence on (1) created by (2), the organizational culture begins to change. But instead of moving towards the desired innovation-

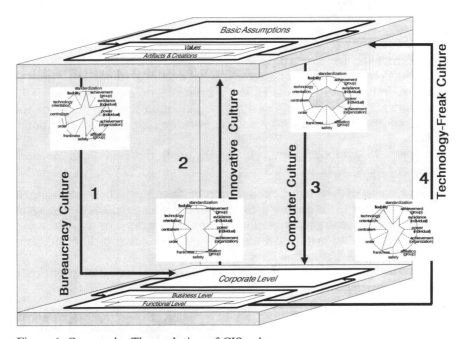

Figure 6: Case study: The evolution of CIS culture

oriented culture, a typical *computer culture* grows: it has an extremely positive orientation towards technology, a strong centralistic tendency, and a strict search for individual avoidance.

4 These new guiding beliefs of (3) combine with (2), leading to a behaviour in which technology by itself becomes the ultimate goal. Since we also reach complete openness and flexibility in the behaviour, this creates a stable culture to be labelled *"technology-freak culture."*

This case is a rather extreme one: but it points out the huge potential of cultural change and the problems of dealing with (CIS)culture on a dynamic perspective.

This dualistic model of cultural change does not only explain the phenomenon of change of a CIS culture, it is also a tool for dealing with change of the overall organizational culture (Scholz/Hofbauer 1990). In this case, more global variables must be used, taking into account the complete spectrum of cultural variables. In addition to this, it must be noted that often the problem becomes even more complicated, since we have to deal with various subcultures, which in turn aggregate into an overall culture.

7 Consequences

Considering the increasing importance of CIS, especially in the area of Personal Computing, everyone agrees on its functional importance. But the symbolic values are, in most cases, overlooked or underestimated. CIS symbolics may serve not only as a tool to determine and to strengthen the organizational culture, but may also support the change of organizational culture.

Before CIS symbolics can actually be used, more in-depth research becomes necessary. In particular:

— We have to understand the connection between the technical facts, their attributes for the user, and their symbolic meaning (which is contingent to environmental and psychological circumstances).
— The full scale of symbolic alternatives must be developed and reduced to the truly characteristic ones.
— Alternative intervention strategies must be analyzed and empirically tested.

The process of creating and developing a CIS may involve verbal and action-oriented symbols. Still, in all cases, a CIS is definitely a *material symbol:* talking about a CIS, introducing the CIS, and experiencing the

CIS; all becomes part of symbolic management. These symbolic procedures allow for describing, enhancing, and changing culture.

One may argue that it is too early to influence organizational culture by means of CIS symbolics. Still there is no doubt that we have to think about the symbolics of the existing or planned CIS. These symbolics do exist, even if the managers in charge of EDP do not believe in organizational symbolism. Even if they do not use the power of the CIS symbolics (yet), we and they should be aware of these symbolics in everyday life.

Taking into account the importance of the CIS culture for the overall culture, the CIS culture could turn out to be one of the key factors in dealing with cultural phenomenons.

References

Argyris, C. (1964): *Integrating the Individual and the Organization.* New York: Wiley

Berger, P. L. and T. Luckmann (1966): *The Social Construction of Reality: A Treatise in the Sociology of Knowledge.* New York: Doubleday

Cohen, A. M. (1976): *Two-Dimensional Man: An Essay on the Anthropology of Power and Symbolism in Complex Societies.* Berkeley, CA: University of California Press

Cyert, R. M. and J. G. March (1963): *A Behavioral Theory of the Firm.* Englewood Cliffs, NJ: Prentice Hall

Dandridge, T. C., I. I. Mitroff, and W. F. Joyce (1980): Organizational Symbolism: A Topic to Expand Organizational Analysis. *Academy of Management Review* 5, pp. 77 – 82

Frost, P. J., L. F. Moore, M. R. Louis, C. C. Lundberg, and J. Martin (Eds.) (1985): *Organizational Culture.* Beverly Hills – London – New Delhi: Sage

McClelland, D. C. (1975): *Power: The Inner Experience.* New York: Irvington

McClelland, D. C. (1985): *Human Motivation.* Glenview, IL: Scott, Foresman & Co.

McFarlan, F. W. and J. L. McKenney (1983): *Corporate Information System Management. The Issues Facing Senior Executives.* Homewood, IL: Irwin

Morgan, G. and L. Smircich (1980): The Case for Qualitative Research. *Academy of Management Review* 5, pp. 491 – 500

Pfeffer, J. (1981): Management as Symbolic Action: The Creation and Maintenance of Organizational Paradigms. *Research in Organizational Behavior.* L. L. Cummings/B. M. Staw (Eds.). Greenwich, CT: JAI Press, Vol. 3, pp. 1 – 52

Pondy, L. R. (1983): The Role of Metaphors and Myths in Organization and in the Facilitation of Change. *Organizational Symbolism.* L. R. Pondy/P. J. Frost/G. Morgan/T. C. Dandridge (Eds.). Greenwich, CT: JAI Press, pp. 157 – 166

Pondy, L. R., P. J. Frost, G. Morgan, and T. C. Dandridge (Eds.) (1983): *Organizational Symbolism.* Greenwich, CT: JAI Press

Porter, L. W., E. E. Lawler, and J. R. Hackman (1975): *Behavior in Organizations.* New York: McGraw Hill

Sathe, V. (1985): *Culture and Related Corporate Realities. Text, Cases, and Readings on Organizational Entry, Establishment, and Change.* Homewood, IL: Irwin

Schein, E. H. (1980): *Organizational Psychology*. Englewood Cliffs, NJ: Prentice-Hall, 3rd ed.

Schein, E. H. (1985): *Organizational Culture and Leadership. A Dynamic View*. San Francisco, CA: Jossey-Bass

Scholz, Ch. (1982): The Architecture of Hierarchy. *Kybernetes* 11, pp. 175–181

Scholz, Ch. (1987 a): Corporate Culture and Strategy. The Problem of Strategic Fit. *Long Range Planning* 20(4), pp. 78–87

Scholz, Ch. (1987 b): *Strategisches Management. Ein integrativer Ansatz*. Berlin: de Gruyter

Scholz, Ch. (1988): Organisationskultur — Zwischen Schein und Wirklichkeit. *Zeitschrift für betriebswirtschaftliche Forschung* 40, pp. 243–272

Scholz, Ch. (1989): *Personalmanagement. Informationsorientierte und verhaltenstheoretische Grundlagen*. München: Vahlen

Scholz, Ch. and W. Hofbauer (1990): *Organisationskultur. Die vier Erfolgsprinzipien*. Wiesbaden: Gabler

Scholz, Ch. and N. Josephy (1984): *Industry Analysis: The Pattern Approach*. Working paper HBS 84–44. Boston, MA: Graduate School of Business Administration, Harvard University

Shull, F. A., A. L. Delbecq, and L. C. Cummings (1970): *Organizational Decision Making*. New York: McGraw Hill

Simon, H. A. (1986): The Impact of Electronic Communication on Organizations. *Organizing Industrial Development*. R. Wolf (Ed.). Berlin: de Gruyter, pp. 251–266

Smircich, L. (1983): Studying Organizations as Cultures. *Beyond Method. Strategies for Social Research*. G. Morgan (Ed.). Beverly Hills — London — New Delhi: Sage, pp. 160–172

Turner, B. A. (1990): *Organizational symbolism*. Berlin — New York: de Gruyter

Car Makers and Marathon Runners: In Pursuit of Culture Through the Language of Leadership

Claudia Piccardo, Giuseppe Varchetta, and Gianni Zanarini

1 Introduction

Our aim in this essay is to analyze the language of leadership in a cultural perspective and suggest that the communications, or "communication products" of social agents whose task it is to guide and coordinate men's actions, should be analyzed as cultural products ("artefacts") that enable us to understand and interpret a culture. Thus, we shall speak of language both as a cultural product and as an instrument used in leadership to create a culture, meaning that a leader can, through language, process and legitimate collective experience by helping to create shared meanings within a culture.

Many studies of the symbolism of organizations have stressed the fundamental role that leadership plays in channelling cultural meaning and establishing a context in which members of the organization can elaborate shared interpretations of such meanings (Peters 1978, Pfeffer 1981, Smircich/Morgan 1982). To the extent that any specific corporate culture gives its members both identity and models for the interpretation of day-to-day experience, a leader's activity in creating, reinforcing, and promoting the growth of a culture can be crucial in ensuring that this experience becomes truly integrative — a way of enhancing the organization's ability to react in the face of the unknown, to respond to external challenges, and to promote its own survival.

This capacity for social planning, which is certainly no less important than the ability to set up formal coordination structures and mechanisms within the organization, is also revealed in language; that is to say, in being able to find "the words to say what something is." One basic task of leadership is the creation of language that can grasp, comprehend, process, and then render explicit those themes which, by the very fact of being made explicit, can give those involved in any particular situation the wherewithal to grasp its significance and place it in an appropriate context or perspective.

This essay will suggest a way of interpreting texts that reveals the cultural significance of language by establishing a "dialogue" with the text itself. The model we describe will then be used to analyze a speech delivered by the leader of a large manufacturing concern.

2 Various Approaches to Text Analysis

Before defining our own model of text analysis, it will be useful to survey the major models described in theoretical and practical text analysis literature. These approaches can be arranged under the three principal headings of *pragmatic*, *hermeneutic*, and *cooperative interpretation*.

2.1 Pragmatic Interpretation

When we feel the need to give a project or task a clear, unambiguous, non-contradictory, binding definition, we commonly speak of "putting something down in black and white." We attribute great power and precision to the black "signs" we write — they seem to stand out against the white background of the paper in a boldly purposeful way. Thus, pragmatic interpretation assumes that what we want is a clear perception of what a text's intention is, of what it "means" in the narrow sense of the term.

Anyone who reads or listens to a text in a pragmatic way will concentrate on "decoding" its message using public codes that give access to its meaning. The message's clarity and effectiveness will be assessed in terms of this code by measuring the redundancy or "wastage" of the message against an ideal model of communication.

The presence of intentionality in a text, and the fact that we want to decode it, are a function of the "operative" level of language, and provide the basis for the pragmatic interpretation of texts (Austin 1962, Watzlawick 1967).

2.2 Hermeneutic Interpretation

Text interpretation becomes more systematic and complex when, after examining the basic operative level of the text, we begin to search for something lying "beyond" the intentionality we have access to through public codes. When this happens, the reader assumes that a text's intentionality may be ambiguous, disguised, or even unconscious, and this lays the text open to a whole variety of interpretations. Of special importance is the fact that what a pragmatic approach would assess entirely in terms of communicative effectiveness or otherwise now acquires meaning at a different level. For example, communicative ineffectiveness or reticence may be seen as a significant indication of an author's unconscious motivation or resistance.

Hermeneutic interpretation is particularly useful in understanding an author's personality, history (Gadamer 1960, Ricoeur 1965) and − of especial relevance to us here − his cultural background and his relations with the institutions that "speak through him." Hermeneutic interpretation has many different applications, but for simplicity's sake we shall distinguish here between "explicative" and "interpretative" applications only. In the former case, we attempt to discover what the text "really" means (e. g. by focussing on the "explanation" of unconscious meanings); in the latter, we recognize that a text carries a whole range of other "voices" that cannot entirely be explained in terms of the conscious or unconscious intentionality of the author, in which case hermeneutic interpretation helps us to isolate and identify "semantic layers" of a fairly broad and well organized type. The search for the meaning of the text thus becomes a rather less straightforward affair than might at first appear − certain "voices" will speak loudly, some will be softer toned, and others will present themselves openly or in disguise. We should also note that there is no objective way of telling exactly when a hermeneutic analysis (composition and decomposition, the reading of "clues," various kinds of observation) is complete.

2.3 Cooperative Interpretation

Using hermeneutic interpretation as his starting point, Gadamer has produced another more highly developed version of the hermeneutic approach which stresses the fundamental importance of the "hermeneutic circle" linking the reader to the text. For clarity's sake, we shall regard this "higher" form of the hermeneutic approach as a method in its own right, and we shall refer to it from now on as cooperative interpretation (Eco 1979, Valesio 1980). In this approach, the reader is not just a "decoder"; he is also a participant in a process in which his fantasies, associations, and intuition contribute to construct the meaning of the text. In many ways, this process is similar to musical interpretation, in which the transformation of the written notes of a musical score actually increases rather than reduces the importance of the notes themselves (their sequence, harmonic structure, rhetorical formulation), insofar as musical meaning cannot exist independently of the notes that convey it.

With the previous two approaches, we saw that questions are asked of the text — the text is "interrogated" in order to discover or decode its meaning. One important premise of this third, more highly developed approach is that the text itself can ask questions of the reader, can subject us to interrogation. This means that the fantasies, associations, and intuitions of the reader play a more important role — after all, how can a "semantic hunt" be possible without the intuition and "sixth sense" of the hunter, without his skill at putting himself in the position of his prey and imagining what he will do next?

In our view, cooperative interpretation not only encompasses and extends the range of the other previous two approaches; it also closely corresponds to what most people's "natural" way of reading is, to what we make of a text when our minds are free of defensive simplifications and rationalizations, the imposed need to "explain" a text definitively, or the fear of finding things that refuse to fall neatly into existing hermeneutic grids.

Later in this essay we will propose certain ways of analyzing texts, and our interpretation will be predominantly cooperative because, in our view, it not only encompasses, but also gives better results than the other approaches we have examined so far.

3 Dialogue with the Text

It will have been noticed that, while advocating the use of cooperative interpretation in text analysis, we attempt nonetheless to construct our own hermeneutic grid, and this puts us, to an extent, in a rather contradictory position. A genuinely interpretative approach tends, of its very nature, to question the validity of "fixed" analytical grids. And yet, it is very useful methodologically to have (while remaining aware, naturally, of its inevitable limitations) some technique that promotes "dialogue with the text" without restricting the subjectivity of the reader's associative procedures.

"Dialogue with the text" is clearly not a literal term — texts are fixed and unalterable, and can neither be changed into something other than what they already are, nor literally made to answer the questions asked of them (or perhaps, rather, a text can supply answers to only certain questions, and then only to a certain extent). Text interpretation passes through stages in which the text is, in a sense, "reawakened" through interrogation, and the fact that certain questions have no answers can be significant in itself, especially when the reader, by closing the "interpretative" circle, as it were "falls asleep" with the text and elaborates a sort of dream based on material it suggested to him.

These interpretative stages have no fixed sequence; the reader's relationship with the text is naturally circular and alternates between phases of "reawakening" or "falling asleep with" the text. For clarity's sake, however, we shall discuss the two stages separately as if they were ordered in a linear rather than circular way, dealing first with elements of a more or less objective kind, and then moving on to examine more subjective, or in a sense, more arbitrary matters.

3.1 Rhetorical Analysis

Ever since ancient times, rhetorical analysis has studied texts systematically (Perelman/Obrechts-Tyteca 1958) to try to discover the "secret" of communication, and it can still give us much help in first identifying and then classifying discourse elements and structures.

Rhetorical analysis can either work outwards and away from basic considerations like the size and complexity of a text's linguistic features, or else burrow down from them to still deeper layers in the text, i. e. analysis can either move outwards from a text's words to its wider features, or vice versa. For the sake of convenience, our later analysis will work down from the overall structure of the text towards the level at which its sentences and words operate.

One of our first concerns should always be the rhetorical framing of the text as a whole. Who wrote the text? For whom? In what context? In which circumstances? With what expectations? With what assumptions about the reader? What seem to be the (explicit or implicit, conscious or unconscious) objectives of the author? What rhetorical strategies does he seem to have adopted? How does he begin, develop, and end the text? What techniques has he used to persuade, influence, or convince his reader?

To give a more satisfactory answer to the last of these questions, we must descend to a lower structural level in the text, which means, essentially, that we have to identify the nature and sequence of the text's themes, its logical structure, its linguistic "constructs" and, above all, the rhetorical figures it makes use of, especially those of thought (irony, reticence) and meaning (such as metaphor, in which meaning is "condensed," or metonymy, in which there is a "shift" of meaning, as when a container is made to stand for what it contains).

We then analyze the actual lexical features of the text. What kinds of words are used? Are they mainly abstract or concrete? If the latter, in which other contexts do the words normally have their literal meanings? Are they, for example, commonplaces of the author's personal historical and cultural context, or archaisms, or neologisms?

It should be noted here that an author's usage can vary during the course of a text, i. e. the lexical features of a text can vary from section to section. For example, a variation in the kinds of words used can mark divisions in the text which, in turn, correspond to its wider rhetorical structure.

3.2 The Reader and the Affective Dimension of the Text

Though various, the previous questions we asked of the text all had something in common — they were all intended to "reawaken the text"; that is, they attempted to draw attention systematically to words, silences, images, figures, and sequences that might otherwise have passed unnoticed. The basic task of collecting and then systematically ordering the basic linguistic features of a text is necessary in first surveying and then interpreting a text.

In cooperative interpretation, this enables us not only to identify the instrumental, operative, or pragmatic features of a text, but also to gauge its affective range (Fornari 1979).

There are two basic affective levels in a text. The first and perhaps most important is the strictly personal experience of the author that prompted him to write in the first place, the level at which affective meaning is embedded in the unique and unrepeatable "personal novel" of the author's life. Then, there is the cultural level rooted in the shared reality to which the author belongs, which has its own "affective constructs" and unique ways of articulating them. Obviously, the author need not be consciously aware that he participates in this "shared affectivity" since it will "speak" through him in any case (Fornari 1979).

No particular method is needed to analyze the affective dimension of a text — rhetorical analysis is enough to enable us to arrive at a cooperative interpretation of it.

It goes without saying that certain features or sections of a text — rhetorical figures of meaning, for example, or rhetorical strategies in general — carry non-literal affective meaning more explicitly than others. For example, we might ask whether the rhetorical structure of a text was consciously adopted by its author or whether it expresses needs, projects, and values that are either personal to the author (although he remains unconscious of them) or part of the culture that speaks through him. We could then ask whether the rhetorical figures he employs are crystallized in the common usage of the language he speaks, are his own personal inventions, or belong to a certain culture. By asking similar questions of the text's lexis, we can build up the "affective meanings" of individual words or sentences into larger "affective constructs." To use our previous metaphor once again, we could say that a text's "affective halo" is, in effect, its "music," and that this is quite distinct from the words themselves (even though carried by them) in the same way that music is expressed through notes but can never be reduced to them alone. In order to understand a piece of music, we must do more than analyze its musical structure, we must also abandon ourselves to the emotions and associations it produces in us.

Similarly, to perceive the full affective range of a text, we must do more than analyze it objectively as an expression of the feelings, imagination, and emotions of an author or the social group he belongs to; we must also be aware of the text's affective meaning as we read it. We then realize that the text not only relates the personal history of its author and the culture he belongs to, but also something of our own personal history and the institutions and culture we belong to. The text's "personal" dimension may seem to have little to do with text analysis as such, but it would be as well to remember that interpretation is inevitably subjective in some ways, and that while this may sometimes limit the efficiency of our reading, it also gives us a "lens" to see features that otherwise might have escaped our attention.

4 Cooperative Interpretation in Action

To show how our approach actually works, we shall now analyze a specific text, a speech given by Vittorio Ghidella, General Manager of Fiat Auto, to mark the unveiling of a new range of Fiat models at the 1986 Turin Motor Show.

Obviously, we cannot provide a detailed analysis in an essay of this length; our aim is simply to give greater practical focus to the earlier theoretical sections of the essay.

We hope the reader will start formulating his own cooperative interpretation of the text as he reads, and, for this reason, the speech we have chosen for analysis is given in full before we offer our own interpretation of it.

4.1 The Leader's Speech

When we last met I spoke of Fiat's recovery, fully aware that we had worked extremely hard, but also very well, to make it happen. I also expressed the hope that I would be able to confirm these results the next time we met, and I think I can say that the promise I made then has been kept: over the past year and a half we have succeeded in consolidating our position not only in the market, but also in terms of market share and economic results.

In the motor industry, the race for success is never won by the hundred metres sprinter; it calls for the determination and stamina of the marathon runner, and I think that we, as marathon runners ourselves, have the strong legs and powerful lungs needed for the job we have to do.

If you will allow me a sporting turn of phrase, Fiat is now out in front with that small group of runners that leads the field, and the continuity of our achievement has had few precedents or parallels in the history of the motor industry. Since 1984 Fiat has invested 2000 billion liras in the research, technological development, and robotization that enables it to go on offering increasingly advanced, truly modern products. Our present Fiat and Lancia ranges, with an average life of 3.2 years, are unquestionably the most modern in Europe, and the significance of this achievement reflects not only the efforts we ourselves have made, but also the competitiveness of the company we work for. A new Fiat model means a product that offers the best of modern technology, maximum comfort, and the most competitive retail price; products fully able to meet customer needs that are also rapidly evolving.

Let us look for a moment at some of the results that have led to this success. As regards market share, we came out ahead in the first quarter of this year (Spain included, this time) with a share of 13.6%. I wouldn't want to make too much of this, however. Being first means the ability to hold a position for a while, only perhaps to lose it at some later date. It means little in itself. What really counts is always being out in front, and we have certainly managed to do that for a good many years now.

The Fiat Uno was the best-selling car in Europe in the first quarter of this year, and is still holding its position as the best-selling car in its market segment. In economic terms, Fiat is highly profitable. I cannot anticipate here results that still await official confirmation, but I will say that they are twice as good as last year's and so entirely satisfactory, especially considering the size and nature of the motor industry as a whole. All our investments during this period were financed with our own capital, and cash flow has been around 11%. Results like these certainly justify my saying that we are up front with the leaders, and that's exactly where we want to remain. The scenario in which we operate at present is a very complex one. Demand is a key success factor for any manufacturer, and of course we have all seen that demand has grown, but it has only been short-term growth. Over the long term, growth has been much slower. I believe that we will certainly see growth over the next few years, but only of a moderate kind. It is true that present macro-economic conditions favour growth, but we are speaking of only a few percent here. And this growth will be subject to extremely wide fluctuations produced by a number of contingent factors: Italian market growth, for example, which was crucially important last year and will be this year; the recovery of the German market after uncertainty created by the prospect of ecological legislation, or the recovery of other European markets like Switzerland and Holland. These are all things which suggest that slow, but hopefully steady growth will nonetheless be subject to wide upward or downward fluctuations that will stretch our flexibility to the limit.

I don't foresee any major market upheavals. True, the Japanese are still with us and are pressing hard, and the Koreans are lurking round the corner with their high competitive potential, but as I said, I still don't foresee any major upheavals, even in terms of mergers or amalgamations. I took part in the negotiations between Fiat and Ford, and I know just how difficult it is to bring together and merge interests of the scale and complexity of those found in the motor industry. The arguments against such mergers are not merely corporate but also legal and fiscal.

In a market that is basically stable though also rather neurotic, in a market that is both stable as well as highly competitive, we can be sure that there are no magic formulas for success. So what strategy must we adopt to remain out in front over the next few years?

Simply belonging to the Fiat group is already an important ingredient for success. The group is extremely healthy at the moment, which means that it can produce synergies and integrations of a very profitable kind. However, when I look at Fiat's internal situation, I am convinced that we must keep on going in the way that we have up to now, by which I mean that we must continue to apply all those rigorous and, if you like, pedantic rules of sound management practice that have rewarded us with the success we now enjoy.

I would say that the common denominator of all these rules of good management can be summed up by one word, or concept: innovation.

Innovation is a very general word that can be used to refer to almost anything: when we speak of innovation in a firm, we certainly think of technological or product innovation, but we should and must think also in terms of innovation in organizational methods and administrative and financial procedures. In a firm, innovation can and must be introduced wherever possible. Let's look at a few examples to see what this really means. If we set up a cost-control system that enables us to calculate the profitability of a product or market in a very short space of time, we will be able to move allocations and sales resources around in a selective way. If our management keeps a careful eye on its floating capital, we can earmark substantial financial resources for product investment, which is another crucial ingredient for success. If we use our financial lever to obtain financial resources at reasonable cost which then enable us to offer both our customers and sales network the kind of leasing, credit, and stock financing facilities they need, then we have another range of possibilities crucial to success. Innovation is an enormous subject that affects every aspect of management, as I said at some length the last time we met. Since some people said then that all I really wanted to do was give you a lecture on company management (although that was far from being the case), I'll limit myself this time to the concept of product innovation.

The automobile is a product that is now morphologically mature, but I would stress the word morphological. A car generally has four or five wheels, a motor, a gear box, a body, and seats. It is perceived as an everyday object, so its features are well known. However, the automobile's apparent maturity actually conceals the fact that it is undergoing radical transformation. It is my firm belief that no other product on the market today is more technologically oriented than the modern automobile. High-tech solutions are being sought in many industries, but we already have them in the products we all sit in every day when we go to work or drive around. We all know about the resins, reinforced resins, and carbon-strengthened resins that the motor industry has borrowed from space technology, or perhaps more accurately, helicopter manufacture, to use in bodywork construction. We know about the optical fibres now being used in electrical systems and motors, and about advanced antielectromagnetic disturbance systems. And of course we've heard all about "electronics." The term is now virtually exhausted, but for me it means the computerized management of highly sophisticated on-board systems. A modern fuel injection system is now not very different, at least in conceptual terms, from the systems that are used to pilot aircraft. We also have the high resistance ceramics now being used in turbines, exhaust ducts, pistons, and cylinder barrels, and these are the ceramics normally used for space shuttles or other similar space applications. I'm not interested in deciding whether or not automobile technology depends on space technology — I'm simply saying that in order to ensure that products are truly innovative in the full sense of the term, we have to commit ourselves one hundred percent to making full use of all the research now being done in laboratories all over the world.

The rate of innovation has accelerated in our industry over recent years, just as it has done in many other areas in the recent or not so recent past. Competition between leading motor manufacturers is limited to those who are able to change product innovation into a recipe for success. Certainly, as I said earlier, everything about a car can benefit from innovation, everything can be improved, but we must be very careful here. In order for innovation to be measurable, to be perceived in concrete terms by our customers in the real world outside, the one that counts, it has to be introduced for a specific purpose, has to be channelled towards an end. While in no way overlooking any research and so also potential innovation available to us, we at Fiat and Lancia have chosen performance as our major area for innovative development. What do I mean here by performance? Performance usually means speed or acceleration, and in historical terms the concept is rather a limited one. Fiat now sees performance as a matter of fuel economy, road-holding, comfort, and a whole series of other features that extend the range of the concept enormously. As I have defined it, performance should be seen as a way of enabling us to offer our customers a positive safety guarantee; that is, they must feel that they are in control of a safe machine that is easy to drive and built realistically for the person who drives it. With this global approach to safety, the achievement of high performance obviously means heavy investment in the development of engines, suspension, aerodynamics, brakes, and on-board electronic control systems — investment in a lot of different areas. While narrowing down our constant search for innovation to the concept of "performance," I have also made a point of referring to all the various sectors in which innovation useful to us may emerge, and this could be seen as a contradiction. But it isn't really. The effort required of us is the same in all cases — what really changes is the approach to the problem. We have to look at the question as a whole, see it in an integrated way. Customers want the kind of performance I have described; and our kind of customer at least wants to be able to travel in all weathers — rain, ice, or sunshine — in maximum comfort and safety with an eye to average speed rather than top speed. In effect, the customer wants to feel happy while driving within the limits of his own natural ability. Our aim is to combine this feeling of security with the concept of "innovation." Seen in this way, innovation acquires real value, in the sense that the customer is happy to invest in a consumer product when he knows he is getting maximum comfort, safety, and financial benefit in return.

We are pursuing this policy in every segment of the market, as the innovativeness and modernity of our product range has recently shown. "Performance" and "positive safety guarantee" mean different things in different products. Fiat tends to emphasize performance plus economy, while Lancia tends to identify performance with stylishness and maximum comfort. We have concrete examples of this: the new Uno Turbo Diesel, which succeeds in combining brilliant performance with remarkable purchase price as well as low running costs and, naturally, a high standard of comfort, or the new Thema 8/32, a beautiful machine that likewise offers a perfect combination of exciting performance and maximum stylishness and comfort.

Having said this, and returning once again to the concept of global innovation which, as I said, has such a wide range of meanings and connotations, let me now say that innovation alone is not enough to guarantee the competitiveness of a product. Amount of innovation is strictly related to both research and development costs and to size of investment. All firms want to be able to say that they invest heavily in machinery, plant, and research and development, but we should be careful here because some firms invest heavily without necessarily being the most successful as a result. The strictly technical aspects of innovation might well seem to be success factors in their own right, but the availability of technical information today is such that new inventions no longer enjoy the caché they once did or, if they do, only for a short while. Sophistication of innovation could also be regarded as a success factor, but we should remember that highly sophisticated makes of only recent times have ceased to be successful. What must we do, then, to get the most out of innovation? Well, innovation has to be chosen in relation to market need, and in a way that makes sense in terms of brand policy and image. In order to acquire real value, innovation must have aims and, as I have said time and time again, it must be planned. I can assure you that it is very difficult indeed to predict the success of any innovation or application when it is implemented on a selective basis. Everything has to be quantified in relation to real, complex market situations which, since they can vary enormously from one moment to the next, call for flexibility of thinking and resources. In short, what you need is a technical vocation, an ability to digest and synthesize, that cannot be acquired in only a brief space of time. Success in our race depends on the abilities of individual men. It is produced by their imagination, dedication, application, and tenacity. In other words, it is the result of the history of a product and the men who represent it.

4.2 A Suggested Interpretation

It is interesting to note (as an aspect of context that illuminates rhetorical framing) that the speech was recorded on video and used inside the company itself; it was shown, in fact, to groups of Fiat managers. We might assume, then, that in terms of the rhetorical intentions and strategies of its author, the text was regarded as valuable to management personnel both inside and outside the company, i. e. the speech was considered especially important for the values that could be transmitted through it.

The author's view, then, is that these values can reinforce both the company's corporate culture, and its external image. Thus, the context in which the speech was given seems to have been a way of reinforcing the author's message inside the company, suitably amplified through the use of mass communications techniques.

However, the speech also assumes the presence of direct interlocutors (audience, journalists). When we look at its structure, we see that they are addressed through references to continuity with the past and statements of the company's credibility and success. Immediately after, this success is linked to effort and commitment using a rhetorical figure which we think is the most significant structural aspect of the entire text: the metaphor of the marathon runner.

Echoes of this metaphor reappear in later sections where the thematic structure of the text (success, the scenario, innovation) is elaborated. Whenever "competition" or "being up in front" is mentioned, the reader (or listener) will immediately be reminded of the opening metaphor of the marathon runner. Thus, a phrase towards the end of the speech ("Success in this race depends on the abilities of individual men") returns us, through a sort of in-built structural loop, to the opening image, thereby emphasizing how the whole text is, in fact, organized around it.

In this opening image, we see that the theme of the struggle for success in the motor industry is introduced in a general metaphor (the race) which Ghidella uses to distinguish between the two classical and best-known types of competition, the hundred metres and the marathon. The marathon is chosen to represent the motor industry since it is the race that separates out the real athletes; it is the most exhausting of all races, and calls for stamina and strength as well as the "dedication, application, and tenacity" mentioned towards the end of the text.

It should be stressed here that the metaphor of the marathon runner is not simply another linguistic device, but a way of underlining and amplifying the affective content of one of the earliest statements of the speech, the need for continuity, stamina, and perseverance in getting, and then, most importantly, staying "out in front."

When we then analyze the lexical content of the text, it is interesting to see how certain words in common use acquire extra meaning when employed metaphorically (in this case, in the context of a sporting metaphor). For example, the word "effort" although usually used of muscle activity, is used here in a non-literal sense, as is the "race" for success. One important aspect of the rhetorical strategy of Ghidella's text would seem to be, then, the fact that it "reawakens" words that are sleeping, restoring their original physical referents.

The marathon is a long race requiring special powers of stamina and concentration in the athletes who run in it. It is also a highly selective race:

many start out, but within the first few miles only a few runners remain in the leading group — the real race is run by only a few of the original competitors. Thus, Fiat is now one of only a "small group of runners," but in order to keep its "stay out in front," it has to keep the competition under constant surveillance because in a marathon race the lead can be lost at any moment.

"We are up front with the leaders, and that's exactly where we want to remain," says Ghidella at one point, and yet any marathon runner is really on his own, is really running against himself. Is Ghidella, then, addressing individuals or the whole team, is he praising the efforts of individuals or those of the whole team? Attention would seem to be focussed on individual men: to win the race, you need to be well-trained individuals with "strong legs and powerful lungs."

Thus, Ghidella is directing his message at each individual marathon runner, and the message is not only contained by but also goes beyond the message he transmits to the journalists present. As we have already suggested, there are good contextual reasons for thinking that this speech was intended both for internal consumption within the firm as well as for outsiders (though perhaps to a lesser extent). Consequently, Ghidella urges each marathon runner to keep on running and not let the fact of being out in front go to his head.

And yet, in a speech also intended for external consumption, it is inevitable that there will be emphasis on the exceptional results the company has obtained, results that have had "few precedents or parallels in the history of the motor industry." So far, Ghidella has adopted the standard rhetorical procedure of giving his audience a string of superlatives: the range is the most modern in Europe, the products embody the best of current technology, they offer maximum comfort and running cost, the Uno is the best selling car in its market segment, and so on.

However, it would be dangerous if all these superlatives gave the impression that Fiat's future was absolutely certain, and in fact Ghidella urges his marathon runners not to lose their concentration and grip: a leading position can be held "for a while, only perhaps to be lost at some future date," and holding it requires sustained effort rather than the quick burst of the hundred metres runner.

Ghidella states that there are "no magic formulas for success," as if to say that nothing can be taken for granted, that the battle can never be finally won. Formulas are no more than shortcuts, seemingly enchanted pathways, but marathon runners have to follow the road that requires the application of all those "rigorous and, if you like, pedantic rules of sound management practice."

In such a competitive market, basically stable but also "neurotic," the only way to stay out in front with the leaders is to desire it obstinately, avidly. The race never lets up, and it's not just a race either — a faintly "criminal" metaphor seems to emerge at one point alongside the basic sporting metaphor. The Koreans are "lurking round the corner" waiting to launch a surprise attack. Defensive tactics are needed because the aggressor is always waiting to strike. This threat introduces a note of anxiety: Ghidella uses the adjective "neurotic" to describe the market, referring to a mental condition that can never be regarded as definitively cured, but which remains as a constant threat, like an enemy lurking around a corner.

However, the threat is followed by a reassurance — a few lines further on he lists success factors, sources of security which include belonging to the Fiat group. After references to illness, the Fiat group is presented as being "in excellent health" and so able to produce important kinds of "synergy and integration." Thus, the loneliness of the marathon runner is reduced by the fact that he belongs to an important group.

And yet, the reference to the Fiat group lasts only a few lines — the reassurance it offers is marginal rather than central to Ghidella's argument. Immediately after, he draws attention to Fiat Auto as such, of which he is the head, and says that it has to keep on going in the way it has up to now, like a good marathon runner. Notice once again how the basic metaphor of the text (the marathon race) can "reawake" and reinforce the meaning of the text's lexis, especially the verbs "go on" and "advance."

At this point we could say that, to use Ghidella's sporting terminology, the model of leadership he presents is that of the ideal winning athlete rather than that of the coordinator or trainer of a team. The team as such is never the main focus of the speech, as we have already seen. Every individual must run his own race and develop "strong legs and powerful lungs." Integration and synergy are important, but they form only the background to the main message that reinforces a culture based on individual effort.

Thus, Ghidella urges his managers to accept effort, anxiety, and loneliness because the reward for their perseverance will be success. He communicates with great motivational force and effectiveness the idea that "it can be done" —, everything he says carries this reassuring affective charge. The reassurance works at two different levels. The first and most important is related to the possibility of becoming a marathon winner by going all out and following the advice, but above all the example, of the leader. The second is related to the ways of coping with the anxieties of competitive running and loneliness that are offered by belonging to a good "team" in "excellent health."

When he moves on to innovation, Ghidella juxtaposes the concept of technical precision with his previous references to fatigue and effort: he mentions carbon strengthened resins, optical fibres, computerized fuel injection systems management, high resistance materials, the ceramics of turbines, exhaust ducts, and so on. Moreover, he is himself an engineer, "one of them"; he knows and loves their product. Once again, he is a model to be emulated.

The idea of a global, integrating objective is now presented with great simplicity and conviction: the customer must have maximum economy, maximum enjoyment, and maximum safety and comfort. The Thema 832, now on show for the first time, symbolizes Ghidella's overall idea — it is "beautiful" and perfectly combines "exciting" performance with "maximum" stylishness and comfort.

The speech ends on a serious note that is emphasized by the structure of the final sentence, where repetition is again used to telling effect. The content of the sentence has already been presented earlier, however: it is individual men who succeed, and to represent the product means sharing the values and commitment of the "technological marathon runner" represented by Ghidella himself.

The whole speech has an affective halo of what we would call "sober euphoria," which it both agrees with and reinforces its message, perhaps even independently of the author's conscious intentions. When he advocates values and strategies, Ghidella first offers himself as a model, the model of the marathon runner for winning engineers.

Obviously, Ghidella's speech is like any other in that its range of meaning can never be completely unified. He speaks as a representative of the Fiat group, as one of the men who, as he himself says, "represent the product," so what he says also gives voice to the culture of the Fiat group. Simultaneously, the fact that he is speaking at the Turin Motor Show affects the tone of his speech, which is perforce celebratory. However, this does not prevent personal elements from emerging in his speech which can produce emotional echoes in his readers or listeners.

Perhaps this also depends on the fact that, as analysts of corporate culture, we are inclined to be rather skeptical about "sermons" or ritual celebrations that are not also expressions of lived personal experience, that are not embodied by the person who makes them.

Only rarely do speakers or writers try to minimize anxiety; they acknowledge it, contain it, and deal with it constructively. From this point of view, the metaphor of the marathon runner seemed particularly resonant and effective: after encountering it early in the speech, we were happily able to proceed to the analysis of the whole text.

References

Austin, J. (1962): *How to Do Things with Words*. Oxford: Oxford University Press

Daft, R. L. (1983): Symbols in Organizations: a Dual-Content Framework of Analysis. *Organizational Symbolism*. L. R. Pondy/P. J. Frost/T. C. Dandridge (Eds.). Greenwich, CT: JAI Press, pp. 199−206

Eco, U. (1979): *Lector in Fabula*. Milano: Bompiani

Fornari, F. (1979): *I Fondamenti di una teoria psicoanalitica del linguaggio*. Torino: Boringhieri

Gadamer, H. G. (1960): *Wahrheit und Methode*. Tübingen: Mohr

Gagliardi, P. (Ed.) (1986): *Le imprese come culture*. Milano: Isedi

Ortony, A. (1979): *Metaphor and Thought*. Cambridge: Cambridge University Press

Perelman, C. and L. Otbrechts-Tyteca (1958): *Traité de l'argumentation*. Presses Universitaires de France *(The New Rhetoric: A Treatise on Argumentation)*. Nôtre Dame: University of Nôtre Dame Press

Peters, T. J. (1978): Symbols, Patterns and Settings: an Optimistic Case for Getting Things Done. *Organizational Dynamics* 7, pp. 3−23

Pfeffer, J. (1981): Management and Symbolic Action: The Creation and Maintenance of Organizational Paradigms. *Research in Organizational Behavior*. B. M. Staw/ L. L. Cummings (Eds.). Greenwich, CT: JAI Press, Vol. 3, pp. 1−52

Ricoeur, P. (1965): *La métaphore vive*. Paris: Seuil

Schein, E. H. (1985): *Organizational Culture and Leadership*. San Francisco − Washington − London: Jossey-Bass

Smircich, L. (1983): Concepts of Culture and Organizational Analysis. *Administrative Science Quarterly* 28, pp. 339−358

Smircich, L. and G. Morgan (1982): Leadership: the Management of Meaning. *Journal of Applied Behavioral Science* 18 (3), pp. 257−273

Valesio, P. (1980): *Novantiqua*. Bloomington: Indiana University Press

Watzlawick, P. (1967): *Pragmatic of Human Communication*. New York: Norton

Part III:
Root Metaphors Embedded in Artifacts

The C.E.O. as Corporate Myth-Maker: Negotiating the Boundaries of Work and Play at Domino's Pizza Company

Richard Raspa

Tom Monaghan, founder and Chief-Executive-Officer of the largest home-delivery pizza company in the world, offers this observation about working:

Have fun in the work you do ... "The play's the thing." I often repeat that line to myself to help focus on the action at hand. No literary reference is intended. I simply take the words and give them my own meaning. When I was working in a [pizza] store, "The play" to me meant the rush [the telephone order for pizza], and handling it was the only thing, the all-important thing. (Monaghan 1986: 34)

To declare that being rushed to do a job is fun reflects the power of Tom Monaghan to mythologize his corporation and his personal success. Can anyone believe that standing on your feet eight hours a night, from 4 p.m. till after midnight, five nights a week, in a tiny store, being paid minimum wage, and more than that, being rushed to repeat the same three of four movements − slapping, shaking, pressing, squeezing sticky food particles into a pan, then cooking the product over a hot oven, cutting it on a cluttered table, and delivering the finished masterpiece in your own car − all in less than thirty minutes, can anyone believe this work is fun? Boring, yes! Stressful, yes! But clearly not enjoyable. Such work in fast-food jobs, we all know, leads down the occupational road to a dead-end. Not only has Thomas Monaghan inspired his employees to believe that work is as much fun as play, but he has gotten fabulously wealthy doing it.

What Monaghan means by play, I surmise, challenges deeply entrenched beliefs in western societies that work and play are separate entities. One is really working when one is serious, putting forth effort, and producing results. One is only playing around when one is enjoying what one is doing, engaged in the·activity in an effortless way, and having no concern for results. Even the premier works in play theory maintains this distinction. Huizinga (1950), Caillois (1962), Rahner (1967) suggest that the domain of play, though a reflection of the social world that gave rise to it, is a closed, self-contained universe of discourse, with its own rules, proceeding according to its own internal logic, quite apart from the conventions of ordinary life.

It may be argued that Monaghan, however, is dealing with food that naturally couples with leisure. Pizza symbolizes a break from the work that is involved in cooking. "Just a phone call away," Domino's advertizes. Order a Domino's pizza and you'll get service and quality food, without the bother of having to slave over a hot stove preparing a traditional meal, then putting out place settings, and having to clean up afterwards. Pizza is sufficient unto itself. So popular has it become that a recent Gallup pole survey indicated that Americans between the ages of 12 and 20 identify pizza as their favorite food, surpassing Big Mac hamburgers, and Colonel Sanders Kentucky Fried Chicken.

Pizza can be eaten with fingers, even played with, as one pulls the mozzarella strings with one's teeth, maneuvering bites to keep the pepperoni, peppers, and mushrooms from falling off the slice. A home-delivered pizza frees the participants to enjoy each other's company. As Roland Barthes (1975: 50) reminds us, eating spontaneously translates into a social experience.

But even beyond the ludic association of pizza and play, Thomas Monaghan is reaching for something more in his organization. More than the standard game metaphor which characterizes organizations as teams, Monaghan's "The play's the thing," is an attempt to transcend the dichotomy of working and playing. Csikszentmihalyi is useful here in suggesting how such a transcendence can be brought forth. Instead of focusing on the differences between work and play, Csikszentmihalyi (1975) argues for investigating the experience of enjoyment which comes from doing something that we love. A common experience occurs when we are doing something we enjoy, even in areas as diverse as playing soccer, playing the piano, or even performing surgery. We experience the flow of the action, a narrowing of consciousness as Abraham Maslow (1971) called it, when everything recedes into the background of awareness and all that remains is the action itself. We are consumed by the performance. In that state we are not conscious of being separate from the action. It is what the Irish poet William Butler Yeats, in another context, summed up in a question: "How can we know the dancer from the dance?" Dance and dancer are fused in the action. For those brief moments we can forget personal problems. We are unaware of the passage of time. In that state the demands for action are clear and non-contradictory, and feed-back is instant. Only when our concentration is broken and we see the action from the outside does reflexivity happen. Then we ask such questions as "Am I doing it right?" or "What am I doing here anyway?" During the flow state we feel in control. And in that state, doing the activity is the reward, not something outside of it, like winning or making money, or receiving social recognition.

To structure work to allow for the experience of enjoyment and flow is, I believe, "The play" Monaghan aspires to. Yet his commercial concerns must take precedence. His business exists to sell pizzas and make a profit:

Our system is simple. Each step is clearly defined and logical. Its real beauty, though, is in the thrill of working as a team when the pace gets really frantic, when the phones are ringing without letup and the drivers are running back out the door right after they come in. Each member of the team has to employ manual dexterity, economy of movement, speed, and quick thinking. If you make a mistake, confuse an order, have a driver unable to find an address, or forget any of the little details that go into the making of a *perfect* pizza, you can mar a whole night's work. People respond to that kind of challenge. It's a game and the ones who have a knack for it go a long way in Dominos. We say they have pizza sauce in their veins. (1986: 18)

Monaghan attempts to evoke the presence of "The play" here, as Witkin and Poupart (1985) might suggest. It begins to approximate the thick description of an athletic event. Managers are coaches. They come up with game plans and design plays for the players. The best coaches and best players are lost in the action of making pizza. They are metaphorically consumed by it. They have pizza sauce in their veins. How can we know the pizza from the pizza makers? Those who can play this game will go far in Domino's. Clearly, play has instrumental value in the organization. The coach-managers frame the work as play, selectively adapting features of the ludic experience to produce results. Presenting the organizational philosophy as play — for example the rule to deliver pizza within 30 minutes of a telephone order — allows Monaghan and his executive staff a source of cultural justification for the way things work around here.

What is the nature of Domino's culture which structures work as a form of play? And what is the relationship between the corporate culture and the culinary artifact? I suggest that the relationship is symbolized by the name Domino. The name of the company is a copy of the name of the board game — Dominos — which name itself is a copy of still another name Dominus, referring to the mask-like hood worn by Cathedral canons during the Middle Ages.

The ancient board game Dominos is played with 28 rectangular pieces. Each piece has one blank face and one face marked with white dots. The marked dots are divided into halves, each half containing from 0 to 6 dots in every combination. The blank half of the domino resembles the half mask dominus. The underlying principle of the game is to match the number of the domino half that has already been played on the table. The game of Dominos is in essence a game or replication, of repetition, reconstruction, or reproduction — all metaphors for copying.

The pizza made at the Domino's organization is a replication of the Italian peasant pie from antiquity. Furthermore, the pizza made at each store is itself a replica of the ideal pizza, photographically diagrammed. In every store, these photographs are prominently displayed over the work area to model perfection and avoid error. They guide action and restrain ingenuity and difference. Their purpose is to assure consistency and predictability in producing the product. The rules for the game are provided by the diagram. "The play" in the store is to "copy" the photo of the perfect pizza. A second photo-diagram notes the 10-point Quality Check: (1) bottom overdone or underdone; (2) top overdone or underdone; (3) round shape; (4) border too thick or too thin; (5) edge too brown or not brown enough; (6) major bubbles or minor bubbles; (7) tails — tail-like protrusions on the edge; (8) portions of pepperoni and other toppings too thick or sparse; (9) toppings too far from the edge or over the edge; (10) red edges.

The construction of a Domino's pizza is neither the art of cooking nor the act of pure play. Both art and play have as an essential ingredient surprise, an ingredient which has no place in this organizational culture. The Domino process is the technology of food production brought to a highly refined form. Here pizza is not created but constructed, assembled, built, produced — copies of the factory process found in manufacturing organizations. Each store is a kind of assembly plant. The pizza dough, cheese, and sauce prepackaged with spices as well as other toppings comes from the food vendor, Domino's commissaries.

What is striking inside a Domino's store is the systematic and tight control of the operation. The two most important steps in building a pizza, Monaghan says, are slapping out the dough and applying the tomato sauce. He describes the dough as alive because it has yeast in it, and you can feel it growing in your hands as you stretch it from the ball and slap it from hand to hand. When it is properly slapped out, it will be perfectly round and snuggle up to the periphery of the pan, and be uniform in thickness.

After the dough is formed in the pan, it is passed along the counter to receive the sauce. A ladle is used as a brush to paint on the sauce: one full scoop of the ladle for small pizzas, and two for the large results in a consistent surface without any ridges. A master saucer will glaze the mixture within one-half to five-eights of an inch from the rim.

Adding cheese involves keen hand—eye coordination. Skillfully done, cheesers are able to grab just the right amount of cheese from the tray and distribute it on the sauced surface of the pizza so that it is uniform in thickness and covers the layer of sauce right up to the edge. The best cheesers use a wrist motion, like dealing cards, that makes the cheese seem to flow like liquid and spread evenly over the entire pie.

The pie is moved quickly along the assembly line as workers shake, sprinkle, and scoop items onto it. Total time for assembly and baking is twelve minutes. Eighteen minutes are left for delivering.

The production of a copy of the ideal pizza is the fundamental task of Domino's assembly-line crews, just as the replication of "The play" is the essential task of managers. Other expressive forms of organizational life are patterns of replication as well. Corporate ceremonies, for instance, are display events which copy and celebrate the essential movements of work life. In each of its business districts, Domino's sponsors an annual Super Seminar to review and plan for the coming year. One of the rituals during this event is a contest to determine the fastest pizza maker. All the managers of the franchises have the opportunity to play: their aim is to beat the current record and slap out a 10 inch pizza and sauce it in under 30 seconds.

While the impulse to copy is the distinguishing metaphor of the Domino culture, framing the way the work gets accomplished, it is the presence of Thomas Monaghan that has given the organization its character. In one symbolic form or another, he plays dominos — the matching game. One of his executives said in an interview that Tom Monaghan's life was a Horatio Alger story. Indeed, the episodes he chooses to narrate in his 1986 autobiography, *Pizza Tiger* (1986) are a copy of the thematic pattern of Alger's heroes. (Horatio Alger was a 19th-century American writer of boys stories. By leading exemplary lives and struggling valiantly against poverty and adversity, Alger's heroes gain wealth and honor.) Tom Monaghan was born in 1937 in Ann Arbor, a small town outside of Detroit. At the age of 4, his father died, and his mother placed him in a Catholic orphanage, where he remained until high school. He entered the seminary to study for the priesthood, but left before he completed high school. For a while he was placed in a Reform School, then he joined the Marine Corps. After an honorable discharge he held a series of low-paying jobs. Then in 1960, on a tip from a relative, he borrowed $ 500.00 and bought a small pizza store. He knew nothing about making pizzas, running a restaurant, or owning a business. What he knew he had was drive. He went through some desperate times — threats of bankrupcy, lawsuits, and unworkable partnerships. Through all the challenges Tom Monaghan has conducted business strictly according to the Golden Rule: Do Unto Others as You Would Have Them Do Unto You.

Today, his organization is made up of over 4,000 franchises in the United States, Canada, Australia, England, West Germany, Hong Kong, and Japan. It posted over $ 2 billion in sales last year, selling over 200 million pizzas. In 1986, the International Food Service Manufacturers Association named Domino's Pizza the fastest growing food service company in history.

In his narrative, Tom Monaghan reproduces himself for his audience as a mythic figure of heroic proportions, who came from poverty and today sits in Board Rooms of such prestigious American institutions as the University of Michigan's President's Club. His myth making has attracted into his circle of friends people of talent and achievement, including the governor of Michigan whom Monaghan persuaded on the 25th anniversary of the company's founding to slap out a pizza of his own and eat it. As he becomes more successful, Monaghan moves into other ventures, including the purchase of the Detroit Tigers, a professional baseball team. He also sponsors a professional car race in the Indianapolis 500 World Cup automobile race, and sponsors Team Tennis, the only co-ed sport in which men and women are equally represented. He owns a yacht, a hunting and fishing lodge, and a private jet. He has founded a classical car museum, paying up to $ 1 million for replicas of classic automobiles. His collections replicate the extravagant accumulation of material things by industrial giants of the 19th and early 20th century, like Henry Ford. With his expensive acquisitions, Thomas Monaghan is making his own inheritance. In his autobiography, he reproduces himself as the ultimate consumer — the state-of-being most highly prized in America: the ability to have what he wants when he wants it. In achieving that, he serves as the Rags-to-Riches *exemplum* for his employees and the wider audience of readers.

In his study of the impact of stories in organizations, Alan Wilkins (1979) says that some kinds of stories are a powerful way to motivate, teach, spread enthusiasm, and compel loyalty. Stories reveal underlying beliefs. As the reader follows the movement of Monaghan's private dreams into the public discourse of his autobiography, the message becomes clear: everyone who works at Domino's is a potential replica of the founder. Moreover, Monaghan plays a kind of rhetorical dominos with the readers. Now that he has presented them with his copy of a Horatio Alger story, readers are invited to match Tom's history with dazzling successes of their own. Even beyond the book, Monaghan encourages belief in the Horatio Alger myth by acknowledging excellent performance with expensive gifts: $ 75.00 Hermes ties, $ 200.00 DuPont pens, $ 800.00 Rolex watches, and even occasionally $ 12,000 solid gold Swiss Patek Phillippe watches — all of which are personal items on his person which he gives away at the moment. It is as if the recipient receives a relic which confers magical powers upon the wearer, thus inspiring him to seek The Play.

The final expression of Tom Monaghan's game is his mythologizing of the corporation's future. Here the playing is paradoxically the most intensely personal and most widely communal in its possible impact. The replications are rich and thick. Domino's Farms is the $ 150 million, 300 acre, futuristic-looking headquarters, the first phase of which has just been completed. Described as combining features of a friendly campus atmosphere with the rural qualities of a working farm within the office complex, it is Monaghan's attempt to integrate work and play. Beautifully landscaped, all the buildings will surround a fifteen-acre lake stocked with aquatic life. Here will stand over one million square feet of corporate office space, consisting of a half-mile long low-rise set of offices. At the center of the complex will be a fifty-four foot tower — the Golden Dome — designed many years ago by Frank Lloyd Wright and given contemporary styling by a local architect. Between the low rise and the Golden Dome will be a re-assembled Frank Lloyd Wright Usonian house. The Wright buildings are either a re-production of an original, or a variation of an original design never produced.

Peacocks, rabbits, and horses will be on the farms and crops will be grown to feed them. The surrounding community will be invited to harvest the fruits and vegetables that grow there. To attract visitors, events are planned for each weekend with the theme "Seasons at the Farm." Hayrides, bonfires, pumpkin carvings, baseball day, and a hot air balloon festival are just a few of them. Finally, a nursing home and an orphanage will be built, each to provide companionship for the other.

Of all the games, Domino's Farms may have the potency to be pure play, if only in the imagination of its founder. While it is true that the working farm is merely a replica of the almost extinct family farm in America, and that its mimetic nature is defined by the corporate context in which it is placed, nevertheless, the farm calls forth in the listener the presence of something profoundly felt. I suggest the Farm is Thomas Monaghan's way of recreating symbolically the experience of home which was so sadly absent in his years at the orphanage. It may be his fullest attempt to replicate the family — the missing half of the Domino.

Do the metaphors which arise in our organizations come out of a coherent center of consciousness that determines how we work, how we think, how we are? Is there a single unifying metaphor, which may be said to constitute our unique epistemological stance in the world? The striking thing about Thomas Monaghan is that his life flows so smoothly out of a metaphoric font, his professional and personal life converging in the play of Dominos.

References

Barthes, R. (1975): Toward a Psychosociology of Contemporary Food Consumption. *European Diet from Pre-Industrial to Modern Times*. E. Forster/R. Forster (Eds.). New York: Harper and Row, pp. 47 – 57

Caillois, R. (1962): *Man, Play, and Games*. London: Thames and Hudson

Csikszentmihalyi, M. (1975): *Beyond Boredom and Anxiety: The Experience of Play in Work and Games*. San Francisco, CA: Jossey-Bass

Huizinga, J. (1950): *Homo Ludens: A Study of the Play Element in Culture*. Boston, MA: Beacon Press

Maslow, A. (1971): *The Farther Reaches of Human Nature*. New York: Penguin

Monaghan, T. (1986): *Pizza Tiger*. New York: Random House

Rahner, H. (1967): *Man at Play*. New York: Herder and Herder

Wilkins, A. (1979): *Organizational Stories as an Expression of Management Philosophy*. Palo Alto, CA: Stanford University

Witkin, R. and R. Poupart (1985): Shadows of a Culture in "Native" Reflections on Work in an Abortion Clinic. *Dragon* 2, pp. 56 – 72

Artifacts in a Bureaucratic Monastery[1]

Janne Larsen and Majken Schultz

> "But videmus nunc per speculum et in aenigmate[2] and the truth, before it is revealed to all, face to face, we see in fragments (alas, how illegible) in the error of the world, so we must spell out its faithful signals even when they seem obscure to us and as if amalgamated with a will wholly bent on evil."
>
> Umberto Eco

1 Introduction

The idea, which we are going to trace and explore, is to understand organizational culture by interpreting physical things and visible gestures in organizations. Our approach is physical-visual: we enter the organization as visitors and describe possible interpretations of the artifacts as we meet them on our way throughout the organization[3].

The data for this expedition is a photo reportage of a public bureaucracy, The Danish Ministry of Domestic Affairs. The photo reportage is used as an entry to the culture. The complete reportage includes more than 160 photos. Thanks to the photographer, Morten Bo, we are able to present a small selection here to visualize the expedition into the organizational culture.

Following Schein, artifacts include material things like rooms, furniture, and decoration, as well as human gestures and visible codes of conduct (Schein 1985). In the literature, artifacts in organizational settings are analyzed from different perspectives. One perspective concerns how artifacts are interpreted by the members of the organization (Morgan et al. 1983): are artifacts interpreted as simple or complex symbols? Are these interpretations consciously or unconsciously created by the members of the organization (Morgan et al. 1983)? Another perspective addresses the functions of the artifacts within the organization: do artifacts have an energy-controlling function or a system-maintenance function to the organization (Dandridge 1983: 72)? From a functionalistic point of view, Schein studies the relationship between artifacts, values, and basic assumptions within the organizational culture (Schein 1985). Finally, the communicative contents of artifacts are analyzed. Artifacts are defined as cultural signals, which send messages to the members of the organization (Daft 1983). The communicative content of the artifacts may be instrumental and relate to work activities. The messages contain "information or meaning that will achieve some rational need for the organization" (Daft 1983: 202). Moreover, the communicative content of the artifacts may be expressive and relate to feelings and emotional needs of individuals in the organization "perhaps by removing uncertainty or providing an object to identify with" (Daft 1983: 202).

We treat artifacts as *cultural signals* with an emphasis on the *expressive communication*. We are interested in the role of artifacts in the creation of meanings and emotions in organizations rather than their instrumental aspects. Using the photo reportage as an entry to the organization, we receive signals from the artifacts, as we walk the corridors, look into the offices, and attend the meetings. By describing and interpreting these signals, we intend to explore the meanings and feelings which the artifacts may evoke to the members of the organization.

In our efforts to explore these meanings and feelings, we use our own creativity as a gateway to reach other people's imagination. In our opinion, a metaphor evoked by artifacts works like the word "an open sesame," in the sense that it triggers curiosity and provokes new insights. A metaphor creates meaning by allowing the interpreter to see something from the viewpoint of something else (Brown 1977, Morgan 1986, Morgan et al. 1983). It can then highlight certain aspects of the artifacts, helping to get a more holistic understanding of the organizational culture in the ministry.

2 The Physical Setting

When you enter the organization, the physical things are the first to welcome you. The outside of the building shown at Photo 1 looks impressive. It reflects the historical ponderous traditions of managing "Les Affaires d'État." The entrance door is overdimensioned. It resembles a gate rather than a door. The heaviness and size of the building express power rather than mere physical strength; just as superordinary strength is symbolized by the ornament above the entrance door and the romanesque shape of halls, windows, and doors. This is not a simple building to be conquered by physical strength.

Not everyone is allowed to enter the building. Perhaps you are an outsider who needs a specific task or a well-defined errand in order to enter the front door. Or perhaps you are an insider entering the front door without obstacles, because you are guided by a strong mission. Perhaps you are

Photo 1

devoted to work for the goals of this house and spend a lifetime behind these walls.

Once you have entered the front door, you are met by a *gate-keeper* — a uniformed man behind glass walls, who is shown at Photo 2. This welcome does not symbolize openness, warmth, or care for the newcomers. On the contrary, you may feel almost suspicious, daring to enter these sacred halls. Like a Kafka-clerk at the lowest level of an endless organization, the gate-keeper may take our destiny in his hand. You will be weighed and perhaps allowed to enter the ministry.

Walking through empty *corridors*, the impressions are created: the white-washed walls, a purity of decoration, and a work-ethic atmosphere. You are met by closed doors, iron-closets, and white, naked walls (Photo 3). It is difficult to see what is going on in the corridors. At each side of the corridors, the subordinates are located behind closed doors which prevent day-light from slipping into the corridors. But once in a while the day-light slips through the large, oval windows and creates a heavenly light in the darkness (Photo 4).

Inside the *offices of the subordinates*, the symbols of individual devotion to hard work are many. The tall and white walls and the deep window frames make them look like monks cells. They contain a chair, a desk, a shelf, a small meeting-table — which is usually covered with files and paper —, a few necessary lamps, and whatever tools subordinates need in order

Photo 2

Photo 3

to serve the bureaucratic order (Photo 5). The subordinates are only "allowed" to have a few things of their own in the office. Too many private belongings may create distractions from work.

These artifacts signal that the subordinates have to commit themselves to an ascetic and simple life. But when you enter the small office-cells from the dark corridors, they are illuminated in a heaven-like way, creating the right vision for the reading and writing usually taking place in the cells. Thus, the hard work takes place in a sacred atmosphere.

At the same time, when you walk into the *offices of the chief executives and the minister*, their richness and glory create a remarkable contrast to the asceticism and frugality further down the organization. At this level, you will find ornamented furniture, paintings, thick carpets, carefully arranged curtains, flowers and beautifully decorated ceilings which express a superfluous abundance compared to the white, plain cells of the subordinates. To enter the area where the minister lives, you do not pass an anonymous gate-keeper, but walk through a large hall of utmost beauty (Photo 6).

Within this atmosphere of asceticism and glory, the artifacts contain several specific messages. The first message is one of *organizational difference*. The differences in office size and in the location of offices are remarkable. Here, difference in location is first of all determined by the

Photo 4   Photo 5

distance to the minister's office. But also variations in amount and quality of furniture and decoration state that distinction is important within this organization.

These artifacts of difference are standardized and formally regulated within the organization. The brown and grey spare furniture, which is shown at Photo 5, is the same within all the numerous small offices. Similarly, the much more comfortable and rich equipment is found within the larger offices. A huge desk, more comfortable chairs, two soft chairs, and large meeting table are the luxurious standard (Photo 7). These things signal how the people working in the various offices are considered by the organization. The numerous subordinates at the lower levels are small and anonymous numbers in an endless row, whereas the few selected managers at the top have their importance celebrated by the artifacts. All of them are reminded that "difference" is an intrinsic value of the organization.

Secondly, artifacts are *signals of style* within the organization, which refer to the ways in which members of the organization express their individuality through physical things. These differences in decoration, selection of furniture, and the arrangement of each office express the individual taste and preferences rather than differences of the organizational hierarchy.

The signals of style are most clearly expressed by the *managers*, because they have the opportunity to make choices different from the grey-and-brown standard. Their individual style is typically expressed through the small details of their offices: posters, selection of couch or soft chairs, the placement of the desk in relation to chairs for visitors, the number of books on the shelves and the selection of lamps. The office styles vary from a classic bureaucratic style with dark, old-fashioned furniture in a comfortable and quite cozy arrangement to a more modern functional and effective style. Photo 7 shows an example of classic bureaucratic style, where the "library atmosphere" is created by all the leather books on the shelf, the old paintings on the walls, and the "fire-place-conversation-position" of the two soft chairs at each side of the small table. On the contrary, the multicolored plastic files, the modern lithographs, and the designer-like couch shown in Photo 8 signal a more modern and light atmosphere in which people meet and talk together.

Thirdly, the artifacts contain messages about *the traditions of the organization*. Traditions are most visible in the paintings of former managers and ministers hanging in corridors and offices. Photo 9 shows how paintings of the ancestors of an office are looking down on the present manager behind a yellow film of dust. These paintings emphasize that this organization has a long history and works within a long time span. The manager is neither the first nor the last person to work here. The old furniture and the decoration of walls and ceilings are other significant signs of tradition. Voluptuous white angels on the ceiling and golden panels show a glimpse

Photo 6

Photo 7

Photo 8

Photo 9

of a glorious past (Photo 6). They may appeal to mixed feelings of proudness and distance. The golden glory of the past makes organizational members imagine themselves as living parts of a proud history, whereas the film of yellow dust on ceilings and paintings symbolizes the long-gone character of past traditions.

All these physical artifacts communicate a *multiplicity of signals.* Here, the multiplicity of signals has been captured by categorizing the communicative content of the artifacts. The categories illustrate that each artifact may send different cultural signals simultaneously. A painting may equally express difference, style, and tradition within the organization. Furthermore, small physical details may open up for a new insight into the organizational culture. The position of the paintings right above the desk enhances the strength of past traditions, just as piles of files on the meeting-table may stress the isolated work situation. The risk of this categorical analysis is that the quality and the ambiguity of the artifacts as cultural signals are lost in the sequential and pinpointing analysis.

3 Small Patterns of "Frozen" Gestures

In this section we turn to another kind of visual artifacts, namely the human gestures. The gestures are exposed in different situations throughout a work day where organizational members meet, formally or informally, for some reason or another. In these situations people, of course, interact with one another, but they also position themselves in space and act versus things like furniture and decoration.

Thus, by focusing on human gestures and trying to extract their meaning, we get closer to recognizing the meaning of organizational life at a larger scale. Again, in the photos we are looking for signals, especially signals revealing the human nature and the nature of human relationships (Schein 1985). The leading questions for the interpretation have been: what do the photos tell us about appropriate behavior in this organization? Can we "decode" normative guidelines from the gestures "frozen" (so to say) in the pictures?

3.1 Gestures Exposed in Different Work Situations

Gestures used to symbolize management
As a manager you signal status and importance by sitting at the end of the table, being the last person to arrive, and thus attracting the attention of the subordinates (Photo 10). Moreover, by "owning" or literally holding on to the papers, while leaning on the table, the manager shows he defines the agenda for discussion.

As a subordinate, you play the reciprocal role: you give attention by waiting for and looking at the manager; you lean back or sit stiffly right-side-up in order to show expectation and acceptance of the manager's right — and duty — to set the agenda.

Gestures used to symbolize efficiency
Apparently, it is important for bureaucrats to look efficient. As a bureaucrat, you may use different signs in order to signal efficiency: always bring a calendar and a notebook when you participate in meetings (Photo 11);

Photo 10

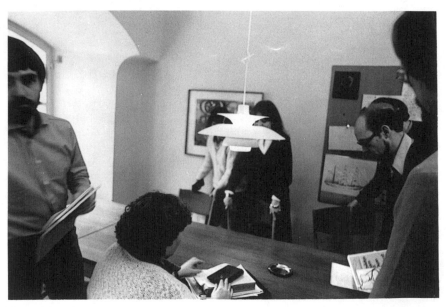

Photo 11

Photo 12

show small signals of impatience during a meeting such as rocking your foot, looking at your watch, reorganizing your papers; look concentrated, serious, and busy — hectic, even — when you leave a meeting, in order to let people know you have important tasks and duties waiting for you (Photo 12). The messages of the efficiency signs are "time is short," "I am an important person."

3.2 Gestures Used to Position Oneself in Relation to Space and Artifacts

Where to sit? Almost all offices have codes of conduct telling who is supposed to sit where. The position may be defined according to distance in status, seniority, sex, etc. Other codes tell how to sit: Photo 10 shows people with their hands at the edge of the table, expressing formality and a little nervousness.

How to deliver a paper to a superior? If two persons are going to deliver a file to a higher ranking person, do not enter like a "messy group" but try to form a line and deliver the file in a quiet and orderly way. Do not expect the superior to look up from his work, as he or she is all too busy to deal with the file right now.

Photo 13

Photo 14

How to present a note to a superior? If you are going to present a note to your manager, enter the room showing you have a good reason for disturbing: hold the note right in front of you for the manager to see (Photo 13). Then, when presenting the note, do not sit down but stand up in a very polite position (Photo 14). Hereby you signal that actually you don't want to take his time — or that you are a listener quite different from an active discussion partner. If the manager wants to have an argument — stay calm and polite, even if he points at you and clutches his head from time to time.

How to relate during informal time-outs? If you are having an informal conversation with a manager of higher status, remember to sit in the sofa — never in the comfortable chair which is usually placed opposite the sofa (Photo 8). If the meeting takes place at the desk, be sure to sit across the manager, but stick to the edge of the chair, and don't lean on the table. If two persons with a different hierarchical status are having a meeting with the manager, the one highest in rank sits directly across the manager, while the lowest in rank is left to a remote corner of the desk.

The small patterns of human gestures described above can be seen as different parts of a deconstructed whole, each part giving meaning to the whole.

Summing up, the gestures shown in the photos uncover a story about spontaneous socialization within the ministry. Following Deal and Kennedy, the gestures can be seen as small rituals, because the "frozen" situations "provide the place and script with which employees can experience meaning and order in chaos" (Deal/Kennedy 1982: 62). Through these small rituals, people are "told" how to relate to colleagues and superiors, how to signalize the organizational virtues, efficiency, and interest, where to sit and how to enter into a superior's office, etc. Small rituals, then, may in our opinion be seen as guide-lines for appropriate bureaucratic behavior. They reveal to us a culture where the basis for structuring human relationships is lineality; power is distributed in accordance with an autocratic system; intimacy and affection among organizational members do not seem to be a basic virtue. On the contrary, the codes of conduct tell that formality, impersonality, and predictability seem to be crucial norms for people's way of interacting with each other.

4 The Metaphor: Monastery

The description and interpretation of physical things have underlined — within an atmosphere of asceticism and glory — the organizational difference, a hierarchy of style, and the importance of history and tradition as cultural messages. Moreover, the analysis of visible gestures has told us about some basic cultural values like order, formality, and predictability. Together, the two expeditions into the different sets of artifacts provide us with some clues for understanding the organizational culture of the ministry. The next step of our analysis will be to use a metaphor as an alternative gateway to organizational culture (Berg 1985, Sapienza 1985) — a holistic and interpretative way of looking at the artifacts, different from the former sequential analysis of each artifact.

Metaphors do not exist *per se*, but require imagination and an attitude of "as if" ...

New metaphors ... are not merely new ways of looking at the facts, nor are they a revelation of what the facts really are. Instead, the metaphor in a fundamental way creates the facts and provides a definition of what the essential quality of an experience must be (Brown 1977: 85).

In our experience, artifacts as a whole trigger a picture which can be interpreted by using another organization — the monastery — as a universe of bureaucratic life and symbols. The monastery defines the essential quality of this organizational culture, as it is communicated by all the artifacts: it is this persistent association that keeps popping up in our minds when we watch the photos.

The "monastery" metaphor is a product of our imagination: it can either be a real gateway to get closer to understanding the deeply rooted assumptions of the organizational culture, or a "deforming lens" which prevents us from seeing what is really valued by the natives. The only way to escape from this dilemma is "to play" with the metaphor, to develop the parallel between the monastery and the ministry in order to interpret important aspects of the organizational life: the more the final picture is internally consistent — and consistent with the cultural artifacts we observe —, the more likely our insight is a "key" rather than a "deforming lens."

In particular, we'll use the metaphor to understand (1) the expected behavior of the bureaucrats; (2) the meaning of more structured, dynamic events, such as formal meetings, which are held on a very regular basis, following strictly defined rules; (3) the fundamental purpose — consciously defined or taken for granted — which seems to give order and meaning to all the activities.

4.1 Passion and Neutrality

In order to enter a dignified, well-established bureaucracy such as an ancient ministry, you have to leave your personal passions, sympathies, and antipathies at the front door. In other words, as a bureaucrat you are supposed to devote your skills, intelligence, and logical thinking to the service of the minister, regardless of the political party in charge.

Stripped of personal compassion, you pass the gate-keeper of the bureaucratic monastery and are welcomed by a rather paradoxical phenomenon:

On the one hand, you must feel a compassionate eagerness to act right, not in an ethical sense of the word, but in a process-oriented sense of the word: not to make the right decision, but to make decisions in the right way. Thus, giving up your personal luggage of small passions, the organization takes you to a single, burning compassion: to act as a neutral tool in the service of The House.

On the other hand, this monotone passion is not allowed to look or sound like a passion. The hard-working, naked, puritan, and grey atmosphere penetrates daily life in bureaucratic organization. Feelings and other kinds of strong emotional expressions are never seen; rather they should be hidden behind expressions of neutrality. Therefore, the demand is to be passionately devoted to the service of the House in a non-passionate way.

4.2 The Duality of Time

Living in a monastery, the beginning of organizational time is the founding of religion, while the units of time are generations, centuries, and reigns of popes and abbots. In a public bureaucracy, the beginning of time is the institution of parliamentarism, while the units of time are the lifespan of laws, decades, and the reigns of ministers and chief executives.

In both organizations, the rhythm of life seems to be repetitive, continuous, and beyond chronological time. The actions of today have taken place in the past, and are to be repeated in the future. The mission is still alive, the play is still performed. The rhythm of time is like a silent and steady breathing, to continue as long as the universe exists.

But time is also divided into very small units throughout a single day. In a monastery, day and night are divided by different prayers. In the early morning, the work day of the monks begins at Matutin, and the end of the working day is marked by Kompletorium. These prayers create breaks in an otherwise hard and secularized working day, which the monks spend in the kitchen, the fields, the stables, the library, etc. The prayers are obligations as well as opportunities for the monks to concentrate on clerical matters and meditate about the meaning of life and the specific goals and "truths" of their monastic order. Thus, staged by ceremonial repetition, the prayers visualize the clerical ethos of the monastery.

In a bureaucracy, meetings are held almost as punctual, repetitive, and continuous as if they were prayers in a monastery. Meetings are the sacred hallmarks of the work day and of the week. Normally, every office has a weekly meeting. The middle managers meet once a week with the chief executive, who on his behalf has a daily meeting with the minister. These meetings may be a way of exchanging information, giving orders, planning tasks, etc. Meetings, however, are also cultural arenas for allocating virtue and status among the participants; a way of paying tribute to values and heroes and of demonstrating power and intellectual craftsmanship.

Monks and bureaucrats, then, both live in formal organizations, where time is punctually structured either by prayers or by meetings. A prayer is a rest from hard work in the monastery, a moment of inner solitude in an otherwise crowded and busy community as well as an act of personal devotion to God. A meeting is a rest from a fragmented and hard working day, a way of sharing information as well as a moment of shared devotion to bureaucratic virtues and political goals.

Thus, time seems to possess a duality in both organizations. One dimension of time is the *endlessly repetition of actions*. Each day is like the other, and the mission or task of the organization goes far beyond the lifetime of monks or bureaucrats. The nature of this dimension is eternity, but it may also be labelled "zero-time," "non-time," or "all-time." In any case, the very notion of time as a transition from one stage to another is absent.

The other dimension of time is the *punctual disruption* throughout the work day by prayers or meetings. People in monasteries and bureaucracies live from prayer to prayer, from meeting to meeting — but simultaneously they are living within a life-long perspective of individual choice which is either to join a monastery for lifetime or to achieve lifetime employment in a bureaucracy.

This simultaneous existence of time as unbroken eternity and as disrupted presence is enhanced by the physical things of the bureaucratic monastery. The artifacts of tradition may be seen as physical manifestations of organizational eternity, just as the white and naked corridors signal timelessness. The bureaucrat in the corridor does not leave any trace vis-à-vis eternity, and the only sign of presence is a painting of the "contemporary minister" in the row of predecessors on the wall.

On the contrary, the artifacts of style may represent the disruptions of presence, as these individual expressions are unique variations in the organizational uniformity. Signs of individual style in decoration are posters, family pictures, etc. in the offices of the subordinates, while the CEOs may also have a choice of furniture, carpets, and lamps. However, only very few subordinates utilize the possibilities for individual expressions. One reason may be that the imposing architecture, the white and naked walls, and the empty corridors create a pressure upon the individual, which destroys attempts to be creative, different, or just something original.

4.3 Knowledge as the Sacred Artifact

Like every other monastery, the ministry possesses sacred artifacts, which are treated like relics by the bureaucratic monks.

In the photo reportage, the sacred artifacts to be found all over the organization are papers, files, lawbooks, and other kinds of stored information and knowledge. Stored knowledge is what makes the bureaucratic world go around: laws are the means and ends of bureaucratic work; information is the formal turning point of all kinds of meeting rituals; ancient knowledge and historical information are preserved and taken care of in bureaucratic routines (Photo 15).

Knowledge, then, condensed into rule making and rule interpretation and stored in countless number of files, is the organizational frame for understanding events and people in bureaucratic organizations.

Thus, a common feature of monasteries and bureaucracies is that the written word — the book — is the sacred artifact of the organization. However, knowledge as a sacred artifact means something very particular to a monastery and a bureaucracy.

— Knowledge in the form of the Holy Book and the law books is seen as the one and only truth.

Photo 15

- Knowledge has an inner logic of its own in the sense that criteria for falsification do not exist. By definition, knowledge is the truth, the fundamental test is not one of critical examination, but one of acceptance and faith.
- Knowledge, in this sense, represents a one-way communication to society. The complexity of the surrounding society is reduced to a simple formula for right and wrong according to the text, i. e. the Bible or the law. If people and phenomena do not fit into the knowledge scheme, alas, it is their destiny, as people are inquisited or prosecuted, and phenomena are banned or ignored.

As it is stored and used in the bureaucratic monastery, the basic message of the sacred artifact is: *One should preserve, not search for knowledge* (Eco 1983). The mission or inner purpose of the secularized activities is to study the Holy Book, the ancient scriptures, and to listen to the true interpretations of them.

5 World-view and Ethos in a Monastic Bureaucracy

The sequential analysis of physical things and human gestures embedded in larger meetings create an alphabet of cultural meanings, while the metaphor leads us to a more holistic and fundamental understanding of the culture. This far in the expedition, we are ready to use the findings and impressions in our reach for the abstract-ideal domain of organizational culture.

Here, with the inspiration from C. Geertz (1973), we have chosen "*world-view*" and "*ethos*" in the description and understanding of different aspects of organizational culture:

A people's ethos is the tone, character and quality of their life, its moral and aesthetic style and mood; it is the underlying attitude towards themselves and their world that life reflects. Their world view is their picture of the way things in sheer actuality are, their concept of nature, of self, of society. It contains their most comprehensive ideas of order" Geertz (1973: 127).

World-view is referring to the cognitive aspects of organizational culture like descriptions of life as it "really is," while ethos represents the moral and aesthetic aspects of the organizational culture. Thus, world-view and ethos are different, very fundamental aspects of organizational culture, which, nevertheless, may be intertwined in the same cultural expressions.

Getting hold of world-view and ethos may, in our opinion, lead to a deeper understanding of the apparently ambiguous character of the culture in the ministry.

The *world-view* catches the puritan and ascetic presence: the self-fulfilling organization based on hard work and regularity which has a number of basic tasks defined by a natural order. The world-view describes the main tasks as nursing and preserving knowledge stored in laws and files. This is done in a serious, calm, and indirect way. It takes a long and carefully planned training to do the bureaucratic procedures right. Thus, the world-view rejects any kind of personal traces in relation to The Sacred Artifact. Rather, "personality" is expressed through marginal deviations in decoration, furniture, and arrangement. In our opinion, the bureaucratic world-view can be summarized in the concept "*naked*": the physical environment is naked; the work is naked in the sense that personal expressions are neither exposed nor allowed; and the puritan atmosphere of hard work is naked in the way that all sorts of non-instrumental activities are seen as superfluous.

The *ethos*, however, describes the mission of bureaucracy: the devotion to Truth and the humbleness towards The House. Bureaucrats do not only keep knowledge in piles of files — they are in touch with a sacred knowledge, and they are the ones who are chosen to fulfil this sancted mission.

The feeling of being chosen is an important feature of bureaucracy, as bureaucrats feel they have been chosen to fulfil a mission, a certain policy. This mission is of such glory and gratitude that it makes them look up to the system only to find that they themselves are a part of the Great System of Order.

Table 1: World-view and Ethos in a Bureaucratic Monastery

Cultural Findings	World-view	Ethos
1. Duality of Decoration, Furniture & Arrangements	Naked	Gold and glory
2. Ambiguity of Work	Work is a neutral function of impersonal procedures	Work is personal devotion to an abstract passion
3. Duality of Time	Presence	Eternity
4. Ambiguity of Organizational Mission	Deducting pragmatic solutions to administrative problems	Preserving the holy truth: Knowledge as sacred artifact

This Great System of Order of organizational culture is based on the passionate devotion to truth and to signals sent by the minister. To make a contribution to The System creates meaning for each bureaucrat.

The opposition to the grey and naked world-view is a richness of *"gold and glory."* In bureaucracy, the ethos contains the mission, glory, and devotion, which seem to be the fundamental dynamics in creating bureaucratic desire. Furthermore, the bureaucratic passion is created by an attachment to the glory of ministers and power.

Although our interpretations originate from only one metaphor, the world-view and the ethos touch fundamental ambiguities of the organizational culture. In Table 1 we have tried to summarize these ambiguous differences between world-view and ethos.

6 Some Concluding Remarks

Throughout the cultural analysis of the Ministry of Domestic Affairs, we have been "faithful" to an explorative method of interpreting artifacts in our attempt to create meaning out of various physical appearances.

Apart from the fact that this method has brought us some important insights into the culture, we would like to point out some of its methodological shortcomings.

First of all, the interpretative method is rather subjective. We have neither interviewed the participants of the organization nor confronted them with our findings. Instead, we have used ourselves as cultural "Geiger counters," creating our interpretations on the basis of visual artifacts and our personal knowledge and experience from living in and studying similar bureaucratic ministries.

Secondly, we have used "monastery" as a metaphor to understand some fundamental features of the culture. In this process, we are guided as well as restricted by our own sources of imagination, curiosity, and free associations.

The restrictions of such an individualistic method are obvious:

— Our findings may not correspond to the insider's interpretations of every day life.
— Our choice of "monastery" as a guiding metaphor may reflect a literary fashion[4] concerning monks and the Middle Age rather than Danish bureaucracies *per se*.
— Our interpretations may be based on personal biases towards bureaucracy rather than on profound knowledge of these organizations. More-

over, our descriptions of mission and knowledge as sacred artifacts may reflect our position in the bureaucracy while working there — at the bottom of the system.

Despite these methodological biases, the method also draws attention to some critical necessities in the process of understanding the symbolic meaning of artifacts.

— In a study of artifacts, such as physical things and human gestures, it is necessary to "deconstruct" and "freeze" various situations and locations in order to grasp the meaning of otherwise elusive and passing moments. Here, the photo reportage has been a useful tool.
— It is necessary to use one's personal imagination in order to grasp the idea of "things meaning something to people." In the case of using artifacts as an entry to culture, the imaginative process is extreme in the way that we have not talked with members of the organization. But still the method illustrates that neither culture nor artifacts can be understood without using one's own creativity as a gateway to reach other people's imaginations. Here, metaphors have proven to be useful tools.

Artifacts may have an impact of their own on the organizational culture. The idea of corporate architecture; the various attempts to create different office environments and the enourmous amount of energy most of us put into our own physical environment in organizations all indicate that artifacts mean a lot to us in our daily life in organizations. The implication is that artifacts should not only be analyzed as superficial expressions of basic assumptions (Schein 1985), but should be understood in their own terms.

Notes

1 We would like to thank the editor, Pasquale Gagliardi, for his excellent and rich comments on our first draft of this paper.
2 This latin sentence means: "We see now through a glass darkly, a rebus."
3 Apart from the photo reportage, we both have several years of practical experience within this kind of ministerial organization. Janne Larsen has been working part time in the Ministry of Industrial Relations and the Ministry of Finance, whereas Majken Schultz has been working part time in the Ministry of Environmental Protection and the Ministry of Finance. Thus, we are not complete strangers in a bureaucratic culture.
4 At the time, when we first used the metaphor "monastery," "The Name of the Rose" by Umberto Eco had created a wave of interest in the Middle Ages etc.

References

Barley, S. (1983): Semiotics and the Study of Occupational and Organizational Cultures. *Administrative Science Quarterly* 28, pp. 393 – 413

Berg, P. O. (1985): Organization Change as a Symbolic Change Process. *Organizational Culture*. P. Frost et al. (Eds.). London: Sage, pp. 281 – 299

Bormann, E. (1983): Symbolic Convergence. *Communication and Organization*. Putnam/Pacanowsky (Eds.). London: Sage, pp. 99 – 123

Brown, R. H. (1977): *A Poetic for Sociology. Toward a Logic of Discovery for the Human Sciences*. Cambridge, MA: Cambridge University Press

Cassirer, E. (1944): *An Essay on Man*. New Haven, CT: Yale University Press

Daft, R. (1983): Symbols in Organizations: A Dual Content Framework for Analysis. *Organizational Symbolism*. L. R. Pondy et al. (Eds.). Greenwich, CT: JAI Press, 1, pp. 159 – 206

Dandridge, T. (1983): Symbols Function and Use. *Organizational Symbolism*. L. R. Pondy et al. (Eds.). Greenwich, CT: JAI Press, 1, pp. 69 – 79

Deal, T. E. and A. A. Kennedy (1982): *Corporate Cultures: Rites and Rituals of Corporate Life*. Reading, MA: Addison-Wesley

Eco, U. (1983): *The Name of the Rose*. London: Picador

Geertz, C. (1973): *The Interpretation of Cultures*. New York: Basic Books

March, J. and J. P. Olsen (Eds.) (1979): *Ambiguity and Choice in Organizations*. Bergen: Universitetsforlaget

Morgan, G. (1986): *Images of Organizations*. London: Sage

Morgan, G. et al. (1983): Organizational Symbolism. *Organizational Symbolism*. L. R. Pondy et al. (Eds.). Greenwich, CT: JAI Press, 1, pp. 3 – 35

Putnam, L. (1983): The Interpretative Perspective. *Communication and Organization*. Putnam/Pacanowsky (Eds.). London: Sage, pp. 31 – 55

Sapienza, A. (1985): Believing is Seeing: How Culture Influences the Decision Top Managers Make. *Gaining Control of the Corporate Culture*. R. Kilmann et al. (Eds.). San Francisco, CA: Jossey-Bass, pp. 66 – 84

Schein, E. H. (1985): *Organizational Culture and Leadership*. San Francisco, CA: Jossey-Bass

Smircich, L. (1983): Concepts of Culture and Organizational Analysis. *Administrative Science Quarterly* 28(3), pp. 339 – 358

Smircich, L. (1985): The Concept of Culture as a Paradigm for Understanding Organizations and Ourselves. *Organizational Culture*. P. Frost et al. (Eds.). London: Sage, pp. 55 – 72

Trice, H. and J. Beyer (1984): Studying Organizational Cultures Through Rites and Ceremonials. *Academy of Management Review* 9, pp. 653 – 669

Van Maanen, J. and S. Barley (1985): Cultural Organizations: Fragments of a Theory. *Organizational Culture*. P. Frost et al. (Eds.). London: Sage, pp. 31 – 53

Wilkins, A. (1983): Organizational Stories as Symbols which Control the Organization. *Organizational Symbolism*. L. R. Pondy et al. (Eds.). Greenwich, CT: JAI Press, 1, pp. 81 – 92

Witkin, R. and R. Poupart (1985): Running Commentary on Imaginatively Relived Events. A Method for Obtaining Qualitatively Rich Data. *Quaderno 5 – 6*. Trento, Italy: Università di Trento, pp. 79 – 87

The Symbol of the Space Shuttle and the Degeneration of the American Dream*

Howard S. Schwartz

> In the South Seas there is a cargo cult of people. During the war they saw airplanes land with lots of good materials, and they want the same thing to happen now. So they've arranged to make things like runways, to put fires along the sides of the runways, to make a wooden hut for a man to sit in, with two wooden pieces on his head like headphones and bars of bamboo sticking out like antennas — he's the controller — and they wait for the airplanes to land. They're doing everything right. The form is perfect. It looks exactly the way it looked before. But it doesn't work. No airplanes land.
>
> From *Surely You're Joking, Mr. Feynman* by Richard P. Feynman

1 Introduction

I am looking at a photograph. Seven smiling people look back at me. Five of them are men, two are women; five are white, one is black, one is oriental. Of the men, two look boyish, one is gray haired and looks older than the rest. They are all dressed in identical coveralls that give no hint at all of the specific characteristics of their bodies. Each coverall has the NASA logo on it. On the table next to them is a model of a space shuttle. Behind them is an American flag. They will be the crew of the space shuttle Challenger, flight 51L.

My imagination takes me past this picture. I see them in space. They cavort weightlessly. They point television cameras out the window and show me how Earth looks from space. Through the marvel of television, I am there with them in the space shuttle, in space. All Americans are with them in space. Even the children are there. For one of these astronauts is a teacher who will conduct classes in space.

There is a feeling of completeness that comes to me with this vision. It is as if my imagination has gone beyond the reconfiguration of common perceptual elements and has entered the realm of the mythic. The picture sings to me: Look what

* First published in *Journal of Organizational Change Management*, reprinted with kind permission of the editor.

American has done! America has transcended its cleavages, man and woman fly together, the races fly together, the ages fly together. Even the children can fly. We are all up there in a machine that manages to be, at the same time, powerful and thrusting, like a phallus, and warm and comforting, like a womb. Earthly cares are overcome. Earth and care are overcome. There are no limits to what Americans can do. Constraint is merely an illusion. I feel on the edge of immortality itself.

I wrote these words in June, 1986 as part of a proposal for the SCOS conference. What I did not know at the time was that the image that came to me from the picture was the image that was supposed to have come to me. As I shall show later, what I had thought of as a spontaneous and creative act of my autonomous imagination was actually the result of a conscious, carefully crafted process of symbol creation that was geared to produce this effect. I was picking up the image of itself that NASA was transmitting.

As Geertz (1973) has observed in his analysis of the Balinese cockfight, through some of their institutions, societies talk to themselves about themselves. Thus:

Like any art form — for that, finally, is what we are dealing with — the cockfight renders ordinary everyday experience comprehensible by presenting it in terms of acts and objects which have had their practical consequences removed and been reduced (or, if you prefer, raised) to the level of sheer appearances, where their meaning can be more powerfully articulated and more exactly perceived (p. 443).

Similarly NASA, and specifically the US manned space flight program, was a way for Americans to talk to themselves about themselves. As Trento (1987) has shown, neither the US military nor the CIA had any interest in manned space flight. The meaning of the space flight program was symbolic from the outset and remained so. In the case of the space shuttle Challenger, as we shall see, the image that I had of the voyage — Americans transcending their differences and their finitude, floating blissfully together in space — was in fact the meaning of the voyage itself.

But when the meaning of social institutions is symbolic, does this not raise the possibility of a rift between the meaning of the symbol and the social reality which it is presumed to reflect? And if so, does that not raise the possibility that a society may become so enamored of the image it creates of itself that the fact that it is only a symbol may be forgotten or repressed? And if that were to happen, could that not make a problem for the very existence of the symbol itself?

For as Goffman has shown (1959), these commentaries, these works of art require a staging, and the staging is not, and cannot be, part of the work of art. If a society were to fall too much in love with what it was telling itself about itself, the staging of the performance might become impossible.

I propose that the symbol of manned space flight that NASA intended, and was intended, to project came to be in contradiction with the social and organizational realities which were necessary for its staging. Briefly put, the symbol of manned space flight had become a symbol of limitless, effortless perfection in which constraint appeared only as an illusion. But the organization of advanced technology cannot take place in an atmosphere of limitless, effortless perfection. It requires a self-critical sobriety in which the consciousness of limitation is ever present. Far from experiencing constraint as an illusion, it must be fully conscious that illusion is a constraint. Under the circumstances it was inevitable that something would give way. It turned out to be the space shuttle itself.

2 Organization and Narcissism

I have (Schwartz 1987 b) discussed the internal working of NASA in terms of a theory about organizations as projects for the return to narcissism (Schwartz 1987 a, c). When this happens, organizational processes typically lose touch with reality, and it is not uncommon to find that, as Richard Feynman said about NASA, those who run the organization behave like children and the adults, who actually do the work, are not listened to.

The purpose of the present paper is to indulge a train of thought which was suggested to me by the commentator Daniel Schorr, who pointed out what tremendous pressure for perfection had been placed on NASA by the news media. For what this suggested was that analyses concentrating solely on what was going within NASA miss the meaning of NASA itself, and particularly of NASA's manned space flight mission. Drawing the boundaries more widely, I realized that NASA was serving a symbolic function within the overall American culture.

In effect, upon NASA had fallen the burden of maintaining the narcissism of a strikingly, and perhaps increasingly (Lasch 1979, 1984), narcissistic American culture. Through NASA, Americans were telling themselves that, despite the drubbing the US army took in Vietnam, despite the fact that American industry could not compete even within the American market, despite the fact that many American cities had become modern instantiations of Hobbes' "state of nature," despite all this — still America was perfect. Thus, this again is narcissism, but on the level of the whole society.

Contemporary theory of narcissism places great stress on Freud's concept of the ego ideal (1955, 1957, Chasseguet-Smirgel 1985, 1986). In the beginning of psychological life, the infant's special relationship with its mother leads the child to an experience of itself as being the center of a loving world. Freud's term for this emotional orientation to the world is "primary narcissism." Displaced from this position by the existential fact of the separation of self and other, the individual's psychological development is conditioned by the desire to return to that happy state. The fantasy of this return is what gives hope in life and represents the meaning of the term "ideal." The image of the self referred to in this fantasy of an ideal state of affairs is what Freud referred to as the "ego ideal."

In the normal case, partly through projection and partly through introjection, the person comes to have a relatively stable image of the person he or she is "supposed to be" or "should be" in order again to become the center of a loving world. This set of obligations provides what we may think of as the conditions for the ego ideal, in other words, the superego. It gives a sense of direction to one's life and especially to those areas of life, such as one's organizational role, that are dominated and motivated by a sense of the appropriate. But between people, and within the same person at different times, the balance between the fantastical aspect of the ego ideal and its obligatory aspect, the superego, may be observed to differ. When the obligatory aspect gains the upper hand and displaces the fantastical, we speak of the person as an obsessive-compulsive. When the obligatory aspect is very weak as compared with the fantastical, we refer to the person as "narcissistic." Such persons may be said to identify themselves with their own ego ideal.

The difference between the narcissistic and the normal case, then, may be seen to have a developmental dimension. The obligatory component develops through the course of a person's life — a course which begins with primary narcissism but which progresses through identifications with adults who are seen as having attained the ego ideal and whom the person strives to become like. Thus, the normal person believes that he or she needs to live up to certain standards, to "become somebody" in order to attain the ego ideal. The narcissist, maintaining an infantile orientation to the world, believes that he or she is already the ego ideal and in one way or another denies those elements of reality which contradict this preferred vision.

One of the most deeply regressive forms of this denial is known to psychoanalytic theory as the "denial of difference." As used by Freudians, the "denial of difference" refers to the infantile fantasy that the mother has a penis. Chasseguet-Smirgel (1985, 1986) points to the function that this serves in the pre-oedipal emotional life of the male child. It allows him to think of the mother as being sexually complete and not sexually requiring the father. In this fashion, the child can conceive maintaining its sense of unity with the mother, a sense which would not be disturbed by the child's recognition that its infantile sexuality will not suffice to keep the mother satisfied. Thus the denial of difference is at the same time a denial of sexual differentiation and something deeper — a denial of the difference between the generations, of children and adults. The child denies that it has to become like the father — that it has to become an adult — in order to have union with the mother. It does not have to do anything. It can have everything just by being what it is.

The denial of difference is the image that spoke to me out of the picture of the astronauts in their unisex flight suits: sexual de-differentiation and generational de-differentiation. Add to this the idea that ethnic de-differentiation represents a denial of rivalry among siblings for exclusive union with the mother and you have the whole photograph.

But at a deeper level, and one which will permit us to return to the proposition that the symbol of manned space flight had become inconsistent with the social reality that would have had to support it, note that the denial of difference is at the same time a denial of the difference between the world and the self, reality and fantasy, achievement and desire, between technology and magic. A society thinking of itself in these terms, living its emotional life on this level, would have lost the motivational basis for technological achievement.

3   The Degeneration of the Symbol of Manned Space Flight

3.1 The Single Combat Warrior

In evaluating the symbol of manned space flight presented in the case of flight 51L, it is useful to compare it to an earlier symbol of manned space flight. In this regard, we are fortunate to have an excellent journalistic account of the generation of this symbol in the form of a book by Tom Wolfe called *The Right Stuff* (1979).

For Wolfe, the symbol called for by the American public, and happily generated by the original American astronauts was the symbol of the "single combat warrior." By launching Sputnik, the first artificial satellite, the Russians threatened, in the words of Senate Majority Leader Lyndon Johnson, to seize "the high ground of space." America was in a panic. When the original astronauts were chosen, during a period in which American rockets did nothing but blow up, the adulation for them was instant. They, our bravest and best test pilots, would ride the rockets into space and symbolically do battle with the Russians, in much the same way that earlier lone warriors had stood for the armies of which they were part and prefigured or replaced the battle between the armies themselves. The public would grant them anything. It would be the loving world of which they were the center. It would fulfill for them the ego ideal.

But note that in this case there is no question of just being oneself. Attainment of the ego ideal here is contingent upon these astronauts *doing something*. And, indeed, doing something pretty impressive. Single combat with the Russians was not regarded as a merely mortal performance. On the contrary, the astronaut would take upon himself the role of a protecting god. He would stand against the hostile forces that surrounded the whole nation and vanquish them. Indeed, at the deepest level, the astronaut would challenge the separation of self and the world that is the root cause of our anxiety and overcome it by overcoming the world. To be sure, as with Geertz' cockfight, nothing of the sort will have taken place. Nonetheless, the very real danger in which the astronauts are placed makes real such overcoming as they may achieve, and at least gives a content to the fantasy. It gives the fantasy an active character.

We can see the active character of the ego ideal in the symbol of the astronauts more clearly by focusing upon the creation of the symbol from the other side — from the side of the astronauts. There, the symbol was one of being a pilot with "the right stuff."

The idea of being seen as pilots, and not simply as passengers was the equivalent of requiring that they be seen as being in control, and not just passive participants (i. e. "Spam in a can"). It would turn the flight from a mere experience into an achievement. This aspect of the symbol was so important to the astronauts that when they realized how much power their iconic stature gave to them, they used that power to force the redesign of their vehicle from a "capsule" to a "spacecraft," by adding elements to it that would approximate as much as possible the control systems of an airplane. If they were to gain adulation, they would gain it by flying.

The idea of the "right stuff," as Wolfe describes it, contains the sort of mythic elements that only the ego ideal possesses. Wolfe likens it to the Presbyterian doctrine of being one of the elect. It was not something that one could gain; one could only prove that one had it. And if one had it, as with Presbyterian grace, one neither had, nor need have, any fear of death. It is clearly a symbol of prevailing over death, of immortality — the ultimate in being the center of a loving world. Moreover, it is immortality that knows itself to be immortality. Analogous to the Presbyterian elect's certainty of his election, to have the right stuff is to have courage without trying to have courage. The proof of the right stuff is perfect calmness in the face of what appears to be absolute catastrophe.

But if the primitive character of the wish is clear enough, what is equally clear is the demanding character of the proof that one has the right stuff.

This proof was nothing short of being the perfect pilot. The death of a pilot meant that he had not had the right stuff. No excuses were allowed. The opposition "right stuff/death" was absolute — even tautological. As Wolfe put it: "There are no accidents and no fatal flaws in the machines: there are only pilots with the wrong stuff" (p. 34). Moreover, the attitude behind perfection in piloting could not be one of complacency. Absolute mastery of detail was required. This is not to deny self-confidence. On the contrary, self-confidence was part of having the right stuff. But in the same fashion, so was an obsessive concentration on detail. Both were expressions of the right stuff. Taken together, the emotional control in the attainment of perfect sangfroid and the perfection in the process of flying itself added to a list of "shoulds" and "supposed to's" that was, perhaps, demanding beyond what human beings could sustain. These people intended to be the center of a loving world, but their concept of being so was in no way a concept of effortless attainment. And it was precisely in those terms that they demanded to be accepted and in which they crafted, consciously and unconsciously, the symbol of themselves and, by extension, of the US manned space flight program.

In comparing the symbol of the original astronauts with that of the astronauts of 51L, we are again fortunate in having a journalistic account of the process of symbol construction. In this case, what was clearly the most symbolic aspect of the program, the so-called "Teacher in Space" program was recorded with a focus on Christa McAuliffe, who was eventually chosen to be the first "teacher in space." The reporter, Robert T. Hohler, was assigned exclusively to cover McAuliffe, and it is clear that they formed a close relationship. He provides a chronicle of the process from start to finish (Hohler 1986).

3.2 The Denial of Difference and Disneyland in Space

The manned space flight program was symbolic in intent right from the beginning. But as we have seen, the symbol constructed of the original astronauts was a symbol of prevailing over death through competence. The contrast with the symbol constructed of the 51L astronauts could not be more striking. Not only does death disappear in this symbol, but competence does as well. For competence in overcoming death has become unnecessary. In developmental terms, the symbol presented here has its home in mental life before the concept of death has yet developed. But if the concept of overcoming death through competence has become unnecessary, it has also become impossible. It has become undefined, meaningless. And the result of this is that it became motivationally impossible. The fact that death itself followed from this regression cannot be surprising. In an enterprise as dangerous as this was, it became inevitable. All of these are aspects of the denial of difference.

Consider the picture of the smiling astronauts. Recall the way this made my imagination soar:

Look what America has done! America has transcended its cleavages, man and woman fly together, the races fly together, the ages fly together. Even the children can fly.

I said before that this fantasy was not my own construct, but was the result of a carefully crafted symbol. Consider Hohler's account:

Its passengers would include Francis Scobee, Judith Resnik, Elisson Onizuka and Ronald McNair, four of the thirty-five astronauts who were selected from a crush of more than eight thousand applicants in January 1978. They were a military pilot, a Jewish woman, an Asian American and a black — *symbols of NASA's commitment to carry America's cultural rainbow toward the stars* (emphasis added; p. 46).

And this about McAuliffe:

On cue, she talked about looking down from the shuttle on "Spaceship Earth" — a Disney concept — imagining a planet where no differences divided blacks and whites, Arabs and Jews, Russians and Americans.

"It's going to be wonderful to see us as one people, a world with no boundaries," she said. "I can't wait to bring back that humanistic spirit" (p. 15).

Now, what is striking to me about these images is not only the symbol of the denial of social differentiation that they represent, but, even more so, the way they manifest the denial of difference in their failure to distinguish the symbol from reality. Christa McAuliffe will go into space and "see us as one people" with no differences between blacks and whites, etc. But of course there are differences, and flying a hundred miles above them does not reconcile them; it only obscures them.

Or consider the idea of sending America's "cultural rainbow" toward the stars. At a time when America's racial groups appear to be becoming irretrievably divided, when America's sexual relationships have become so problematic that a recent writer has spoken of our youth as "the unromantic generation," when heavily armed neo-Nazi sects are trying to organize the secession of the American Northwest, the idea of America's cultural rainbow as being a unity in diversity is simply absurd, and the idea of bringing it into being by flying people in space is bizarre. Indeed, from a psychoanalytic point of view it is precisely the tensions between these groups that make the symbol of their resolution attractive. What gives this image its clinical cast is the failure to distinguish between symbol and reality.

Returning to Geertz' analysis of the cockfight, with Geertz we saw that the cockfight, stripped of consequences, could become a form of art. The same can be said of the space shuttle phenomenon. But it is worthwhile to note that the Balinese did not think that the separation of the cockfight from the surrounding social reality constituted a *replacement* of that reality. In the case of American culture, the symbol appeared to represent precisely that. Indeed it would seem that setting the stage for this play of the imagination in space has behind it the idea that distance can establish imagination as an alternative reality which has as much claim on the psyche as the world in which we live. This is the denial of difference in a particularly acute form.

The denial of social differentiation is an aspect of the denial of difference that puts the sense of reality into a precarious position. But at least as a fantasy it gives a positive sense of direction to the process and a content that is at least relatively harmless. Much more insidious are those aspects of the denial of reality that directly undermine the possibility of competence. The selection of Christa McAuliffe as the teacher-in-space provides a case study of how this happened.

If the sense of competence were to be reinforced; if Americans were telling themselves something about the necessity for being able to do something in order to participate in utopia and fulfill the ego ideal, the selection of the astronauts would have been made on the basis of a perceived difference, an achieved difference, between the astronaut and the ordinary person. But as Hohler makes plain, the selection of McAuliffe was intended to give precisely the opposite message. Thus, whatever the wisdom or lack of wisdom of the teacher-in-space program itself, many of the other finalists had considerable accomplishments to their credit. McAuliffe had none. McAuliffe was selected, I propose, because she was just like everybody else and because she was proud of it:

Christa was not the brightest of the ten finalists. One of them was a prize-winning playwright and poet, and another had been invited by the French government to study language, literature and culture there for a year. Most of them had graduated from schools more prestigious than Christa's alma mater of Framingham State College. One had even graduated Phi Beta Kappa from Stanford University.

On paper, some of them seemed to push Christa to the back of the class. There was a former fighter pilot, a film producer and a woman who, among other adventures, had climbed the Andes and Himalayas and crossed the Atlantic in a thirty-one foot sailboat. Several of them knew much more about space and science than Christa knew, and the projects most of them had proposed for the six-day journey made Christa's idea of keeping a diary look rather ordinary.

Which of course was the difference. Christa was the girl next door, and more. No other finalist matched her potential for getting NASA's message across (p. 10, emphasis added).

And what was the message and why could she get it across so well?

She was even a Girl Scout. Who better to sell the wonders of space than a woman who once sold more Girl Scout cookies than anyone in her neighborhood? And she still had the touch. She was bold, charming and convincing, and when she said in her teacher's voice "I want to prove that space is for everyone," people believed her (p. 6).

She told Lathlaen [another teacher-in-space finalist] she had done her best to convince NASA that she could "humanize the technology of the space age" by showing the world that "there are real people up there" (p. 6).

When a reporter asked her why she wanted to go into space .... She talked about her journal, about how her perspective as an ordinary person would "demistify" the space program and about her vision of the world as a global village, of one people living together (p. 106).

With a push from NASA, the media had stumbled upon a new concept: the teacher as hero .... Through it all, Christa was one of us (p. 180).

Her selection, in other words, expressed the message that the American public did not have to do anything to experience utopia in space, but that they could do it just as they were. Americans were telling themselves through the medium of McAuliffe that they did not have to do anything in order to attain the ego ideal, to be perfect — they already were perfect and it was only their temporary boundedness to the world that caused their anxiety. Space flight is simply the realization of that perfection. The meaning of Christa McAuliffe's selection, I submit, was the expression of American narcissism. Her primary task would be its legitimation.

Thus, if I am correct, the selection of Christa McAuliffe as the teacher-in-space represented a critical aspect of the denial of difference. It represented the denial of the difference between the generations — of the fact that one has to learn to do something, to attain competence, in order to attain perfection.

But showing how the regressive character of the ego ideal in its most acute form is exemplified by McAuliffe's selection requires that one more observation be made. What needs to be finally understood is that the image of the shuttle was intended to appeal to children, and at the same time to the child in each of us. In this respect, we simply cannot forget that there are virtually myriads of ordinary occupations. The symbolism of choosing the teacher from among these needs further explanation. It seems to me that this symbolism needs to be understood in terms of the universality of the symbol of the teacher. Each of us has had teachers and children have teachers still. But in seeing this what we also see is that the universality of the symbolism of the teacher is based upon the universality of childhood. Christa McAuliffe would come back from space, and then her job was to spread the news. But she would spread the news to children and to the child in each of us. McAuliffe's mission was to put the symbolism of space flight into a perspective that made sense within the cognitive orientation of the child.

McAuliffe's thought concerning Barbara Morgan, who was to be McAuliffe's backup, evinces her attitude on the place of children in space clearly enough:

She arrived at the space center with a camera dangling from her neck, her eyes aglitter and her dark-brown, shoulder-length hair pulled back on one slide with a clip. She looked like a child on her first day at Disneyland, Christa thought. She looked like she belonged on the shuttle (p. 98).

Thus, NASA had chosen to cast its ideal as a child's ideal. Ultimately, it seems to me, it was this transformation in its image that most closely represented the rift between NASA's image of itself and the reality that it required. For there is no place in the child's world for the sort of painstaking care that space flight requires. In a word, the child's view of the world does not recognize technology. Technology is not defined within it. What is defined within it is magic. Symbolizing itself on this level, NASA's image became incompatible with itself. We shall return to this shortly, but first it will be useful to observe what we can about the transformation of the symbolism of manned space flight from that of the single combat warrior to that of Disneyland in space.

4 The Succession of Symbols

If the symbol of space flight had changed from test pilot competence to ordinary American mediocrity, one might anticipate a clash between these symbols. Surely the test pilot would not let the dramatization of their ego ideal be overcome without a struggle. In fact, there is evidence of such a struggle, but it appears to have been rather feeble. Thus, McAuliffe's encounter with Dick Scobee, the mission commander:

Scobee had worried her. She knew her meteoric flash across the media sky had bred contempt among a few people in the space agency. She knew her promise to "humanize" space travel had not sat well with astronauts who also claimed to be human. And she knew she was an outsider who had been thrust into one of the world's most exclusive clubs without a vote by its members. Little had frightened her more than the crew rejecting her as a public relations ornament .... She wondered most about Scobee.

At first glance, she thought, he seemed like the astronauts of her youth, wholesome and handsome, tall, blue-eyed and ruggedly built with a square jaw and an air of self-confidence. And right from the start Scobee left no doubt that he was in charge, that Christa was a member of a team that had been chosen for a space mission, not a joy ride.

"Those are no firecrackers they'll be lighting under our tails," he told her. "Those things are for real."

But soon he eased up, and Christa realized he was not the macho jet jockey she had feared. He was much like her, an ordinary person who had accomplished the extraordinary, the first enlisted man to rise through the ranks to the astronaut corps (p. 149).

And it appears from Hohler's account that Scobee would not have disagreed with this unheroic assessment:

When he returned from his first shuttle mission in 1984, he told the students at his former high school, "If I can do it, anybody can."

Scobee had come to NASA headquarters to review the preliminary plans for Christa's shuttle lessons. He talked with her for a while and began to see a little of himself in her, a person of modest background *and modest talents* who had maintained her humility in the face of extraordinary success (pp. 149–150, emphasis added).

In understanding the full significance of these judgments, it is useful to consider what "extraordinary accomplishment" and "extraordinary success" mean here. Remember in this regard that Christa McAuliffe had not done anything yet and that, indeed, given that there was to be nothing requiring competence in the task she was to undertake in space, she would not do anything even then. The conclusion must be that the accomplishment consisted in being selected itself. Thus, the traditional formulation in which adulation arises from achievement has been replaced by a short-circuit: adulation *is* the achievement. One need not do anything to be somebody.

This is a point that calls for some elaboration. In our earlier discussion we saw that, in the normal case, the individual is connected to the fulfillment of the ego ideal through the superego. An obligation, a deed, stands between the separate individual and the individual as center of a loving world. But in the case of McAuliffe, the instrumental deed seems to have become superfluous. McAuliffe experienced herself as already the center of a loving world, and her selection merely confirmed this predestined appointment. It does not go too far to suggest that McAuliffe experienced the connection between herself, as she was, and the world that loved her as essential. She could call forth the loving response of others just by being herself. She was their meaning, indeed their very cause. Hence, she could take pride in the fact that she was selected by others and see it as her own accomplishment, even despite the fact that she knew that she had done nothing to earn it. Here again is the denial of difference, this time in the form of the denial of the difference between the self and others. In such a fashion the celebrity replaces the hero and competence is interred.

But sad to say, the fact is that the symbol of competence had been dying for some time. Wolfe (1979) describes part of this process:

The prestige of the Astronaut absolutely dominated flying, and the Air Force was determined to be the prime supplier of that breed ...

To tell the truth, the brass had gone slightly bananas over this business of producing astronauts. They had even set up a "charm school" in Washington for the leading candidates. The best of the young pilots ... flew to Washington and were given a course in how to impress the NASA selection panels in Houston. And it was dead serious! They listened to pep talks by Air Force generals .... They went through drills on how to talk on their feet — and that was the more sensible, credible part of the course. From there it got right down to the level of cotillion etiquette. They were told what to wear to the interviews with the engineers and astronauts .... They were told what to drink at the social get-togethers in Houston .... They were told how to put their hands on their hips (if they must) ...

And the men went through it all willingly! Without a snigger! The brass's passion for the astronaut business was nothing compared to that of the young pilots themselves. Edwards [Air Force Base — the Air Force test facility] had always been the precise location on the map of the apex of the pyramid of the right stuff itself. And now it was just another step on the way up ...

The glamor of the space program was such that there was no longer any arguing against it. In addition to the chances for honor, glory, fame and the celebrity treatment, all the new hot dogs could see something else ... the Astronaut Life .... The *Life* contract ... $ 25,000 a year over and above your salary ... veritable *mansions* in the suburbs ... free Corvettes ... and the tastiest young cookies [i. e. girls] imaginable .... The vision of all the little sugarplums danced above the mighty ziggurat [i. e. the test pilot's ascent to his ego ideal] ... and all these young hot dogs looked upon it like people who believed in miracles ... (p. 413).

Thus, over a period of time, the astronauts themselves had abandoned their own ego ideal of competence in the overcoming of death. From an ego ideal which they could conceive of creating through their own actions, of realizing themselves in, they had adopted that of the organization man — an ego ideal created outside of themselves, fitting someone else, and to which they could approximate only through an act of subservience. Competence in the face of death had become, not the condition for their ego ideal, but simply a selection criterion, among many others, in the pursuit of an ego ideal whose content had become the simple consumption of commodities. They had, indeed, become just like everybody else.

5 From Religion to Animism

In his classic study on the origins of religion, *Totem and Taboo* (1938), Freud differentiated among three "systems of thought": the animistic (mythological), the religious, and the scientific, which he found both in the historical and the individual developmental order. Among the characteristics differentiating these stages is variation in the attitude toward what he calls the "omnipotence of thought":

In the animistic stage man ascribes omnipotence to himself; in the religious phase he has ceded it to the gods, but without seriously giving it up, for he reserves to himself the right to control the gods by influencing them in some way or other in the interests of his wishes. In the scientific attitude towards life there is no longer any room for man's omnipotence; he has acknowledged his smallness and has submitted to death as to all other natural necessities in a spirit of resignation (p. 875).

In this differentiation it seems clear enough that the "single combat warrior" view of manned space flight belonged to the religious stage of development. Here, the astronauts were seen as gods who could protect the people and upon whom the people could depend, or at least upon whom they could depend if the gods were kept in the proper frame of mind. That this is so is seen all the more in Freud's location of the religious phase in the developmental period of dependence on the parents. Thus, from this perspective, the shift of symbolism from "single combat warrior" to "Disneyland in space" can be seen as a regressive shift from the religious phase to the animistic.

A key element in Freud's analysis of animism is the concept of magic. I have argued that when the concept of space flight was cast in the child's perspective, the concept of technology was lost and replaced by the concept of magic. It is possible to amplify this point on the basis of Freud's observations and to show what it involves.

On magic, Freud (1938) quotes J. G. Frazer to the following effect:

Men mistook the order of their ideas for the order of nature, and hence imagined that the control which they have, or seem to have, over their thoughts, permitted them to have a corresponding control over things (p. 871).

He adds that the instrumental factor, the factor that leads primitives to believe that they can accomplish things through magic, is evidently the power of the wish: "We need only assume that primitive man had great confidence in the power of his wishes" (p. 872). Thus, the primitive feels that by representing the fulfilled wish, a state comparable to the child's play, he has brought it about. Moreover:

If play and imitative representation suffice for the child and for primitive man, it must not be taken as a sign of modesty, in our sense, or of resignation due to the realization of their impotence; on the contrary, it is the very obvious result of the excessive valuation of their wish, of the will that depends upon the wish and of the paths the wish takes.

And then: "In time the psychic accent is displaced from the motives of the magic act to its means, name to the act itself" (p. 872).

Again, Freud directly equates the animistic phase with narcissism, in the sense that the overvaluation of psychic acts which give rise to magic accounts for "the unshaken confidence in the capacity to dominate the world and the inaccessibility to the obvious facts which would enlighten man as to his real place in the world" (p. 876).

Thus, it is the narcissism of the animistic phase that makes magic seem natural and makes science impossible within it:

Animism, the first conception of the world which man succeeded in evolving, was therefore psychological. It did not yet require any science to establish it, for science sets in only after we have realized that we do not know the world and that we must therefore seek means of getting to know it (p. 877).

Finally, Freud notes that:

Only in one field has the omnipotence of thought been retained in our own civilization, namely in art. In art alone it still happens that man, consumed by his wishes, produces something similar to the gratification of these wishes, and this playing, thanks to artistic illusion, calls forth effects as if it were something real (p. 877).

This last passage enables us to return to the original terms of our inquiry, in which we compared the US manned space flight program with Geertz' Balinese cockfight, seeing them as art forms. We asked what would happen if a symbol which had become incompatible with the social reality necessary for its staging were actually adopted to replace the reality. This appears to be what has happened here.

6 Consequences of the Degeneration of the Symbol

Looking at the transformation in the image of manned space flight, from the single combat warrior to Disneyland in space, and seeing it as representative of a deeper shift from the religious to the animistic system of thought, gives us ample material to consider the loss of technological capacity that gave rise to the space shuttle catastrophe.

Consider the astronauts as single combat warriors, seen as gods, and seeing themselves as bearers of the right stuff that will enable them to prevail over death through competence. There is no conflict here between the message and its staging, the symbol and the technology that makes it possible. On the contrary, the astronauts, knowing that the technology must work perfectly if they are to survive must have obsessive concern with just that technological perfection. This is an aspect of their competence. Moreover, with regard to others who are involved in the technological process, that obsessive concern must manifest itself as a deep motivational thrust. For while it perhaps goes too far to say that NASA and other aerospace workers felt that they had to protect the single combat warriors, they certainly felt themselves as having a stake in the warriors' victory. They knew very well that the mission was dangerous and that victory was not assured but required their best efforts if it was to be attained. Moreover, the astronauts' role as god/parent/protector gave them authority. These were gods that had to be loved, honored, and obeyed, if they were to protect. And competent work on the part of the aerospace workers would constitute this love, honor, and obedience.

Thus, Wolfe (1979) tells this story concerning Gus Grissom, one of the original astronauts:

Gus Grissom was out in San Diego in the Convair plant, where they were working on the Atlas rocket ... and then the astronauts [were] supposed to say a few words, and all at once Gus realizes it's his turn to say something, and he is petrified. He opens his mouth and out come the words: "Well ... do good work!" It's an ironic remark, implying: "... because its my ass that'll be sitting on your freaking rocket." But the workers started cheering like mad. They started cheering as if they had just heard the most moving and inspiring message of their lives: *Do good work!* After all, it's little Gus's ass on top of our rocket! They stood there for an eternity and cheered their brains out while Gus gazed blankly upon them .... Not only that, the workers − not the management, but the workers! − had a flag company make up a huge banner, and they strung it up high in the main work bay, and it said: DO GOOD WORK (p. 147−148).

How can anything like this take place with regard to Disneyland in space? In the narcissistic world in which NASA had come to live, there was no death. There was not even any danger. Certainly there was no more danger than one would find on a good roller-coaster ride − existing for the purpose of exhilaration. Moreover, perfect workers could not make mistakes. Indeed, there was not even any necessity to pay attention. After all, if the ritual forms were followed, the magic would assuredly take place. Wishing would make it so. The symbol had become incompatible with the possibility of its staging and had been chosen over it.

In referring to the power that the primitive and the child place in magic, we are going back to what we have already said about the "denial of difference." Here again is the failure to distinguish reality from fantasy that led people to believe that if they could send a harmonious social mixture in orbit around the world that they had created social harmony. Put in this connection, the space shuttle became itself a magical instrument, akin to a magician's wand. Its purpose was to transform the wish into the reality, and it did not need to be fussed over in order for it to be able to do that.

To be sure, the space ship had had to prove its efficacy, but it had already done so during the early days of space flight when it took men to the moon. Having proved its capacity to create magical transformations, nothing remained to be shown.

Within this context one could find the sorts of abuses of organizational process that the Rogers Commission (Presidential Commission 1986), Trento (1987), and Schwartz (1987b) found at NASA: appointments to technical position based purely on politics, loss of technical capacity to properly oversee contractors, submission of schedules that could not be met, commitment to projects that were grossly underfunded, extreme miscalculation of risks, suppression of unpleasant information, degeneration of organizational processes into empty rituals, and so on.

In a word, I submit that what we have seen was a neurotic regression of the symbolic structure in which the American people saw manned space flight and through it themselves. From a religious framework where danger was acknowledged, possibility of failure was present, and competence was required; to an animistic system in which safety was assured, perfection was assumed, and nothing was required at all. In the first system, technological achievement was possible. In the second it was not.

7 Regression in Organizational Culture

I claim that a regression has occurred in the symbol of manned space flight and that this regression is part of a larger shift in American culture. If this is so, one should be able to find evidence of this regression in other cultural areas. By way of doing so, I shall suggest evidence of such a shift in American organizational culture.

In an article that began as the 1981 Presidential Address to the American Academy of Management, Cummings (1983) described the rise of what he called "management by ideology." According to his view, management by ideology is supplanting what he called "management by information."

Management by ideology differs from management by information in a number of ways, according to Cummings, the most important of which for present purposes is this:

Management by information encourages participants to engage in hypothesis *testing* about aspects of their organizational existence: to query, to question, to ask, to explore, and, most of all, to learn. Management by ideology as a logic encourages a participant to accept hypothesis *confirmation* and *affirmation:* to accept, to believe, to commit, to expound accepted doctrine, and even to glorify, and never to question, except in private, sanctioned arenas and audiences (1983: 533).

It seems clear enough that the shift from management by information to management by ideology represents a shift from an orientation toward reality to an orientation toward fantasy. As such, it appears to manifest the same regression we have seen in the image of manned space flight. But more than that can be said of it.

The timing of Cummings' observation suggests that he is referring to the same transformation in organizational culture that has seen the rise of "symbolic management" as an important focus of organizational change, supplanting, at least in part, earlier organizational change strategies, such as job enrichment.

Organizational change strategies tend to invoke what I have called the "organization ideal" (Schwartz 1987 a, b, c). This is an idea of an organization serving as an ego ideal. In the organization ideal, organizational participants are conceived as perfectly integrated into organizations that are perfectly adapted to their environments. In the organization ideal, individuals do spontaneously and out of desire what the organizational system requires. The organization ideal presents utopia in the form of an organization.

The organization ideal is represented in traditional theories of organizational change by notions such as "self-actualization," (Argyris 1957)[1] which imply that at the peak of individual and organizational development, there can be a unity of individual happiness and spontaneity, on one hand, and maximal performance and productivity, on the other. In current theories of "cultural management" it is represented by such ideas as the "excellent organization" (Peters/Waterman 1982) and the "strong culture" organization (Deal/Kennedy 1982). But notice that there is a difference between the traditional and current theories.

In the traditional theories the idea of the organizational participant as resident in utopia is clear enough. Thus, for example, Hackman et al. (1975) liken working at an enriched job to playing golf. But even if the utopian element is a fantasy, it is at least conceived as a fantasy in which one can participate only by doing something. Entry into the utopia represented by the symbolically managed excellent organization, by contrast, is conceived of as being only a matter of participating in the organization's culture — that is to say, of believing and valuing certain things. Thus, as with the regression from "the single combat warrior" to "Disneyland in space," the necessity for satisfying the demands of the superego, the obligation to do something as a requirement for participation in utopia has become lost.

8 Conclusion: Against the Manic Defence

In attempting to understand the shift from management by information to management by ideology, Cummings (1983) offers the following explanation:

Now there is a reemergence of management by ideology because of turbulence in environments, because of rapidity of change, because of the increased sophistication of the receiver of facts, and ... because distortion and intentional untruths are a common, daily fare for many organizational participants (p. 533).

And he adds:

Without this return to management by ideology, the only alternative would be alienation, resentment, and despair (p. 533).

There is no need to dwell overly long on Cummings' referent. The United States, which in 1945 truly was the center of a loving world, has lost both that centrality and that love. What Cummings observes is the fact that American organizations have not responded at all well to this loss.

It has brought out problems which were always there, but which were never thought to matter very much. Within the context of our narcissism, these problems have come to seem insurmountable. Rather than giving up the narcissism and attempting to grapple realistically with these problems, we have given up realism and reinforced our narcissism. Following Klein (1975) psychoanalytic theory call this the "manic defence." The regression of the symbol of manned space flight and the regression in organizational culture are elements of this manic defense.

But while, clinically, the manic defence can be sympathetically understood, on the practical level it cannot be countenanced. As the tragedy of the Challenger has shown, it takes us in precisely the wrong direction. Reality will not be mocked.

Note

1 For a critique of this usage of the term "self-actualization," see Schwartz (1987c).

References

Argyris, C. (1957): *Personality and Organization: The Conflict between the System and the Individual*. New York: Harper and Row

Chasseguet-Smirgel, J. (1985): *The Ego Ideal: A Psychoanalytic Essay on the Malady of the Ideal*. First American edition, P. Barrows (Translator). New York: Norton

Chasseguet-Smirgel, J. (1986): *Sexuality and Mind: The Role of the Father and the Mother in the Psyche*. New York: University Press

Cummings, L. L. (1983): The Logics of Management. *Academy of Management Review* 8(4), pp. 532 – 538

Deal, T. E. and A. A. Kennedy (1982): *Corporate Cultures: The Rites and Rituals of Corporate Life*. Reading, MA: Addison-Wesley

Freud, S. (1938): Totem and Taboo. *The Basic Writings of Sigmund Freud*. A. A. Brill (Translator/Ed.). New York: Modern Library, pp. 807 – 930

Freud, S. (1955): *Group Psychology and the Analysis of the Ego*. Standard edition, Vol. 18. London: Hogarth

Freud, S. (1957): *On Narcissism: An Introduction*. Standard edition, Vol. 14. London: Hogarth

Geertz, C. (1973): *The Interpretation of Cultures*. New York: Basic Books

Goffman, E. (1959): *The Presentation of Self in Everyday Life*. New York: Doubleday Anchor

Hackman, J. R., G. Oldham, R. Janson and K. Purdy (1975): A New Strategy of Job Enrichment. *California Management Review* 17, pp. 57 – 71

Hohler, R. T. (1986): *"I Touch the Future …": The Story of Christa McAuliffe*. New York: Random House

Klein, M. (1975): A Contribution to the Psychogenesis of Manic-Depressive States. *Love, Guilt and Reparation & Other Works, 1921 – 1945*. M. Klein (Ed.). London: Hogarth, pp. 262 – 289

Lasch, C. (1979): *The Culture of Narcissism*. New York: Warner Books

Lasch, C. (1984): *The Minimal Self*. New York: Norton

Peters, T. J. and R. H. Waterman (1982): *In Search of Excellence: Lessons from America's Best-Run Companies*. New York: Harper and Row

Presidential Commission (1986): *Report of the Presidential Commission on the Space Shuttle Challenger Accident*. Washington, DC: United States Government Printing Office, June 6

Schwartz, H. S. (1987 a): Antisocial Actions of Committed Organizational Participants: An Existential Psychoanalytic Perspective. *Organization Studies* 8(4), pp. 327 – 340

Schwartz, H. S. (1987 b): On the Psychodynamics of Organizational Disaster: The Case of the Space Shuttle Challenger. *The Columbia Journal of World Business* XXII (1), pp. 59 – 67

Schwartz, H. S. (1987 c): On the Psychodynamics of Organizational Totalitarianism. *Journal of Management* 13(1), pp. 38 – 51

Trento, J. J. (1987): *Prescription for Disaster: From the Glory of Apollo to the Betrayal of the Shuttle*. New York: Crown

Wolfe, T. (1979): *The Right Stuff*. New York: Farrar, Strauss, and Giroux

Part IV:
Artifacts and Organizational Control

The Aesthetic Imperative of a Rational-Technical Machinery: A Study in Organizational Control Through the Design of Artifacts

Robert W. Witkin

Working life in a modern organization imposes a definite aesthetic discipline on people. It can be observed in organizational constraints and expectations in respect of dress and personal presentation, in modes of address, and in office manners. Aesthetic discipline can also be observed in the design of buildings, furniture and furnishings, in the organization of physical space, in the use of colour and texture, and in organizational artifacts of all kinds. So pervasive is the aesthetic control imposed on individuals by the existence of the modern organization, that it is surprising that the styling of organizational artifacts has been virtually ignored in theories of organizations. The present paper develops a view of the aesthetic imperative inherent in the ideal-typical modern organization. I have in mind, here, the kinds of large formal organizations that many of us are familiar with in our daily lives and which, at a theoretical level, have been analysed ideal-typically by Weber and others, as bureaucracies, as rational-technical machineries for administration and for the production of goods and services and for the generation of profits (Weber 1948).

1 The Organization as a "Geometrical Spectacle"

The history of industrial design charts the inexorable progress of rationalization and standardization of products and resources as reflected in design (Heskett 1980, Sparke 1986). The present century has seen the emergence of the "machine aesthetic" in which the rational and technical features of mechanisation have been exploited to the full in realising a sensibility of a type "appropriate" to the demands of modern organizations. Most conspicuous in this aesthetic is the dominance of simple geometry. It is clearly expressed in a quotation from an early design periodical "Le Rappel à L'Ordre" cited by Reyner Banham (Banham 1960).

If we go indoors to work ... the office is square, the desk is square and cubic, and everything on it is at right angles (the paper, the envelopes, the correspondence baskets with their geometrical weave, the files, the folders, the registers, etc) ... the hours of the day are spent amid a geometrical spectacle, our eyes are subject to a constant commerce with forms that are almost all geometry.

Sociologists and organizational theorists, however, have concerned themselves little with this revolution in design. They have had much to say about the rational structure of relations in the modern organization. No doubt, the geometrical spectacle provided by the design of modern buildings and organizational artifacts is seen as entirely consistent with their observations on the social structure. This consistency has been very much taken for granted. It has not been analysed as significant or problematical in determining organizational life, although it is clear to anyone that the revolution in industrial design has involved a massive transformation of the living and working environment of whole populations. In approaching the aesthetic dimension of organizational life as both significant and problematic, the present paper offers a tentative approach to understanding its significance in the determination of organizational life and relations.

There are a number of reasons, however, for the scant attention that has hitherto been afforded to the study of artifacts and of aesthetic factors in organizational life. An appreciation of the most important of these may help in laying the foundation for the view of the aesthetic imperative developed here. In the first place, the very conception of the organization as a rational-technical machinery for the achievement of certain empirical ends emphasises cognitive process, even scientific reasoning, as the basis of mental life in organizations. The sensuous, non-rational, and artistic or aesthetic life finds no room in this conception of the organization. Actually, this tendency is even more general and is characteristic of classical sociological conceptions of modern society as opposed to traditional society (e. g. Durkheim 1933, Tonnies 1957), psychological theories about adult cognition as opposed to childhood thought (e. g. Flavell 1963), and even of the design of secondary school curricula as opposed to primary school curricula (Witkin 1986). In all of these dichotomies, there is an implicit theory of progress in which rational, scientific cognition is seen as characteristic of the "advanced" state and sensuous aesthetic thought, of the "primitive" state (Witkin 1983). It is not surprising, therefore, that the closer an organization approximates to the quintessential character assigned to it by organizational theorists, the more the aesthetic dimension is excluded by theoretical definition. Of course, it is recognized that socio-emotional factors are involved in organizational life but these are seen essentially as secondary and as a problem for rational manipulation and management.

2 The Trivialisation of the Aesthetic Dimension of Organizational Life

This exclusion of the aesthetic from conceptualisations of both modern organizations and modern societies has meant that phenomena which are clearly recognized to be aesthetic tend to be conceptually trivialised. Thus, the aesthetic is closely identified with sensuous gratification, with the experience of pleasure, and of pleasing the senses. While these are certainly important in aesthetic experience, this aspect has to be seen in the context of the importance of the aesthetic as a mode of understanding, as a mode of knowing, and as intelligence (Dewey 1934, Langer 1967, Reid 1969, Witkin 1974, 1983). It is the separation of the sensuous aspect of aesthetic experience from knowing and understanding that has led to the trivialisation of the aesthetic domain. Thus, the artifacts with which modern organizations are "furnished" are seen as more or less pleasing, "modern," "stylish," and so forth; their aesthetic impact is recognized in two senses, as an aesthetic interpretation of technical function and also in terms of the company's "image" with its more important clients or customers; but this impact is seen as secondary, as adornment, as packaging, dress, or front for the organization or for its products. It is a matter of presentation rather than substance. It is only when the aesthetic dimension is seen as an integral part of the substantive relations of organizational life, as being fundamental in the organization's development, structure, and functioning, that it ceases to be trivialised. It means, however, that we have to see action itself, even the actions through which a rational-technical machinery is produced and reproduced, as an aesthetic accomplishment. Furthermore, we have to see why such an aesthetic accomplishment is essential to life in a modern organization.

The tendency, everywhere, has been to relegate the aesthetic to the sphere of consumption and conspicuous leisure. Not surprisingly, it is here that sociologists have treated the aesthetic in an altogether more serious way, for example in the work of youth subcultures carried out at the Centre for Contemporary Cultural Studies in Birmingham. The styles of the various youth movements since the war have been shown to have a serious content

grounded in the class experience of young people seeking to resolve fundamental contradictions posed by the erosion of community and territory in
post-war reconstruction and development (Cohen 1972, Hall/Jefferson
1976, Hebdidge 1979). The dress and music, the types of drug use, and
typical activities of different youth groups cease to be seen as bizarre
entertainment or aberration and are treated instead as instances of complex
cultural creation, articulated about the central problems of existence for
real groups in society. The complex web of sensuous display, of sensuous
symbolling, and aesthetic language developed in such groups is treated as
homologous to the focal values and life concerns of the particular group.
Ironically, because "the magical recreation of community" is centred on
consumption and leisure processes, and does not reach into the production
process, it is treated as essentially a doomed attempt at a resolution of the
problems which give rise to it. Work on youth styles certainly points the
way to the kind of serious sociological attention that aesthetic factors
deserve, but an exclusive preoccupation with aesthetic values at the level
of consumption must be overcome if we are to realize more clearly the
important role played by aesthetic factors throughout society.

Insofar as organizations design the situations of action for their members
in a sensuously coherent and consistent way, they call out in individuals a
certain "presence," a structured tension, a readiness for action, and a
preparedness for experience, which corresponds to the sensuous values
manifested in the design of the situation. Physical artifacts are integral to
the design of situations in organizations, and they play an important part
in calling out "appropriate" attitudes and responses in members. Through
the design of situations, which embraces not only the design of artifacts
but the entire socio-cultural context of action, organizations indicate, in
the "presence" they awaken, how they are to be lived by their members.

3 Aesthetic Design and the Problem of Agency

While we frequently pay attention to the results or effects of actions in
organizations, we show remarkably little concern with the nature of the
action itself, with its qualities as agency, as skilled performance of various
kinds. Each type of action, diplomacy, collective bargaining, accounting,
risk taking, and so forth can be seen as aesthetically structured in terms of
its "rhythms," its "pitch" or "amplitude" or "harmonics." The aesthetic
structure of action realizes a distribution and ordering of energies. Action

takes place in situations, and action situations specify the demand characteristics of "agency" in the situation, that is, the qualitative structure of the
action called for.

Action which we would label "diplomacy" is formed, styled, and delivered
in a different way from that of, say "cost accounting." Organizational skills
such as those cultivated in personnel departments and departments of
organizational development differ from the entrepreneurial or marketing
skills of business departments. The structured tension with which action is
performed, its rhythms and textures, in short, its aesthetic qualities, is
grounded in the action situation and is mediated by physical artifacts. The
demand characteristics of the situation are made "visible" in the aesthetic
qualities manifest in the actions of those involved in the situation and *in
the aesthetic qualities of the physical artifacts from dress to furniture which
mediate that action.*

What is essential for the individual generating skilled action of a particular type, is that there should be some continuity (homology) between the
structured tensions (aesthetic qualities) visible in the action situation and
those which inhere in his or her performance. It is this very homology or
continuity between the ordering of energies constituting the action of the
individual and the ordering of "energies" present or implicit in the action
situation, which enables the individual to *bring to mind* the sensuous import
of his action in the situation and to regulate it accordingly. To be effective
in the situation, that is, to "deliver" action of the type and quality required,
the individual must find within himself the structured tension which corresponds to the visible demand characteristics of the action situation. Physical
artifacts play an important role here in their power to reflect these demand
characteristics. They constitute "perceptua" which provide the elements of
a "symbolic system" or "language" through which action can be "brought
to mind," and through which its import in the situation can be grasped.
The intelligent structuring of energies in action demands this continuous
effort to realize a continuity, a resonance between the affective import of
outer forms and the inner sensuous tension that is the life process of the
subject. Only thus can the subject turn about on that inner sensuous tension
and order it in ways that will realize its possibilities in the world.

The design of organizational artifacts and of the material environment
of the organization plays a part, therefore, in determining and constraining
the possibilities for sensuous ordering that are realizable in the situation.
By indicating its affordance of certain types of action and, by implication,
its impedance of others, the design of organizational artifacts calls out in
the subject a certain presence. The personal bearing and presentation of an
individual, the way he moves, dresses, and holds himself in relating to
others, the aesthetic structuring of his action, realizes, at a sensuous level,
this "presence" which constitutes the subject's "being-in-the-situation."

4 Evoking a Presence

There is a great deal said in the organizational literature about motivation and incentive, and this has tended to obscure the role of "style" and of "presence" in the development of skilled performance. Action takes place in situations. A given action has a sensuous import in the situation in which it takes place. That sensuous import is on the "outer" side of the action. On the "inner" side of the action is the sensuous tension in which the action originates. An actor may be said to manifest presence in the situation to the extent that he realizes a resonance, an homology, between the "inner sensuous tension" and the "outer sensuous import" of his actions in the situation.

The *organizational presence* realized by a typist, for example, involves much more than an incipient readiness with respect to the disposition of eye, hand, and body in the execution of the action of typing. These physical movements are nested in a structure of social interactions and relations, an incipient readiness with which the typist orients herself in organizational relations, and it is her aesthetic perception of the resonance between the sensuous ground of her own organizational operations, and the sensuous import of those operations in the total action situation, which she draws upon in constituting her organizational presence. Such a presence is realized in and through the flow of organizational encounters and interactions in which the individual is involved and from which she acquires her sense of herself in action. These encounters, inherently social in character, are mediated by the physical environment, including physical artifacts.

Presence, in this sense, should be identified with skillfulness and with intelligence. It is in and through realizing presence in the situation that the individual successfully negotiates the complex demands of a flow of "encounters" in which there is continuous variation in the sensuous demands made upon him. There is a sensuous structure or order to the flow of encounters that goes to make up organizational life, a certain continuity or symmetry. In realizing, in his own bearing, actions, and movements, a sensuous structure that is homologous with this order, that is resonant with it, the actor achieves a sense of both self and situation as integral. Such a realization is an aesthetic accomplishment, an ordering of sensuous values in expression. The value structure of an organization, manifest at the level of social interaction and of the physical artifacts which mediate such interaction, calls out a presence in the actor that is the locus of its continued recreation.

The presence which an individual realizes in a situation is in itself an intimate "knowing" or "understanding," an "intelligence" with which he shapes his actions. I have, elsewhere, called this intelligence, "the intelligence of feeling" (Witkin 1974) in order to draw attention to the epistemological significance of affect. The presence of the individual as a subject, in a dynamic and active sense, is the only direct and immediate *knowledge* of the felt life that he or she can have. Because we are accustomed to thinking of knowledge as knowledge of "things," we are perhaps less prepared for the recognition that the presence cultivated by an actor on stage, or captured in a painting, a poem, or a piece of sculpture, no less than the presence cultivated by the chief executive of a multi-national company is, in itself, a mode of knowing and understanding upon which the individual depends for orientation in, and an adequate grasp of, the real world. Furthermore, the activation of this presence, this knowledge, is essential to skillful behaviour and interaction, to interpersonal perception and judgement, and to personal relations of all kinds (Witkin 1990). Organizations, therefore, have a real interest in ensuring that they evoke presence in their members that is appropriate in the context of their objectives, and, to that extent, the design of situations and the artifacts that are integral to them is more or less pursuant to that interest.

5 The Aesthetic Imperative of a Rational-Technical Machinery

Organizations differ in their purposes, in their environments, and in their cultural contexts. These differences are reflected in the design of artifacts. It matters whether an organization is making steel or offering financial services, whether it is a small organization or a large multi-national and so forth. The type of business, the type of client, and the importance of the organizational premises in resepect of contact with clients and customers of different types may all affect the aesthetic presentation, the styling of artifacts, and the aesthetic organization of space. In referring, therefore, to an "aesthetic imperative," I do not mean to imply that there are not important aesthetic differences among organizations at the level of artifacts. On the contrary, there are clearly important differences in the aesthetic dimension of artifacts within the same organization. Because of the nature of the argument that follows, it is important to take this qualification seriously. I am not attempting a comprehensive account of organizational artifacts. Rather, in line with the arguments of the classic organizational theorists such as Weber, I am considering only some of the most essential and typical tendencies of modern organizations and asking how these are reflected in the design of organizational artifacts. In effect, this amounts to considering what are the essential aesthetic correlates of a rational-technical machinery, where this latter term is intended to embrace the most ideal-typical characteristics of modern formal and bureaucratic organizations.

For the purpose of analysis, I shall distinguish between two aspects of the aesthetic imperative of a rational-technical machinery. Both are concerned with the organization's use of sensuous values to realize an "organizational presence" in their members. The first concerns the *suppression* of those sensuous values which realize elements of the life process of the members that are excluded from the business of organizational life. These can involve severe constraints on the use of colours and textures, for example, and, in the present context, a suppression of the sense of volume, of mass, and of rounded form in favour of the rectilinear and planar. Organizations do not embrace all of one's existence and frequently take care to ensure that members develop an organizational presence, free from "contamination" by their involvement and presence in other contexts and situations. Forms of aesthetic suppression are seen here as corresponding to important constraints on social relations and upon the life process within organizations. However, they are not seen as merely reflective of such constraints on social relations but as dynamically implicated in their realization.

The second aspect concerns the positive *cultivation* of certain sensuous values that directly express or realize the organizational presence demanded — for example, those qualities of line, form, and colour that serve to realize the sensuous values of rational-technical production. Again, the realization is seen as more than a mere reflection of such values and as actively implicated in their development.

6 The Room at Unilever

To focus attention on certain aspects of the aesthetic dimension of modern organizational life that I consider to be important, I have chosen to describe one particular room in which I recently addressed a group of business consultants. I regard the room as more or less unremarkable and as typical of many such rooms in organizations all over the world. It very much accords with the generalization made by designers cited earlier, in which "our eyes are subject to a constant commerce with forms that are almost all geometry." A description of this room will serve to illustrate both the suppression and cultivation of aesthetic values in a rational-technical machinery.

The room is on the fourth floor of a multi-storey rectangular building and is situated at one end of the building. It is about nine metres long by about three metres wide and is entered from a corridor. There is continuous window, on three sides of the room. The windows have two sets of blinds, one set of narrow horizontal plastic strips (Venetian blinds) and, in front of them, a set of much wider vertical strips. The vertical lines are extremely dominant, perhaps because they are to the fore and go right around three sides of the room. One is, nevertheless, still aware of the continuous horizontal lines behind them which also bound the room on three sides. The remaining side to the room consists of a wall, white in colour, from the top half of which projects a solid white rectangular fronted block, some four metres in length, with small rectangular ventilation grilles at regular intervals along the entire length. There is a long rectangular table, white in colour, which runs the length of the room, a smaller rectangle nested within the larger one of the room itself. Actually, the table is made up of several small tables that have been bolted together.

Along both sides of the table and, at one end, there are chairs, rectangular in shape, and with seats and back and arm rests padded and covered in a shiny, black vinyl material. The strong vertical and horizontal lines of the chairs, together with the smooth hard appearance of the coverings, give a visual impression of lack of comfort. In fact, the chairs are comfortable to sit in. Behind the chairs, at one end of the table, there are two flip chart boards, white in colour and rectangular in shape. Their flat vertical planes rise above equally flat-looking metal frames. They are supported at their base by two pairs of tiny legs descending from two horizontal bars. The supports only serve to accentuate the flatness of the boards, a flatness which is echoed in the strong smooth white plane of the table and the white planes of the wall. It is as though the room has been purged of the appearance of volumes. The floor is of a tough hard material that gives the impression of being smooth mottled stone. At the far end of the room is a coat stand. It is made of metal and, although it has something of the traditional shape, with its central column and curving arms on which to hang clothes, it is altogether sharp and stabbing in appearance. Its curves are attenuated, straightened, and somewhat spikey. The metal circlet for holding umbrellas looks sharp enough to cut your hands. The only other curves that I could see in the room were those of the circular chunky ash trays at intervals along the table. So strong was the linear and planar impression conveyed by this room that these ash trays seemed almost anomalous.

Around the table sat seven men and two women. Dark suits and plain or striped shirts and tastefully blending ties predominate in my impressions. They were dressed in a manner that would be thought appropriate in any large modern organization anywhere.

7 The Suppression of Sensuous Values

In a traditional community, there is no radical disjunction between the production of goods and services and their consumption. They are integral. The modern organization, however, as classically conceived, abstracts production from consumption, and brain from hand and body, in a way that would not be possible in a traditional community. The organization, considered as a rational-technical machinery, is an instrument of production. There are, of course, other ways in which to conceive of organizational life. Work experience and working relations may, in themselves, be seen consumption terms, as something that intrinsically gratifies a need. In treating the formal organization as essentially an instrument of production, however, the classical sociological view accepts, as primary, the instrumental character of the organization, without necessarily denying that there may be other, secondary, characteristics. The room at Unilever is for talking heads, not for those who work with their hands and their bodies, and it is designed as a production resource, not as a consumption utility.

Rooms, such as the room at Unilever, are remarkable for what is omitted at the level of sensuous values. There is an absence of real colour, for example, or of textural variety, of soft or rounded forms, and of an impression of volumes. The unrelieved rectilinear planes, the dominant white, the strong vertical and horizontal lines, seem part of an aesthetic imperative that deliberately suppresses sensuous values that are centred in the being of the individual as a living "subject"; values which are, therefore, expressive of the body, its moods and tensions. The more that sensuous values must express the multitudinous and complex states of being of the subject, the more that use must be made of colour and of textural varieties, and the more prevalent is a softening of surfaces; a softening which occurs both in tactile values themselves and in the optical appearance of such values. Thus, in the room at Unilever, the coverings of the chairs were comfortable to the touch, but they were designed to convey a rigidity and hardness, optically.

It is possible to see this aesthetic imperative as simply a particular instance of "modernism" in design, as lionised in the writings of Le Corbusier, Walter Gropius, and others. Modernism, in this sense, refers to a "machine aesthetic" in which simplicity, rationality, and standardization are the principle tenets. In this way, the modernist designer may be said to have made a virtue out of the necessity imposed by the conditions of mass production and mass consumption. In stylistic terms, modernism involved the abandonment of the natural world and of the individual as the symbolic sources of the language of mass-produced objects and its replacement with the metaphor of the machine and the mechanical environment (Sparke 1986).

The suppression of volume in the room at Unilever is particularly interesting. We are treated not only to a "spectacle of geometry" but to one in which there is an overwhelming predominance of rectilinear planes. One way of analyzing this phenomenon is simply to invoke a technical functionalism. Modern organizations developed vast administrative systems centred on the production of written documents, the management and movement of paper. The paper on which organizations work is both rectilinear and flat. It requires to be housed and transported in containers suitable for the purpose, filing cabinets, correspondence baskets, and so forth. While this is undoubtedly true, it by no means exhausts, or even confronts adequately, the meaning of the revolution in design for the people who live and work in modern societies. Furthermore, the emphasis on the linear and planar emerged among artists in the early years of the century and represented a profound cultural shift that could hardly be reduced to the exigencies of managing paper. When Picasso and Braque effected the Cubist revolution, they turned their backs on the fully volumetric tradition that had dominated in the visual arts in Europe for five centuries, and evolved a new kind of spatial reading in which naturalistic appearance was sacrificed for a synthesis of the real "moments" in which objects appear. The juxtaposition of planes and restrictions on colour in the Cubist paintings have certainly had a profound influence on all design including industrial design.

Furthermore, there is a literature which sees this distinction between the volumetric and the linear-planar as fundamental in the history of art and as linked to social factors (Hauser 1951, Witkin 1983, Wolfflin 1932). Hauser, in his monumental Social History of Art, makes the issue central. His concern is not so much with the modern geometrising tendencies in European art as with past traditions and traditions elsewhere, for example those of neolithic civilizations, of ancient Egypt, or of "primitive" societies. Hauser identifies the planar and geometric styles with aristocratic and hieratic societies. Where there is a developed urban middle class and an associated rise in individualism, he sees naturalistic representation as predominating. There are two aspects to this association. At the level of content, naturalistic representation permits the depiction of a high degree of individuation, of personality, and of particularity. From the standpoint of the producer of the art it may be said to grant significance to a particular point of view, an individual's perspective on the world. By contrast, the geometric and planar represent a de-individuating tendency in art in which formula (often hieratically imposed) and tradition predominate.

From my own point of view, however, the most important function of the planar and geometric modes of representation is to be found in the possibilities that they afford for establishing a purely formal and ideational order. Volumes exist in real space. They have a materiality that must be taken account of. They are never purely formal. A structure of action that is oriented to formal administration, to the rational-technical, is at home with linear and planar forms, for they permit the degree of abstraction of head from body, of management from execution, that is implicit in the development of the modern large-scale bureaucracies. De-individuation is implicit in this aesthetic also. Insofar as volumes have interiors, they have "body," an inner authority with respect to the disposition of their surfaces in relation to the surfaces of other bodies, *and to the body of the observer.* Where the emphasis is on the formal and "ideal," the exigencies of formal relationships require that individuation be suppressed and, it is argued here, the suppression of volume plays an important part in that.

The annihilation of inner freedom, authority, and initiative, which is achieved aesthetically in the suppression of chromatic and textural variety and of volume, is, paradoxically, conducive to the sense that everything is under control and as one wills it to be. There is such a strong boundary between work and leisure in our society that, for many people, there is the feeling that it is only when they are outside the organization that they can be themselves, that they can free the possibilities of the inner life or express themselves or realize their potential for experience. In discussing the more extreme case of the "hippy" culture, Paul Willis has drawn attention to the barrier between the "straight society" and the world of enlarged sensibility which lies on the other side and to which access is sought through the use of drugs. Here, it is argued that "straight society" is marked by an illusion of autonomy, a suppression of the subject, and a deprivation of the senses implicit in rational-technical domination, which masks the real state of being a "determined variable in the world." The straight society was seen as one in which people's sensibilities had been so irrevocably reduced by the compulsive urge to barricade experience away.

To the head (hippy), the 'straight' consciousness, the everyday assumption of auton-omy in the world, in fact, meant limiting consciousness to a microdot in the full spectrum of potential states of consciousness. That dot which an accidental turn of history — the discovery of rational-technical analysis — had magnified into the whole known world of thought. If you could trust yourself to leave that tight circle of apparent certainty, then you would be free to enter vast new experiential areas (Willis 1976).

8 The Cultivation of Sensuous Values

The suppression of sensuous values in the room at Unilever can also be conveyed in positive rather than negative terms, that is, in terms of the cultivation of certain values of importance in an organizational context.

There is, for example, a preference for clean lines, plain and smooth surfaces, and sharp contrasts, which is reflected not only in the physical artifacts in the room as well as the room itself, but also in the attire of members using the room. Thus, it is not really accidental that suits with strong patterning, loose folds, or roughness of texture are not really as acceptable as a blue or grey suit, cut with clean lines that makes a definite figure-ground contrast; and which is worn with a contrasting light-coloured shirt, usually white, and blending tie. The shirt and tie establish the same sharpness of line and contrast at the collar. Patterning, where it does occur is more likely to take the form of thin vertical stripes in either suit or shirt.

In his classic essay on "The Metropolis and Mental Life," Georg Simmel argued that the principle demand upon the personality of the modern urban dweller, pursuing his livelihood in organizations, was to appear incisive and to the point, as someone whose talk and actions were practical and effective, who did not digress, or take up more of other people's time than was necessary, who was fitted for a life in which "money economy has filled the days of so many people with weighing, calculating and numerical determinations with a reduction of qualitative values to quantitative ones" (Simmel 1964, p. 412). Certainly, the imperatives for dress in a modern organization would appear to reinforce that impression aesthetically. The dress itself announces that which is incisive and to the point. However, there is more to it than that. Formal organizational attire, like the room at Unilever, suppresses volume — in this case "body." The sensuous life of the body is excluded from the individual's organizational presence. It is not legitimately "expressed" in his attire or manner of presentation. The power and charisma with which presentation and appearance may be invested becomes very much an organizational rather than a personal attribute, having its source in organizational relations and functions and in a rational-technical aesthetic.

The development of an organization as a rational-technical machinery gives rise to an aesthetic imperative characterized by those familiar elements of the modernist design, the sharpness and simplicity of line, the suppression of colour, the smoothness and hardness of tactile values, and the preference for planar forms. By such means, the room at Unilever, and rooms like it everywhere, successfully achieve, at an aesthetic level, the separation of head from body, of rationality from sensuous values, of production values from consumption values, and of organizational function from personality.

References

Banham, R. (1960): *Theory and Design in the First Machine Age*. London: Architectural Press

Cohen, S. (1972): *Folk Devils and Moral Panics*. London: McGibbon & Kee

Dewey, J. (1934): *Art as Experience*. New York: Capricorn Books

Durkheim, E. (1933): *The Division of Labour in Society*. Glencoe, IL: Free Press

Flavell, J. H. (1963): *The Developmental Psychology of Jean Piaget*. New York: D. Van Nostrand

Hall, S. and T. Jefferson (Eds.) (1976): *Resistance through Rituals — Youth Subcultures in Post-War Britain*. Wolfeboro, NH: Hutchinson

Hauser, A. (1951): *Social History of Art*. New York — London: Random House

Hebdidge, D. (1979): *Subculture — The Meaning of Style*. London: Methuen

Heskett, J. (1980): *Industrial Design*. New York: Thames and Hudson

Langer, S. (1967): *Philosophy in a New Key*. Cambridge, MA: Harvard University Press

Reid, L. A. (1969): *Meaning in the Arts*. Winchester, MA: Allen and Unwin

Simmel, G. (1964): The Metropolis and Mental Life. *The Sociology of Georg Simmel*. K. H. Wolff (Ed.). London: Free Press, pp. 409 — 434

Sparke, P. (1986): *An Introduction to Design and Culture in the Twentieth Century*. Winchester, MA: Allen and Unwin

Tonnies, F. (1957): *Community and Society*. New York: Harper and Row

Weber, M. (1948): *From Max Weber: Essays in Sociology*. H. Gerth/C. W. Mills (Trs.). London: Routledge & Kegan Paul

Willis, P. E. (1976): The Cultural Meaning of Drug Use. *Resistance through Rituals — Youth Subcultures in Post-War Britain*. S. Hall/T. Jefferson (Eds.). Wolfeboro, NH: Hutchinson, pp. 106 — 118

Witkin, R. W. (1974): *The Intelligence of Feeling*. London: Heinemann Educational Books

Witkin, R. W. (1983): The Psychology of Abstraction and the Visual Arts. *Leonardo* 16(3), pp. 200 — 204

Witkin, R. W. (1986): Living Art and Educational Work. Keynote address to the National Conference of the Canadian Society for Education through the Arts. Reproduced in *Artstrip*, Vol. 5(2), pp. 5 — 25. Exeter, England: University of Exeter School of Education

Witkin, R. W. (1990): The Collusive Manoeuvre: A Study of Organizational Style in Work Relations. *Organizational Symbolism*. B. A. Turner (Ed.). Berlin: de Gruyter, pp. 191 — 206

Wolfflin, H. (1932): *Principles of Art History*. New York: Dover

Linguistic Artifacts at Service of Organizational Control

Barbara Czarniawska-Joerges and Bernward Joerges

> That we can make the stars dance, as Galileo
> and Bruno made the earth move and the sun
> stop, not by physical force but by verbal
> invention, is plain enough. That we by like means
> also make things what they are in respect other
> than motion has now begun to be clear
>
> (Goodman 1984: 34).

1 Linguistic Artifacts

In the present paper we want to follow Goodman's lead and go further, claiming that not only things are made by verbal inventions but also that verbal inventions themselves are treated as things. We shall scrutinize this phenomenon in the context of organizations.

It is conventional to speak, in organizational contexts, about instruments of control. But if the organizational control function, at least in its personalized forms of leadership, is management of meaning (Smircich/Morgan 1982), then it has to have adequate instruments at its disposal.

Three exemplary verbal tools used to build shared meaning are labels, metaphors, and platitudes. Labels tell *what* things are, they classify; metaphors say *how* things are, they relate, give life; platitudes conventionalize, they standardize and establish *what is normal* (Czarniawska-Joerges/Joerges 1988).

In what sense do they function as tools? This is possible due to the capacity of language to create and stipulate realities of its own. Such a power of language is called *constitutiveness* (Bruner 1986).

We create realities by warning, by encouraging, by dubbing with titles, by naming, and by the manner in which words invite us to create "realities" in the world to correspond with them. Constitutiveness gives an externality and an apparent ontological status to the concepts words embody (Bruner 1986: 64).

If words are tools for reality construction, then it is understandable that they acquire a "material existence" themselves. Alternatively, but in the same vein, we can say that, as their use is always metaphoric in character, they tend to become reified because the most basic metaphors are of a simple, graspable, and physical kind (Lakoff/Johnson 1980).

Let us trace the ways in which organizational "verbal inventions" create reality and how they themselves become commodities which are produced, sold, and bought, like other organizational artifacts.

2 Labels

Labeling, or naming, is calling things into being. By giving something a name, we perform a linguistic act of creation; things without names do not exist, at least not within the realm of social action. The process of labeling people attracted attention of many authors (for a recent example, see Mary Douglas' analysis of the process of creating new groups of people by inventing new labels, 1986). Although we use labeling on things and people alike, it is the naming of social phenomena that is of interest here, as it stabilizes the flux of social life and helps to create the realities to which it applies.

Much (...) worldmaking consists of taking apart and putting together, often conjointly; on the one hand, of dividing wholes into parts and partitioning kinds into subspecies, analyzing complexes into component features, drawing distinctions; on the other hand, of composing wholes and kinds out of parts and members and subclasses, combining features into complexes and making connections. Such composition or decomposition is normally effected or assisted or consolidated by the application of labels (...). Thus, for example, temporally diverse events are brought together under a proper name or identified as making up "an object" or "a person"; a snow is sundered into several materials under terms of the Eskimo vocabulary (...). Identification rests upon organization into entities and kinds (Goodman 1978: 7−8).

This process was early identified within the political sciences. Labeling, or the linguistic structuring of (social) problems, is a forceful formula for influencing through language.

Political and ideological debate consists very largely of efforts to win acceptance of a particular categorization of an issue in the face of competing efforts in behalf of a different one; but because participants are likely to see it as a dispute either about facts or about individual values, the linguistic (that is, social) basis of perceptions is usually unrecognized (Edelman 1977: 25).

Weick (1985) pointed out the role labels play in organizational life.

Labels carry their own implications for action, and that is why they are so successful in the management of ambiguity. Consider these labels: that is a cost (minimize it), that is a spoilage (reduce it) ... that is a stupidity (exploit it) and so forth. In each of these instances a label consolidates bits and pieces of data, gives the meaning, suggest appropriate action, implies a diagnosis, and removes ambiguity (Weick 1985: 128).

Effective labeling (i. e. that which becomes accepted by others) is one of the sources of organizational power (Smircich/Morgan 1982, Weick 1985). Labels are also the most unobtrusive means of control; it takes a great deal of self-reflectiveness to become suspicious of a classification or of a name. "What's in a name?" asks Juliet, "That which we all call a rose, By any other name would smell as sweet" (*Romeo and Juliet*, Act II, Scene 2). But Romeo knows better and points out that the name one has can decide one's fate ...

In what follows we shall use some examples of labeling in organizations taken from our own and other's studies.

2.1 "Decentralization"

An exploration of the Submunicipal Committee reform in Swedish municipalities (Czarniawska-Joerges 1987) revealed the use of labels in organizational change processes. Employed as control means, they helped to insert wanted changes and to combat opposition.

The most portentous label was that of "decentralization," as it applied to the reform as a whole. Now, designate something as "decentralization" in the 1980s sounds as beneficial as labeling something "centralization" had been in the 1960s' debate on public administration. Decentralization is, by definition, good. However, almost indistinguishable organizational or political changes may be called "centralization" or "decentralization," depending on the designs of label-users and on prevailing trends (see for example DiTomaso's depiction of Reagan's reform of state administration, 1985). Already the classic decentralization studies, such as Blau's (1970), demonstrated the relativity of the concepts of centralization and decentralization; a problem which is often solved, just like in the case of the Submunicipal Committee reform, by a platitude saying: "Every decentralization requires some centralization, and vice versa ..."

Labels govern by removing ambiguity, claimed Weick (1985). But labels diverge on the degree of their tangibility, and therefore in the amount of ambiguity they can eliminate. Compare "this is a spoilage" and "this is a decentralization." It is manifest that the former is bad and the latter is good, but the specificity of following action differs greatly. Spoilage must be reduced, and there are probably only so many ways of doing it, but decentralization can be approved of, loved, helped, achieved, implemented, and so on and so forth. Broad, abstract labels of this kind are very useful as control tools because they permit an *ad hoc* redefining of actions to be undertaken. "This is a spoilage" indicates a value (spoilage is wrong) and points towards a concrete action (reduce it). "This is a decentralization" also indicates a value (decentralizing is right) but unfolds a wide scope of possibilities (we might even have to centralize to be able to decentralize ...). The label gave the meaning to the whole of the reform; by labeling it a decentralization, a setting of positive attitudes was created, furthermore impeding likely criticisms.

2.2 "Leadership"

An interesting case illustrating the complexities of labeling is the history of the "leadership" label in the Swedish public sector. For many years, not only in Sweden but everywhere else, organization researchers concentrated on "management," an impersonal process of organizing the flows of people, things, and money towards a desired outcome, leaving "leadership" to small group, psychological research, or, at a larger scale, to the political sciences. In the early 1980s the interest in "leadership" and in charismatic managers accompanies a growing fascination with "corporate culture" (for an excellent example, see Deal and Kennedy 1982). We are not able to analyze the process of introducing these labels into the U.S. context of organizing, hence we shall limit ourselves to tracing the consequences of this trend visible in Sweden. The private sector imported the "leadership" notion from the U.S.A., together with many others. Some 20 years ago, the public sector would have paid no attention. At that time, public sector was the public hero, whereas private business was the public villain. "Leadership," smacking of totalitarianism and personality cult, was a word to be avoided. But times changed. Nowadays public sector is the wasteful controller, hostile towards those whom it should protect, whereas private business appears the savior and defender of all liberal values. The public sector follows humbly in the footsteps of private business, all leadership gurus arriving from the U.S. book their seminars both with business and public administration, and "leadership" is positively in.

As the label infiltrated the walls of the public sector, it is not surprising that "leadership" turned out to be one of the important aims of "decentralization." If, however, we dare to scratch the labels and have another look, it would seem that "decentralization" and "leadership" do not go well together. If citizens are to have more say, the last thing they need is charismatic leaders — be they politicians (who should concentrate on reflecting demands and not dictating them) or administrators (who should be efficient servants, and not the rulers of souls). One would think that decentralization should decrease the amount of, and need for, leadership. However, the proponents of "leadership" claim that it takes place through activation of followers, and therefore leadership and decentralization should support each other ... Labels do not have contents of their own; it all depends on to what we accord them.

2.3 "Excellence"

A label that we all recognize is that of "excellence," for which we are all searching. As Fischer and Mandell put it,

... excellence has become the present-day cultural jargon of merit. Isn't excellence "what we do best?" asked President Reagan rhetorically in his recent State of the Union Address. It "makes freedom ring" (1988: 11).

Fischer and Mandell discuss the rhetoric of excellence as the way of relegitimating meritocracy in the American educational system, but they notice that it penetrated almost every field:

We are enticed on all fronts to embrace a world of "excellence": from micro-wave ovens that provide us with a "galaxy of excellence," to the Philadelphia Orchestra which invites us to "subscribe to excellence," to self-discovery and personal growth seminars that offer "blue-prints for excellence," to Indiana University's claim to "embrace excellence" in the classroom as well as on the court (1988: 11).

When analyzing the function of "excellence" as a label, we must ask, however, whether excellence is what *we* do best, or whether it is what the U.S. citizens do best. In fact, the Swedish public sector swallowed "leadership," but it seems to have choked on "excellence." Its meritocratic frame of reference does not agree well with an egalitarian climate. Peters and Waterman's book is called in Swedish "På jakt efter mästerskapet" (Hunting the mastership). The "hunting" metaphor creates a Viking touch (on Viking organization theory, see Czarniawska and Wolff 1986), and "mastership" is a more limited concept than "excellence"; it is trainable, and therefore open to everybody.

2.4 Labels and Trends

Labeling is not accomplished once-and-for-all or, to fall back on Goodman again, decomposing is an inseparable part of composing. Labels change their places in classificatory schemes as the general frames of reference change, and therefore different things are given the same labels, or else same labels carry different meaning. When public opinion in Sweden pushed the public sector off its pedestal of a "do-gooder" and put the private sector in its place, things that were "bad" became "good" and vice versa. In the 1960s, "centralized control," "detailed regulations," "planning," "specialization," "investigation studies," and "investments" were all positive labels in the context of the Swedish public sector (and not only there. For the Italian "top list" of labels of the 1960s, see Gagliardi 1988). Now they are all "bad." In their place came labels like "service-mindedness," "know-how," "profitability," "effectiveness," "management philosophy," "net-works," and strategic decision making," which are the new favorites. Trends ("a trend is a range of actions from which an observer constructs a label," Edelman 1988: 16) emerge as new master-labels.

3 Metaphors

If labels create existences, metaphors endow them with attributes and therefore structure action.

(...) the process of metaphorical conception is a basic mode of symbolism, central to the way in which humans forge their experience and knowledge of the world in which they live (Morgan 1980: 610).

Metaphor is an operation by which "aspects of one object are 'carried over' or transferred to another object, so that the second object is spoken of as it were the first" (Hawkes 1972: 1). Eco asserts that metaphors can be acceptable, rewarding, or defaulting. Metaphors are perceived as *acceptable* if they evoke a desired association but fail to exert an aesthetical influence, like when we say that organizations are political systems (for metaphors of organization, see Morgan 1980). In contrast with these, metaphors that create new associations are received as *rewarding*. "Organizations as garbage cans" is a good example of such a metaphor (Cohen/March/Olsen 1972). Metaphors feel *defaulting* (or deceiving) if it is difficult to come upon the desired association, and when it happens, the result is not very illuminating. We see "organizations as seesaws" as such a metaphor. Finally, there are metaphors which are not really metaphors anymore, as they are "matching something that our common knowledge has long since matched, and without exciting results" (Eco 1979: 4). These are metaphors turned into platitudes, as, for example, "organizations as hierarchies" is.

Until not so long ago, metaphors remained a subject matter of literary criticism, semiotics, and hermeneutics. As organization researchers became interested in these fields, metaphors moved into the focus of organizational attention. It has been suggested that the "metaphors of the field" can become a tool for comparative analysis of different organizations (Manning 1979) and that research paradigms are situated in master-metaphors of organization (Morgan 1980). The more cautious authors warned against a "metaphor overdose" (Pinder/Bourgeois 1982), but, in our opinion, such voices fall on deaf ears.

Our intention is to concentrate on metaphors of the field, i. e. those used by the actors, on the assumption that they are much more than just decorative figures of speech (Morgan 1983). They are not only symbols: if they serve the function of symbolic expression, they are also instrumental, like in control uses, and therefore bridge the expressive and the practical orders in organizations (Harré 1981). "Metaphor is no decorative rhetorical device but a way we make our terms to multiple moonlighting service" (Goodman 1978: 104).

How exactly does such a moonlighting proceed? Look, as an example, at the function metaphors serve in the spreading of new ideologies. Metaphors impart new meanings by molding them into romantic messages. Their role involves reducing uncertainty produced by the confrontation with the new. They refer to something which is better known than the object in question. In that sense, they can be seen as short-cuts in explication, evoking a single image which encompasses the most important elements of a phenomenon or object in question. They are also seen as attractive because their "orna-mental" characteristics fulfill a need for colors and life in organizations which tend to be rather dull, It is the expressive and not reflective power of metaphors which is most important, both in symbolic and in functional contexts (Geertz 1964). That is why a metaphor "is often most effective when it is most 'wrong'" (Thompson 1980: 233). Metaphors "produce, prior to knowledge, something which, psychologically speaking, we could call 'excitation'" (Eco 1979: 87).

3.1 Metaphors and Change

In the Submunicipal Committee reform, metaphors aided the understanding of the idea of change and increased its attractiveness. By summoning colorful associations, they educated and motivated organizational actors.

"Rich flora of experiments" is a good example of a well-coined metaphor. It projects a picture of something multifarious, vibrant, organic but also uncontrollable, hard to get across, slightly dangerous, and various actors emphasized different aspects of the metaphor. A less successful metaphor was that of "blowing life into dead party organizations," which was dangerously close to a platitude "we have made a living democracy." Metaphors, after long use, petrify and become labels, or die and become platitudes. This statement, however, is in itself metaphoric, as metaphors do not do anything — it is we who do things to them. And what we do depends on who we are. Our favorite metaphor, "living under a cold starlight of scarcity" (which Swedish municipalities apparently did) was judged a platitude by our Swedish colleagues, who had many opportunities to learn it by heart before we ever came to Sweden.

3.2 Metaphors and Managerial Philosophies

A Swedish company was severely threatened by a decline caused by the oil crisis (Czarniawska-Joerges 1988). The new President instituted a new life and a new ideology to the company and, while doing it, put the linguistic artifacts to a proficient use. A metaphor which he used often was "gardening" as symbolizing his attitude towards personnel development.

There are two basic philosophies about development. One is so-called engineering philosophy and the other is gardener philosophy. If you have an engineering philosophy about development you look upon people as pieces of metal that you put into a lathe and then into a grinding machine and then into a lathing machine and then you put them into the oven to harden the surface and then perhaps you grind them again and finally you have a piece that fits perfectly into the organization chart. The only mistake with that particular philosophy is that it is poorly wrought. There is no way that I can develop you, and there is no way you can develop me. You develop yourself if you want to do it and if you feel inclined to do it. If the environment is such that you feel that you want to develop yourself. Therefore, it is much better to take a gardener attitude. You look upon the company as a garden with plants all around. Then it is the responsibility of the gardener to walk through this garden and water the plants, give them a little extra soil, perhaps fertilizer sometimes, and perhaps one plant is sitting there in the shade and needs more sun, so you pick it up and move it into the sun, and if someone in the sun doesn't want this he should be put in the shade, and perhaps somebody in the sandy soil should be moved over and put into some other kind of soil, and sometimes you have to remove some undesirable plants that hinder the growth of the others ...

The metaphor caught on, as demonstrated by the fact that almost all actors were using it. They described their company as a kind of a "hothouse" where for all the "plants" the best conditions to develop were created.

3.3 Metaphors and Worldmaking

Metaphors are used for worldmaking in a double sense of the word. To begin with, they create a version of the world, shared by those who accept it. This means that they also create "thought-worlds" (Douglas 1986), groups of people who use a given metaphor to structure their actions. A study on consultants in the Swedish public sector (Czarniawska-Joerges 1990) showed how metaphors created a vision of the world (for example, of organizational identity: a "teacher" and not a "guardian," or of the environment: a "market" and not a "hierarchy") and, by virtue of their attractiveness, acted like powerful magnetos towards various actors and groups of actors, creating new groupings. Similarly, the metaphor of Sweden as an "information society" made people from local government think of information needs of the citizens, the entrepreneurs of computers that can be sold, and the unions of information distribution and information rights. The metaphor created for them a common area where they had a basic common language, and yet they could preserve their own perspective and interests.

4 Platitudes

In literary criticism, platitudes are seen as a blemish, a flaw in the art of creative writing.

Literature subjunctivizes, makes strange, renders the obvious less so, the unknowable less so as well, matters of value more open to reason and intuition (Bruner 1986: 159).

Platitudes do just the opposite: they objectivize, make strange into familiar, doubtful into obvious, and by involving values close the gaping door of the unknown. They can be seen as verbal rituals, utterances whose meaning lies in the act of repetition. They familiarize by relating concrete things or happenings to commonsensical generalizations. These characteristics of their functioning suggest a similarity between platitudes and rituals, both of them being linkages between a specific present and the accumulated past.

And that is why in verbal interactions the role of platitudes is drastically different from the one they play in a literary text. They facilitate interactions by reduction of uncertainty (Hendricks 1987). In a situation characterized by a great deal of uncertainty, interpersonal tensions are bound to arise. A use of platitude suggests a good will, a wish to find a common ground (before differences can be safely explored), very much like hand-shaking does. Platitude can be seen as an opposite of a metaphor, but in organizations they both fulfill the same function in a different way: they remove ambiguity by relating the new to something which is better known (metaphor) or to something which is very well known (platitude). The relation between them is close, and their meaning depends on the experience of an observer: what for some is a bold metaphor, for others is a dull platitude.

In organizations, platitudes alleviate shocks produced by daring metaphors and astonishing ideologies. Like safety-valves, they taper off tension when it builds up too high. Their obviousness encourages consensus, and their sharedness soothes social frictions. That is why platitudes, contrary to a commonsensical picture, are the stuff of which leadership is formed:

To maintain adequate support and acquiescene, aspirants for political leadership and for social acceptance must choose from a circumscribed set of banal texts (Edelman 1988: 113).

Platitudes do not carry change and innovation; they cushion it. Such was the role they performed in the Submunicipal Committee reform. Indeed, it is reasonable to expect many platitudes in a situation of change, which by definition is filled with uncertainty. There was a whole set of platitudes that seemed to cover all the major problems of the reform. And so those who doubted the need for a sudden decentralization were to learn that "democracy is not given once and for all, and every generation must build it anew." Those who observed that things did not change much were told that "democracy has to take its time." We know by now that "every decentralization requires a corresponding centralization and vice versa," and so forth. Some actors were putting such platitudes into the inverted commas, by various rhetorical devices like laughing or adding "as one says." This served to stress their competence as speakers (who do not usually tell platitudes) and to indicate to which side they belonged in a given problematic area.

Again, political scientists observantly noticed this use of platitudes and other rituals:

In politics, as in religion, whatever is ceremonial or banal strengthens reassuring beliefs regardless of their validity and discourages skeptical inquiry about disturbing issues (Edelman 1977: 3).

This statement evidently applies to all organizations, not only those of overtly ideological character.

5 Linguistic Artifacts as Tools of Control

What kinds of reality are created by linguistic artifacts? Labels, metaphors, and platitudes are important tools of power forging. Power in organizations belongs to those who can define reality for others, and who can convince others that things are what they think they are, are like they think they are, and are normal when they think they are normal. Linguistic artifacts enable leadership to manage meaning by interpreting, coloring, and familiarizing, as opposed to traditional control methods: commanding, fighting, and punishing.

All this takes place in the course of organizational talk, which "imposes structure, conceptualizes, ascribes properties" (Goodman 1978: 6). But surely talk is an interaction, and a transaction: to assume that it is leaders who talk to the silent rest is to oversimplify. The rest talk back. Hence, let us take a look at the interaction itself and the role of linguistic artifacts in it.

We agreed that linguistic artifacts are used for management of meaning. This formulation leaves open, however, the issue of who manages what and for whom. It can be interpreted in at least two ways: as managing the meaning *for* other people and managing the meaning *of* others, the meaning that others have (Figure 1).

The first interpretation seems to be closer to the intentions of the authors who introduced the concept (Smircich/Morgan 1982), as its continuation in the idea of "enacted environments" (Smircich/Stubbart 1985) indicates. Organizational actors need some shared interpretation of reality to be able to carry out their collective actions. Managers reduce uncertainty, for themselves as well as for others, by saying what is there, what it is like, and what is normal. If this process is to proceed smoothly, those who are managed must abdicate their ambitions to arrive at their own interpretations of the situation. Or, in a classic formulation, "willingness to suspend one's own critical judgement in favor of someone regarded as able to cope creates authority" (Edelman 1988: 20, after Herbert Simon). An *abdication of meaning* is an act of trust on the part of the followers or, alternatively, a gesture of despair and frustration.

Usually, however, the non-managers are not *tabula rasa* to be freely written upon: they perform their own enactments, incomplete and faulty as they might be, with their own linguistic tools, and their sense making can be very different from that of managers. Still, if there are no shared meanings, collective action is impossible. And here is where the second interpretation of the "management of meaning" comes in. Managers try to manage subordinates' meaning by convincing them that their, managers', enactment is a more valid or a better basis for collective action. Such an *imposition of meaning* can be accomplished by persuasion or by force, with the aid of linguistic artifacts or material ones. But no matter what means are used, it is clear that control — and power — involves the imposition of one's own definition of reality upon others (Brown 1978).

Both abdication and imposition of meaning take place in organizations in their pure form; but the most common situation is perhaps that of a *negotiation of meaning*, where many and different attempts at imposition of meaning (coming not only from the formal leaders) lead inevitably to compromises, exchanges, and bargains. When successful, negotiation increases the amount of shared meaning; when unsuccessful, it leads to imposition and conflict, or abdication and apathy. In all these operations, linguistic artifacts play a prominent role.

As they are used as tools to build shared meanings, they themselves are treated as tools, i. e. as things. We shall now look in more detail into the two relations this implies: that of use, and that of property.

The former one is well explicated in Elaine Scarry's theory of the interior structure of the artifact (Scarry 1985). Artifacts for her are sites of *projection* and sites of *reciprocation* of human

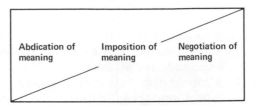

Leader defines the meaning

Abdication of meaning — Imposition of meaning — Negotiation of meaning

Group defines the meaning

Figure 1: Different types of management of meaning

action. A designer projects a perception about human sentience ("humans suffer from their body weight") onto an artifact ("a chair"). The artifact refers back to human sentience ("chair is to relieve the suffering from the body weight") and invites a reciprocative action ("sitting down"). Similarly with linguistic artifacts: calling something "a reform" projects into a name the feeling of human fallibility and a need for betterment. When accepted as such ("this indeed is a reform"), artifacts invite reciprocation ("reforms should be supported and carried through").

Artifacts are not only used but also, at least temporarily, they belong to somebody. In this sense linguistic artifacts can be seen as possessions (in claiming this, we follow Abelson's example, who claimed that "beliefs are like possessions," 1986).

In the Submunicipal Committee reform mentioned before, a group of actors in each local government acted as "ideology owners": through inventing, appropriating, or buying they owned a set of ideas which constituted the reform. This gave them the property rights to linguistic artifacts connected to ideology: "decentralization," "breathing new life into the dead party organizations," and "each decentralization requires some centralization" all belonged to them. The "believers," i. e. those actors who espoused the ideology of the reform, were allowed to use these artifacts. Not so the "heretics," i. e. actors who were labeled so because they were expected to oppose the reform, as it threatened their positions. Some of them, however, contrary to expectations, were enthusiastic of the reform and picked up the pertaining artifacts. This was met with embarrassment, like when a sudden bankrupt tries to claim his property, not knowing what everybody else does, that he lost it overnight.

Even worse was the case of "skeptics" and true "heretics" who would steal the artifacts and use them subversively, often by putting them into inverted commas of irony: decentralization became "a so-called decentralization," metaphors were punctured until they resembled platitudes, and platitudes were ridiculed. But they would not do it in public: the artifacts did not belong to them, after all.

For their true owners, the artifacts were tools for creating a common reality. In case of "ideology owners," they were tools of imposing their version of reality upon others, and therefore tools of control. For the second-hand owners, the "believers," they were badges of belonging and ordering devices in the complexity of reality.

Until now we looked inside organizations, watching the use of linguistic artifacts. Now it is time to trace their way into organizations. Sometimes they are internally produced; most of the time they come from the outside. Like any other artifacts, they are bought from outside suppliers.

6 Supply

The supply side of linguistic artifacts is dominated by consultants who are the most prolific producers, but also processors of raw materials and half-products which can be found in research results. We therefore decided to concentrate on consultants as the main suppliers of labels, metaphors, and platitudes used in organizational control processes.

The 1984—86 issues of the *Journal of Management Consulting* serves us as one data source. As stated in its editorial, "*Management Consulting* is written and edited primarily for readers actively engaged in the design, development and delivery of management consulting services." It is, in other words, a journal were consultants write about consulting for consultants and not for managers, as for example the Swedish *Ledarskap/Ekonomen* which we have therefore used to a lesser degree.

In the editorial and in many articles, the supply—demand metaphor which we use as a leading metaphor in this paper is also used very often. The authors speak about product development, idea selling, direct selling techniques, etc., thereby demonstrating that these are "metaphors of the field."

6.1 History

Martin Bower, a McKinsey consultant who was also the first president of the Institute of Management Consulting, in the first number of Volume 1 tried to delineate the historical forces that launched management consulting:

During the Depression ... the urge to "try anything" was strong, and for this and other reasons, companies did begin to employ consultants. Once a few companies had experienced the value of independent management advice, the force of emulation took over. One company followed another in retaining consultants, and consultants of competence and high standards multiplied. As companies of greater and greater status became "users," the field began to live down the opprobrious term "business doctors." Gradually the bandwagon effect helped executives surrender their prideful insistence "We don't *need* outside help." Although pride still keeps some managers from retaining consultants, such managers are an endangered species, and quality of consulting work of perceived value is gradually making them extinct ... (Bower 1982: 5)

As we can see, the battle was half won when a derogative metaphor gave field to a positive message. And that took quite a long time, as the first consulting firms came at the turn of the century (Arthur D. Little 1886, McKinsey 1910). Since the 1968, the Institute of Management Consulting certifies management consultants, and, adds Bower, "... as leaders flourished, charlatans vanished." Home craftsmanship gave way to professional production. Let us take a closer look at it through the eyes of persons involved.

6.2 Products

Articles, panel discussions, interviews with leading consultants, and other materials in the Journal confirm that main products are labels, metaphors, and platitudes. The two former are often called "insights, ideas, images." Speaking about their clients' problems or about themselves, the authors seem to be breathing metaphors. One company advises a "cookie cutter approach to consulting," another claims that "business strategy is a large chess game." A chief executive officer of a consulting firm says that "hiring MBAs is like buying fine wines," and another confesses that his first consulting experiences were like "taking a girl for a walk through a minefield you didn't know was there." This production seems to be based on one basic skill: associating. Unlike managers and researchers, consultants seem to have a free hand in associating, bisociating, and in general trying on various creative tricks. Managers may fear being taken literally; for researchers it is not "good style." Consultants fill the gap.

   Their product is of the package type: product plus service. There are, basically, two types of packages. One is called "the infusion of creative thinking" by one of the consultants and "the injunction of metaphor" by Morgan (1986). The products are labels and metaphors (labels have very often a flavor of metaphor); the service is to show how to relate them to organizational life. A friend of ours, recently head of a very new, very dynamic, and very unstable organization, was faced with growing numbers of problems that made him both nervous and depressed. After two hours of talk with a well-known consultant he came to us, his eyes shining: "Do you know who we are? We are a deviant learning system!" The label-metaphor helped him to justify and explain the troublesome happenings to himself and to his subordinates.

Another kind of package can be called "facilitation package." If the "creativity" package was more of a problem-solving or intellectual type, this one is oriented toward human interactions and communication problems. Labels and metaphors again, but mostly platitudes, help to get the air go from bags of accumulated grievances, to reopen blocked communication channels.

6.3 Control

Consultants describe their function as "infusion of creative thinking," "facilitation," time-compression," but they do not mention issues of power and control. They may sometimes mention conflicts — which are a part of their job, anyway — but search for power awareness is futile. Allan A. Kennedy (the co-author of "Corporate Cultures") illustrates the work of consultants in a series of drawings (Figure 2). The metaphor is cosmic. The organization at the first stage is a constellation of randomly located stars — they differ in size and distance, but there is no trace of hierarchies or any other solar systems. Consultants arrive, supposedly, from another galaxy, and they start to infuse their new waves of thinking. This mental invasion (this metaphor is ours!) encompasses more and more stars, to initiate a consensus which grows ... At the point when consensus embraces most of the stars, the work is done. Consultants board their space ship and go to another galaxy.

Yet, commonsense knowledge of organizational practice indicates that this heavenly picture does not include the most important traits of organizational reality. Consultants are usually called by somebody, and it would be surprising indeed if the person who initiated the action expected them to prove that he or she was wrong. That happens very often, as an unexpected result (unexpected by the caller, that is), but the dynamics of the real situation is then much more complicated. One can imagine a whole continuum of possible developments concerning power. On the one extreme would be a situation described to one of the authors by a chief executive officer, who said quite openly that he employed consultants to stood up decisions that he feared might be unpopular. Such an action does not presume corruption, bribing, or other unethical steps. Within the existing plethora of consultants, he explained, one can always find those whose general line is in agreement with what the leader wanted. And not only consultants: in one of the municipalities under study, a group considering a cautious approach to Submunicipal Committee reform recommended a referendum. A group of the enthusiasts of the reform then organized a seminar with a group of political scientists who were known for criticizing the ritualism of referenda. At the time we last talked to them, the opponents were considering another conference, with scientists of an opposite stance in the matter.

The other extreme is the situation where consultants team up with people who are the main opponents of the caller or, alternatively, when the caller did not know what the problem was and did not like what was revealed. Both extreme situations are, however, reluctantly described both by the consultants and their clients.

One reason for neglecting power issues may be related to the fact that most consultants have a power background, as managers and academicians have. It has been frequently observed that managers, and other people in power, tend not to notice the power background (Morgan 1986). This brings us to another issue, namely a striking similarity between consultants and their clients.

6.4 Producers and Buyers

Bruce Henderson, the chief of the Boston Consulting Group, in an interview published in the Journal, repeatedly stressed that consultants are very much alike their clients, with one difference: they are not blinded by being inside. This widened horizon enables them to compress time for their clients by performing "impressionistic jumps" which result in insight that clients could achieve only much, much later. This jump is not, however, effected by more accurate information or other devices to increase rationality.

In fact, it may be only predictions founded on impressionistic observations that are worth their cost ... If nearly perfect data are required in order to make an acceptable prediction, the time and effort required to get the data will rob the process of its contribution to time compression ... Intuition is the keystone of consulting (*Journal of Management Consulting* 1984, Vol. 1/1).

In other words, if you need information that can be provided by a computer, buy yourself a computer instead of consulting services. Consultants sell hand-made tools, pieces of craft, if not of art.

7 Demand

The question arises what the clients are prepared to pay for those. The popular picture would want it that the demand for management consultants is enormous and therefore the prices are exorbitant. What do the consultants say?

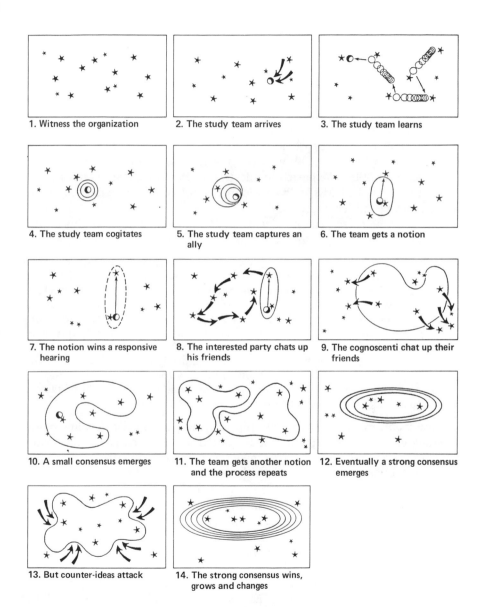

Figure 2: The cosmic metaphor of consulting

7.1 Salaries

Although prices are sometimes mentioned in connection with consulting services, there is not much factual information. One aspect which was relatively easy to investigate was salaries paid by consulting companies to MBA graduates. The stereotypical picture is that these young people are ridiculously overpaid compared with all other graduates, and therefore more and more people choose consulting, hence depriving industry and commerce of line specialists and good managers. This issue was a topic for a panel discussion reported in the *Journal of Management Consulting* (Vol. 1/1). The data showed that of the Harvard Business School class of 1981, 21.4% went into consulting. However, argued the panelists, the most obvious reason was not obvious at all. In 1981, an average MBA base starting salary was $ 31,600 in consulting firms as compared to a general average of $ 29,200. We hasten to add that in the same year McKinsey was offering $ 50,000 to MBAs from Sloan School of Management. Averages are somewhat misleading.

After having presented their defensive data, the panelists generally agreed that consultants' salaries are very high and chose another line of defense:

... what is it about the consulting profession that causes us to pay what many consider to be exorbitant salaries? I think it's simply a matter of supply and demand. The people who are willing to be on the road and gone from home all week, to work fourteen or sixteen hours a day, to be on call all the time, tend to gravitate toward investment banking and the consulting profession. There aren't too many folks who are willing to do that. Frankly, we have to pay them what it takes to get them into the firm.

The real question is whether clients will pay the markup that's required to make a firm an economic success. If the clients didn't pay the daily rates demanded by these salaries, we wouldn't be able to pay the salaries, and that would be the end of it (Robert M. Sontheimer, of Resource Planning Associates, Inc.).

Before we move to clients, let us stop for a while with the first line of the argument. Contrary to the statistics quoted in the same panel discussion, the discussant tried to project an image of a profession with a very limited pool of candidates, due to extremely harsh working conditions. What is more, the image presented here is not of a producer trying to sell products and services to the market, but an emergency service, like a fire brigade, or "Red" Adair's oil fire services. In other words, the services are indispensable and very difficult to render.

This is a very common argument, which could be used against our subsequent reasoning. According to this line of thought, consultants do not produce labels and metaphors, but offer concrete and often technical services. Is this so? *Ledarskap/Ekonomen* (No. 12, 1986) reviewed the consultant market in Sweden and found that there were very few companies

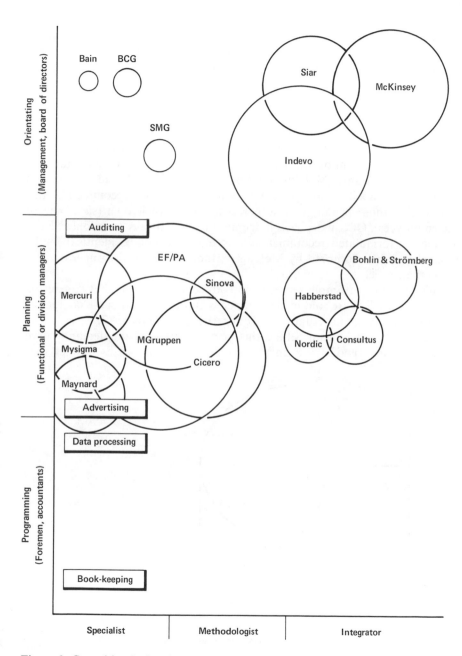

Figure 3: Consulting in Sweden

that operated on a programming or operational level. Most of them acted on symbolic levels: planning and general orientation. As far as status was concerned, the highest status was accorded to "integrators" (as opposed to "specialists" and "methodologists") who operated at the orientation level and dealt with labels and metaphors (Figure 3).

7.2 Demand Curve

A county council in Sweden employed McKinsey at a SEK 1 million fee to prepare a program of improvements and effectivity increase for medical services in the county. McKinsey did as it was asked, collected the fee, and the county council is now a proud owner of a list of recommendations exactly like those produced by other councils on their own (say some of the employees). Of course, such judgement can be always questioned. Even identically formulated recommendations may still not be identical in the sense that, when authored by McKinsey, they will have a stronger control value than others.

This anecdotal example serves to introduce a hypothesis that consulting goods and services are sold in accordance with the demand curve characteristic for prestige goods (Figure 4, Kotler 1983, Williams 1982).

What is the mechanism behind this peculiar shape of the demand curve at its high-price end? "A brand," says Jones (1986), "is a product that

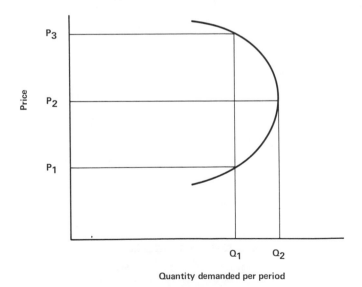

Figure 4: Demand curve for prestige goods

provides functional benefits plus added values that some consumers value enough to buy" (p. 29). Joan Robinson leaves no doubt as to what these values are:

... various brands of certain article which in fact are almost exactly alike may be sold as different qualities under names and labels which will induce rich and snobbish buyers to divide themselves from poorer buyers (1950: 180–181).

That may be well so, agrees Jones, but there is no reason to only blame the sellers:

If people buy higher priced merchandise in reasonable large quantities in the belief that it is better than a lower priced item partly by the fact of its higher price, they will presumably get greater satisfaction from the more expensive article than they would have gotten from the cheaper one; and if this situation is deplored, people's psychological makeup is surely more at fault than the actions of oligopolists (Jones 1986: 36).

Whoever's fault is greater, the fact is that the combined efforts of oligopolists and buyers' snobbery create the prestige good demand curve.

Or maybe "snobbery" is a label which does not offer sufficient insight. James G. March, when discussing the role of consulting, reminds us of Dale Carnegie's theory of relations between sellers and buyers. Carnegie claimed that there were only two types of goods in our societies: self-esteem and substantive goods. Self-esteem is in continuous shortage in relation to substance, so that anyone who can offer any amount of it can expect a very advantageous rate of exchange (March 1984). And we might add that the rate of exchange is in itself an element that can contribute to self-esteem.

Another aspect of prestige goods is that the name of the manufacturer stands often for a brand. This phenomenon, however, is very little discussed. Jones dismisses the value of manufacturer's name and reputation as merely symbolizing other, more important values, such as the experience of the brand, the kind of people who use the brand, the appearance of the brand, and a belief that the brand is effective. In contrast, other sources indicate that corporate advertising supersedes product advertising and company-image overshadows brand-image (Bernstein 1984). Additionally, other linguistic phenomena facilitate this process; as Lakoff and Johnson (1980) point out, one of the most frequent metonymies in our culture is exactly that the producer represents the product. Consulting counts as goods when coming from well-known consulting firms, and only leading consulting firms can demand exorbitant fees. Of course, beyond a certain threshold it is impossible for small companies or some public agencies to pay the fees, and therefore the demand curve bends again. But, generally speaking, the attraction lies in the brand. McKinsey can be seen as the Rolex of consulting.

However, prestige goods are usually also of practical use. Rolex watches show not only status, but also time, and goods brought in by consultants are put to work in the company. As it is only top management who can decide to pay exorbitant fees, it is top management who has all the rights to use the products purchased. But, as we have seen before, various groups of actors appropriate linguistic tools and might be even using them for subversive purposes. However, as with the use of other artifacts, one must claim a minimum identification with the organization to be allowed to use the artifacts. People who are known to use organizational artifacts for private purposes or, worse, for ridiculing organization, will sooner or later find out that their access to stickers, pens, or labels is limited. The control tools must not be used for counter-control.

7.3 Brand Strategy

If the analogy between consulting and prestige goods is correct, then the same factors can be seen as decisive for success.

One factor that contributes to a product's being considered a prestige item is that relatively few people can possess it. People in higher social strata buy high-priced items as symbols of their social status. The most common way to monitor ownership is limited supply and attendant high price (Williams 1982: 360).

As we are dealing with a specific market, some exceptions are obvious. Limited supply does not seem to be a common method: in fact McKinsey subcontract their orders if needed. Keeping a high price is an obvious way, but it is not enough to produce few goods and then overprice them in order to create a prestige good. It is the amount of resources allocated to marketing addressed to a well-chosen market niche that creates a successful brand-image. As formulated by a marketing consultant (quoted by Jonsson):

People have faith in names which are often heard or read. A name which is often repeated will soon be associated with a given product or a given brand. People have an instinctive feeling that "this must be good." This concerns both palpable things and abstract phenomena. In spite of less known producer's efforts to compete through lower prices, the well known brands always have good sales. People willingly spend a few cents or dollars more to buy a brand that they learned to appreciate. This prestige stand was achieved through advertising, which is, after all, just one of the marketing techniques (Jonsson 1978: 377).

If it is true that Peters and Waterman sent out 2,000 copies of their book free, the same mechanism seems to be in operation. The marketing can sometimes require other resources apart from finance: giving speeches, writing articles, and becoming visible in civic affairs are strategies successful consultants recommend to the beginners. Once the brand-image has been created, one of the factors helping to sustain it is the fact that companies are unwilling to admit having paid a high price for not-so-good consulting (*Ledarskap/Ekonomen* No. 12, 1986).

Unfortunately, most research on brand image and prestige goods is carried out within the framework of consumer behavior studies (see e. g. Jonsson 1978, Williams 1982). These studies, valuable as they are, are of limited use in our case. In the first place, the marketing of consulting is much more a social, opinion-building process than the marketing of ordinary goods. Secondly, the marketing attempts are not directed to aggregates of individuals, but to groups of various kinds, hidden behind an anthropomorphic image of an "organization." While organizational purchase may to a certain extent be seen as analogous to individual buying behavior, the extent to which the analogy holds remains an empirical question. Using metaphors has its disadvantages.

One possible source of information, consultants themselves, seem to suffer from an acute euphemism-syndrome in this matter. In No. 3, Vol. 1 of the Journal, one of the readers expresses what seems to be a common problem in a letter to the editor: "Selling is not a dirty word, neither is making money an obscene phrase ..." He then proposes to abandon euphemisms like "Practice Development," "Personal Selling," and "Client's Zone of Readiness" in favor of "making a profit," "defining services," "identifying markets," "packaging services," "selling," etc. Seemingly this is a war of straightforward labels against pompous metaphors. But like in the case of control uses of linguistic artifacts, the euphemisms seem to be getting an upper hand. "Power" and "money" are two concepts which consultants prefer not to notice.

8 A Need for Self-Reflection

We have started in this paper — and indeed, the whole thinking process — from the user's end, as it were. While visiting organizations, we observed the use of linguistic artifacts for control purposes. Intrigued with the phenomenon, we tried to trace these linguistic tools to their origin. This brought us to the supplier's end, and we were trying to reconstruct their relationship using the supply—demand metaphor.

In the course of our analysis we kept asking ourselves: do consultants know that by producing labels, metaphors, and platitudes, and by injecting them into organizations, they facilitate control processes? Do they follow the use of their products? We doubt that. The *Journal of Management*

Consulting reveals (much to our surprise) a very vulnerable group of professionals, who have uneasy feelings about what they do and what they are paid for. Articles on anxiety, assertiveness, and phenomena like the "Thorn handicap" (a rabbit crossing the road at night caught in the glare of lightning, from Richard Adams' "Watership Down") abound in the Journal. This basic insecurity seems to be balanced by a firmly held idealistic picture of consultants as organizational therapists, who bring relief and creativity into organizational dreariness. Like arms dealers, they prefer not to know the details of use of their pretty toys. Peace is the ultimate aim and only that matters. Power and control are horrors not to be discussed in decent company. Many cope with political issues by ignoring them.

One might emphasize the fact that management consultants *by definition* serve those in power, and therefore there is nothing problematic in that fact. Greiner and Metzger propose the following definition, formulated from the client's perspective:

Management consulting is a temporary infusion of outside and credible talent to provide new ideas and additional personnel to the client organization, as well as to serve the special interests of those hiring the consultant (1983: 9).

The authors are very serious and uncompromising in dealing with ethical issues connected to consulting, but it soon becomes clear that they are limited to one class of problems only: that of breaches of loyalty towards the client. What if client's interests are incompatible with the interests of other groups?

Because of our interpretive affinity, our final recommendation is easy to foresee. Basically, there is nothing wrong with consultants forging control tools, as long as they know what they are doing (assuming, of course, that the management and the managed know it, too). However, it is much easier to realize that a pay scheme has something to do with control than to see the connection in case of metaphors, labels, or platitudes. Also, unobtrusive control is often much more effective and more difficult to oppose than traditional, visible organizational control. Therefore, a broadened self-reflectiveness should be an important goal to achieve for all suppliers of linguistic artifacts — be they consultants or researchers.

References

Abelson, R. P. (1986): Beliefs Are Like Possessions. *Journal for the Theory of Social Behaviour* 16(3), pp. 223–250

Bernstein, D. (1984): *Company Image and Reality. A Critique of Corporate Communications*. Eastburne: Holt, Rinehart and Winston

Blau, P. (1970): Decentralization in Bureaucracies. *Power in Organizations*. M. N. Zald (Ed.). Nashville, TN: Vanderbilt University Press, pp. 201–218

Brown, R. H. (1978): Bureaucracy as Praxis. Toward a Political Phenomenology of Formal Organizations. *Administrative Science Quarterly* 23(3), pp. 365–382

Bruner, J. (1986): *Actual Minds, Possible Worlds*. Cambridge, MA: Harvard University Press

Brunsson, N. (1985): *The Irrational Organization*. London: Wiley

Bower, M. (1982): The Forces That Launched Management Consulting Are Still at Work. *Journal of Management Consulting* 1(1), pp. 4–6

Cohen, M. D., J. G. March, and J. P. Olsen (1972): A Garbage Can Model of Organizational Choice. *Administrative Science Quarterly* 17, March, pp. 1–25

Czarniawska, B. (1985): The Ugly Sister: On Relationships between the Private and the Public Sectors in Sweden. *Scandinavian Journal of Management Studies* 2(2), pp. 83–103

Czarniawska, B. and R. Wolff (1986): How We Decide and How We Act – The Assumptions of Viking Organization Theory. *Organizing Industrial Development*. R. Wolff (Ed.). Berlin: de Gruyter, pp. 281–304

Czarniawska-Joerges, B. (1987): *Reformer och Ideologier*. Lund: Doxa

Czarniawska-Joerges, B. (1988): *Ideological Control in Nonideological Organizations*. New York: Praeger

Czarniawska-Joerges, B. (1990): Merchants of Meaning. *Organizational Symbolism*. B. A. Turner (Ed.). Berlin: de Gruyter, pp. 139–150

Czarniawska-Joerges, B. and B. Joerges (1988): How to Control Things with Words. Organizational Talk and Organizational Control. *Management Communication Quarterly* 1, November, pp. 170–193

Deal, T. E. and A. A. Kennedy (1982): *Corporate Cultures: The Rites and Rituals of Corporate Life*. Reading, MA: Addison-Wesley

DiTomaso, N. (1985): The Managed State: Governmental Reorganization in the First Year of the Reagan Administration. *Research in Political Sociology*. R. G. Braungart (Ed.). Greenwich, CT: JAI Press, pp. 1–39

Douglas, M. (1986): *How Institutions Think*. Syracuse, NY: Syracuse University Press

Eco, U. (1979): *The Role of the Reader. Explorations in the Semiotics of Text*. London: Hutchinson

Edelman, M. (1977): *Political Language. Words That Succeed and Policies That Fail*. New York: Academic Press

Edelman, M. (1988): *Constructing the Political Spectacle*. Chicago: The University of Chicago Press

Fischer, F. and A. Mandell (1988): Relegitimating Meritocracy: Educational Policy as Technocratic Strategy. *Telos* 76, pp. 1–15

Gagliardi, P. (1988): L'organizzazione dell'impresa innovativa. *L'Impresa Innovativa*. C. M. Guerci (Ed.). Milano: Edizioni del Sole 24 Ore, pp. 155–170

Geertz, C. (1964): Ideology as a Cultural System. *Ideology and Discontent*. D. Apter (Ed.). New York: The Free Press of Glencoe, pp. 47–76

Goodman, N. (1978): *Ways of Worldmaking*. Hassocks, Sussex: The Harvester Press

Goodman, N. (1984): *Of Mind and Other Matters*. Cambridge, MA: Harvard University Press

Greiner, L. E. and R. O. Metzger (1983): *Consulting to Management*. Englewood Cliffs, NJ: Prentice-Hall

Harré, R. (1981): Philosophical Aspects of the Macro-micro Problem. *Advances in Social Theory and Methodology*. K. Knorr-Cetina/A. V. Cicourel (Eds.). Boston: Routledge and Kegan Paul, pp. 3—18

Hawkes, T. (1972): *Metaphor*. London: Methuen

Hendricks, J. (1987): Lastige klanten, een interactioneel gezichspunkt. *M&O* 41(1), pp. 6—21

Jones, J. P. (1986): *What's in a Name?* Aldershot: Gower

Jonsson, E. (1978): *Teori för företagets marknadsföring — en kritisk granskning fran samhällsekonomisk synpunkt*. University of Stockholm Research Report N. 113, Stockholm

Journal of Management Consulting (1984): 1(1); 1(2); 1(3); 1(4)

Journal of Management Consulting (1984/5): 2(1)

Journal of Management Consulting (1985): 2(2); 2(3); 2(4)

Journal of Management Consulting (1986): 3(1); 3(2)

Kotler, P. (1983): *Principles of Marketing*. Englewood Cliffs, NJ: Prentice-Hall

Lakoff, G. and M. Johnson (1980): *Metaphors We Live By*. Chicago: The University of Chicago Press

Ledarskap/Ekonomen (1984): 10

Ledarskap/Ekonomen (1986): 1—2; 3; 4; 5; 6—7; 8—9; 10; 11; 12

Manning, P. K. (1979): Metaphors of the Field: Varieties of Organizational Discourse. *Administrative Science Quarterly* 24, pp. 660—671

March, J. G. (1984): Organizational Consultants and Organizational Research. Talk delivered at the annual meeting of the Academy of Management

Morgan, G. (1980): Paradigms, Metaphors and Puzzle Solving in Organization Theory. *Administrative Science Quarterly* 25(4), pp. 605—622

Morgan, G. (1983): More on Metaphor: Why We Cannot Control Tropes in Administrative Science. *Administrative Science Quarterly* 28, pp. 601—697

Morgan, G. (1986): *Images of Organization*. London: Sage

Peters, T. J. and R. H. Waterman Jr. (1982): *In Search of Excellence*. New York: Harper and Row

Pinder, C. C. and V. W. Bourgeois (1982): Controlling Tropes in Administrative Science. *Administrative Science Quarterly* 27, pp. 641—652

Robinson, J. (1950): *The Economics of Imperfect Competition*. London: Macmillan

Scarry, E. (1985): *The Body in Pain. The Making and Unmaking of the World*. New York: Oxford University Press

Smircich, L. and G. Morgan (1982): Leadership: The Management of Meaning. *The Journal of Applied Behavioral Science* 18(3), pp. 257—273

Smircich, L. and C. Stubbart (1985): Strategic Management in an Enacted World. *Academy of Management Review* 10(4), pp. 724—736

Thompson, K. (1980): Organizations as Constructors of Social Reality (I). *Control and Ideology in Organizations*. G. Salaman/K. Thompson (Eds.). Milton Keynes: The Open University Press, pp. 219—240

Weick, K. E. (1985): Sources of Order in Underorganized Systems: Themes in Recent Organization Theory. *Organizational Theory and Inquiry*. Y. S. Lincoln (Ed.). Beverly Hill, CA: Sage, pp. 106—136

Williams, T. G. (1982): *Consumer Behaviour: Fundamentals and Strategies*. St. Paul, MN: West

Failed Artifacts*

Barry A. Turner

1 Introduction

The creative, fabricating, manipulating activities which individuals and organizations are incessantly involved in are normally considered in a favourable manner in our society. In such a technologically interventionist society, activity directed towards the modification of the world is generally assumed to be good, while passivity, a reluctance to modify our material surroundings, is less good. The current growth of concern for the environment means that we may not go quite so far as the nineteenth-century engineer who, on encountering a previously undiscovered American valley, remarked "How beautiful! What a wonderful place to build a railroad!" but we still prize artifacts and give priority to their construction. But though we prefer to talk more about success than about failure, with technology you can make mistakes. All artifacts have a purpose, but they may not always succeed in achieving their purpose.

In this essay, I would like to explore some ways of considering the process of artifact making, and some of the ways in which we deal with failures in technical projects, looking especially at contrasts between our cognitive, calculative response to such failed outcomes, and our affective response. To start with, it may be helpful to review some of the research on accidents of various types with which I have been involved for some years.

2 Failed Artifacts

Although it is not usual to look at them in this way, accidents and man-made disasters are closely bound up with the failure of artifacts of one kind or another. In focussing research upon the organizational preconditions

* I would like to acknowledge support provided by both the University of Exeter and the European Community Joint Research Centre, Ispra, during the preparation of this paper.

associated with man-made disasters, I have developed a model which recognizes that large-scale disasters originate from multiple sources and from multiple errors (Turner 1978). Failures of foresight of this kind can be seen to arise from complex forms of information breakdown, usually in an organizational context. A variety of errors, slips, and false assumptions build up in the "incubation period" prior to a large-scale failure, creating an accumulating set of latent preconditions. This process continues until a trigger incident or precipitating event brings together the various forms of predisposing factors, in such a manner that their effects combine to produce a disastrous outcome.

Typical varieties of latent preconditions can be identified within the incubation period: events may be unnoticed or misunderstood because of erroneous assumptions; because of the difficulties of handling information in complex situations; or because of a reluctance to fear the worst. Safety rules and safety precautions may be disregarded or violated, and old or inadequate safety precautions may not be updated properly. Within these very broad types of preconditions, more specific sub-categories can be identified, revealing patterns of preconditions which are associated over and over again with large-scale failures and man-made disasters (Turner 1978). Although the disasters originally examined occurred in the 1960s and 1970s, more recent incidents such as the failure of the Challenger shuttle, the capsizing of the ferry "The Herald of Free Enterprise," and many others can be seen to have developed in accordance with this model of large-scale failures.

We should note, though, that this model stresses the state of knowledge before a major failure and emphasizes the surprise caused by the failure. Thus it is a strongly cognitive view of accidents, which focusses upon acute, unintended incidents rather than chronic, non-surprising conditions (Gephart 1984). It emphasizes knowledge and ignorance prior to an incident rather than behaviour and reactions after the incident, and it does not focus attention upon the emotional aspects of failure. Since the argument is made that large-scale, man-made disasters in contemporary society do not occur without access to the resources of organizations of various kinds, almost all of the preconditions can be expected to be found within one organization or another. Large-scale failures occur when organizations make large-scale technological mistakes. After such corporate surprise, after the disaster, collective cognitive adjustments need to be made to allow organizational personnel to understand and to accommodate to failure.

The original development of this model examined a range of fires, explosions, collisions, and epidemics. More recent research has concentrated more obviously upon the failure of artifacts, in a five-year programme which has looked at the preconditions associated with building failures.[1] The study examined decision making by engineers and designers responsible for buildings which had subsequently failed because of a lack of structural integrity. The original model, combined with a parallel one developed by Blockley (1980), has retained its usefulness in guiding analysis of complex multi-organization professional design relationships, and it has also formed a basis for developing hierarchical computer representations of the lessons learned. Building these representations into an intelligent knowledge-based "artificial intelligence" system will help to guide future designs and make them less likely to fail (Pidgeon/Blockley/Turner 1987).

These approaches to the understanding to artifact failure rely heavily upon making a search for a cognitive representation of the events preceding the failure and then understanding the transformations which this cognitive representation undergoes before, during, and after the failure. Although some aspects of the analysis will be unclear or even disputed by the parties involved, the aim is to develop a relatively "objective," commonly agreed way of analyzing past errors which may then point to possible techniques for avoiding such mistakes in the future. But, in spite of this emphasis upon seeking for improvements in professional practice, it is interesting to note that it was not at all easy to locate cases of failure where all of the principal professionals involved were willing to talk to us. We had very good contacts with the structural engineering community, and in some cases we were aware that cooperation was made difficult by legal action relating to the case, or by the possibility of such action in the future. But there was also a reluctance to talk about failures in which individuals or their professional practices had been involved. Not surprisingly, too, those who saw themselves as "innocent parties" were more willing to talk than those who could have been seen to be blameworthy in some way.

It was somewhat easier to gain access to cases where no individuals had been killed or injured as a result of the building collapse, and to get people to talk about the more complex failures provoked by combinations of errors, rather than about those resulting from a single mistake. The published accounts of the research (Pidgeon/Blockley/Turner 1986, 1988) show patterns in which no single individual or group of individuals can clearly be seen to be responsible for the artifact failure, the breakdown characteristically coming about as a result of interactions between many actors in the system. These analyses are not particularly untypical, however, since, as has already been noted, the most common forms of complex system failures are those which involve contributions from many groups and individuals. Technological and legal constraints and precautions have blocked off the simpler forms of breakdown which emanate from a single cause or a single error.

The research which has been briefly summarized above makes it clear that it is both possible and useful in today's technologically complex world to carry out analyses which examine the state of knowledge available before a failure and which are intended to increase our understanding of the manner in which "technological surprise" is associated with the failure of artifacts. There are many aspects of such failures which remain unexplored, however, and in the remainder of this paper, I would like to try to understand better some of these alternative facets of failed artifacts.

3 The Nature of Artifacts

One enticing path to be followed is that which has been mapped out by writers trying to specify and thus to clarify the abstract features associated with artifacts, considered as a general class of phenomena, so that we can see if these help us to deepen our understanding of the failure of artifacts. Two rather disparate writers, Polanyi and Kubler, have offered different perspectives which are worth some consideration. The philosopher Michael Polanyi examines the way in which the creation of "contrivances" differs from the process of scientific inquiry, while Kubler's concern with the series of artistic representations produced over centuries leads him to look for ways of understanding and ordering these arrays of artistic "things."

Polanyi considers contrivances to be "classes of objects which embody a particular operational principle" (1958: 328). This principle is a general one, something which cannot be reduced to the physics or chemistry of a particular contrivance for we are dealing here with technology rather than with science. The person who specifies the operational principle also specifies a purpose for the contrivance, either implicitly or explicitly, and thus cannot escape a consideration of whether the purpose involved is thought to be reasonable, of whether she or he endorses that purpose. Contriving, Polanyi points out, can thus never be impersonal, because some initiator and executor is always involved in its process[2]. Thus, "Technology comprises all acknowledged operational principles and endorses the purposes which they serve" (Polanyi 1958: 329).

The complete knowledge of a machine as an object — that is to say knowledge in terms of its physical constitution and structure — tells us nothing about it as a machine. We see this point exemplified from time to time with great clarity when antique dealers or museum curators ask for comments from the public on some contrivance from the past whose purpose is unknown. The object will evidently have been manufactured, and presumably was intended to serve a purpose, but this purpose may not be divined without additional information about the intentions of its maker.

If the purpose is known, however, what Polanyi calls the "stratagem" embodied in a particular contrivance can be assessed as a rational means of securing that purpose. The operational principle of the contrivance, machine, or artifact serves as an ideal — the ideal of a machine in good working order. It sets a standard of perfection against which an artifact or contrivance can be judged to be a more or less perfect typewriter, locomotive, clock, plate, or building. Moreover the operational principle also embodies a contrasting conception of a machine that is out of order — it specifies a non-functioning artifact. When a train is derailed, when a building collapses, or a plate breaks, these things behave against the rules laid down for them within the conception of their operational principle. "So, while this conception credits certain events as orderly performances, it condemns others as failures ... The operational principles of machines are therefore *rules of rightness*, which account only for the successful working of machines but which leave their failures entirely unexplained" (Polanyi 1958: 329; emphasis in original).

Technology then, for Polanyi, is embodied in rules of rightness, and it teaches a rational way to achieve an acknowledged purpose. An operational principle can be distinguished from a scientific law by the characteristic that it can *succeed or fail*. All engineers or technologists, therefore, will share a concern about the possibility of failure in their projects. If the stratagem which they use to achieve a particular purpose is successful, it will succeed in accordance with its own premeditated internal reasons. These cannot, however, account for failure, which will have to be related not to *reasons* within the stratagem but to some types of unforeseen external *causes*.

From this discussion we can realize clearly that artifacts are teleological constructions, objects which embody goal-oriented operational principles specified for them by the person or persons who contrived them. The specification of the purposes and operational principles of artifacts is essentially a human activity, and it is this activity which sets out the criteria for the success or failure of the artifact.

These observations on the process of the creation of artifacts apply to the process of engineering in its broadest terms. As well as producing contrivances, the engineering process itself is a goal-oriented contrivance, one which requires for its operation the purposeful combination of energy and information. Information is needed to guide the construction process, to shape it to a prearranged or improvised stratagem or design; and energy is needed to activate the process of changing the material world accordingly. *Engineering*, we might say, is made up of the combination of *energy and information*. When a stratagem fails, when the technology is inadequate, energy has still been used in an attempt to shape the material world, but at some point the information embodied by the stratagem has proved to be inadequate or inaccurate. We might express this in summary terms by saying that *failure* arises from the combination of *energy with mis-informa-*

tion (Turner 1978). In this way we can see a very clear connection between Polanyi's concern with the human process of contrivance and our previously outlined model of man-made disasters.

In his "history of things," Kubler (1962) has a rather different concern. He wants to develop a system of formal relations which will help to connect the visual aspects of many types of artifacts including works of art: tools and expressive creations, replicas and unique examples, all materials worked by human hands under the guidance of connected ideas developed over time. He starts from the premiss that all such artifacts are desired things. An individual decides to create something or to ask someone else to do so to meet a need.

The specification of a desire for the creation of an artifact may be considered as the specification of a problem which creates a class of possible solutions to that problem. Kubler argues that the design process can be seen as exploring possible solutions from the class of solutions which has been specified in this manner. In terms of this problem-solution framework, each specified solution is seen by Kubler to limit the number of remaining possibilities unless and until the problem is reformulated[3]. Each sequence of possible solutions:

... corresponds to a conscious problem requiring the serious attention of many persons for its successful resolution. There are no linked solutions without there having been a corresponding problem. There is no problem where there is no awareness. The contours of human activity as a whole are therefore congruent with those of the totality of formal sequence ... Stated differently: every new form limits the succeeding innovations in the same series (Kubler 1962: 38, 54).

Kubler uses this way of thinking about the exploration process to look at formal sequences of artifacts, at the relationship between prime objects and replications, and at the importance of serial position, age, and change within a given series. Once a solution to the problem has been initiated, it becomes possible to extend and propagate this solution in a variety of ways: by means of invention and variation based upon the original; by replication which may either be faithful or suffer change through historical drift; by processes of discard and retention, obsolescence and ritual, and through reactions to the onset of "aesthetic fatigue"[4].

Kubler distinguishes works of art, the primary artifacts with which he is concerned, from some of the contrivances which are at the centre of Polanyi's attention, commenting that works of art are not tools, although he acknowledges that many tools share qualities of fine design with works of art. A work of art, he comments, has no preponderant instrumental use, and its technical and rational foundations are not pre-eminent. By contrast, in an "object of use, the technical organisation or the rational order of a thing overwhelms our attention" (Kubler 1962: 16). Against Lodoli's comment that only the necessary is beautiful, he sets Kant's reply that the necessary cannot be judged as beautiful, but only right or consistent.

The perspective which we gain here upon artifacts is again one of personal involvement in the creation process, via the realization of a desire, expressed as a problem with a set of possible solutions to be considered. The failure of an artifact is determined in relation to individual or collective judgements about just how appropriate a solution is to meet the problem posed; and in relation to the extent to which, with time, any perceived correctness or appropriateness will gradually drift off target, as sequences of novel solutions are generated and modified.

For the present discussion, both writers emphasize especially the extent to which there is a personal involvement in the whole of the process of the initiation and creation of artifacts. If we are to describe this process in cognitive terms, as we were doing in the model of man-made disasters set out at the start of this discussion, we also have to realize that this cognition and its contexts are overwhelmingly human ones. Theories and models which disregard this quality are likely to prove misleading in one way or another. By the same token, if the process of failure is to be seen in cognitive terms, this cognition again has to be recognized as human, and the context of it will mean that responses to failure will seldom be solely calculative ones.

In one respect, however, the accounts offered by both of these writers neglect a crucial aspect of failure with which we are concerned here. In our complex, organizational society, the important artifacts and certainly the important artifact failures fall within the province of the modern organization, whereas both Polanyi and Kubler automatically concern themselves with the individual contriver or the individual artist seeking a solution to a problem specified by a need. To fully transfer their discussions to large-scale artifact failures, we need to consider the processes of contriving, or of combining desire and action at an organizational level. In one sense it is not too difficult to make this transference, and to see organizations or groups within organizations acting in a manner which is analogous to these contriving, desiring individuals. We are familiar with the kinds of organizational processes which serve to simplify the world, according to a bounded rationality or a cluster of bounded rationalities so that an organization can be seen as acting somewhat like an individual (MacKenzie 1987, Simon 1957, Turner 1978). The creation of organizational artifacts can then be seen to proceed as the groups directing the organization harness the energy and the resources of the organization in order to create things which they desire.

Matters become less satisfactory, however, when we look at the ill-defined or ill-structured problems (Simon 1969, Turner 1978) which are at the source of so many large-scale contemporary failures. Here the clarity of Kubler's formulation that "man-made things are desirable ... because ... nothing gets made unless it is desirable" (1962: 1) can be applied with difficulty to many contemporary corporate artifacts. We would propose that broadly similar processes operate as the organization strives to deal with dimly discerned problems on the periphery of its day-to-day concerns, with a much more vaguely defined class of solutions. However, even when we have invoked the simplification process associated with bounded rationality, such a formulation begs many questions about who, about what group, regards an object as desirable. It neglects the whole range of developments made by planners and decision makers at a distance, and it neglects the unpleasant side effects and the unintended consequences of creating the desirable. Further, even if an approach to an ill-structured problem is broadly agreed, it may, in the event, prove inadequate to meet the "desire." In Polanyi's terms, the stratagem may be insufficient to meet the demands of the relevant operating principles.

Matters become even more complex when we consider multi-goal, multi-actor settings where the stratagems of different parties may cross, intersect, or conflict. In such settings, groups concerned with different aspects of the perceived problem may work on solutions to the problem which prove to be incompatible. Also, different parts of the material world may be called upon from different directions to make incompatible contributions to more than one stratagem. In such systems the successful working of a stratagem will thus be dependent upon the goals, the point of view, and the perceptual framework to which it relates. What is an artifact failure for one group may be counted as a success by another. The successful channeling of a meandering river by the water navigation authority may upset those who want to fish in the river, or to observe water birds in the shallows at the edge, while a pattern of management of the river which waterskiers might regard as a successful one might well conflict with the desires of all of the other groups mentioned.

Whilst it is true, in a sense, that someone, somewhere, must have "desired" every artifact, our world is full of artifacts which are difficult to connect directly to any personal desires. Many of them seem to be merely the physical by-products of a desire for money or some other form of advantage. With a certain number of reservations, though, it is possible to think of both individuals and groups embarking upon the creation of contrivances, making artifacts to fulfil given purposes and to answer needs. We also recognize, perhaps more clearly now than before, that all of these technical and aesthetic problems are not necessarily tackled with appropriate stratagems. With both well-structured and ill-structured problems, with single actor, multi-actor, and organizational problems, the possibility of failure, error, or inadequacy exists.

How can we handle this possibility? Polanyi has already pointed out that failure is inexplicable from *within* a given stratagem, so that we have no option but to look outside, either at the surrounding context of the stratagem's development, or, in what may come to the same thing, at the framework within which the stratagem was developed. One way of looking at the possibility of failure is to tackle it in a Popperian sense as a sequence of conjecture and refutation: each design, stratagem, or solution which comes to be embodied in an artifact is seen as a conjecture, and while the satisfactory performance of the artifact up to the present time is no guarantee of its continued functioning in the future, a failure gives us something clear to work with in the form of a refutation (Blockley 1980). Indeed, Popper argues that we should *seek* to have our conjectures refuted in order to advance understanding (Popper 1969). As we might anticipate from our earlier discussion of the *personal* nature of cognition, however, and as a host of Popper's critics have also pointed out, most people find it difficult to get their conjectures to remain as conjectures, without developing a deeper degree of commitment to them, a commitment which makes them unhappy to see their ideas refuted.

More complex interpretations of the failure of a plan or a stratagem within a given paradigm are also available. For example: we can see the information developed by failure at one level being transformed, at an appropriate transition point, into information at another level. This input can then be incorporated into a new paradigm which circumvents the original difficulty or makes it irrelevant (Bateson 1973, Turner 1978). Expressing this argument at a biological level, Bateson comments:

But as Nature avoids (temporarily) what looks like irreversible change by accepting ephemeral change ... death itself is avoided by a quick change from individual subject to class. Nature allows old man Death ... to have his victims while she substitutes that more abstract entity the class or taxon, ... finally if death should have his victory over the species, Nature will say "Just what I needed for my ecosystem" (Bateson 1980: 142–145).

But just as death is not neutral for those individuals who undergo it, neither is the experience of failure. If we step back and are able to take a sufficiently detached view of any failure, we can view it merely as a problem of information flow, of instructive, corrective feedback processes, however grave the consequences. But since people are always involved, one way or another, in failures of artifacts, this detached analysis is difficult to attain and, if reached, may at times be inhuman. We face the conflicting demands of needing to reflect objectively upon failures in order to learn from them individually and collectively, and of having to recognize the impact which particular artifact failures may have upon those involved with them.

4 Victims of Failed Artifacts

One of the minor surprises to which I was subjected in my early days as a fieldworker in organizations related to the fear of failure. While studying organizational control systems, concerned to find out about the goal-related behaviour of managers, my usual questions aimed to determine how they structured their behaviour in relation to their goals (Turner 1970). One day, though, when I asked a slightly different question about what made a manager feel vulnerable, this produced, to my surprise, a completely different set of responses. The new responses not only connected rather poorly with the earlier ones, but they also seemed to be more vivid, more readily accessible to the manager and to make a different kind of sense. Many activities were more readily explicable as protections *against* the possibility of various kinds of failure, rather than as rational strategies *for* the achievement of a goal. I used the idea of vulnerability more frequently from that point on since it was often more productive to persuade people to talk about the outcomes they *feared*, the outcomes which made them feel vulnerable and which they were concerned to avoid. Even though such "defensive thinking" is condemned by management writers, most members of organizations do not seem to be immune to it. It is true that some of these responses could be defended as contingency plans developed within a rational paradigm, but others seemed to be more somatic, more concerned with protecting the being of the manager than with promoting organizational goals — these managers were concerned to avoid, one way or another, becoming victims of failure.

When artifact failures occur, their effects are not normally limited to the material domain, for they create victims. Victims of failure do not constitute a single type. It is possible to distinguish, for example, between the immediate victims killed or injured in a failure, if there are any; the family and friends of this group; those on the site of the failure who escaped without physical injuries; rescuers and emergency services involved in the distressing task of dealing with the dead and injured; and the designers and planners of the system which failed.

The manner in which artifact failures tend to be considered in our society underestimate the impact and the stress which such failures can impose upon individuals, especially when they are looked at solely from the point of view of the cognitive, "accident as corrective" point of view outlined above. For immediate victims involved in a major incident and for their families, the emotional trauma will be severe. After an initial "disaster syndrome" where survivors are docile, unresponsive, and undemanding, not exhibiting any emotional reactions, survivors' subsequent reactions will vary according to a variety of factors. These include cultural elements, the survivors' sense of loss with regard to others who may have perished, and their own relief and guilt at being spared. Some of the survivors may also see the suffering and loss experienced by others as part of their own personal burden, and this perception will strongly affect their own behaviour (Wolfenstein 1957). The need for counselling following such incidents as the Bradford and Hillsborough football stadium tragedies in Britain, where numbers of the crowd were burned or crushed to death, has now become accepted, but even with such assistance, the impact will be long-lived. One of the survivors from the Cocoanut Grove nightclub fire in the United States was reported to be still receiving treatment twenty years later and, even so, had to arrange her life to avoid soft furnishings and similar materials which reminded her of the bodies over which she had climbed in her escape (Turner 1978).

An interesting recent study of French electricity workers involved in accidents with no readily explicable causes offers a detailed exploration of the impact of failure upon the victims of industrial accidents. Collis and Fillion (1988) tried to look behind the events reported in order to try to get a better idea of the meaning, for the victims, of these accidents. They argue that accidents constitute personal failures for a worker, for a work team, and for managers. For this reason, in the organizations studied, they became a taboo subject, which could not be freely talked about[5]. "Human weaknesses must not exist in places where reliability is supreme." In lengthy interviews, these workers offered rich accounts of their normal work life surrounding the accident, but a very impoverished account of the accident itself: they spoke of it only as bad luck, as fate, or as destiny. When pressed, however, they produced dramatizations of the accident they had been involved in. Thus, for example, a worker who had been accidently crushed by a machine talked about the experience of being crushed releasing all of the hatred which he felt for management and his fellow workers: another who was injured by a shovel striking a wall felt that this expressed his clashes with management. The worker's analysis of what happened to him in his accident can be used to bring to light a latent malaise in which the contradictory pressures of individual motives, tense inter-personal relationships, and difficult work conditions are expressed.

Collis and Fillion also judged the safety rules associated with work activities in the electricity industry to be associated more with rule following than with work expertise. They advocate the development of a new logic of safety by means of the "discovery of the full meaning of safety rules." Proposing the development of work group assistance in both the control of anxiety generated by dangerous situations and in the analysis of accidents, they are pointing in the direction already being taken by a number of companies which regard themselves as being in the forefront of contemporary safety practices. To create "high reliability organisations" (La Porte

1987, Weick 1987), they try to promote an atmosphere in which accidents and near-miss failures can be discussed freely and openly, and used as a means for learning (du Pont 1984, Shell 1988). Recent safety developments in Japan also try to involve workers in recording for their work group not only near-miss accidents, but also those occasions on which they *sensed* danger — the *hiyaro-hatto* approach (Kitagawa 1989). At an individual and a work-group level such initiatives seem to some extent to combine a recognition of the personal vulnerability which individuals may experience with the need for a collective cognitive assessment of the flow of events and of desirable future changes which may help to prevent failures[6]. Following the Chernobyl failure (OECD 1987), attention began to focus upon the "safety culture" of industrial workers both inside and outside the nuclear industry, and further examination of the cultural aspects of safety will intensify the need to embrace both the cognitive and the symbolic aspects of behaviour concerned to avoid serious failures (Turner 1989).

When we move away from the shop floor to look at some of the other categories of victims already mentioned, we can see that those not directly involved in dangerous artifact failures may nonetheless not be immune to their effects. If we are looking at large-scale failures which involve contemporary organizations, we need to be especially aware, too, of their potential effects upon the designers and planners of artifacts. Research[7] into the long-term feedback cycle triggered off by inquiries into major accidents has thrown up some incidental findings which indicate that designers and planners frequently demonstrate emotional as well as cognitive responses to such incidents (Toft 1990, Turner/Toft 1988).

Responsible managers were interviewed in 23 organizations which had been the subject of public inquiry recommendations, following their involvement with major fires or explosions ten years previously. The intention was to determine the effects of these recommendations upon the organizations after this lapse of time, but one point which was immediately striking was the emotional impact which the major accident had had upon those interviewed:

Even after an interval of ten years or more, these effects appear to be massive and enduring. One senior manager did not wish to talk about the incident which his organization was involved with, because it still upset him to think about it, even though his organization bore no responsibility for the accident. As a result of the effects of the accident, some of those interviewed reported that their connection with the accident had triggered a major shift in preoccupations and activities. One architectural practice, for example, has shifted the emphasis of its work so that the bulk of its work was concerned with safety matters, whilst an individual in another practice responded to the shock of discovering the fire potential of furniture used in his building by spending several years designing safer alternative fittings (Turner/ Toft 1988: 303).

The managers interviewed also seemed to recall the failure incident with considerable clarity after this long lapse of time. Memory research would lead us to expect systematic distortion in such retrospective accounts, and it was not possible to confirm independently the *accuracy* of their recall. Nonetheless, informants' discussions of what had happened had a very vivid and immediate quality: they had no difficulty in presenting this clear account of what had taken place, and of the consequences for themselves and for their company. It was evident that they had all carried away and retained in a very accessible form their own personal lessons from the incident.

5 The Costs of the Failure of Artifacts

When, following a failure, we try to consider the learning which an organization rather than an individual undergoes, at first sight it might seem that here, at least, we can concentrate upon a rational, calculative response to the event, disregarding the emotional responses of individual members of the corporate body concerned. This is not so, however, for a number of reasons. The first, and perhaps most obvious reason is that the idea of organizations as rational, calculating entities is not one which can be accepted without qualification. Discussions such as those of Perrow (1972) or March and Olsen (1976) have stressed the inadequacy of rational models of organization and the complications of ambiguity. Moreover, the recent rise of interest in organizational culture has stressed ceremonial, ritual, and the part played in organizational affairs by symbolisms of all kinds (Pondy et al. 1983, Turner 1990). But also the process of organizational learning is not in itself a simple one. While organizations can be considered to undergo forms of learning, they do not always move readily towards "intelligent behaviour": they may comprehend matters too slowly, make erroneous inferences, and even demonstrate "superstitious learning" (Levitt/ March 1988). It is possible to outline desirable patterns of feedback and learning for organizations and for the societies in which they operate, but the evident complexities of such schemes are increased by the need to take account of the shifting ecology produced by the simultaneously adapting behaviour of other organizations, and, increasingly, of other societies[8] (Levitt/March 1988, Turner/Toft 1988: 308 – 9).

A further reason to doubt the proposition that organizations will react rationally to the possibilities and to the consequences of failure is demonstrated by a study of company expenditure on insurance (Spencer 1990) which set out to test economic models of insurance-related behaviour in the field of consumer liability. Economic models developed theoretically suggest that companies will balance expenditure on insurance and safety against expected losses in the case of a failure or accident. In the sample of small and medium-size British companies examined by Spencer, however, she found no link at all between such economic predictions and corporate response to the possibility of failure in the consumer field. The companies were unable to identify separately expenditure which was related to protection against potential consumer liability claims, or expenditure devoted to improving product *safety* as against other aspects of product quality.

Also, in cases where a product failure had involved actual or potential harm to the consumers of their product, they responded, on the one hand, with a remarkable degree of personal and corporate distress to the idea that anyone should have been harmed through the use of their product; and, on the other hand, with an increase in expenditure to prevent a recurrence which was disproportionate to any figure which might have been arrived at by "rational" economic calculations of appropriate corrections. They undertook this expenditure both from a feeling that the company needed to act strongly to protect its public image with consumers, and from a personal feeling on the part of senior managers that they did not wish to be involved in professional activities which had the potential for causing significant harm to others as a result of product failure. Companies studied which made responses of this kind included a cosmetics company, a baby food company which experienced a case of contamination, and a garage equipment manufacturer which completely redesigned one of its products after learning that someone had been injured whilst using it.

Not all companies may be expected to respond in such a manner — but the clearest example of a company which *did* make a calculative response to potential hazard demonstrates vividly the limits of ostensibly rational preparations for failure and shows how extensive such estimates need to be if any kind of a full accounting is to be made. The damaged tanker *Exxon Valdez* spilt 11 million gallons of oil into Prince William Sound, Alaska in March, 1989, in what has been called the most expensive industrial accident on record. According to press and other reports, Exxon had previously limited the amount of insurance it paid for potential oil spills in the Alaskan region, based upon the costs which it might expect to incur in a clean up. In the event, not only have both their pre-accident and post-accident estimates proved to be well below the actual costs of the clean-up, but it is now clear that they took no account of a wide range of consequent losses. Five months after the spill, the costs of the clean-up had already reached ten times that of the company's first post-accident estimate, reaching $ 1.3 billion. In addition, the company had suffered a boycott on petrol sales as a protest against what was seen as its lack of concern for the environment, it still had to face suits for damages from the State of Alaska and 100 private suits, and it had returned the lowest second quarter profit figures for 20 years (*Guardian Weekly*, August 6, 1989: 9, Valdez Oil Spill 1989).

Once again, at the organizational level, we are led to conclude that although rational calculations of the possibilities, the consequences, and the costs of potential failures of major artifacts are not at all to be ruled out, this by no means covers the whole picture. Individuals and those complex entities, organizations, have many reasons for exhibiting a range of responses to the possibility and the reality of artifact failure, ranging from personally and collectively felt emotions, through issues of professional integrity and corporate image, to disbelief in adequacy of the economic or accounting models available.

6 Discussion and Conclusions

Daniel Bell (1980) has argued that culture serves to guard continuity in human affairs, while the influence of technology governs change — from the effects of the invention of the stirrup upon patterns of warfare to the consequences of the computer for patterns of organizations. In this view, not only will technology and technological artifacts always be disruptive, constantly creating crises for culture, but this disruptive effect might be expected to be exacerbated when artifacts fail. This opposition of technology and culture is an appealing one — in Bell's writings it consciously echoes Marx's base and superstructure opposition, although the distinction is put to quite different purposes. But if I try to use it to tie together the preceding discussions of artifacts and the symbolic aspects of their failure, I realize that it is an opposition which is difficult to apply here. Looking closely at culture, it is clear that much of it is concerned with artifacts of one kind or another, and looking closely at technology, it is evident that it is pervaded by cultural considerations.

This realization also helps to make clearer the illusory nature of the opposition which we have been chasing through this essay, an opposition between culture, with its symbolic qualities, and rational technical thought, as a logical, cognitive exercise. There is no denying that the main thrust of the disaster and accident models of both Blockley and myself are heavily biased towards the cognitive, and at one point I was tempted to argue in a kind of reversal of Bell's position, that rational cognitive analysis was naturally more appropriate. *before* an artifact failure, while affective and emotive responses followed upon such a failure. This would have made it possible to link Kubler's examination of a "problem-solution" explanation for formal systems of artifacts and Polanyi's ideas of stratagems and operating principles with my own approach (and that of Blockley) — indeed, I have drawn upon their work precisely because I could see their compatibilities.

The illusion, though, lies in several points — one is the misleading nature of a separation based upon "before" and "after" failure. Failures succeed one another, so that the period before one failure is always the period after another. A further difficulty is that this recruitment of Polanyi to the rational cognitive cause neglects the central point of all of his positions, that knowledge is essentially *personal* knowledge, the whole thrust of his thought having been to deny that it is helpful to try to separate out cognition from the person whose cognition is being considered. Moreover, he argues that a significant portion of the relevant knowledge in any situation, including scientific and technical situations, is tacit knowledge which those concerned find it difficult or impossible to articulate.

It is, perhaps, little wonder, then, that this attempt to explore studies of accidents and disasters, and more particularly studies of buildings as failed artifacts, bring us back once again to the recognition that failure is not a simple matter of the calculation of costs and benefits. It is a much more complex and emotive issue, but not just because the *aftermath* of technological failure engenders cultural responses which are personal and emotional, or because these merge with issues of public confidence and public image. The affective and symbolic responses of the organizational actors are as much concerned with the creation of artifacts and with the generation of stratagems as are their cognitive responses. Human activities before and after artifact failures are all concerned with rational understanding and emotional response, with personal knowledge and with passionate understanding (Polanyi 1958, Solomon 1983, Turner 1988).

Human projects, including the creation of physical artifacts, are mainly propelled and guided by knowledge and information derived from individual or collective cognitive frameworks, but it is always misleading to consider this knowledge as impersonal. The project then occurs as a personal form of knowing, passionate manipulation of the world, and failures, too, must for someone be personal failures, failures of this knowing passionate manipulation. It is true, as we have noted above, that the mechanisms of our complex technological society create a series of separations between desire and execution, so that the location of the human concerns and feelings relevant to a particular artifact may be rather difficult to identify, particularly in view of the enhanced possibilities which contemporary mass media offer for the *simulation* of projects and their failure (Baudrillard 1988, Rosen 1990).

At a cognitive and information-based level of analysis, it is clear that failures may earn a kind of *post hoc* justification if helpful feedback occurs, and especially if they provoke some kind of higher order learning. But it is important not to see either the preconditions or the consequences of artifact failures as being solely concerned with detached sequences of information processing. Whether we want to talk about the personal involvement of those who set in motion the process of "contriving" by developing stratagems and operating principles to fulfil a given, personally endorsed purpose, or to refer to the needs and desires of those who initiate the creation of sequences of artifacts to solve the problems posed by their desires, it is clear that the processes of the production of artifacts are intensely human ones, involving all facets of *homo faber* and not just the rational cognitive ones.

By the same token, artifact failures must be seen not merely as occasions for making adjustments to information sets, but as major or minor occasions for the signalling, in a culturally, emotionally, and symbolically traumatic manner, the collapse of a project — the frustration of hopes, the dashing of aspiration on whatever scale is involved. In any study concerned with organizational symbolism we would expect to find such a concern both with artifacts and with their failures as symbolic entities.

Notes

1 Carried out jointly at the Department of Civil Engineering, University of Bristol, and the Department of Sociology, University of Exeter, and supported by a grant from the Joint Committee of the Economic and Social Research Council and the Science and Engineering Research Council.
2 When talking about "contrivances," Polanyi refers to tools, machines, and technical processes, and offers as examples clocks, typewriters, locomotives, and cameras. However, the discussion need not be so restricted, since, as we shall argue below, and as Polanyi argues elsewhere, all artifacts are purposive and can be regarded as simple machines or contrivances — a plate has no moving parts but it is contrived to serve a multiplicity of purposes relating to the tasteful, convenient, and hygienic serving of food. However we may wish to qualify the comment, we have to acknowledge, with Le Corbusier, that "a house is a machine for living."
3 One unwritten chapter in the history of design and technology which would exemplify Kubler's point is the series of contrivances produced over the past twenty years to process credit cards: the need or the desire is for a contrivance which will take an impression of the credit card details, name and number, together with corresponding information from the vendor. The physical stratagems adopted to meet this need have passed through an interesting series of solutions during the period, from machines which required so much force to operate that they were almost impossible to use, through lighter machines, to the motorized

or automated models currently in use. Few of the solutions to this design problem, however, have the elegance of the solution devised by dining car staff on British Rail, who reduce the needs or desires to be satisfied by the artifact to its essentials and take an impression of the card by placing the invoice over the card on the tablecloth and briskly rubbing the side of a ball point pen over it.

4 Although the mode of analysis is rather different, it is interesting to note here Witkin's (1971) demonstration that artists generate what he calls a "holding form," a working note, sketch, or model, in order to create a physical but symbolic statement of their "desire" which will also help to guide their actions as they repeatedly try to tackle a given artistic problem. Given that the class of possible solutions to their current "problem" will have affinities one with another, the holding form serves as a mnemonic, a specification, a label for the *set* of solutions which the artist might consider to be acceptable in relation to that problem.

5 Note the contrast between this comment and the practices in "high reliability organizations" discussed below, where there is a *requirement* to talk about failures.

6 For an interesting discussion of the manner in which we handle danger in our everyday life, see Rip 1989; on parallel processes in occupations known to be dangerous, see Turner 1981.

7 Doctoral research carried out at Exeter University by Brian Toft, with financial support from the Economic and Social Research Council.

8 The variety of patterns of behaviour which complicate learning above the individual level is extended in discussions by Bateson, where he considers cases in which immediate benefit at one level becomes a calamity at the next highest level. He comments that "We can learn and learn to learn and possibly learn to learn to learn. But that is probably the end of the sequence" (Bateson 1980: 176). He also makes a useful if rather subtle distinction when he separates out *feedback* from *calibration*. In feedback, correction can occur within the single act. In calibration, there is no possibility of this, and the entire operation must be improved by repeating a larger class of actions, successive experiences being packed like Chinese boxes in the context of information from all previous relevant experiences (Bateson 1980: 203 ff.).

References

Bateson, G. (1973): *Steps to an Ecology of Mind: Collected Essays on Anthropology, Psychiatry and Epistemology*. St. Albans: Granada

Bateson, G. (1980): *Mind and Nature: A Necessary Unity*. London: Fontana

Baudrillard, J. (1988): Simulacra and Simulations. *Selected Writings*. M. Poster (Ed.). Cambridge: Polity Press, pp. 166–184

Bell, D. (1980): Technology, Nature and Society. *The Winding Passage: Essays and Sociological Journeys, 1960–1980*. Cambridge, MA, pp. 3–33

Blockley, D. (1980): *The Nature of Structural Design and Safety*. Chichester: Ellis Horwood

Collis, Th. and F. Fillion (1988): When Considering Safety: Beware of Danger! Paper presented to the Annual Conference of the Society for Risk Analysis, Laxenburg, Vienna, November du Pont (1984): *Safety and Occupational Health: A Commitment in Action*. Employee Relations Department, E. I. du Pont de Nemours and Company, Wilmington, Delaware

Gephart, R. P. (1984): Making Sense of Organizationally Based Environmental Disasters. *Journal of Management* 10(20), pp. 205 – 225

Kitagawa, H. (1989): The Role of Safety Managers and Safety Officers – An Overview. Paper presented to OECD Workshop on Prevention of Accidents Involving Hazardous Substances: Good Management Practice. Berlin, 22 – 25 May

Kubler, G. (1962): *The Shape of Time: Remarks on the History of Things*. New Haven, CT: Yale University Press

La Porte, T. R. (1987): High Reliability Organizations: The Dimensions of the Research Challenge. Working paper on Public Organizations, Institute of Governmental Studies. Berkeley, CA: University of California, March

Levitt, B. and J. G. March (1988): Organizational Learning. *Annual Review of Sociology* 14, pp. 319 – 340

MacKenzie, D. (1987): "Micro" versus "Macro" Sociologies of Science and Technology. Paper presented to the Annual Conference of the British Sociological Association. Leeds University, 6 – 9 April

March, J. G. and J. P. Olsen (Eds.) (1976): *Ambiguity and Choice in Organizations*. Bergen: Universitetsforlaget

OECD Nuclear Energy Agency (1987): *Chernobyl and the Safety of Nuclear Reactors in OECD Countries*. Paris: OECD

Perrow, C. (1972): *Complex Organizations: A Critical Essay*. Glenview, IL: Scott Foresman

Pidgeon, N., D. I. Blockley, and B. A. Turner (1986): Design Practice and Snow Loading: Lessons from a Roof Collapse. *The Structural Engineer* 64A, pp. 67 – 71

Pidgeon, N., D. I. Blockley, and B. A. Turner (1987): Hazard Assessment in Structural Engineering. *Reliability and Risk Analysis in Civil Engineering*. N. Lind (Ed.). International Conference on Applied Subjective Probability, 5. Canada: University of Waterloo, Institute for Risk Research, Vol. 1, pp. 358 – 365

Pidgeon, N., D. I. Blockley, and B. A. Turner (1988): Site Investigations: Lessons from a Late Discovery of Hazardous Waste. *The Structural Engineer* 66(19), pp. 311 – 315

Polanyi, M. (1958): *Personal Knowledge: Towards a Post-Critical Philosophy*. London: Routledge and Kegan Paul

Pondy, L. et al. (Eds.) (1983): *Organizational Symbolism*. Greenwich, CT: JAI Press

Popper, K. (1969): *Conjectures and Refutations: The Growth of Scientific Knowledge*. London: Routledge

Rip, A. (1989): The Danger Culture of Industrial Society. *Communicating Health and Safety Risks to the Public: International Perspectives*. R. Kasperson/P. J. M. Stallen (Eds.). Dordrecht: Reidel, Ch. 13.

Rosen, M. (1990): Crashing in '87 – Power and Symbolism in the Dow. *Organizational Symbolism*. B. A. Turner (Ed.). Berlin: de Gruyter, Ch. 8, pp. 115 – 135

Shell Safety Management Programme (1988): The Hague: Royal Dutch Shell International

Simon, H. A. (1957): *Administrative Behavior*. New York: Free Press

Simon, H. A. (1969): *The Sciences of the Artificial.* Cambridge, MA: MIT Press, see esp. "The Architecture of Complexity," pp 84−118

Solomon, R. C. (1983): *The Passions: The Myth and Nature of Human Emotion.* Nôtre Dame, Indiana: University of Nôtre Dame Press

Spencer, J. (1990): *Product Liability and Producers' Behaviour.* Unpublished research report. Exeter, UK: University of Exeter, Faculty of Law

Toft, B. (1990): The failure of Hindsight. Unpublished doctoral thesis. Exeter, UK: University of Exeter, Faculty of Social Studies

Tuite, R. J. (1989): Communicating with the Public about Major Accident Hazards: An Industry Leader's Conclusion. *Communicating with the Public about Major Accident Hazards,* H. B. F. Gow and H. Otway (Eds.) London: Elsevier. pp. 142−159.

Turner, B. A. (1970): Control Systems: Development and Interaction. *Industrial Organization: Behavior and Control.* J. Woodward (Ed.). Oxford: Oxford University Press, pp. 59−84

Turner, B. A. (1978): *Man-Made Disasters.* London: Wykeham Press

Turner, B. A. (1981): Organizational Responses to Hazard. *Risk: A Seminar Series.* H. Kunreuther (Ed.). International Institute for Applied Systems Analysis. Collaborative Proceedings Series CP-82-S2. Laxenberg, Austria: IIASA, pp. 49−85

Turner, B. A. (1988): The Academy and the Intelligence of Feeling. Paper presented to the Erasmus University Lustrum Conference on Critical Thought. Rotterdam, November

Turner, B. A. (1989): How Can We Design a Safe Organization? Paper presented to the Second International Conference on Industrial and Organizational Crisis Management. New York University: New York, 3−4 November

Turner, B. A. (1990): *Organizational Symbolism.* Berlin: de Gruyter

Turner, B. A. and B. Toft (1988): Organizational Learning from Disasters. *Emergency Planning for Industrial Hazards.* H. B. F. Gow/R. W. Kay (Eds.). London: Elsevier, pp. 297−313

Valdez Oil Spill (1989): Keynote Session. Second International Conference on Industrial and Organizational Crisis Management. New York University. Hon. S. McAlpine, L. G. Rawl and Admiral P. A. Yost, speakers. November 3−4

Weick, K. (1987): Organizational Culture as a Source of High Reliability. *California Management Review* XXIX (2), Winter, pp. 112−127

Witkin, R. W. (1971): *The Intelligence of Feeling.* London: Heinemann

Wolfenstein, J. (1957): *Disaster: A Psychological Essay.* London: Routledge and Kegan Paul

Part V:
De-Constructing Artifacts

Theory as Artefact: Artefact as Theory

Stephen A. Linstead and Robert Grafton-Small

> *Theory* — 1597 [late L. *theoria* contemplation, speculation, sight]. 1. Mental view, contemplation 2. A conception or mental scheme of something to be done, or of the method of doing it; a systematic statement of rules or principles to be followed 3. A scheme or system of ideas or statements held as an explanation or account of a group of facts or phenomena ... statement of the facts on which (a subject) depends, or of its principles or methods, as distinct from the *practice* of it 4. Without article: Systematic conception or statement of the principles of something; abstract knowledge, or the formulation of it: often used as implying a more or less unsupported hypothesis: distinct from or opposed to *practice* 5. In a loose or general sense: A hypothesis proposed as an explanation; hence, a mere hypothesis, speculation, conjecture; an idea or set of ideas about something; an individual view or notion.
>
> *Artefact* — 1821 ... An artificial product.
> — from *The Shorter Oxford English Dictionary*, Third Edition, 1983.

1 Introduction: Theory and Artefact

In this chapter we wish to turn our attention to an apparent paradox: that theory, which is traditionally characterised as the abstract antithesis of concrete practice, of which artefacts are the even more concrete outcome, is itself an artificial product, an outcome of a process of *theorising*. Furthermore, not only do artefacts embody theory in the processes of their production, but the understanding of an artefact by those who consume it literally or symbolically is only made possible by the application and use of implicit and explicit "theories" about the nature of artefacts in general. Theory is a product of lived relations in the social world, and artefacts become meaningful in the context of theorised social relations.

Our argument, in short, is that *all* understanding is structured, and hence theorised (cf. Derrida 1980 on "writing"). This theory is neither abstract nor ahistorical, but is the outcome of a *process* of theorising and therefore a cultural artefact which reflects the experience, the history, the symbolism and language of human actors. It is an inescapable condition of human existence and therefore grounded in our perceptions of both the social and the concrete world. This process is not merely reflective of objective social facts, however: it is simultaneously constitutive of those "facts," "relationships," "selves," and the form of life of which it is a part.

Theory may be seen in terms of the paradoxical nature of language and its artificial ability to separate meaning and non-meaning by ordering relationships within particular lexical frameworks (Deleuze and Guattari 1984, Derrida 1980, Lecercle 1985). Any ordering in this way is also a confusion in that it suppresses other alternative views of the world, establishing its articulated version as meaningful in preference to unformulated alternatives. Theory, constituted in language, can determine practice; however, it is not only a *cause* of action or utterance, but also an *effect* of experience, an explanation occasioned by experience and proposed as its origin. Nietzsche (1966) argues that the common assumption that causes are both logically and temporally prior to their effects rests on a reversal of the chronological sequence of actual experience. For example, feeling a sudden pain, we may be *caused* to look for the *cause* of the pain: seeing a pin, we may make the inductive link pin = pain which reverses the perceptual sequence, pain − pin (Gowler/Legge 1984: 6).

The fragment of the outside world of which we become conscious comes after the effect that has been produced on us and is projected *a posteriori* as its "cause." In the phenomenalism of the "inner world" we invent the chronology of cause and effect. The basic fact of "inner experience" is that cause gets imagined after the effect occurred (Nietzsche 1966: v.3 p.804; quoted in Gowler/Legge, ibid).

The theory of causation remains important, as theory is the medium uniting cause and effect. It is merely reversed in this *deconstruction*. In the process, it illustrates that theory is not an innocent and inevitable outcome of experience, a window on truth − it is itself a device, an artefact, simultaneously expressive and constitutive of lived relations, and may be used as a tool to justify, preserve, or redefine those relations. Power and knowledge are bound together in theory.

The exchange, or reciprocity, of properties between cause and effect is parallelled in this chapter by a similar transaction between theory and artefact. Artefacts are certainly used in the process of sense making and theorising, and our awareness of the nature of the object-world (particularly in conditions of mass production and consumption) is an important part of our making and making sense of social relationships and identities.

However, understanding artefacts involves theorising them appropriately, whilst recognising that they also embody theoretical positions and relationships as a result of their production. Our entire understanding is mediated and made possible by objects, artefacts which embody theory in their production yet influence theory and theorising through their everyday use, their consumption, and re-consumption. This perpetual revaluation, constitutive of our sense of our own and others' identities, is termed by Lévi-Strauss *bricolage* (Lévi-Strauss 1966). In making the world, we make ourselves; in thinking the world, we think ourselves.

Deconstruction then uses reversals, inversions and paradoxes to gain new insights into taken-for-granted understandings (Gowler/Legge 1984: 7).

In what follows, we apply a deconstructive approach to explore the paradoxes inherent in the relationship between theory and artefact. We begin by discussing the reflexive paradox generated by all forms of formal theory, and in examining the process of theorising consider the link between theory and the form-of-life of the theorist. This takes us to an examination of some informal but explicit theory found in some current texts on "managerial success." We move on to examine more implicit theory in data obtained from a commercial truck company and a firm of architects, in which the product and its negotiated meaning lead us beyond the confines of merely verbal discourse and up to the boundaries of semiotics. We continue this progression to consider a cinema advertisement in which the product itself, as artefact, is not mentioned or shown but is nevertheless understood by the audiences to whom the advertisement is shown. We explore the nature of the "real" product of the ad., which we see as being a form of theorising, a set of relations, or a conceptual space for the viewer/ consumer to occupy. Researchers, being themselves consumers, are similarly active theorists and yet irredeemably part and product of that which they survey.

2 Theory and the Reflexive Paradox

We wish to begin by examining the paradox which bedevils all forms of theorising and which supports our approach of concentrating on informal, non-scientific theorising in our analysis. We are about to argue that no form of theory, hypothetico-deductive, anarchic, or dialectical for example, can escape the paradox of self-reference — that is, it cannot guarantee its own truth. In order to do that, a theory must assume a realm of certainty, an arena of presence, of that which is undoubtedly known, its parameters determined by meta-theory, or the "metaphysics of presence." To know is to become blind: we become blind by making choices or by existing in a condition of a choice having been made, whether by us or for us, directly or by implication. The use or effect of theory in determining such conscious and unconscious choices is our interest in this chapter.

Having examined the flaw in different types of theory, we also consider Blum's analysis of theorising as a process, where he looks at the differences between theorising and a persuasive, other-directed process in search of community; and theorising as a disclosure, an open-ended exploration in search of self, expressive of a form of life. We offer some modifications to Blum's view before our analysis of our "data."

The post-modern condition of uncertainty is one which has been likened to the position of classical scepticism (see for example Derek Pugh's contribution to Gareth Morgan's *Beyond Method* (1983: 45−49) in which he claims to have heard the arguments before and to nevertheless be an "unreconstructed positivist"). To such a commentator, the claim "We cannot know anything" has been dismissable because of its reflexivity, in that its author claims to know that he cannot know. Insoluble, unreal, and apparently trivial, these reflexive paradoxes have been regarded as harmless logical puzzles, to be put away whilst ordinary and purposeful scientific life goes on. However, as Lawson (1985: 19) illustrates, reflexive paradox is present "at the root of our most fundamental theories": a deconstructive approach takes not the sceptical view of detachment (for example to acknowledge the "causation" can never be demonstrated and leave the matter there) but one of "unwarrantable involvement" in "systematically employing the concepts or premises one is undermining" (as in reversing the path of causation to see effect as cause, cause as effect). As Culler remarks, "deconstruction uses the very principle it deconstructs" (1983: 87−88), and far from being detached is implicated in the very criticisms it voices.

The reflexive paradox which is encountered in such claims as "We cannot know anything" or "There is no truth" arises because such statements cannot be both true *and* refer to themselves. Hence they must be held to belong to a *different class of statement*, to that "limited region" of statements to which they refer, if they are to be asserted as truth.

So long as the statement can belong to a higher order, a *meta-level*, the self-reference can be avoided and the paradox evaporates (Lawson 1985: 17, our emphasis).

If we wish to avoid paradox at any level, we must establish a limit to that level and then resort to a level beyond it, which could (and did in the case of Russell) lead to a complex hierarchy of meta-meta and meta-meta-meta-levels. Nevertheless, it remains impossible to make any *general* claim held to affect all levels including its own. The strategy of limiting the bounds of the claim has the implication of defining an arena of truth, of the knowable, or even the self-evident — and it is this "metaphysics of presence" that Derrida, in particular, contests.

It is in this vein that Lawson (1985: 19) looks at the claims of logical positivism, which have become almost synonymous with the "natural scientific" mode of theorising, very much the privileged mode of thought in twentieth century Western culture (Blum 1974: 303).

In the case of the logical positivists truth and meaningfulness were defined in terms of satisfying criteria derived from the scientific method. According to this view, "only empirically verifiable statements are meaningful." However, this statement is itself not empirically verifiable (Lawson 1985: 19).

It is impossible to escape from this trap by altering the criteria for "empirical verifiability," or even by suggesting that the statement is not a claim, but a proposal. Such a proposal would amount to proposing that reflexivity was not a problem, and removing the discomfort by pretending it did not exist. We are left with the problem that "unless this central principle of verifiability can avoid self reference in some way it must be regarded as meaningless" (Lawson 1985: 19). However, counter-claims that nothing is verifiable and hence "anything goes," such as those made by Feyerabend (1978), or the paradigmatic theory of Kuhn (1962) (in which the rules for determining scientific truth are themselves determined by the social practices of scientists) are subject to similar problems.

The denial of the supremacy of science, however, implies the denial of the supremacy of his own theory as well. Thus Feyerabend's claim that there can be no criteria for overall rational acceptability appears reflexively undermining in a way that parallels the opposite claim made by the logical positivists, that a set of criteria, which they had provided, must be satisfied in order for a statement to be deemed rationally acceptable (Lawson 1985: 20).

In other words, the certainty of Feyerabend's denial is as questionable as the positivists' counter-assertion, and other theoretical positions can fare no better. Relativistic theories of knowledge, involving some form of social, cultural, or linguistic determinism, suffer a similar fate — at what level can a theory avoid self-reference and be accepted as true? Is not a deterministic theory itself culturally determined?

The move of avoiding self-reference by the provision of a meta-level inevitably induces a realm of possible certainty which provides what may be called *a ground, a foundation, or an absolute*. A theory which declares the limitations of context is thus forced to find a means of escaping the limitations of that context (Lawson 1985: 20, our emphasis).

Lawson also argues that Hegel and Marx, in their attempts to avoid resorting to a meta-level by incorporating self-reference, are equally unsuccessful: Hegel's account of the unfolding of the *Phenomenology of Mind* effectively introduces the meta-level in the form of the cumulative "Book" of knowledge which Derrida criticises; Marx's dialectical solutions still leave some doubt about the character of the dialectical theory itself. James, Dewey, and Wittgenstein profess to make no claims about the world in general or even of language itself. However, such a backing away from making claims in an attempt to avoid paradox (which is not always acknowledged by interpreters of Wittgenstein) has influenced a generation of microsociologists.

3 Theorising and the Self

Derrida, following Nietzsche and Heidegger, does not regard reflexivity as eradicable, or as avoidable, or as requiring solution. Paradox, he claims, is unavoidable. He therefore pursues the contradictions in the writing of others, revealing or de-constructing their attempts to create an "arena of certainty," whilst turning his own deconstructive gaze back on his own writing. We are left with no proposed alternative by Derrida, other than an awareness that the proposition of alternatives is doomed to contradiction. The problem is not how to eradicate reflexivity, but how to proceed in writing or theorising in the light of that reflexivity.

In a paper which stands somewhere between Wittgenstein and Derrida as an attack on the "scientific" conception of theorising, Blum (1974: 301) begins:

All versions of theorising convey as an essential part of their meaning a tacit stipulation concerning the adequacy of a favoured method of analysis, of a preferred solution to the problem of "seeing (sociologically)." At certain points, different proponents of different versions of theorising find it impossible to talk together because they differentially decide where to stop doubting. Such decisions are expressions of the form of life of the theorist, which he seeks to persuade others to accept and which he argues for as a condition of his existence as a theorist (Parenthesis added).

The decision to stop doubting is one which requires either faith or metatheory insofar as they are separable; it is also one which Derrida never makes. Blum observes that we have become accustomed to regarding theory as relating to affairs external to the theorist, primarily being engaged in reference or description. This, he argues, is a degenerate usage of a term which originally meant far more than this, and exhorts us to treat theory as, "doing a display of mind" (Blum 1974: 304): "Through theorising the theorist searches for his self, and his achievement in theorising is a recovering of this self." Wittgenstein, Blum argues, claimed exactly this when he denied that he produced "theories."

His entire enterprise was devoted to showing how any concrete and degenerate version of theory always necessarily glossed the form of life which made it all possible, and that to show such a form of life is simultaneously to find one's self (Blum 1974: 305).

He moves on to suggest that Wittgenstein's activity of "calling to mind" what we know, a recovery of what we have all along is a way of "seeing," which is associated with a way of living. In re-constituting our way of life, in seeing it differently, we reformulate it. Hence the importance which has in the past been placed on form, or method, by positivist theorists amongst others.

Blum attempts to explore why "correct form" — i.e. arranging the world in the "correct" way (mirrored by theorising after the "correct" method) should be the preferred outcome of theorising.

Apart from it being its own justification, it could be said to lead to "correct" or "true" statements about the world; to be compelling or persuasive to an audience; and to standardise vocabulary. All these last three justify theorising on the grounds that it leads to the production of a collective — it orientates toward an audience, it seeks to achieve agreement. It seeks to remove doubt, to be persuasive — indeed a persuasive character is essential to such theories as they seek to transform an audience's way of looking at the world. Blum suggests that the relationship between theorist and audience in positivism is a persuasive one — its analytic character is that of a form of life which requires unity. "Bias" threatens such unity and hence must be eliminated.

He then suggests that an alternative version of theorising is to explicate the form of life, to undress language, to "show another possibility for seeing." Bias is to be celebrated, refashioned, carried to its limits — indeed the theorist will even "provide methods for its production." The audience is analytically irrelevant here, he argues, for display is important rather than persuasion.

From my perspective, any other conception of theorising is degenerate, concrete and practical, since it locates its own justification in terms of the services it renders; its contributions to other concrete selves, its effects upon an audience; to formulate one's self as an achievement of theorising is to render one's common-sense audience· irrelevant; it is to destroy the audience for one's theory (Blum 1974: 308).

We would perhaps wish to change Blum's emphasis here, to stress the idea of formulation of the self as reflexive rather than objective. That is to say, we would wish to draw on our readings of Foucault (1979), Barthes (1981), and Derrida (1980) to recognise the textual features of theorising — to acknowledge that a text creates "spaces" for the "subject" (authorial voice) and reader to occupy. There is a tension between authorial space and the "real" author just as there is tension between the discursive positioning of the analytical "reader" and any actual readership. Readership/authorship are part of the duality of production/consumption and themselves have artefactual qualities. Theorising then is less of a closed self-exploration which makes its specific audience irrelevant than a debate over self, a struggle between the implicit and explicit demands of a variety of "audiences" and possible "authors/selves" whose traces intersect within the discourse. The formulation/recreation of self through theory is a paradoxical struggle — self is re-created, created, and simultaneously destroyed: through deconstruction we may see how this is done, and with what consequence, but deconstruction itself is no less flawed as a process. Blum cites Wittgenstein perceptively when he says:

no proposition is beyond doubt while at the same time every description ultimately presupposes some proposition that is not doubted ... every theory rests upon a stipulation that can be distrusted from the perspective of another theory (Blum 1974: 317).

Our argument, and one which is perhaps characteristic of the shift from modernist to post-modernist analysis, is that these tensions do not exist only when viewed from these other perspectives but are present as implicit or explicit contradictions within the theoretical text itself. It follows then that any text is a battleground of perspectives, rather than a neutral object on which these perspectives are imposed.

3.1 Up the Junction

Perhaps an illustration would be helpful here. Ferdinand de Saussure uses a celebrated example to indicate the importance of structural differentiation in linguistic meaning which is cited by Giddens (1982: 12):

We say that the "same" Geneva-to-Paris train leaves Geneva every day at 8.25 p.m., even if from one day to another the engine, coaches and personnel are different. What gives the train its identity, Saussure argued, is the ways in which it is differentiated from other trains: its time of departure, route, etc. Similarly in language the identity of linguistic units, whether these be vocalisations or written terms, depends upon the differences or oppositions that separate them from one another, not upon the intrinsic content.

Thus the train may be recognised as itself because it is going nowhere else at no other time; it is differentiated by its destination and sequential positioning. However:

The identity of the "Geneva-to-Paris train" cannot be specified independently of the context in which the phrase is used: and this context is not the system of differences themselves, such as Saussure mentions, but factors relating to their use in practice. Saussure implicitly assumes the practical standpoint of the traveller, or the time-tabling official, in giving the identity of the train; hence the same "train" may consist of quite distinct engines and carriages on two separate occasions. But these do not count as instances of the "same" train for a railway repair engineer, or a train spotter (Giddens 1982: 16).

Giddens' introduction of changing perspective as a result of social rules, or roles, is nevertheless only a half-way house to the recognition of multiple simultaneous perspectives. Giddens' awareness is of "coding," but as Cicourel (1973: 111) notes:

Our human experiences continually outstrip our ability to express them in speech acts. We must assume that a number of tacit properties are operative or plausible when we code, recode and then use information to communicate with others. The organisation of memory and the intuitive procedures we use to interpret an interactional setting are strained by the indexical structure of language. Our ability to assign meaning to utterance is contingent on an understanding of various possible sources of information in a complex setting.

Thus, if the "Geneva-to-Paris train" were accorded the cachet of, say, The Orient Express, the important point might not be the rolling stock or the destination but who was booked into which compartment. Even then, as Wolfe (1977: 177−178) explains, those who were on the train for the sake of being there may well not admit it.

Even people who lend themselves to the fashion pages ... are not going to be caught out today talking about fashion in terms of being fashionable. They talk instead of ease, comfort, convenience, practicality, simplicity, and, occasionally, fun and gaiety (for others to share).

The "Geneva-to-Paris" train as a text then, is the ground for many a definitional struggle between possibilities which are both emanated from the external positioning of the various audience selves viewing it, and imminent within the text itself. In the analysis which follows, we attempt to tease out some of the similar tensions in our chosen texts.

4 Management Theorised: Heroes and Villains

The theorising which we have discussed is, of course, born of continuing attempts to make meaning and to resolve problems in a world of endless variety. The essential problem of making meaning, through language or any other symbolic structure, is that of establishing an order. Whatever order is established in such "textual" creations is always temporary, arbitrary, and never absolute, carrying embedded within it the paradox of its own necessity — the threat to subside into disorder at any moment. Hence order is never the "natural" order — it is subject to re-creation, sustenance, maintenance, and re-negotiation with theory and practice in mutual support/contradiction.

Mary Douglas (1975) has addressed some aspects of this problematic in examining the nature and importance of boundaries between purity (order) and danger (disorder) (see also Linstead and Grafton-Small [1985] and Linstead [1985]). That which deviates from the established order, in any social conceptual scheme, has the potential to be both creative and destructive — it may produce chaos or it may produce order as it requires the readjustment of the whole scheme for its accommodation. It has power, it has mystery — heroes and villains alike are equally charismatic and frequently difficult to distinguish. If we were to borrow the parlance of mainstream organisational behaviour and talk of "resistance to change," we would need to observe that such resistance arises not simply because of a human predilection for the comfort of the known, or a perhaps irrational fear of the unknown — it is a product of the inherent ambiguity of known/unknown, of good and bad, of new order/disorder which is inescapably at the heart of our interpretative schemes. When Deal and Kennedy (1982) and Peters and Waterman (1982) exhort us to create heroes, they neglect to acknowledge that we are simultaneously creating villains; our "cultural manipulations" may seek to prefer the hero interpretation but the villain is created on the same spot. As the Hero becomes the "Other," the step to pariah is but a short one. From apotheosis to abomination is a common path, and the more powerful, charismatic, and "magical" the hero, the easier the transformation.

"Change agents" and consultants involved in the promotion of organisational re-ordering have sought to become less threatening by acquiring some of the legitimating attributes of the "professional": formal training, theoretical and conceptual frameworks, codes of practice. As we have outlined in a previous paper (Linstead/Grafton-Small 1985), purity (the moral order) is threatened by dirt or impurity (disorder, that which is outside the moral order). Difficult, unresolvable problems, heresy, diseases, all pose threats to our customary way of life, our system of knowledge/belief, our physical and moral health. Those with the ability to intervene, to immerse themselves in disorder to create order on our behalf have great power, but also pose a great threat — how can this power be contained, channelled, circumscribed by criteria for its application to make it safe? Professionalism is the rational-scientific response: shamanism the primitive response.

Professionals intervene to solve problems of disorder (which, as such, threaten the social order) and create order. They work on behalf of society and because of their gifts, knowledge, and training can surround themselves with impurity without becoming tainted. Heroes are more problematic because they must first create or stimulate disorder before resolving the chaos they themselves have instigated. Their magic is more powerful because it is more problematic and ambiguous — professional change agents help to guarantee the quality of change but they don't create or energise it, for that is done by heroes.

This perhaps accounts in part for the current rash of managerial bio-graphical theorisations; the ideological rationalisation of powerful social forces and industrial upheaval; the combinations of homespun logic and gutsy familiarity which offer us the featherbed of "organisational kitsch" (Cooper 1986) against the reality of rapid and fundamental technological and social change. Let us turn our attention to some of these heroic apologia.

4.1 Happy Talking: Talking Happy Talk

Our examples here come from sources which seek to exemplify the nature of heroic endeavour. We may be reassured when we see these things that their perpetrators are heroic; if we were heroes ourselves, we should do those things. Our first example, however, possesses more mystique than programme, and concerns the character of Victor Matthews, who worked as M. D. of Trafalgar House in harness with his close friend, Nigel Broakes. The source is a best-selling book (in the UK academic world), *Exploring Corporate Strategy* by Gerry Johnson and Kevan Scholes (1984), but they are paraphrasing and citing original material presented by D. F. Channon in a case study of the Company (Stopford/Channon/Constable 1978). Broakes is speaking about the proposed acquisition of the Beaverbrook Newspaper Group, and relates that one decision-making factor "at the forefront of my mind, was the desire to see Victor once again engrossed with a challenge — something that would gratify and occupy him, leaving free part of his time for all the rest of Trafalgar."

Having acquired Beaverbrook, Matthews, installed as chairman, was immediately involved in an industrial dispute with the Fleet Street Unions. Nigel Broakes:

... Victor produced a list of 18 conditions without accepting which, those men who had been sacked, would not be re-engaged. The crisis reached its peak on a Saturday, by which time we had lost several hundred thousand pounds. Victor telephoned me four times; the third call was just after lunch and I asked him where he was: "At home, doing the washing up," he told me ...
"They seemed to have agreed to everything," he said, in doleful tones.
"Then why do you sound so depressed," I asked.
"Because it's been too easy," he replied.

Clearly, Trafalgar House's acquisition strategy was, at least in part, designed to provide a challenge to Victor Matthews (Johnson/Scholes 1984: 319).

An interesting feature of this account is the way in which it resolves oppositions through the hero figure. First of all, Matthews' essential humanity is stressed — prodigy though he be, his childlike qualities make him unusually dependent on the kindness of strangers. Poor soul, he needs a challenge, he needs to be gratified, he is even capable ultimately of being doleful. Pathos is introduced — some of us may even begin to feel sorry for this languishing talent.

Our focus is drawn to the individual and his needs; the implications of the size of the Trafalgar Group and its objectives are left unexplored. Matthews, of course is the representative of a collective which is capable of withstanding a loss (in revenue) of "several hundred thousand pounds": yet this collective is represented only in its abstract vulnerability. The alternate collective, the "unions," is presented solely *in toto* as a threat. Heroically, Matthews makes a stand of no less than eighteen conditions without which "those men who had been sacked would not be re-engaged." No mention of how many men, nor of who sacked them, but the implication is of the essential humanity of Matthews, who is willing to reinstate if only they accept his conditions. His eighteen conditions indicate his toughness: he is a hard bargainer but basically compassionate and reasonable. His domestic humility even extends as far as doing the washing-up (apparently with a telephone beside the sink).

The implicit metaphor here is the game. No mention of social justice, the merits or demerits of managerial causes, the nature of conflict, or the cost to individuals. We must note here the reversal of individuality/collectivity in the account — management are individuals, but the company loses money; the union is a collective, but individuals lose their jobs and wages. It is this which makes the presentation of Matthews as the sporting hero who likes a good match, every game going to the fifth set or final over, so distinctly managerial, for it is only managers as such who have the luxury of playing the game without losing their livelihood. There are few union members, or even leaders, who could be legitimately said to relish a long drawn-out conflict. Even Arthur Scargill of the British National Union of Mineworkers would be unlikely to complain of the ease of a strike victory.

One might also speculate as to the status of the eighteen conditions. Although they function here as a measure of Matthews heroic stature, we might wonder what proportion of them would have been in the end negotiable, and what perceptions of the balance of power led the unions to capitulate.

We are left with a curious paradox which returns us to the earlier theme of Matthews' need for challenge. Although the brave and talented hero was vanquished the evil ones, they had better get their act together quickly and put up a better fight next time, for if Matthews does not get a decent game soon, he may, as Broakes feared before the acquisition, seek other opposition ("I had to face the possibility that we might lose Victor altogether"). What will be the eventual price of this man's ego needs? Several hundred thousand more pounds? A demoralised work-force? Might it be cheaper or more worthwhile to co-operate with the unions? Who are the heroes and villains in this blurred scenario?

4.2 You Can All Join In

Our next examples come from *The Winning Streak* (Goldsmith/Clutterbuck 1985), one of a series of "recipe" books, loosely based on the assumption that companies broadly defined as "excellent" (having a collective heroic stature) must be executing some activities which guarantee their success. The pragmatics of such corporate heroism calls for an indicator to the less-than-excellent as to what they might do, ostensibly to become excellent. In fact, what happens is that the mystification is perpetuated and less-than-excellent companies are given a vague indicator of boundary markers as to what separates them from the high performers. Perhaps what really makes the difference is the deferential need to know where the boundaries are, which indicates problems with the centre of their schematic. Below we have a discussion of one company's approach to a key activity in the heroic endeavour: participation.

STC's employee participation was similarly put to the test when the workforce had to be slimmed by one-third. The cause was a sudden slamming on of the brakes on capital expenditure in the telephone service. "The government cut back and the Post Office cancelled two years out of our five year forward order programme. It was a major exercise in consultation all the way," says Cooper.

A lot of the managers said, "All this participation is for the birds now, isn't it?" We said: "No, the real test is in the bad times." Consultation doesn't mean asking people to agree their factories should be closed. That's our decision. In one case a factory was to be shut and its production moved to the other end of the country. We said: "You may not agree with our decision, but we will tell you why and how we made it. If you can provide us with new information, or other ways we could tackle the problem, we will see if they can work." They put up lots of alternatives.

The factory manager complained, "Every time I knock down a suggestion, they come up with another one. When will it end?" After two or three weeks, however, the union representatives agreed that, although they didn't like the decision it was time to talk about minimising the social consequences of the closure.

During the whole of this volatile and traumatic cutback — of some 7000 employees across the country — the company lost only one man-hour per worker through strikes or stoppages. "The employees knew," says Cooper, "that while we do care about people, we are absolutely hard-nosed about facts" (Goldsmith/Clutterbuck 1985: 68−69)

One is first struck by the coyness of the euphemisms displayed: the work-force, although not overweight, had to be "slimmed" — the fat collective dwindles, rather than draw attention to the 7,000 individual lost livelihoods. The external cause was a rational one, if a little precipitous — the "brakes" were "slammed on" as public expenditure was, by implication "running away." Although the environment was treating them less than kindly, our heroic corporation did not let go their values, although they found that they had to provide firm moral guidance to their perhaps more expeditious lieutenants. The paternalism of the faceless corporation — "we" — advising the hapless managers through the liminality of their moral adolescence is touching.

Consultation, we are advised, is not about decision making. That is the province of the corporate "we" — which does not appear to include management. If, however, it is not about decision making, it must be about engineering the acceptance of decisions already made, and hence its apparent moral burnish fades a little. The homiletic, decision-making, anonymous "we" (one wonders here if a small Greek chorus of directors performed at these gatherings) addresses "they," and having framed the debate and its parameters by having already made the decision, offers to take into account any additional information, or other alternatives, which significantly must be *added*, and are hence marginal. "They" must therefore overturn an existing framework rather than develop according to their own logic: they are "rigged out in" the language "of our accusers, humiliated and condemned by it" (Barthes 1973: 46), subjected to an established method of theorising whose guarantee is a positivistic epistemology.

It appears that the point of this consultation is not to generate alternatives but to exhaust them. The manager who sees his job as "knocking down" suggestions (the very word specifies and trivialises the nature of the contribution expected) is not gainsaid by the corporate "we." The work-force representatives, presumably by now less corpulent, eventually are intellectually fatigued and re-draw the boundaries. The whole structure of this episode, presented as the face of the caring corporation, is in fact the opposite. The care which is lavished upon "facts," upon the apparently rational-logical, is nevertheless done in emotive language which evokes the kinship group. The paternalistic elders of the corporate "we," the rather impetuous, perhaps late adolescent, managers requiring guidance; and the work-force, needing to be herded and shepherded, with a patience masquerading as wisdom, in the face of hostile elements. The power structure is clearly drawn and laid down — the elders communicate with the elements and hand down the decision divined from the facts. The managers open their office doors and wait for nature to take its course. And although it is difficult (it is also important for these directors that they not be seen to take any "easy" options), everyone faces up to the facts. The managers' final statement could be reversed in the context of this account, in view of the primacy accorded to a particular form of theorising to the exclusion of other considerations in decision making: "while we do care about facts, we are absolutely hard-nosed about people."

4.3 Roll Out the Barrel

Our final example in this section comes from the same book and allows us to indulge in some exegesis.

Another way of developing involvement is an active drawing in of people to practical efforts that go beyond their immediate job. One company has trained delivery men to "sell" the company as they go around, for example, while parts of Allied-Lyons' brewing division have actively involved the whole spectrum of employees in gaining new custom. For example, Tetley Walker, an Allied-Lyons subsidiary, has increased market share in the free trade area with the help of ordinary employees. When the salesmen pitch for new business at working-men's clubs or leisure centres, they take with them draymen, brewers and a variety of white-collar workers. The personnel manager explains how he can advise the client on industrial relations matters and staffing; the tele-sales staff explain how they take orders and the company surveyor describes how he can help them to get the best value for money out of repairs and extensions. Each of these people makes it clear why getting the club's custom is important to him or her.

Explains Tetley Walker free trade sales director Roger Parker: "We wanted to put more in front of them than just a salesman with a smart car. We wanted them to see the drayman who makes sure the beer arrives on time and the technical services man who fixes their cellar equipment if things go wrong."

Apart from gaining the company new business, the all-in approach has helped open the employees' eyes to commercial realities. "It has shown them that customers are not won over as easily as they supposed," says Parker (Goldsmith/Clutterbuck 1985: 65–66).

This account, in itself, is somewhat improbable. Delivery men are, we know, frequently exhorted to "sell" the company as they go round — the extent to which they are able to do this and the nature of some of their other activities is beautifully illustrated in Jason Ditton's (1977) treatment of bread salesmen. Apart from the unusual prospect of a motley group desperately trying to "sell" the company in the club bar, the use of the working men's club as an example allows us to illustrate the situation from our own research.

A project conducted for the Economic and Social Research Council and written up in the *Club & Institute Journal* (Edwards 1987, Linstead 1987a, b, Linstead/Edwards/Rippon/Turner 1986, also Linstead/Turner 1989) explored the relationships between brewing companies and Working-Men's Clubs in the U.K. (approximately 4,000) through loan-financing. It appears that throughout the 1960s the brewers sought to extend their free-trade market by offering cheap loans to clubs in return for an exclusive purchasing agreement (tie). This financed an enormous expansion in the club sector, contemporaneous with both EEC and UK concern with the monopolistic features of the tied-house system. Since 1974, the brewers have diverted their money into other areas (they are currently in the middle of a three-year £ 2 billion [£ 2 million per day] programme of refurbishing public houses) and have been less patient with clubs — loans are called in, mortgages foreclosed, premises taken over (many converted into brewery-owned or -dominated proprietary clubs or leisure centres); interest rates become punitive and discounts less frequent. Since 1979, over 300 clubs have gone out of business.

Such is the concern that the clubs nationally have successfully negotiated with banks to buy up certain brewery loans over a longer term (new EEC regulations limit the conditions of loan related ties) and are negotiating as a national body for discounts in order to remain viable. Distrust of the brewers is widespread, and is reflected in the recent Monopolies and Mergers Commission Report on the industry (1989). The important point here is that it is generally recognised as having been the "logic of the trade" for 20 or 30 years that the way to get new business in clubs was to "buy-in" and offer loan finance, and that the way to defend "your clubs" from poaching was to keep increasing their credit obligations. Allied-Lyons, as one of the dominant Big Six brewers, were as formative of this logic as any other brewer.

Despite any internal contradictions which may be deconstructed in this account, it appears that the brewers were seeking to mystify their own employees even as they sold the company, for not only are customers "not won over as easily as they supposed," they are not won over in that way at all. "Commercial reality" as it appears in this account, again presented with positivistic deference to external logics and paradoxical helplessness as regards methods of response, is a myth: those presenting "facts" have conversely as little regard for "fact" as they have considerable energy for fiction. But, of course, the distinction itself is reflexively paradoxical, drunk or sober.

Reflexivity poses a threat to this distinction, and in so doing threatens facts, reality and truth, but so does it also threaten fiction, myth and falsity (Lawson 1985: 10).

5 The Object in Question

So far we have discussed the embeddedness of theorising in practical self-interest, emergent social relations, and the struggle for control and addressed the artefactual qualities of theory. In this section, we look at the importance of artefacts themselves in the process of theorising everyday commercial relations.

5.1 Scantrux Ltd.

The data in this and the following example were collected by Bob Grafton-Small as part of his field-work amongst marketing managers (Grafton-Small 1985). In this case, the principal respondent was the Branch Manager of one of a chain of garages in the North-East of England, operated by Scantrux Ltd., importing agents for a range of well-known Scandinavian heavy goods vehicles. That so many of the staff were keen to talk about their work in fairly specific terms is perhaps a reflection of the Customer Services Manager's boast:

Our "artics" and "flat backs" are generally acknowledged to be well up in a highly competitive market. The manufacturer has a fine reputation for quality, reliability and service, which is where I come into it, and drivers who use these vehicles speak equally highly of them. They like the power, the style and the comfort, which is next door's responsibility.

This straightforward division forms the basis of the company. Whilst the Customer Services Department sells the vehicles in their orthodox form and runs the office, "next door" is devoted to servicing lorries, major repairs, and the construction of "custom" or bespoke bodywork made to a customer's specifications and then fitted to a standard chassis.

Divers drivers arrived at intervals throughout the morning of the interview, to collect vehicles which had been put in for servicing or modification. All the lorries involved were ready and waiting as company policy dictated that customers should be telephoned when their charges were ready for collection. The Customer Services Manager was insistent:

It doesn't do our reputation any good at all to have people hanging about or phoning up for work we're supposed to have done. Even so, there's more to it than simple Public Relations. A clear policy towards the customers is also a matter of discipline. It means that everyone in the firm has an idea of what they should be doing and why. It also helps us to get the bills paid because customers who feel they've been treated responsibly tend to respond in a similar manner.

The emphasis on "customer service" is characteristic of the company's history. The initial importation compaign had been based on setting up more garages and spares depots than were warranted by contemporary sales levels. This was a deliberate and successful attempt to ensure that those lorries which were sold would stay on the road for as long as possible and so keep hauliers' overheads down whilst gaining the Scandinavian vehicles an impressive reputation. Subsequent increases in sales had not affected the policy of "spares and service first," for as one of the salesmen pointed out:

If customers can get spares easily and cheaply, then their "artics" or whatever stay on the road, which is good for us, and our mechanics can help to sell the company and its products to potential customers before they meet a salesman. This overcame a lot of the original inertia in what is still a very traditional market. It's selling by word of mouth which is very effective if it's working in your favour. Our custom body business is based on it and that's why we put such an emphasis on service. Our lorries are expensive initially but customers don't mind paying a lot of money for something they are sure will do the job. In fact, this is an area in which our reputation has given us quite an edge. We keep in front even though there's a lot of good vehicles about.

Take Foden's for example. They're big in Europe but don't mean a light here, primarily because no one believes in them. They're a driver's favourite and quite a few hauliers still pay far too little attention to their drivers. We make lorries for the international routes so we're known all over the world and whenever hauliers or drivers speak well of us, we sell lorries. This also means listening to our own mechanics, which is something else other people don't seem to do. The mechanics obviously know an awful lot about how an individual vehicle is actually performing. We take note of what they say and if something looks unsatisfactory we send it back to Sweden with our spares orders. They might make a component change or alter the maintenance schedules or even redesign the part if it's a big enough problem but whatever they do it helps us to see to it that customers never have reason to complain about us.

The other salesman was equally forthcoming:

You have been getting the technical side of it from David? He's good, you know, but even he doesn't always know why people buy our vehicles. There's a sort of snow-ball effect which sweeps in business once you've passed a certain point. As long as you don't do anything stupid or try to sell rubbish, a lot of customers buy your trucks simply because they're on the road. They see them rolling. They fancy the driving jackets we give to their drivers. It becomes a guaranteed correct decision which is great for me personally. I use this approach in selling to committees or local government. Even they have heard of Swedish winters so I point out that many of our trucks have extra power driven attachments to beat snow, ice and cold weather generally. They buy the lorry with all these fittings which might not get used more than once in its entire life time. The drivers can simply uncouple the hydraulics and put more power onto the road. They'll get more than 90 mph (145 kph) from our biggest tractor unit and that's with a load up. Yes, power is very important with these people.

I think a lot of our bigger stuff sells because the buyer is so impressed with the power and size of the thing that it doesn't matter what he needs, he simply can't say no. And of course the competition helps. Look at the brochures, the magazines ... the roads are full of great names: Mercedes Benz, Rolls-Royce, SAAB, Seddon Atkinson. Most of them are aero engine makers and famous for it. That's why the servicing is so important. Once you've got the power you want it on the road. After all, that's your name in 10 foot (3 metre) letters doing 60 (95 kph) up the middle lane.

The climax of this argument was a free sample, a run round in a turbo charged twelve-litre tractor unit driven by one of the workers from the "custom" body shop. He said that the salesman had not only underestimated the value of a service which provides guaranteed "bespoke" bodywork, which was understandable given his interest in "chassis and standard rigs," but that he had also omitted one important point. Whilst it was true that the Scandinavian lorries were capable of 90 mph (145 kph) when fully laden, the manoeuvre was not to be recommended: it would take a "32 tonner" with excellent air brakes a mile or so to stop in a straight line. Less with just a tractor. The tone of the driver's voice made Grafton-Small look at the speedometer. He thought of the ease with which they had reached 80 mph (130 kph) and realised some measure of the excitement to be had from machines like this. As the driver said afterwards when they rolled back into the yard, "That's why you've got to take care ... if anything goes wrong it's always the driver or his licence that gets buggered."

The manager of the "Custom Bodyshop" seemed surprisingly forthright given the impression created by the Customer Services Department.

We're not Mulliners and there's nothing as grand as "bespoke coachwork" in here. It's just a matter of doing simple things properly, putting the rubbing strips in the right place for whatever size palettes the customer uses, things like that. The metal work doesn't often amount to much because most of our customers want reliable alloy boxes. They're not even bothered about air dams or stream lining. Some of our regulars have their own requirements but we've got templates cut to their specifications and it's just a matter of putting all the bits together. I suppose that if I were asked I'd have to say that most of the interesting work we get in here comes from crashes. God forbid that anyone should get hurt but there's quite a challenge in straightening out a bent wagon and getting it roadworthy again.

The Branch Manager, who finished for the weekend at 12.30 on a Saturday, admitted that he would rather talk to Grafton-Small than risk getting caught by a last minute customer. They were having coffee in the manager's first floor office, when Bob asked if the manager ever got any repairs or faults that were too much for even his specialist mechanics to handle.

Well, it's a matter of cost really. We can put anything right if the customer is willing to pay for it but occasionally it's better all round if we don't bother. We can't always afford to have skilled labour tied up on difficult jobs. We've got one in at the moment and it's a disgrace. George has been on it all morning. There's over 2,000,000 kilometres on the clock and the haulier who runs it has a reputation for double booking; from the state of this tractor unit he deserves it. Anyway, George is his last hope because if he can't get it to run then no-one can.

This explained the series of laboured diesel rumblings and sudden silences which had been echoing round the yard all morning. The Manager obviously didn't take the job too seriously for he opened his window and shouted at a figure below: "What's the matter George? I can't hear that engine."

George was sitting in a armchair made from a pile of old lorry tyres. He was sipping a mug of tea and smoking a cigarette. He was filthy. His overalls were covered in grease and oil; his face and hands were glistening with sweat and dark excrescences from the abandoned engine. He was in no mood for levity. "Fucking thing's fucked ... so fuck it."

Our main concern in presenting this vignette is a simple one — how do we understand George's utterance? It is an almost completely indexical sentence — the words are in the right places, they have the form of meaning, but the sense of the same root changes with each word. We must be able to relate them to traces of meaning from other similar occasions of their use. But also we must relate them to George's context and to similar contexts in order to realise that it is more than a simple oath of frustration.

George's outburst represents the Other of the manager's discourse and the salesman's spiel. Beneath their presentation of the organisation as highly customer orientated, devoted to service, disciplined and well ordered ("everyone has an idea of what they should be doing and why"), rational and responsible, with a product embodying power (itself a double-edged concept), quality and reliability, and a sensitive approach in listening to drivers and their own mechanics, there is a tension, a thinly disguised vulnerability. What are the boundaries of the discourse? Implicit within it are the assumptions that customers are naturally responsible and reasonable, that their demands can be met, and that if treated well and spoken to they will respond sensibly and appropriately with purchase and unexcessive after-sales demands.

But the environment is after all competitive and it is in the nature of organisations like Scantrux to make it so. If the demands were too easily satisfied, they would lose their distinctiveness. They also acknowledge the possibility that the customer might be a fickle prima donna, or a cowboy who simply plays one dealer against another to milk the benefits. Their own ordered response, a policy and a reputation, is in part a defence against unreasonable demands and hence disorder — they establish what they do well in order to protect themselves from the implicit threat of the customer who is not right, who wants more than they can give. Although they claim to listen to the drivers and mechanics they do not, it is clear, *sell* to them. Hence the salesman who talks about additional power and speed is selling the trucks *symbolically* — as the firm's driver pointed out, speeding with a full load is dangerous and the risks are taken by the drivers. Unrealistic relations with the environment can result in the importation of disorder — customers can expect drivers to go faster because they have the power, the dealer can expect his mechanics to fix machines that have been thrashed in an unholy fashion. In each case disorder promotes a split between the levels of the organisation, but it is a tendency already implicit in the distribution of power. There is also a solidarity related to occupational structures — the mechanic knows the lot of the driver who is a victim of the collusion of sales/customers — as a result, life gets difficult for them both. It is no accident that there is a tension between the avuncular Branch Manager and George, and that he looks down from his first-floor window on to exhausted George's makeshift armchair. Their physical surroundings reflect their position, supporting the manager's right to speak. The idea of skill and quality is undercut by the custom bodyshop man who claims that most of their work is routine and the only real challenge is when unreal demands occur — an accident, or, in George's case, a breakdown. Thus the interest and challenge of the job depends, ironically, on the customers periodically making excessive demands, threatening the order of the organisation, underlining the fragility of its capacity to respond. This is reflected in the possibility of "organisational breakdown" — lack of discipline, lack of reliability, and failure to respond which is the implicit threat behind the salesman's and manager's discourse.

George's utterance is made just after the manager has sealed himself in as a protection against last minute customer demands. George himself has been struggling with the results of these all morning. He wears the scars of his frustration. He understands the product and what should be expected of it, although he cannot own one, but his occupational kinship group provides the skill to intervene when products fail to underpin the social and economic relationships they are there to support. However, when those relationships themselves are fractured by excessive cost-cutting, excessive demands on drivers, excessive demands on the product, and excessive demands on George, provoking the tensions already present internally within the organisation, the boundary is exceeded. George's mildly insubordinate oath therefore rescues the threatening situation by both underlining the organisational order, in drawing the boundary to exclude the unreasonable customer, and by redoubling on itself in an ironic suggestion of the distance between mechanics, drivers and managers, who may themselves be unreasonable. This is done by a dramatic and conspicuous, but playful, display of the sloppiness which would, if framed seriously, be seen as the greatest threat to the organisational purpose.

5.2 Fraser, Railton, and Springfield

The architect today is first, it seems, a professional man. He cannot, and this is of fundamental importance, see his project through on his own. Its physical making is in the hands of a vast number of contributory trades, crafts and even professions. He has, however, to see it through, and this has necessitated (as in fact the process of designing itself necessitates) his familiarity with, and understanding of, every trade involved. More than that he should be aware of the limits of potential in all these trades so that he himself can exploit and even extend them in creative designing (Martienssen 1976: 18 – 19).

The following is based on a series of interviews with a firm of commercial architects and offers insights into the mediation of order by negotiation. The introduction to this firm came from an environmental designer who had recently graduated from the Royal College of Art and then moved to the North of England where he was now employed by Messrs. Fraser, Railton, and Springfield in their eponymous partnership. Their service covered everything from an enquiry by a client to the completion of whatever work would embody those requirements.

Mr. Fraser, the senior partner, was quite happy to talk about his business.

There's a lot of competition on everything from furnishings and interiors to entire sites. I insist on more than professional competence from my designers, they have to be flexible, and I won't work with builders who can't stay within a budget whatever the contract. I negotiate all the additional allowances, penalty clauses, and surcharges and that's bad enough without your own people screwing up the details.

This ability with contractual minutiae had apparently been gleaned from Mr. Fraser's 30 years in architecture dealing with, as he put it,

Clients who don't realise what the design process involves. They have no idea of what it costs for just a set of drawings and the relevant estimates. I have to convince them that the money will make a worthwhile difference.

When pressed on this, several of the designers said that because clients might not understand the design process, they had to learn to trust the group to turn their money into a creditable asset. However, one of the senior draughtsmen explained that such was not always the case.

The large breweries are by far the most particular. They keep huge manuals of fabrics, colours and shapes which mustn't be used. There's also a list of approved accoutrements, a very tight budget, seating and capacity limits, a definite idea of "house style" and an expectation of good work done on schedule.

The designer who introduced us to the firm agreed, but felt much less certain of the partner's appreciation of the difficulties inherent in a site. Our confidant's responsibilities for a project would normally be expected to cover the choice, purchase, and installation of whatever constituted the job. He thought that whilst Fraser and the other partners might get the contracts, he kept them.

All that old sod does is a fast sales and P. R. job over an expensive lunch. We pick up the pieces of his bloody disastrous tendering though half the time I don't know how or why we manage. There's not enough "blue sky" (no limits) work to take the monotony out of this hacking for the breweries. It might mean steady money but it's as uninspiring as their keg, which is fitting, I suppose, but hardly worth the tens of thousands it costs to give all these pubs flock wall paper and vile carpets. I dunno ... you wish sometimes they'd let you use blue and yellow in a bar ... green beer might taste of something.

The final treat was to be invited to a site meeting to see the design group's "continuous market research" in progress. According to Mr. Railton, this meant leaving the customer as many options as possible for as long as possible. The designer who provided the entry into F.R.S. called it "the fudge factor" whereby deliberately low tenders could be jacked up to profitability by dextrous use of the special effects clauses. The builders involved, in a rare uncharitable moment, called it "pissing about." It became clear as the meeting went on that many builders avoided this sort of work whenever possible. Others found it exciting and tendered for it with relish. Should one of the former have the contract, as was the case here, it fell to the designer to placate the builders, the partners being involved occasionally to reassure the customer of the service being given and to spot any last minute alterations which might facilitate payment.

The meeting was over the construction of a new and expensive set of offices for a steel company. A major part of the contract insisted on the use of stainless and chromed steels in as wide a manner as could be tastefully imagined. This immediately caused some friction as the company was going through a very public bad patch and the idea of costly new offices running old plant might well appear tasteless. Fraser, however, felt that he could present the company's pride in itself in a way that the steel executives would appreciate. He also believed he could galvanise designers and builders into producing something the company would be proud of. After the meeting, which had been a triumph for the partners, one of the jobbing builders buttonholed the designer.

"Are they serious? Using all these flash steels? They're bloody hard to work with and damned expensive when you can get 'em. Besides we've got no experience of steel, not on this scale."

The designer, who had originally been very excited by the project, was similarly unsure but for different reasons. He had recently seen some photographs in an international design magazine.

"Well, nobody has. That's part of it or at least it was. There's a big pagoda in Japan with a stainless steel roof ..."

"Bloody wonderful! Trying to convince everyone they're doing all right by copying the Japanese. No offence, lad, but this is the last time I work with any of this mob. They're puddled. How can you go on like this wi' no money?"

The designer then went on to describe the way in which the steel company would be presented:

Adventurous but not foolhardy, hence the special steels, and confident but not boastful or unreliable, so it's display without ostentation. They should be really pleased with what they're getting, providing Fraser doesn't annoy them too much with his bloody manoeuvering. There's room for development so when this starts looking tired they'll have us back. As for their employees, well, I don't know, I suppose they get sold it the way Fraser and Railton convinced me.

In this case we have an example of how corporate image, embodied in the architecture of a company, is both the outcome of a process of negotiation between specialists and simultaneously the embodiment of the Other which makes such a negotiation necessary. The company in question at the end of the case was losing money, cutting back on labour, and creating high unemployment both in the industry and in the area. The industry as a whole was in decline. Yet the company management chose to channel their efforts into a public display of confidence which was both expensive and technologically difficult — a displacement of the challenge of wresting order from a difficult economic environment to a problem of technological order, with which they were more at home. Not only does ostentatious display of this sort call attention to its purpose and the threats which confront the company, it fails to take into account the key issue of users' meanings — the people who work there, and even those who consume it symbolically by walking past it every day. It is, however, not surprising when the process by which the decision was arrived at is considered. Fraser's own operation is an uncertain one, and he uses the environmental uncertainty to control his designers internally. Failure to work within tight budgets is "screwing up." These budgets are of course dictated by the "objectivity" of completion, yet Fraser is remarkably possessive and secretive about the special way his deals are done. He inhabits the organisational boundary between two forms of ignorance — the designers who don't understand cost constraints, and the customers who don't understand design. Ultimately, with no means to assess in advance the competence of a highly technical profession, the customer has to rely on trust — the architect, in common with all professionals although it is rarely realised, has an important problem in developing this trust.

This can lead to boundary collusion between salesman and customer — "a fast P.R. job over an expensive lunch" — and reflect back on the internal tensions within each operation — "we pick up the pieces of his bloody disastrous tendering." The process of servicing the contract being problematic is backgrounded, the power dimension being explicit as the architects are treated in the same way as the jobbing builders — there's the job, there's the price, do it. The architects, however, cannot choose not to do it as the builder can, although builders who don't like the work must sometimes take it because they have to.

The different perceptions of Railton's "continuous market research" ("keeping the options open" to the client, "the fudge factor" to the architects, and "pissing about" to the builders) embody both an ironic measure of insight into the implausibility of the practice and a good measure of self-interest. They do, however, expose the precarious way in which those who participate in the construction of a corporate image are themselves open to redefinition.

Perhaps the final insight into the process of displacement at work here belongs to the architect who realises the way in which he has just been sold an idea which is both difficult to achieve and of questionable value, who suggests that the employees of the steel company will be sold it in just the same way. This is a fine example of organisational kitsch "which turns the disturbing into something that is pleasing and pacifying" (Cooper 1986). The expense is therefore not important, and the threatening environment which makes the expenditure unwise is precisely the reason why it is accomplished: it reassures. It suggests the desirable qualities, it invites the response "surely there can't be much wrong with a company than can dress itself like this?" It makes the company "agreeably presentable to themselves." And of course the architects feel a similar agreeable self-satisfaction, until it is deconstructed, or the builders tell them to stop "pissing about," or the company goes under with that self-satisfied smile still playing round its corporate lips.

6 Picture This

In the preface to the Fourth Edition of "Decoding Advertisements" (1985), Judith Williamson reflects on the developments which have taken place in advertising since the book was written:

... advertising also began to show far more skilful, self conscious use of "semiotics" (whether under that name is irrelevant), so that many of the formal practices of advertising which in this book I found I was teasing out as IMPLICIT in the ads, and not EXPLICIT ... Form is becoming far more important in the overt "content" or meaning of ads: (on p. 22) I show the connection of creamy coffee with a "mild" cigarette, effected by picturing the two together. Today, Silk Cut can make a similar reference by using the colour and typography evoking, THROUGH FORM ALONE, the famous "glass and a half of full-cream dairy milk" which, ANOTHER ad has told us, go into Cadbury's chocolate. All this is the semiotician's dream — and also her or his nightmare. For where do you go next, when the notions that some of us struggled over years ago in Saussure and Barthes now seem to be part of public imagery and a source of increasing refinement in, not just academia, but the media? (Williamson 1985: 7)

In our previous examples we have seen how theory is created with the broad purpose of legitimising and lionising whilst having the additional effect of pre-empting criticism and maintaining the status quo: far from being a description of the "realities" of business life, it is an aggressive next step in the discourse of domination. In the advertisement we analyse below, theoretical familiarity is essential for proper understanding, and a model of theorised relations is a product of a sophisticated interaction.

A case in point (*Design Week* 1986: 6) involves the use of paintings by J. M. W. Turner in the designing of labels for a new range of wine. Whilst the keepers of these works, the Tate and the National Galleries, have monitored this process most carefully, some of the reproductions have still been cropped though not "Peace: Burial at Sea" which Turner himself framed "like a threepenny bit" and John Lewis, the designer in question, would not. Given these modifications and the size of the labels, the end results are clearly far more than mere copies or a simple pastiche of Turner's work for, in effect, they represent a series of explicit quotations. One or two questions are left unanswered, even so. Is it necessary for potential customers to recognise individual pictures or is it simply a matter of some vague reference to Turner as a cult personality, the embodiment of high culture, or some disembodied sense of individuality, worth, and "Englishness"?

Clearly, Christopher Frayling (1986) has something of the sort in mind when he reviews a campaign to develop the corporate image of Shell Oil and wonders "if you're looking for a short-cut image of 'braving the elements,' the 'romance of the sea,' and 'rain, steam and speed' for your corporation, then what could be more effective than an animated version of Turner's seascapes?"

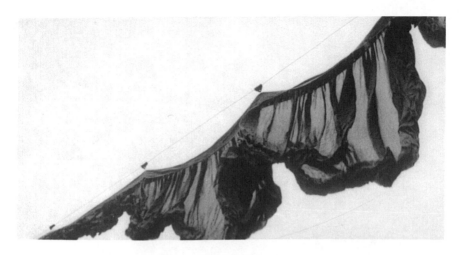

These remarks are themselves remarkable for the unconscious or, who knows, even conscious ironies implicit in an animation based on a seascape by Turner, an artist renowned for his ability to capture the essence of elemental fluidity in a single painting. Setting aside for the moment the punning anachronism of an oil rig tapping Turner's oils, one might also wonder at the historical inversion whereby cartoons were once the sketches an artist made in preparing an idea for the larger canvas and yet nowadays that self-same canvas is regarded as the basis for a series of sketches. Shades, perhaps, of Eco's (1986: 7 – 8) superabundance?

Frayling goes on to consider the aftermath of *Ways of Seeing* (Berger 1972) and notes that whereas Berger could demonstrate an explicit reliance by commercial publicists on the language of oil painting, this is no longer possible: "When artists, film-makers, architects and advertisers all seem to be part of a 'post-modernist' culture of quotations, things are beginning to get far more complicated." Indeed they are. Moreover, Frayling believes that this complexity is not simply the outcome of art history being studied as a visual lexicon, for the advertising industry asks, as a matter of everyday practice, a lot of questions about its audience – which are precisely the questions that art historians have traditionally ignored. Nor, he asserts, is it possible to assume a high visual literacy amongst the public; there is too much evidence to the contrary. It may be a matter of using eye-catching newness as something which reads in a diffused sort of way as art, but if so, Frayling wonders, at what level do these advertisements work?

We wish to turn now to the analysis of a singular piece of advertising, produced to promote Benson and Hedges' "Silk Cut" cigarettes by Saatchi and Saatchi. The advertisement lasts three minutes, contains no mention of the product at all, and consists of a considerable number of men and

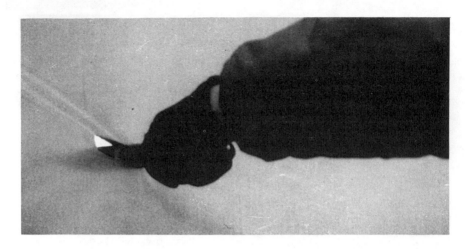

machines being employed to erect a purple silk curtain across a snowy
Scottish glen, and to slash that silk ceremonially with a gleaming blade.
The health warning at the end of 180 luxurious seconds and a reputed three
million pounds is the only clue to the nature of the product.

In Britain, cigarette manufacturers are restricted by law to advertising
in the press and the cinema and similarly bound to conclude each and
every ad with a Government Health Warning, yet this apparent proscription
of unbridled "free" speech has not only been accepted by the likes of
Saatchi and Saatchi but thereby subverted and overthrown. This overthrow
is apparent in at least two ways.

Firstly, the ad is designed to use the cinematic medium to the full, which
gives the ad agency access to visual, aesthetic, and social languages that
are beyond other advertising media, especially the televisual ones denied
by law. Secondly, the Health Warning, which was intended as a salutary
afterward or moral, with distinct overtones of Léger's (1973: 10) Modernist
dictum, "This will have killed that," is now used as a last-ditch solution
for those still lost in the advertiser's semiotic maze.

The significance of our unpicking lies in the way the ad offers "intelligence" and "wit" to its viewers for even if the ad-makers' codes and clauses
are left undeciphered, members of the audience can flatter themselves that
they have at least recognised the existence of a code! By the same token,
the visual and aural "bricolage" of the ad offers separate readings to each
of its various audiences.

Non-smokers are distracted, amused, and, perhaps unwittingly, encouraged to mitigate their criticism of smoking. Smokers of "Silk-Cut" are also
encouraged but in different ways, for despite the sponsor and the ad itself,
the product in question is not "sold" in its own terms as smoking. The

basis of "Silk-Cut's" appeal is rather the tapestry of "Art values" that also muffles popular antagonism to tobacco. The ad is civilised, clever, and witty and so, by implication, are those who smoke "Silk-Cut." After all, smoking is banned in many cinemas nowadays, yet here we have a group of smokers who will not only refrain from smoking, and so privilege the well-being of others, but will sponsor ads, and thereby a cinema, which denies them their very identity.

Whilst other smokers may thus appear to be easy recruits to "Silk-Cut" as a brand, the ad's promotion of a number of seemingly contradictory but nevertheless "positive" interpretations has special appeal for such as an audience of the teenagers who form a significant part of Britain's cinema-going public. A number of them will be nascent or novice smokers and this ad will surely do much to massage any feelings of guilt or uncertainty.

These ideas hinge on an understanding of the ad as both a process and a medium of transformation. Thus the "voice-overs" in the video are critics talking about the original work by Christo which is being parodied and parallelled by the ad. In 1977, Christo "wrapped" 24 miles of California with an 18-foot high white nylon curtain, a process which took years to complete, given the negotiations involved. The ad compresses this series of transformations — money into nylon, time into art, landscape into ornament — into a mere three minutes whilst inverting the colour scheme, for clearly the curtain is the purple of mountains and the mountains themselves are the white of Christo's original hanging. That purple and white are also the colours of a "Silk-Cut" packet is, literally, not worth mentioning. A passing reference is far closer to the spirit of discourse. Similarly noteworthy is the snippet of "snake-charmer" music which plays when the furled curtain is drawn from the truck. One might also wonder at the plays on "elevation" and purple "the imperial colour," just as the coincidence of environments is surely no accident. These semiotic games are vital for they give the ad a terrible coherence. The ad plays on subsumed understandings of both "Art" and smoking — no-one needs to be told what it is just as no-one would admit to being puzzled until they saw the Health Warning — and distances other cigarettes in the same way that it distances undesirable attributes and connotations. The point is not that these qualities are simply old-fashioned or muddle-headed but that they are not applicable — they are part of an inappropriate account. This notion is in itself significant for, in addition to its obvious audiences, the ad is a medium for a number of privileged dialogues, privileged in the sense that, whereas the cinema audience may make what they will of another's filmic account, there are also those who consciously made the film itself. An indication of this interplay can be gathered from the following:

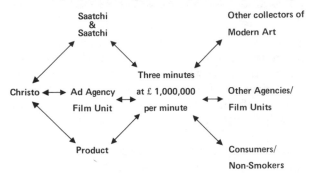

So Charles and Maurice Saatchi, owners of the biggest collection of contemporary art in Britain (estimated value in excess of £ 140 million), can flaunt their taste and their collection whilst making their clients, Benson and Hedges, the makers of "Silk-Cut," look impressive. Similarly, the entire range of advertising and technical staff involved can show off to their peers in other agencies throughout the world yet justify their salaries at the same time. These are, of course, extensions of the semiotic "slippage" whereby the consumer of "Silk-Cut" appreciates that the last thing the cigarette stands for is a smoke!

The same slippage is also evident elsewhere. The moving effort of raising the curtain stands in implicit contrast to the ease of a cigarette; the tensions of man-made beauty in a naturally beautiful landscape and the vandal's work in the tearing of the curtain, the valley as a tearing of the hillside.

We might summarise then by saying that viewers of the advertisement are

1. Invited to participate in a code/vocabulary of sophisticates. The emphasis here is clearly on community — in understanding the various refer-

ences, one is identified as part of a group which includes smokers, if not part of the world of smokers.

2. By implication, smoking becomes a normalised activity. It is naturalised, but, through the naturalisation of artifice and the implication of community, metaphorically rather than by mere simplistic metonymic allusion (for example: the "Come to Marlborough country" ads). The audience is one with the world which erects the curtain across the glen — not with the glen itself.

3. A position of "smoker's friend" is offered to the audience — and even if the audience is unable to read the detailed coding of Christo, they should be able to recognise it *as* a code, signifying arty sophistication if nothing else.

4. The ad takes the disturbing or potentially problematic (smoking) and makes it natural or comforting in the manner of kitsch: in so doing it trivialises the bold, expansive, and perhaps disturbing statement of Christo's art into the literal significations and narrow coding of a cut-in-silk.

5. The enormous expense in the endeavour of art which is identified with smoking conceals a corresponding lack of concern with other expenses incidental to smoking such as health care. Additionally, although the curtain image is a part of a fairly restricted language game, the enormous expense is also a part of a larger discourse of power, which has a historical dimension. The arrogance of spending so much money on an ad which does not mention the product, but yet most audiences will understand, is considerable.

In conclusion then, the outcome of this ad is a position, an environment which will sustain smoking as a valued or at least tolerated activity — it works specifically to promote the audiences' theorising through a visual discourse. Just as our other examples seek to sustain or establish material relations through the production and reproduction of conceptual schemes, our ad works in a similar way confirming that the production/consumption duality present in material artefacts is similarly and simultaneously present in those theoretical artefacts which inevitably accompany their creation and re-creation.

References

Barthes, R. (1973): *Mythologies*. London: Paladin
Barthes, R. (1981): The Theory of the Text. *Untying the Text*. R. Young (Ed.). London: RKP, pp. 31–47
Berger, P. (1972): *Ways of Seeing*. Harmondsworth: Penguin

Blum, A. (1974): Theorizing. *Understanding Everyday Life*. Jack D. Douglas (Ed.). London: RKP, pp. 301 – 319

Cicourel, A. (1973): *Cognitive Sociology*. London: Penguin

Cooper, R. (1986): Notes on Organizational Kitsch. Paper presented to conference on "Aspects of Organisation," Lancaster, January

Culler, J. (1983): *On Deconstruction: Theory and Criticism after Structuralism*. London: Routledge and Kegan Paul

Deal, T. and A. Kennedy (1982): *Corporate Cultures*. Reading, MA: Addison-Wesley

Deleuze, G. and F. Guattari (1984): *Anti-Oedipus*. London: Athlone Press

Derrida, J. (1980): *Writing and Difference*. London: Routledge and Kegan Paul

Derrida, J. (1982): *Margins of Philosophy*. London: Harvester

Design Week (1986): 1(10), p. 6, 28 November. London

Ditton, J. (1977): *Part-time Crime*. London: Hutchinson

Douglas, M. (1975): *Purity and Danger*. London: Routledge and Kegan Paul

Eco, U. (1986): *Faith in Fakes*. London: Seeker and Warburg

Edwards, V. (1987): The Clubs and the Brewers. *Club and Institute Journal* March, p. 6

Feyerabend, P. (1978): *Against Method*. London: Verso

Foucault, M. (1979): What is an Author? D. F. Bouchard (Transl.). *Screen* 20(1), pp. 13 – 33

Frayling, C. (1986): *Campaign* 31st October. pp. 50 – 53. London

Giddens, A. (1982): Structuralism and the Theory of the Subject. *Central Problems in Sociological Theory*. London: Macmillan, pp. 9 – 48

Goldsmith, W. and D. Clutterbuck (1985): *The Winning Streak: Britain's Top Companies Reveal their Formulae for Success*. London: Penguin

Gowler, D. and K. Legge (1984): The Deconstruction of Evaluation Research: Part 1, The Way Forward? *Personnel Review* 13(3), pp. 3 – 13

Grafton-Small, R. (1985): Marketing Managers: The Evocation and Structure of Socially Negotiated Meaning. Unpublished Ph. D. thesis, CNAA. Sheffield City Polytechnic

Grafton-Small, R. (1989): Smoke Signals: Semiotics and the Art of Cigarette Advertising. Paper presented to 18th Conference of European Marketing Academy, Athens, April

Grafton-Small, R. and S. A. Linstead (1987): Artefact as Theory: All Roses Lead to Milano. Paper presented to 3rd SCOS International Conference on "The Symbolics of Corporate Artifacts," Milan, June

Johnson, G. and K. Scholes (1984): *Exploring Corporate Strategy*. London: Prentice-Hall

Kuhn, T. (1962): *The Structure of Scientific Revolutions*. Chicago: University of Chicago Press

Lawson, H. (1985): *Reflexivity: the Post Modern Predicament*. London: Hutchinson

Lecercle, J. J. (1985): *Philosophy Through the Looking Glass*. London: Hutchinson

Léger, F. (1973): *Functions of Painting*. London: Thames & Hudson

Lévi-Strauss, C. (1966): *The Savage Mind*. London: Weidenfeld and Nicholson

Linstead, S. A. (1985): Breaking the Purity Rule: Industrial Sabotage and the Symbolic Process. *Personnel Review* 14(3), pp. 12 – 19

Linstead, S. A. (1987a): Brewery Loans and EEC Legislation. *Club and Institute Journal*, January, pp. 3—5

Linstead, S. A. (1987b): The Clubs and the Future. *Club and Institute Journal*, April, pp. 1—6

Linstead, S. A. and R. Grafton-Small (1985): The Everyday Professional: Skill in the Symbolic Management of Occupational Kinship. *The Symbolics of Skill*. A. Strati (Ed.), Quaderno 5/6. Trento: Università di Trento, pp. 53—67

Linstead, S. A. and K. Turner (1989): Competitive Strategy and Collective and Action in the Brewing Industry: The Growth and Decline of the Working Men's Club in the UK. *Management Research News*, 12(4—5), pp. 40—54

Linstead, S. A., V. Edwards, G. Rippon, and K. Turner (1986): *Pricing and Loans in the Brewing Industry: Social Effects of EEC Legislation on Registered Members Clubs*. Report to the Economic and Social Research Council, F09 25 0067, two volumes

Martienssen, H. (1976): *The Shapes of Structure*. Oxford: Oxford University Press

Monopolies and Mergers Commission (1989): *The Supply of Beer: A Report on the Supply of Beer for Retail Sale in the United Kingdom*. Cm651 HMSO

Morgan, G. (Ed.) (1983): *Beyond Method: Strategies for Social Research*. London: Sage

Nietzsche, F. (1966): *Werke*, Vols I—III. K. Schlecta (Ed.). Munich: Hanser

Peters, T. and R. Waterman (1982): *In Search of Excellence*. London: Harper & Row

Pugh, D. (1983): Studying Organizational Structure and Process. *Beyond Method: Strategies for Social Research*. G. Morgan (Ed.). London: Sage, pp. 45—56

Stopford, J. M., D. F. Channon, and J. Constable (1978): *Cases in Strategic Management*. Chichester: John Wiley and Sons

Williamson, J. (1985): *Decoding Advertisements* (4th ed.). London: Marion Boyars

Wolfe, T. (1977): *Mauve Gloves and Madmen, Clutter and Vine*. London: Corgi

The Authors

Per Olof Berg (born in 1946) received his Ph.D. in business administration from Lund University, Sweden. He is an associate professor at the Lund University with a joint appointment at the Copenhagen School of Economics. He has been a visiting scholar at Stanford University and at UCLA (1975), and a visiting professor at Insead (1981/82) and at ISTUD (1985). He is presently the Head of MOPS (Management and Organization in Postmodern Society), a research program at Lund University involving seven research projects. He was the founder and the first chairman of the Standing Conference on Organizational Symbolism. His publications include a number of articles and books in the field of organization sciences. His address is: University of Lund, Department of Business Administration, Tunavagen 35, 22363 Lund, Sweden.

Claudio U. Ciborra (born in 1951) is currently on leave from the University of Trento, Italy and teaches at the Institute Theseus in Sophia-Antipolis, France. He has a degree in electronic engineering from the Polytechnic of Milan. He has been visiting as a research scholar and professor the Graduate School of Management at UCLA, the Institutes of Informatics of Oslo University and Aarhus University, Harvard University and New York University. His main research fields are the interaction between information technology and organizations; the foundations and models of software engineering and the emergence of new organizational forms, such as strategic alliances and the network corporation. In his research work and consulting he applies innovative approaches based on transaction costs theory and organizational learning. His address is: Università di Trento, Italy.

Barbara Czarniawska-Joerges (born in 1948) is associate professor of business administration at Stockholm School of Economics, Sweden. Her research focuses on control processes in complex organizations. She has published widely in the area of business administration in Polish, her native language, as well as in Swedish and English, including *Controlling Top Management in Large Organizations* (1985) and *Ideological Control in Nonideological Organizations* (1988). Her articles have appeared in *Scandinavian Journal of Management Studies, Organization Studies, Journal of Management Studies*, and *Accounting, Organizations and Society*. Her address is: The Economic Research Institute, Stockholm School of Economics, Sveavagen 65 − Box 6501, 11338 Stockholm, Sweden.*

Deborah Dougherty (born in 1950 in Syosset, New York, USA) received her bachelor's degree in sociology from the College of William and Mary in Virginia, a master's degree in applied behavioral science from Wright State University in Ohio, and a Ph.D. in management, organization studies, from the Sloan School of Management, MIT. She is currently assistant professor of management at the Wharton School of the University of Pennsylvania. Her present research concerns how people in large firms make sense of new, emerging markets and incorporate that knowledge into product design. Previously, she was a head start teacher, a social worker, and an administrator. Her address is: Management Department, The Wharton School, University of Pennsylvania, Zoll Steinberg-Dietrich Halls, Philadelphia, PA 19105 – 6370, USA.*

Dennis Doxtater (born in 1941) is a licensed architect who teaches social science theory and application at the College of Architecture, University of Arizona, USA. Academic background includes an M.A. in socio-cultural anthropology and a doctoral degree in architecture which emphasized anthropology and environmental psychology. In addition to the presently described work in analysis and design of U.S. office buildings, this author has worked as an architect with the U.S. Peace Corps in Peru and done research on traditionally built environments in Andalusia, Spain, Norway, and in the U.S. Southwest Anasazi (ancestors of the Pueblo Indian cultures). Current work focuses on the cultural, spatial basis of form in Swedish offices. His address is: College of Architecture, University of Arizona, Tucson, Arizona 85721, USA.

Pasquale Gagliardi (born in 1936) is professor of organizational behavior and director of ISTUD – Istituto Studi Direzionali, Belgirate, Italy. He graduated in law from the Università Cattolica del Sacro Cuore in Milan. After working in private industry, he joined the "Centro di organizzazione aziendale" of the University of Padova where he taught organizational behavior from 1964 to 1969. Professor Gagliardi is a consultant to many large Italian corporations. His current research concerns organizational culture and cultural change. His address is: ISTUD, Istituto Studi Direzionali, Via Mazzini 127, 28040 Belgirate, Italy.

Robert Grafton-Small (born in Birmingham in 1950), of Scots and English descent, though raised on the Welsh Marches and currently in a basement in Glasgow, is a tenured academic in the Biggest University Department in Marketing in Europe (University of Strathclyde). His background, his nature, and his education in various Victorian cities, including Sheffield where he was first overwhelmed by Stephan Linstead, have left him ideally suited to a life-long pursuit of the arcane and the ambiguous. Dr. Robert believes himself to be a bachelor and in this, if little else, he is probably right. His address is: University of Strathclyde, Department of Marketing, Stenhouse Building, 137 Cathedral Street, Glasgow G4 ORQ, Great Britain.*

Mary Jo Hatch (born in 1950) attended the University of Colorado where she studied architecture, and Indiana University where she received her Bachelor of Arts degree in English literature and the MBA in finance. Her Ph.D. work was done in the field of organizational behavior at Stanford University. Prof. Hatch teaches organization theory at San Diego State University in California, USA. Her papers on physical structure and corporate culture have been published by *Administrative Science Quarterly*. Prof. Hatch's most recent research effort involves a longitudinal field study of a middle management team operating under conditions of high uncertainty. The focus of this research is on the interrelationship between work issues, interaction patterns, and performance. Her address is: College of Business Administration, San Diego State University, San Diego, CA 92182–0096, USA.

Bernward Joerges (born in 1937) is professor of sociology at the Technical University Berlin and a senior researcher at Science Center Berlin. His research focuses on science studies, large technical systems, technology in everyday life, and energy conservation. He has published books and articles on these topics in German. In English, he has co-edited *Public Policies and Private Actions: A Multinational Study of Local Energy Conservation Programmes* (1987) and *Consumer Behavior and Energy Policy* (1984, 1986). His articles have appeared in the *Journal of Economic Psychology, Journal of Consumer Policy, Technology and Culture*, and *Journal of the Theory of Social Behaviour*. His address is: Science Center Berlin, Reichpietschufer 50, 1000 Berlin 30, FRG.

Kristian Kreiner (born in 1947) received his MBA at the Copenhagen Business School and his Ph.D. at the Technical University of Denmark. His research interests have included organizational decision making, organizational culture, and project management. Currently he is engaged in a major empirical study of international collaboration in high-tech fields, with a special focus on EUREKA projects. His address is: Copenhagen Business School, Institute Org./Ind. Sociology, Blaagaardsgade 23B, DK 2200 Copenhagen N, Denmark.*

Gideon Kunda (born in 1952 in Tel Aviv, Israel) received his undergraduate and master's degrees from the Hebrew University of Jerusalem, in economics and psychology, respectively, and a Ph.D. in management, organization studies, from the Sloan School of Management, MIT. At present he is a lecturer in the departments of Sociology and Labor Studies at Tel Aviv University. His book entitled *Engineering Culture: Culture and Control in a High Technology Organization* is forthcoming from Temple University Press. His address is: New York School of Industrial and Labor Relations, Cornell University, Ithaca, NY 14851—0592, USA.

Giovan Francesco Lanzara (born in 1946) is associate professor of theory of complex organizations at the University of Bologna, Italy. He holds a degree in civil engineering from the University of Pisa, and a master's degree in design and planning from Harvard University. He has formerly taught at the University of Bari, Italy. He has been a visiting professor at Aarhus University, Denmark, and a visiting scholar and research associate at the Massachusetts Institute of Technology, USA. His major research interests and published works concern the analysis and design of complex systems, organizational behavior and learning, design theory and practice. At present he is engaged in developing action-oriented methods for innovation and change in private and public organizations. His address is: Università degli Studi di Bologna, Dipartimento di Organizzazione e Sistema Politico, Via Petroni, 33, 40126 Bologna, Italy.*

Janne Larsen (born in 1956) is human resource manager at The National Association of Local Authorities in Denmark. She received her master of political science from Copenhagen University, was awarded a Fulbright scholarship and spent a year as a visiting scholar at Stanford University. She has worked as a consultant at The National Association of Local Authorities in Denmark, then as a consultant in charge of the National Training Program for CEO's in the public sector. She has published a paper an organizational change. With Majken Schultz she has co-authored a book on the use of social science research within different organizational cultures in a Danish Ministry. Her address is: The National Association of Local Authorities in Denmark, I-LP, Gyldenloevesgade 11, 1600 Copenhagen V, Denmark.

Stephen A. Linstead (born in 1952), a thoroughbred Yorkshireman with experience as an industrial baker and semi-professional folk singer, has — in addition to his prodigious range of academic and professional qualifications — recently been appointed as a senior teaching fellow at the University of Lancaster. Previously the Head of a local Polytechnic Department of European Business, he is now 37 years old and very much at home in Barnsley with his wife Eileen and their three children. He also has to live with the nagging suspicion that something, somewhere has been left undone, probably by his co-author.

Wanda J. Orlikowski (born in 1958) is an assistant professor of information technologies at the Massachusetts Institute of Technology in Boston. She is interested in the role of concrete artifacts in everyday life. Her research addresses how humans design and use such artifacts in organizations, the mechanisms by which these artifacts are implemented and institutionalized, and how they come to enable and constrain social relations in the workplace. Her address is: Information Technologies Group, E 53 – 329, Massachusetts Institute of Technology, 50 Memorial Drive, Cambridge, MA 02139, USA.

Claudia Piccardo (born in 1950) is researcher and teacher at ISTUD (Istituto Studi Direzionali, Belgirate, Italy) in the area of organizational behavior and human resources management. Her main research interests are in the field of cultural analysis of organizations linked to the psychological root of culture and to its political impact. She is a fellow of Ariele (Italian Association for the Development of Psycho-socio-analysis). Her address is: ISTUD – Istituto Studi Direzionali, Via Mazzini, 127, 28040 Belgirate, NO, Italy.*

Richard Raspa (born in 1940), Ph.D., is professor of communication at Wayne State University in Detroit, Michigan. He was a Fulbright scholar, Ellsworth fellow, and has published three books in communication and folklore. His last co-authored book, *Italian Folktales in America: The Verbal Art of an Immigrant Woman* (1985) won the Botkin Prize, an international award for the best first book in the field of folklore. Currently he is studying the organizational culture of the Detroit Symphony Orchestra, and at work on a study of the organization as theater metaphor at the Stratford Shakespeare Festival in Canada. His address is: Wayne State University, 475 CJI (CLL), Detroit, MI 48202, USA.

Michael Rosen (born in 1956) is the president of Sundered Ground, Inc., a real estate development firm in New York City specializing in residential housing. He is also an adjunct assistant professor of management at New York University, where his studies focus on the interrelationship of symbols and meaning to power, control, and consent to the labor process in formal organizations. His address is: Sundered Ground, Inc., 512 Broadway, Room 5M, New York, NY 10012, USA.*

Brian Rusted (born in 1953) teaches communications studies at The University of Calgary, Alberta, Canada. His research interests involve the ethnography of communication, visual communication, and cultural studies in organizational settings. He directs the Research Project in Canadian Studies and Communications, and is vice-president of EM/Media, an artist run, media production cooperative. His current work involves exploring video as a medium for conducting and distributing qualitative and critical research. His address is: The University of Calgary, Faculty of General Studies, 2500 University Drive N.W., Calgary, Alberta T2N 1N4, Canada.

Joseph Sassoon (born in 1946) is a researcher in the Department of Sociology of the University of Milan. Publications include: "Ideologia e interdipendenza nel sistema internazionale. Un esame dei modelli teorici," *Quaderni di Sociologia* (1980–1) 3: 367–392; "Ideology, symbolic action and rituality in social movements: the effects on organizational forms," *Social Science Information* (1984) 23: 861–873; "Principio di vertigine e immaginario della distruzione," *Quaderni Piacentini* (Nov. 1984) 14: 95–104; "La retorica dell'immagine pubblicitaria" (1987, unpubl.). Author's address: Dipartimento di Sociologia, Università di Milano, Via Conservatorio 7, 20122 Milano, Italy.

Kim S. Schmahmann (born in 1955) is an architect running his own practice in Boston, where he tries to engage client and architect in an interactive, participative design process. The intent is to bring to consciousness the ways in which the built environment influences people's lives, so as to produce a building that is supportive of the social relations in which it is embedded, and sensitive to the community with which it will interact. His address is: Urban Design Centre, 12 Greenough Lane Ph-B, Boston, MA 02113, USA.

Christian Scholz (born in 1952) is full professor of business administration at the University of Saarland in Saarbrücken (F.R.G.), teaching organization theory, human resource management, and information management. After receiving his master's degree and his Ph.D. at the Regensburg University (F.R.G.), he there completed his habilitation in 1986. For his Ph.D. thesis he won the Thurn-und-Taxis award. Having participated in the Individual Studies Program at the Harvard Business School (1982), he conducted a research project on industry analysis at the same institution. He is author of several books, including *Strategic Management* (de Gruyter, 1987) and *Human Resource Management* (Vahlen, 1989), both in German. In addition, he has published in several professional journals, including *Long Range Planning, Kybernetes, Omega, European Journal of Operational Research, Zeitschrift für Betriebswirtschaft*, and *Zeitschrift für betriebswirtschaftliche Forschung*. Besides working in the area of personal computing and the design of expert systems, one of his current research interests is comparative management, where he participates in the "International Industry Observatory" (together with researchers from several European countries). One of his specific research interests deals with computerized information systems under the perspective of organizational culture. His address is: Universität des Saarlandes, Im Stadtwald, D 6600 Saarbrücken 11.

Majken Schultz (born in 1958) is an assistant professor of organizations and industrial sociology at the Copenhagen Business School. She received her master of political science from Copenhagen University and holds a Ph.D. in organizational theory from Copenhagen Business School. She is a member of the board of the Standing Conference on Organizational Symbolism. She has been studying public organizations as cultures from different theoretical concepts of culture and published a book and papers on this issue. Currently, she is studying organizational settings, defined as innovative, and the formations of cultures across organizational boundaries. With Janne Larsen she has co-authored a book on the use of social science research within different organizational cultures in a Danish Ministry. Her address is: Institute of Organisation and Industrial Sociology, Copenhagen Business School, 23 B Blaagaardsgade, 2200 Copenhagen N, Denmark.*

Howard S. Schwartz (born in 1942) went to Antioch College and got a bachelor's degree from there. He also got a master's degree in philosophy from the University of California at San Diego and a Ph.D. in organizational behavior from Cornell University. He teaches at Oakland University, but he has never been convicted of a felony. His address is: Associate Professor of Organizational Behavior, School of Business Administration, Oakland University, Rochester, MI 48063 – 4401, USA.

Burkard Sievers (born in 1942) is since 1977 professor of organization development in the Department of Business Administration and Economics at the Bergische Universität Wuppertal in West Germany; in addition to his academic work he is consulting to enterprises as well as to non-profit institutions; he is scientific director of the "Standing Conference for the Promotion of the Learning of People and Organizations (MundO)," a network in the tradition of the Group Relations Programme of the Tavistock Institute of Human Relations. His address is: Bergische Universität, Gesamthochschule Wuppertal, Postfach 10 01 27, 5600 Wuppertal 1, FRG.

Barry A. Turner (born in 1937) is reader in the sociology of organizations at the University of Exeter, U.K. For many years he has been engaged in research into the organizational causes of large-scale accidents, and also into the cultural features of organizations. He has recently completed a year as a visiting scientist at the EC Joint Research Centre, Ispra, Italy. He is also currently the chairman of the Standing Conference on Organizational Symbolism. His address is: University of Exeter, Department of Sociology, Amory Building, Rennes Drive, Exeter EX4 4RJ, England.

Giuseppe Varchetta (born in 1940) is responsible for organization and management development activities in a multi-national company. He is also teacher at ISTUD (Istituto Studi Direzionali, Belgirate, Italy) in the area of organizational behavior and human resources management and president of Ariele (Italian Association for the Development of Psycho-socio-analysis). He is the author of a number of publications in the field of human resources management and education. His address is: UNIL-IT S.p.A., Via Privata N. Bonnet, 10, 20154 Milano, Italy.

Robert W. Witkin (born in 1941) is senior lecturer at the Department of Sociology, University of Exeter, U.K. He is the author of *The Intelligence of Feeling*, a study of the teaching of the creative arts in secondary schools and a number of other publications on subjects of aesthetic interest. In recent years he has extended his interest to the study of organizations, and has carried out studies of work cultures in organizations as diverse as a financial services company and an abortion clinic. He is currently completing a book on *Modern Art and Modern Social Structure* and also (with his colleague Robert Poupart) a book on abortion entitled *A Woman's Birthright*. His address is: University of Exeter, Department of Sociology, Amory Building, Rennes Drive, Exeter EX4 4RJ, England.

Gianni Zanarini (born in 1940) is professor of physics at the University of Bologna, Italy. His main research interests are in the field of complexity in natural and cultural systems. In particular, he has been studying in depth the dynamical systems approach to artificial intelligence and the psychological roots of organizational cultures. Among his most recent publications: *Introduction to the Physics of Complex Systems*, 1987, Pergamon Press and *Complex Systems and Cognitive Processes*, 1989, Springer Verlag. His address is: Università degli Studi di Bologna, Istituto di Fisica "A. Righi," Via Imperio, 46, 40126 Bologna, Italy.

de Gruyter Studies in Organization

An international series by internationally known authors presenting current research in organization